MATERIALITIES OF
COMMUNICATION

WRITING SCIENCE

EDITORS Timothy Lenoir and Hans Ulrich Gumbrecht

CONTRIBUTORS

Mark R. Anspach

Jan Assmann

Andreas Ballstaedt

Stephen Bann

Karlheinz Barck

Klaus Dirscherl

Monika Elsner

Wlad Godzich

Charles Grivel

Hans Ulrich Gumbrecht

Alois Hahn

Wulf R. Halbach

Friedrich Kittler

Niklas Luhmann

Jean-François Lyotard

Jan-Dirk Müller

Thomas Müller

Helmut Pfeiffer

K. Ludwig Pfeiffer

Albrecht Riethmüller

Bernhard Siegert

Vivian Sobchack

Peter M. Spangenberg

Martin Stingelin

Francisco J. Varela

Paul Zumthor

MATERIALITIES OF COMMUNICATION

EDITED BY

Hans Ulrich Gumbrecht and
K. Ludwig Pfeiffer

TRANSLATED BY William Whobrey

STANFORD UNIVERSITY PRESS

STANFORD, CALIFORNIA 1994

Stanford University Press, Stanford, California
© 1994 by the Board of Trustees
of the Leland Stanford Junior University
Printed in the United States of America

CIP data appear at the end of the book

Monika Elsner, Thomas Müller, and Peter M. Spangenberg, "The Early History
of German Television: The Slow Development of a Fast Medium," originally
appeared in the *Historical Journal of Film, Radio, and Television* and is reprinted with
permission of the editor.

Jean-François Lyotard, "Can Thought Go on Without a Body?" originally appeared in *Discourse* 11, no. 1 (Fall–Winter 1988–89): 74–83.

A much shorter version of Vivian Sobchack, "The Scene of the Screen: Envision-
ing Cinematic and Electronic 'Presence' " appeared as "Toward a Phenomenology
of Cinematic and Electronic Presence: The Scene of the Screen," *Post Script* 10,
no. 1 (Fall 1990): 50–59.

With the exception of these three chapters and the introductory chapter by
K. Ludwig Pfeiffer and the closing chapter by Hans Ulrich Gumbrecht, which
were written especially for this book, the other chapters in this book were
translated from the German versions originally published in either Hans Ulrich
Gumbrecht and K. Ludwig Pfeiffer, eds., *Materialität der Kommunikation* (Frankfurt a.M.: Suhrkamp, 1988) or Hans Ulrich Gumbrecht and K. Ludwig Pfeiffer,
eds., *Paradoxien, Dissonanzen, Zusammenbrüche: Situationen offener Epistemologie*
(Frankfurt a.M.: Suhrkamp, 1991).

Contents

❖❖❖

Contributors

Mark R. Anspach was educated at Harvard, Stanford, and the Ecole des Hautes Etudes en Sciences Sociales. He is currently a research scholar at the Centre de Recherche en Epistémologie Appliquée in Paris, where he is studying the circular logic underlying various cognitive and social processes. He is the editor of *Vengeance*, a special issue of the *Stanford French Review*, and co-editor of *Tiresias and the Critic*, a collection of essays by René Girard forthcoming from Stanford University Press.

Jan Assmann is Professor of Egyptology at the University of Heidelberg. He is director of the Ramesside Tombs research project in Luxor, Egypt, and coordinator of several working groups. The author of many works on ancient Egyptian religion and literature, comparative religion, and the general theory of culture, he recently finished a book about writing, cultural memory, and political imagination in ancient societies.

Andreas Ballstaedt is Assistant Professor at the Institute for Musicology at the University of Frankfurt am Main. His fields of interest include music theory (eighteenth to twentieth century), popular music, and the history of musicology. He is co-author of *Salonmusik: Zur Geschichte und Funktion einer bürgerlichen Musikpraxis* (1989). He has also written articles on Beethoven, terminological problems of twentieth-century music history, Johann Strauss's waltzes, and Chopin in German criticism.

Stephen Bann is Professor and Director of the Centre for Modern Cultural Studies at the University of Kent, England, where he has taught since 1967. His recent books include *The True Vine: On*

Visual Representation and the Western Tradition (1989), and *Interpreting Contemporary Art* (co-editor with William Allen, 1991). His translation of Julia Kristeva's *Proust and the Sense of Time* was published in 1992.

Karlheinz Barck is Professor of Romance Literatures at the Humboldt-Universität zu Berlin. His working fields include modern Spanish and French literature and literary theory and aesthetics. He has made contributions to *Gesellschaft, Literatur, Lesen* (1973), *Funktionen der Literatur* (1975), and *Künstlerische Avantgarde* (1979). He has edited German versions of Góngora (1974), Rimbaud (1973), Miguel Hernández (1972), Ortega y Gasset (1987), and French surrealism (1986). He is currently editor-in-chief of the *Historical Dictionary of Aesthetic Categories.*

Klaus Dirscherl teaches French, Spanish, and Portuguese literatures at the University of Passau. His main interests are the history of sensibility in the French Enlightenment and its continuing manifestations into the twentieth century; modern poetry in Spain, France, and Portugal; and the culture and mentality of Franco's Spain. He has published, among other books, *Zur Typologie der poetischen Sprechweisen bei Baudelaire* (1975), *Der Roman der Philosophen: Voltaire, Diderot, Rousseau* (1985), and *Die italienische Stadt als Paradigma der Urbanität* (editor, 1989).

Monika Elsner studied Romance philology at the universities of Bochum and Barcelona. Since 1986 she has been employed in a media research project, Early History of German Television and Its Predecessors, within the German Research Council's Special Collaborative Program 240, Aesthetics, Pragmatics, and the History of Television, at the University of Siegen. She is writing a doctoral dissertation on the Argentine tango and its reception in Europe (1907–30), with a special interest in phenomena of coupling between the human mind and body and relations of body experience and technical media.

Wlad Godzich is Professor of Emergent Literature and Director of the Department of English at the Université de Genève. After working in medieval literature, he has concentrated on issues of literary theory and comparative literature. Currently he divides his time between studies in emergent literature, the physics and economics of values, and contemporary European studies.

Charles Grivel is Professor of Modern French literature at the

University of Mannheim. He has written numerous articles on the avant-garde and contemporary literature, including detective novels and popular fiction, as well as the theory of reading. His book *Le fantastique* (1983) is concerned with literary fear and the fantastic. He is also interested in the relationships between image and text. Professor Grivel is a member of the editorial board for *Revue des Sciences Humaines* and is on the board of directors of NOESIS.

Hans Ulrich Gumbrecht is Albert Guérard Professor of Literature at Stanford University. He has taught at universities in Bochum, Siegen, Rio de Janeiro, Berkeley, Montréal, and Buenos Aires, and at the Ecole des Hautes Etudes en Sciences Sociales in Paris. His most recent works include *Eine Geschichte der spanischen Literatur*, in two volumes (1990; forthcoming in English), *Making Sense in Life and Literature* (1992), and *1926: An Essay on Historical Simultaneity* (forthcoming).

Alois Hahn has been Professor of Sociology at the University of Trier since 1974. Since 1992 he has been a member of the Comité National, CNRS, Paris. His fields of research include sociology of religion and health and family. Recent publications are "Zur Soziologie der Beichte und anderer Formen institutionalisierter Bekenntnisse: Selbstthematisierung und Zivilisationsprozeß" (1982), "Bekenntnisformen und Idenitätsentwicklung" (with H. Leitner and H. Willems; 1986), "Kann der Körper ehrlich sein?" (1988), and "AIDS und die gesellschaftlichen Folgen" (with W. H. Eirmbter and R. Jacob, 1992).

Wulf R. Halbach has worked at the University of Bochum and at the Cultural Research Institute in Essen with emphasis on communications technologies in the humanities. He now is a collaborator at the Institute for Technology Transfer in Ulm. He has published articles on fiction and simulations theory as well as American literary criticism. His book *Fiktion und Simulation* is forthcoming.

Friedrich Kittler is Professor of German at the Humboldt-Universität zu Berlin. In 1987 the second edition of his *Aufschreibesysteme 1800/1900*, which has since appeared in English as *Discourse Networks 1800/1900* (1990), was published. Other major works include *Grammaphon Film Typewriter* (1986), *Alan Turing, Intelligence Service: Schriften* (co-editor with B. Dotzler, 1987), and *Mutter, Vater, Kind* (1990).

Niklas Luhmann is Professor Emeritus of the University of

Bielefeld and is now directing a risk research institute in Lecce, Italy. Among his most recent works are *Liebe als Passion* (1982), *Soziale Systeme* (1984), *Ökologische Kommunikation* (1986), *Die Wirtschaft der Gesellschaft* (1988), *Reden und Schweigen* (1989, with P. Fuchs), *Paradigm Lost: Über die ethische Reflexion der Moral* (1990), *Die Wissenschaft der Gesellschaft* (1990), and *Beobachtung der Moderne* (1992).

Jean-François Lyotard is a member of the Collège Internationale de Philosophie. He teaches philosophy at the University of Paris VIII and at the University of California at Irvine. In the 1950's and 1960's he was active in the group Socialisme ou Barbarie. His major philosophical works include *Economie libidinale* (1974), *La condition postmoderne* (1979), *Le différend* (1983), and *L'inhumain* (1988).

Jan-Dirk Müller was Chair of the Department of Medieval German Literature at the University of Hamburg from 1984 to 1991 and is now teaching at the University of Munich. His books and articles include *Romane des 15. und 16. Jahrhunderts* (1991); *Höfische Literatur—Hofgesellschaft—höfische Lebensformen um 1200* (with G. Kaiser, 1986); and *Wissen für den Hof: Der spätmittelalterliche Verschriftlichungsprozeß am Beispiel Heidelbergs im 15. Jh.* (forthcoming).

Thomas Müller has studied Romance philology, modern history, and political science, and received his M.A. from the University of Bochum. Since 1986 he has worked on the research project Early History of German Television and Its Predecessors, within the German Research Council's Special Collaborative Program 240 at the University of Siegen. He is completing his doctoral dissertation on the fascination for the aviator as a collective symbol between 1909 and 1939.

Helmut Pfeiffer is Professor of Romance Literatures at the Humboldt Universität zu Berlin. He has written numerous articles on the literature of the Renaissance, the literature and literary theory of the nineteenth century, and, above all, aestheticism and modern literature. His publications include *Roman und historischer Kontext: Strukturen und Funktionen des französischen Romans um 1857* (1984), *Der Nutzen der Kunst: Kunsttheorie zwischen Geschichtsphilosophie und Gesellschaftstheorie* (1988). He was Managing Editor of Journal Poetica.

K. Ludwig Pfeiffer has been teaching at the University of Siegen since 1979. From 1989 to 1992 he was director of the university's

Graduiertenkolleg. He has taught at the University of Houston; University of California, Davis; Kansai University, Osaka; Colorado College; University of California, Irvine; University of California, Santa Cruz; and Stanford University. His major works include *Sprachtheorie, Wissenschaftstheorie und das Problem der Textinterpretation* (1974), *Wissenschaft als Sujet im modernen englischen Roman* (1979), *Bilder der Realität und die Realität der Bilder* (1981), and, as co-editor, *Materialität der Kommunikation* and *Paradoxien, Dissonanzen, Zusammenbrüche* (1991). His current interests include the study of opera.

Albrecht Riethmüller is currently teaching at the Free University Berlin. His main areas of interest are the history of music (especially of Greek antiquity and of the eighteenth to twentieth century), history of music theory, music aesthetics, musical terminology, and music and politics. He has published extensively on the history of music theory, music aesthetics, and the interrelationship of music and literature and music and politics. His books include *Die Musik als Abbild der Realität: Zur dialiektischen Widerspiegelungstheorie in der Ästhetik* (1976) and *Ferruccio Busonis Poetik* (1988).

Bernhard Siegert is Assistant Professor at the University of Bochum. From 1987 to 1991 he was a member of the German Research Council's project on media and literature. He is co-founder of the international workshop "Übertragung und Gesetz: Interdisziplinäre Analysen zur Theorie und Praxis von Institutionen." His work and interests include the history and cultural impact of the telephone and communication by mail, and the history of communications technology in general. His forthcoming articles include work on communications around 1500 in relation to the European colonization of America.

Vivian Sobchack is Professor of Film and Associate Dean of the School of Theater, Film, and Television at the University of California, Los Angeles. She is the author of *The Address of the Eye: A Phenomenology of Film Experience, Screening Space: The American Science Fiction Film* and, with Thomas Sobchack, *An Introduction to Film.*

Peter M. Spangenberg graduated from the University of Bochum and completed his Ph.D. at the University of Siegen with a dissertation on medieval French miracles. He has taught at the universities of Siegen, Bochum, Essen, and Mannheim. His research has centered on literary theory, media analysis, medieval literature, and early media changes from manuscript to print.

Martin Stingelin has studied German literature and history in Basel. His publications include "Nietzsches Wortspiel als Reflexion auf poet(olog)ische Verfahren" (1988) and "Gehirntelegraphie: Die Rede der Paranoia von der Macht der Medien 1900. Falldarstellungen" (1988).

Francisco J. Varela has taught at the University of Colorado, the University of Chile, and the Brain Research Laboratories at the New York University Medical School. Since 1986 he has held the Fondation-de-France Chair for Cognitive Science at the Ecole Polytechnique, Paris. Along with H. Maturana, he developed a theory of biological autonomy. This, along with other theories, has had repercussions in numerous fields and has been the object of intense international discussion. He has recently published *The Tree of Knowledge: The Biological Roots of Human Understanding* (with H. Maturana, 1987).

Paul Zumthor taught at the University of Montreal from 1972 until his retirement, in 1980. Among his many articles and books are *Histoire littéraire de la France médiévale* (1954), *Langue et techniques poétiques à l'époque romane* (1963), *Essai de poétique médiévale* (1972), *Le masque et la lumière: Poétique des grands rhétoriqueurs* (1978), *Parler du moyen âge* (1980), *Introduction à la poésie orale* (1983), and *La poésie et la voix dans la civilisation médiévale* (1984). Professor Zumthor is also an accomplished novelist.

MATERIALITIES OF
COMMUNICATION

K. LUDWIG PFEIFFER

The Materiality of Communication

I

" 'Matter doesn't exist,' said Berkeley, who suffered terribly from diarrhea." This joke, if it is one, is quoted, from J. O. Wisdom's *The Unconscious Origin of Berkeley's Philosophy* (1953), in *Les immatériaux* (Lyotard et al., 1985, vol. *Epreuves d'écriture*, 130). *Les immatériaux*, three volumes of manifold, not to say heterogeneous, content, was published for an exhibition of that title in the Centre Georges Pompidou from March 28 to July 15, 1985. The conceptual fate of that enterprise is significant. It began, in April 1983, with the aim of examining "matter in all its states." Once it became clear, however, that the notorious "new technologies" were as much technologies of distribution as technologies of production, the emphasis quickly changed. The entrance hall to the new world now seemed to be constructed of "immaterial" materials ("matériaux 'immatériels' "). These, in turn (January 1984), under the impact of a "dematerialization of production," were superseded by a general perspective of "immateriality" (See ibid., vol. *Album*, 8–17).

A raid on matter in all its states thus turned into a Baudrillard-esque criticism of (Marxist or other forms of) materialism. "Nature," according to Jean Baudrillard, had been elevated into the grand design of reality, both natural and supernatural, during the Renaissance. Production—that is, a seemingly imposing world of objects, products, goods—became the fetish of the Industrial Age. In criticizing, quite understandably, its totalitarian modes, Marx neglected, nevertheless, the growing importance of less tangible "things," technologies, and procedures. These—information codes, stylistic variations instead of "substantially" new products, a rhetoric advertising hard facts instead of producing them—took over in the twentieth century (see Baudrillard 1976).

The "materiality of communication," then, looks like a return to the obsolete. Both in *Les immatériaux* and in Baudrillard, however, there are other, somewhat submerged stories. The fall of matter and materialism does not lead to the immaterial pure and simple; rather, it *branches into* the immaterial *and* its material "sites" or "supports" (French "supports"). Instead of substantial objects and their meanings, we get information overload and a new hardness of "supporting" materials, a new "performativity" of things and bodies (Lyotard et al. 1985, vol. *Album*, 19, 26–27). Human beings, like things, have become interfaces in a technological world—and many boring, historically superfluous things have been said, since Foucault, concerning the death (or the impoverished forms of life) of the "subject." But subjects or things were never, in any substantial sense, simply given. There have been, indeed repeatedly been, substantialistic interpretations of matter (human and otherwise) and meaning, but not much more.

Substantialistic amalgamations are no longer possible. Where they occur, they smack of archaic fanaticism. Still, even Baudrillard keeps talking about things (and even passions)—things and human beings that/who have found ways to escape dogmatic and/or boring amalgamations with meanings, or more nobly put, the "dialectics" of substance and significance (cf. Baudrillard 1983). Instead, they have come to present "themselves," that is, themselves as surfaces, to an almost obscene degree. In that sense, "expression" and "interpretation," the leaps of the soul and the pet activity of certain cultural worlds, have reached, as Beckett put it in *Molloy*, the end of their elastic.

We have come or (looking at the ancient Greeks as one example) reverted to dynamic contexts of *performance* (which may attract or disappoint) and to meaning *effects* (which may be fascinating or misleading but hardly right or wrong). Where do we find conceptual powers for an exploration of the shift that, as always, is not confined to the present but must expand retroactively, too? "Materialities of Communication" is a name (and the present volume a local habitation) for a *scene of multidirectionality*. It gains cohesion, a negative one certainly, by distancing itself from habits whose importance we have come to overestimate, that is, from habits of overestimation themselves. The main culprit, in that galle(r)y of habits—the "ballast that chains the dog to its vomit" (Beckett again, in his 1931 Proust essay)—was, and to some extent is, the "privileging of the semantic dimension" (Frank 1980: 9). Cosmologies, philosophies of history, of ethnic, period, or national spirits, and, finally, of communication, hermeneutic and otherwise, have been allies and successors in that privilege. Meanwhile, some iconoclasts, including Jacques Derrida (but the movement started much earlier and more powerfully with, for instance, the philosophy of language of Fritz Mauthner), had become aware that centers of meaningfulness in philosophy had to be demoted to the rank of mere metaphors (see Derrida 1974, 1974/75). But in that type of criticism, the driving powers behind conceptual, interpretational metaphors remained hidden. Logocentrism, to be sure, like the Cartesian ghost in the machine another skeleton in the Western closet, was nailed to the cross. But the deconstructive move was of no (real—if that word can still be used) avail. The picture painted by that "critique" (and it might have been better to leave the pathos of the term to the past) is historically misleading, perhaps downright wrong. Logocentrism, like "that fatal knife, / Deep questioning, which probes to endless dole" (Meredith, p. 47, Sonnet L), depth interpretations, that is, of various Marx- or Freud-inspired sorts, and finally those interpretational hangovers in (re)politicized versions of structuralism and poststructuralism, are themselves *effects*: effects, among others, of situations, media, and technologies of "communication." Communication here is not supposed to connote understanding, coming to terms, mutuality, exchange. It unfolds as an open dynamic of means and effects. In a philosophico-linguistic vein, Gilbert Ryle's *Concept of Mind* (1949), Ludwig Wittgenstein's *Philosophical Investigations* (1953), and W. V. O. Quine's *Word and Object* (1960) had tried to exorcise that Cartesian ghost in the machine, whose obituary, in evolutionary and creative terms, was then written by Arthur Koestler (in large part, incidentally, at Stanford's Center for Advanced Study in the Behavioral Sciences; see his *The Ghost in the Machine*, 1967). Both Ryle and Wittgenstein had adopted a *therapeutic* stance in order to provide cures for the maladies of meaning and the illusions of the spirit. In that respect they recommended, and did not combat, multiple sclerosis.

II

The therapeutic stance does not befit our present enterprise. That stance represents, its analytic rigor notwithstanding, residues of an anthropologizing trend (concerned with dispositions, motives, even mental events like images) that does not open but rather blocks views of the productive layers and mechanisms of meaning effects or their relative absence. This may become clearer if we look at a dramatic and exemplary switch in the depth interpretations of the therapeutic domain itself. I am referring to the transition from Freud to Lacan (and relying heavily, for that purpose and for the sake of a *model construction*, on Borch-Jacobsen 1988, 1991). For Freud, the mind was no longer master in its own house. Yet he was not able to effectively dislodge that mind and its cultural manifestations. The new pretenders to power, the unconscious and its drives, remained chained in the human basement. Whatever their individual urgency, there was no enduring cultural space for them. Consequently, as Derrida showed, a system of metaphors outlining a topography of spiritual sublimations continued to be active (Derrida 1967). Jacques Lacan, on the other hand, was enmeshed in a debate on the implications of *posthistoire*. That concept proved, and continues to prove, much richer in suggestions for our enterprise than that of postmodernism. The latter can, in fact, partly be seen as a pretentious evasion of *posthistoire*'s challenge. *Posthistoire* and its most noteworthy representatives—first Hegel and later A. Kojève (ironically Lacan's absolute master) and A. Gehlen—do not preach an end of history. *Posthistoire* suggests, for the time after the "great transformation" (Karl Polányi) in the late eighteenth and early nineteenth centuries, an end of substantial changes in history and in its interpretations. In that sense, Hegel did present a philosophy of history. But it was one that buried its own future. Closer to ourselves, Kojève, in his *Introduction à la lecture de Hegel* (1947), diagnosed the end of free, meaningful, history-making or epoch-making individual action in any emphatic sense. The impact of (first) the American and (then) the Japanese experience provided evidence for a *flattening-out of profiles of significance*, individual, historical, or programmatic/ideological. The Japanese in particular seemed to embody a deep-seated indifference toward intentionalistic or "ideological" interpretations of history and human action. With regard to accumulated interpretational loads, the Japanese and, willy-nilly and often unconsciously, the rest of us too have literally become "snobs." This is a background against which Lacan's despecification of the semantics of human drives assumes crucial importance for the present enterprise. In Lacan, Freud's (let us assume) well-defined, sexualized forms of unconscious energies dissolved into amorphous Desire. That Desire, it is true, may be resemanticized. But for that, it needs cultural (including technological) mechanisms, in which it acquires fictitiously well-defined shapes. Desire is nothing in itself; it always turns into the desire for the desire of the Other, that is, into the shapes it takes in domains of generalized otherness. Otherness may show up in heavily personalized forms (whence Girard's "mimetic" desire, envy). But personalization too is "just" an effect. Desire has become immensely "baitable"; it is lured on by images and simulacra (of authenticity . . .) in which it takes on, for better or for worse, some transitory shape or paranoid reality. Deprived of intrinsic meaning and substance, it falls prey to the floating fictions in which the imaginary appears to "materialize." Feelings of self are soaked in the images of others, petrified into an uncanny world or museum of images and statues. Freud, in constructs like the Oedipus complex, committed the fallacy of misplaced concreteness.

Kojève did not abandon the Hegelian analysis of consciousness for nothing. His interest swung over to a "human reality," somehow similar to Martin Heidegger's mediation between theory and practice in the concepts of *Dasein* and *Sorge*, rigorously cut off, however, from Hegel's self-consciousness-connection. Thus, there is no drive for Lacan that is not already represented. Yet the corresponding "representatives," the museum of images and statues, are steeped in a strangely unreal, uncanny light. They are less signified than signifiers themselves, inviting and undermining the unstable interpretations they seem to warrant. As signifiers, they point to the inarticulable; they demand, much in the manner of John Austin's speech acts, *performance* rather than interpretation. Performances are judged in terms of their "felicity," that is, rather in terms of rules and styles than of meanings. This is why the quasi-mathematical formulas with which Lacan, following the model of Claude Lévi-Strauss, came to map the psychoanalytic field, "are true magic formulas, supposed to be all the more effective for being devoid of meaning" (Borch-Jacobsen 1991: 162; cf. 7, 11–16, 49–50, 101, 143, 176). If it were possible, then, to look at signifiers in isolation, one would be interested not in their meaning but in their "materiality" (thus Lacan already in the 1954/55 Seminar II). This is a crucial point: it entails that materiality cannot simply replace meaning. It also follows, however, that the signifiers, in their latent materiality as source and support, will produce meanings as their effects (Borch-Jacobsen 1991: 178). Not replacement, but a reorientation of interest. We may leave open the question to what extent Lacan's approach includes nonlinguistic signifiers. Signifiers, in any case, and their interrelations ("wiring") cannot be treated as data. They are equivocal themselves. For any hermeneutics, however, the consequences are fatal, because the signified effects are liable to endless slippages.

III

I am exploiting a Lacanian perspective because it supplies us with a motivating model. Communication is envisaged less as an exchange of meanings, of ideas about . . . , and more as performance propelled into movement by variously materialized signifiers. It is enframed into hardwares, guided by rules and styles, and "crowned" by signified effects that, once sufficiently routinized, can appear as realms of their own. To hold, as Derrida did in *Grammatology*, that signifier and signified cannot be isolated against each other, would constitute a minimal claim of the program. The deconstructionist project uncovered implications of the minimal claim, pursuing the infinite play of meanings as traces without ultimate origin and control. The present enterprise takes another direction. It is concerned with potentials and pressures of stylization residing in techniques, technologies, materials, procedures, and "media." This point may perhaps be more easily driven home for socially or culturally important performances like rituals. For quite some time, a focus on symbolic interpretation has blurred their qualities as forms of spectacular, aestheticized autodynamics—on which meanings of all kinds can certainly be grafted, but not inherently bestowed (see Hamerton-Kelly 1987). The same is true for the social exploitation of dance. Here, the 1920's and 1930's cherished doctrines of its organic, natural essence; they were equally ready to tumble into left- or rightwing exercises and ideologies. On the other side of the spectrum, it seems clear that "literature" has been both overly engulfed in and by interpretation and, in some of its forms, abetted that tendency itself.

"Materialities" may also function as an overall metaphor for the joint impact of institutions (the church, educational systems) and the media they predominantly employ (rituals, books of special kinds, etc.). It is interesting to see, for instance, when and how the smaller, handier format of books within the framework of medieval universities transformed these books into targets of study and interpretation (see Le Goff 1985, chap. 1, on the urban Renaissance and the birth of the intellectual; and chap. 2 on the book as an instrument). It is sobering, though, to witness the survival of petrified exegetical and interpretational habits. It is only this survival, buttressed by an economically not unimportant book culture, that makes plausible its opposite, too: the Cassandra-like laments on or the gleeful technological prophecies of the death of the book. There is little warrant either for the luxuriance of interpretation or for the burial of what is still, in principle, a strong medium. We are witnessing, rather, shifts in media configurations for times in which the language of "literary" books (primary and secondary) can do justice neither to dimensions of cultural visuality nor to what A. Leroi-Gourhan called, in a hauntingly romantic phrase, "the rhythms of life." The spiritualization of literature was plausible for periods in which, like late nineteenth-century Germany, the cultural deficiencies of a politico-social lag and high-speed technological progress were all too manifest. It is not for nothing that a period of positivistic epistemology and booming natural sciences produced global "standpoint"—and "worldview"—philosophies. The rise, as well as its twentieth-century decline, of Wilhelm Dilthey's and other forms of hermeneutics comes as no surprise in such a context.

A sort of intuitive resistance to attribute, to ourselves or to others, actions that do not "represent" some intention or meaning may—given institutions and media—easily harden into compulsions to see meanings, and particularly hidden ones, everywhere. To do so may be a fairly general symbolic gesture; it may unavoidably haunt religion as theology and justice as written law. Its special elaboration and institutionalization—with the help of specific ("canonized") books and their continuous reinterpretation—in historical, philosophical, and literary contexts may still command legitimacy and respect. Today's mixtures, though, of institutional inertia, cultural lag, and sporadic relics of fascinating interpretation present a problematic picture. It is gripping, for instance, to see W. Iser reflect upon contemporary media and the ways in which they have superseded books as cultural paradigms—and then to retreat into a "literary" anthropology of the fictive and the imaginary (Iser 1991: 10–12). Here, the imaginary is protected against psychological and social encroachments. In its ceaseless fall from concreteness, however, it is reinvested with the pathos of an intangible spirituality. To ascertain its status as a literary prerogative has become a baffling task.

Advanced positions that, like Iser's, have abandoned the cult of interpretation, but not the culture of the literary book, are caught in conceptual dilemmas. In the German context, these had come to a head already in the 1920's and 1930's. In his "Habilitationsschrift" *Real and Unreal Spirit* (1978 [1931]) Gehlen asserted that Hegel knew what he meant when he talked about the spirit and the like— and, today, it seems important to underline the talk, since the editing and publishing history of Hegel and others has "written" significant chapters of its own on the adventures of materialities and ideas. Today, according to Gehlen, we can no longer mean what we say when we use these and similar terms. Hermeneutics never made up its mind whether, and to what extent, it was to be taken as an existential performance (*Daseinsvollzug*) or a mere interpretation of existential relics preserved, somehow, in books. Dilthey was aware that the urge to go "significantly" (theoretically, interpretationally) beyond the diverse material conditions of life and its routinized understanding sprang up in times of great historical movements (like the Reformation), in which neither conditions nor routines could be taken for granted; that afterward that urge "vanished back into the dark" (Pöggeler 1972: 11; Weimar 1975: 26). In any case, the domains of the spirit (that is, those domains in which, for lack of alternatives, it makes sense to use that language) have shrunk; the concept of the imaginary itself indicates that we no longer know what the imagination is. This is why the imaginary can be handed over to the slings and arrows of media of all kinds; its literary code has been reduced, at best, to a very restricted one.

Thus, a strong sense of the loss of the object pervades the classic texts of the German humanities in the 1920's and 1930's. The lost object was replaced, for a while, by the idea that the humanities and their interpretations were but pawns in fierce life struggles (see Rothacker 1965: 4–16 for the vanishing concept of spirit; and 109–13 for the life struggles within the substance of the humanities). Finally, the sometimes existential sense of loss exploded in catastrophic resurrections of the object. And it has become a trivial, if necessary, pursuit to scourge Heidegger, Rothacker, Gehlen, and others for their Nazi involvements. It was equally easy, after World War II, to brush aside both loss and resurrection and to act, within frameworks of institutional inertia, as if nothing had happened. "Improvements"—methodological, theoretical, or political—were installed, but were installed internally. They were undertaken in order to optimize the paradise regained of the literary object—even if they were conducted from an "external" (Marxist, etc.) point of view.

Still, for thinkers better inured to the struggles of life than literary people themselves, the humanities, even if carefully tended, could never shake off the suspicion that they were producing mere ideas, fantasms without communicative or cultural impact (see Schelsky 1963). In 1934, Julius Kraft had declared the impossibility of the humanities (see Kraft 1977). Present-day talk about their "unavoidability" (Marquard 1986) does not undercut the force of this diagnosis. It merely lends a voice to the intuition that there might be something—meaningful, spiritual, existential?—beyond the steel-like cages of technology and the sciences.

IV

But what? In his *Decline of the West*, Oswald Spengler had ventured to assert the demise of research, as a higher, spiritual or intellectual, ideal, for both the humanities and the sciences (1972, 1: 548). The "soul of culture" was surfeited with the orgies of a scientific spirit celebrated for more than 200 years. Narrowness and the drying up of grand creative enterprises had become universal. Gehlen, more specifically, treated the humanities with ironic condescension. They presented a sorry sight: vague capacities of understanding always on the move, indeed on the prowl for something to be interpretationally, critically . . . victimized. Yet these capacities kept proving indifferent and inconsequential with respect to their alleged objects; they spread out masses of "literature" for nobody's enjoyment nor anybody's suffering (1978: 343). A new initiative though, Gehlen thought, was shadowed forth in an indistinct willingness, important for the future, to drop the concept of individual consciousness, to blur the distinction between mind and matter (324). Here, prospects for an undogmatic research into hard and soft forms of materiality might have loomed large. Unfortunately, in an existentialist and later political swerve, Gehlen moved on to a program of cognition based on "action" hopefully and, as it turned out, disastrously not divorced from "life." Action having turned crude, indeed brutal and "inhuman," and forms of the material thus having been discredited again altogether, the humanities, after World War II in (West) Germany, aspired toward respiritualization. Nicolai Hartmann tried to reformulate Hegelian notions, desperately looking for the substance and habitations of what he called the "objectified spirit" (cultural domains, the state of the art in scholarly or scientific disciplines, etc.; see Hartmann 1949: 200–205). Afterward, in 1960, Gadamer (*Truth and Method*) constructed traditions within which the spirits of culture communed with each other (if only in books). Here, indeed, the dematerialization of vague capacities was driven home with a vengeance. Criticism of ideology, reception theory, and deconstruction have not altered *this part* of the situation.

V

Three methodological orientations have continued to exercise some stronger attraction for the editors of the present volume. One, unfeasible here, was anticipated by Egon Friedell (among others) in precisely those times in which the sense of the lost object had imposed itself. This was the project, realized by Friedell in charming, if highly erratic, "unscholarly" ways, of a *cultural history* less burdened by fictions of the spirit, considerably less boring than many present-day investigations into material culture, definitely less dogmatic than some schools of cultural materialism. In some ways, Friedell's cultural history presented affinities with the new historicism. There was a sense of historical contingency, of the pull exerted by institutions and technologies, a feeling for the long-term, quasi-spiritual impact these as well as life forms may create, a feeling also, on the other hand, of the occasional strength something one feels compelled to call spirit or morality may periodically acquire (Friedell 1969). In its almost total indifference to notions of historical truth or adequacy, it was also different from the second orientation. There, *technological hardware*—in production, recording, storage, and reproduction—"exercises influences" on or in fact "determines" what poses as semantic, symbolic, spiritual, or emotional worlds. Work on this conception was willfully brilliant with Marshall McLuhan, so willfully indeed that "human" priorities (media as "extensions of man") still loomed large. This conception changed, with Elizabeth Eisenstein's work on the printing press and similar projects, into a normalized paradigm of research. It turned, with Friedrich Kittler's "writing" on discourse networks (the English term does not quite capture the technological implications of *Aufschreibesysteme*), on the gramophone, the typewriter, and so on, into a powerfully somber paraphysics in which Friedell's "European soul" gasped its last few breaths. Strong as their single impact may be, these works are not fully adaptable to inquiries like those collected here. The historical range and the communicative drives of "materialities" are immense; to sketch their pluridimensionality and interleavings requires manifold conceptual detours. Certainly, one would like to know what kind of autodynamic wirings or analogues of them there are—if there are any—that test perception, guide behavior, evaluate experience, caring little or nothing for the pathetic semantic textures we weave around them. There are the brain, the hormones, and other circuits that produce, in ways still fairly obscure, electric and chemical binarisms. But if it is one of the deadlocks of brain research that the steps from there to what still appears as meaningful cultural worlds *are extremely hard to take and yet have to be taken*, it behooves "literary" people (like most of those in this volume) not to abandon prematurely some striving toward the "nobleness of life" (Antony in Shakespeare's *Antony and Cleopatra*, 1.1.36)—even if it consists only in "literature."

Thus, the human body does not possess any inherent significance. But its positions and performances deploy symbolic repercussions; these may be reflected in elementary categories of grammar or expand into cultural relevance. This is why, *pace* Derrida, conditions of relative orality and literacy, why writing seen both as performance and as system(s), can be examined in terms of psychophysical, indeed culturally normative implications (see, for one example, Goldberg 1990). Within writing systems themselves, the relative differences between "alphabetic" and more "pictorial" scripts oscillate uneasily between quasi-material and cognitive drifts (see Gumbrecht and Pfeiffer 1993).

The point, then, of the present enterprise is not a search for the reality of the material or the materiality of the real. We are looking for underlying constraints whose technological, material, procedural, and performative potentials have been all too easily swallowed up by interpretational habits. These habits have been overdeveloped and overprivileged and have, to some extent, veered out of control. Our own options are therefore not unhinged by a correct insistence on the immateriality of modern art or of an age of electronics in general. The concept or, if you will, the search metaphor of materiality points to a gap that, by and large, has considerably widened in modern times. It is a gap between information overload, interpretational sophistication, and a radical evanescence of semantic stability. One may hold discrepancies like these responsible for the crudeness, indeed the archaic quality, of behavior in many domains, for example, the political domain. The striking behavioral affinities between archaic and late, highly technologized cultures have been, for quite a while, the targets of conservative cultural criticism (see Gehlen 1957, 1975). A perseverance neither in the cult(ure) of interpretation nor in reductive technologisms but, perhaps, an exploration of the *dimensions in between* may move us away from what has equally turned sour— cultural nostalgia and technological euphoria.

MEDIA OF COMMUNICATION
AND HISTORICAL THRESHOLDS

JAN ASSMANN

Ancient Egypt and the Materiality of the Sign

Iconicity and World Reference

World Reference and Language Reference

If writing is language made visible (*Visible Language* being the name of a related periodical), then hieroglyphic writing is more than a writing system. It refers not only to the Egyptian language but also to the "world," that is, to objects and events. Hieroglyphics can represent these independently of a specific articulation of a single language. Anyone who expressed this thesis prior to 1822 would have received only a tired shrug of the shoulders. This was the *communis opinio* concerning the function of the hieroglyphic writing system. It was precisely in this that one saw its advantage. Since the system's signs did not have any sound value, it was not bound to any specific language. These signs did not establish the reference to reality by way of a particular language and its "double articulation" but were able to represent "things" directly and abstract concepts via metaphoric and metonymic representations.

In 1822 Jean-François Champollion published his decipherment of hieroglyphics based on his discovery of the sound value of hieroglyphs. This breakthrough established that hieroglyphics is not picture writing but a "visible language" like every other script. From this point on, a thesis such as the one advanced above would have been branded a blatant heresy. The only difference between hieroglyphics and common alphabets lies in the fact that the writ-

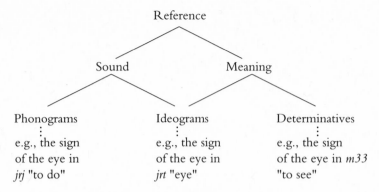

Fig. 1. The principle of double codification

ing does not operate exclusively on the level of phonological articulation but on the level of semantic articulation as well. In other
words, there exist not only "sound signs" but also "sense signs" and
"sound + sense signs." Figure 1 presents a representation of the
principle of "double codification" (see Schenkel 1971, 1981, 1984).

Ideograms refer to words as units made up of sound and meaning. Phonograms refer to (a complex of) sounds that disregard the
meaning. It therefore becomes possible, for example, to transfer
the image of the eye with the sound value $jr<.t>$* to the word
$jr<.j>$ "to do," which has the same sound value. One can also
write the image of a house with the sound value pr for the word
$pr<.j>$ "to go out," that is, for unrepresentable denotations.[†] Determinatives refer to classes of meaning: for example, the sign of
the eye refers to everything that has to do with seeing, the sign of
the house to all concepts of space, the sign of the sun to concepts
of time.

*The $<.t>$ is a feminine ending that is not included in the sound value of the
sign.

[†]The "sound value" of the letters is limited to the consonants and does not
include vowels. In this way, the scope of transferability is significantly increased.
The practice of writing only the consonants may have appealed to the Egyptians
on the basis of the structure of their language. Their language, like other Semi-
tohamitic languages, binds lexemic meaning to "roots" with fixed consonants and
forms inflections by changing the vowels, so that consonants are constants and
vowels are variables. H. G. Fischer has drawn attention to the exceptionality of
this practice in the history of writing, which was adapted in later consonantal
scripts by the Hebrews and Arabs from hieroglyphic writing (see Fischer 1986:
25–26).

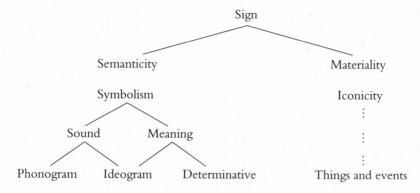

Fig. 2. The semanticity vs. the materiality of the sign

The system can manage with about 700 signs by combining these three functions. Compare, on the other hand, the incredible number of signs in scripts such as Chinese, where the ideographic element is stronger. "World reference" is not included in this scheme. All functions, including ideograms and determinatives, refer to the language. It is a common mistake to see a direct, extralinguistic reference to reality in these signs (as does, e.g., te Velde 1985/86). Sense is also a linguistic category. Sense signs refer either to "sememes" (word meanings, ideograms) or to "classemes" (word-class meanings, determinatives). They refer in any case to language and to the level of its semantic articulation of reality, not directly to reality itself. We would like to keep this basic distinction in mind and keep the scheme free of any language-independent world reference. Wherein, then, lies the assumed "world reference" of Egyptian hieroglyphic writing? It lies in the *materiality* of the sign and not in what we call its *semanticity*. We will accommodate this reference not within but outside the scheme, which, with its three functions, is limited to semanticity (see Fig. 2). It may seem surprising to interpret the iconic reference of Egyptian hieroglyphics as materiality. The concept of materiality brings to mind the purely material, such as stone or paper, engraving or coloring, rather than a characteristic such as iconicity. What I mean is this: every sign has two aspects, the aspect of its function within a sign system, by which it can refer to a specific meaning, and the aspect of its physical manifestation, by which it can indicate this meaning. The concept of semanticity includes everything from the first aspect that is necessary and important for the functioning of the sign as a sign. The concept of materiality includes the second aspect and everything that serves as a physical carrier of meaning. This carrier can be formed one way or another without necessarily influencing the functionality of the sign. An "R" can be chiseled in stone, written on paper, carved in bark, printed in Gothic, Bodoni, Garamond, or Helvetica type without having its meaning, its reference to the phoneme [r], affected in the least. Its distinctiveness is crucial: it must not be confused with a "P" or a "B." Everything else belongs to the materiality of the sign, which, although necessary for the indication of the meaning, does not add anything to the meaning by its specificity. In this sense, the iconicity of hieroglyphs is an aspect of their materiality that can be shed with no change to their language-referential meaning. Egyptian cursive scripts took this path and developed within the independent laws and paths of graphic systems. Hieroglyphic writing maintained its pictorial realism. This shows that this sign system is not a "visible language" in the complete sense, but is more than just a script, involving more than just language reference. This "more" is based on its pictorialness; it is therefore "world reference."

The Origin and Development of Hieroglyphs

It is a mistake to believe that writing was invented to record language. This possibility only gradually presented itself after hundreds if not thousands of years of experience with scriptlike recording systems. Sumerian writing goes back to "calculi," or counting stones. These were small clay models that had numerical or objective meaning and were used to record not linguistic but rather economic communications and transactions and to register ownership and other claims on land, animals, and grain (see Schmandt-Besserat 1982a, 1982b). Iconicity did not play a particularly great role since the signs were very abstract from the beginning.

In contrast to the Sumerian case, Egyptian hieroglyphic writing had its origins in a recording system in which iconicity was important from the beginning. Its purpose was political rather than economic communication, the recording of acts of special political significance (see Fig. 3). Two goals were of primary importance. The first was to secure the result of these acts permanently by

Fig. 3. Ceremonial slate palette of King Narmer (ca. 3000 B.C.) (SOURCE:
H. Müller-Karpe, *Handbuch der Vorgeschichte II*, Munich, 1968, pl. 26)

depicting them in stone and depositing them in a sacred place. This
placed the record in a physical situation that was both permanent
and open to the divine world. The second was to create a means for
chronological orientation by recording the major event of a given
year and naming the year after that event. This is the origin of
Egyptian chronography and the recording of history. The first goal
is also the origin of all monumental architecture and pictorial art.
The only meaning of such art was to expose and to develop the
physical situation as a "sacred space of permanence." And it is also
the origin of hieroglyphics that remains a genre of pictorial art. It is
reserved for the "writing of divine words," as it is called in Egyptian, for recordings in the sacred space of permanence.[1]

Protodynastic pictorial narrative uses picture-signs on two
distinctly different physical scales. The large pictures portray a
"scene," and the small pictures identify actors and places by including names. The small pictures therefore refer to *language* (names),
the large pictures refer to the *world* (acts). It would be a mistake,

however, to categorize only the small pictures as "writing." The large pictures also act as writing. After all, the entire complex picture "writes" a name, that is, the year named after that particular event. This type of recording is successful only when both types of signs, the small ones with language reference and the large ones with world reference, work together. Neither of the two "media" is self-sufficient in recording the intended or any other meaning. The small signs do not yet make up a writing system but are simply a constituent of a complex recording system.

A new stage is reached when the "large" signs are integrated into the inventory of the "small" ones. This is the origin of determinatives. The determinative is originally nothing more than a "picture" reduced to script size that joins the preceding phonogram as annotation. The reference of these sense signs only gradually becomes generalized from sememes to classemes. The word for "beetle" is originally determined by the picture of a beetle. Only later is the word for "beetle" determined by the picture of a bird as falling into the sense class "flying animals," and even later by the picture of an animal skin as falling into the more general sense class "animal."

Picture and Writing: Interdependence and Complementary Multimediality

A typical example should suffice to make clear to what degree the spheres of world representation and language recording influenced each other. I take this example from the tomb of Count Paheri in El-Kab, dating to the early New Kingdom (middle of the second millennium B.C.), in other words, to the middle of Egyptian history. Figure 4 shows the west wall of the tomb (southern part). Figure 5 replaces the hieroglyphs with translations. Important in Figure 4 are the following characteristics.

1. The complete *flexibility* of the writing. With the change in writing direction (right to left, horizontal to vertical), the writing is able to adjust completely to the composition of the picture and the direction of the figures, that is, to the "sense" of the scene (see Fischer 1977a, 1986; Vernus 1985).

2. The *fluid transition* between caption (the text integrated into the picture) and illustration (the picture integrated into the text) in the framework of mutual "determination."

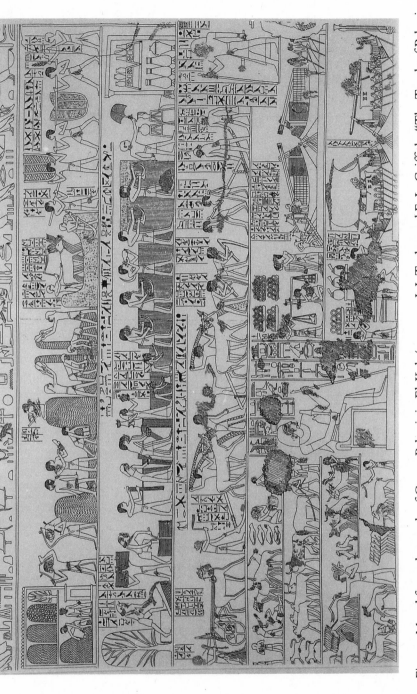

Fig. 4. Mural from the tomb of Count Paheri, in El-Kab (SOURCE: J. J. Taylor and F. L. Griffith, "The Tomb of Paheri at El-Kab," in E. Naville, ed., *Ahnas el Medineh* [*Heracleopolis Magna*], London, 1894)

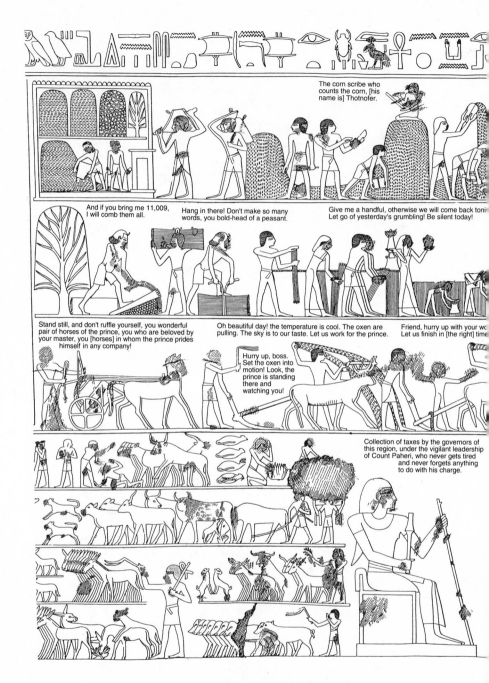

Fig. 5. Mural from the tomb of Count Paheri (Fig. 4), with English captions

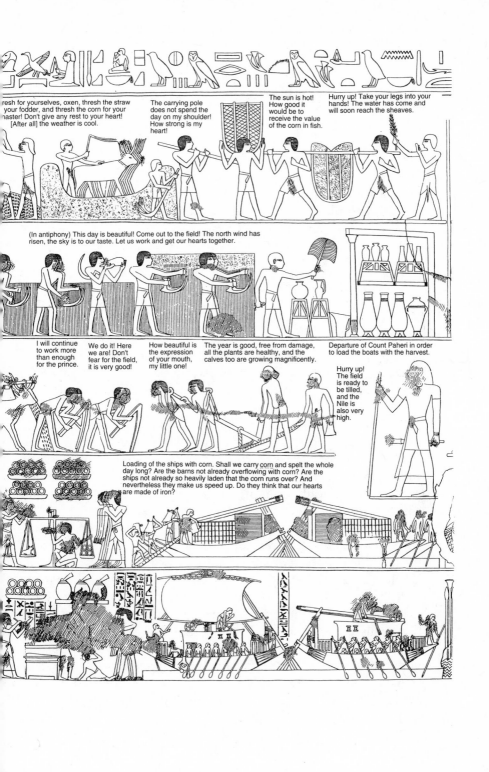

resh for yourselves, oxen, thresh the straw your fodder, and thresh the corn for your master! Don't give any rest to your heart! [After all] the weather is cool.

The carrying pole does not spend the day on my shoulder! How strong is my heart!

The sun is hot! How good it would be to receive the value of the corn in fish.

Hurry up! Take your legs into your hands! The water has come and will soon reach the sheaves.

(In antiphony) This day is beautiful! Come out to the field! The north wind has risen, the sky is to our taste. Let us work and get our hearts together.

I will continue to work more than enough for the prince.

We do it! Here we are! Don't fear for the field, it is very good!

How beautiful is the expression of your mouth, my little one!

The year is good, free from damage, all the plants are healthy, and the calves too are growing magnificently.

Departure of Count Paheri in order to load the boats with the harvest.

Hurry up! The field is ready to be tilled, and the Nile is also very high.

Loading of the ships with corn. Shall we carry corn and spelt the whole day long? Are the barns not already overflowing with corn? Are the ships not already so heavily laden that the corn runs over? And nevertheless they make us speed up. Do they think that our hearts are made of iron?

3. The *three functions* of the writing. The first is to *explain* the picture (scene titles in the infinitive, e.g., "Departure of Count Paheri to load the ships"). The second is to *identify* the persons (annotations of names, e.g., "the grain accountant, who counts the grain, Thotnofer"). The third is to supplement the rendering of speeches, that is to *record sound*, in multiple media.

In this way, these complex reading pictures are produced as a unique phenomenon in art history. They address not only the inner eye but also the inner ear[2] and, in the richness of the connection between picture and writing, go far beyond what is possible in the area of modern picture narratives (comics).[3]

Inscriptionality: Physical Presence and Situational Grounding

Semiotic Interference

Every sign has two sides: the semantic side, namely, its meaning, and the material side, namely, its physical form. Not only does a sign sense have to take physical shape in order to manifest itself, but this physical shape, in which lies Aleida Assmann's dialectic of presence and absence (A. Assmann 1988: 238–39), must also be diminished in its own importance; that is to say, it must be *semantically neutralized*. The participation of the material can never be silenced but can only be made latent. The material aspect of the sign is never categorically insignificant but always more or less latently cosignificant (see Fig. 6).

As Aleida Assmann shows, readability is decreased by actualized co-meaning. The reading gaze, which normally sees directly through the materiality of signs to the sense that is shown in them, is halted by the elaboration of the form in a physical manifestation. "The impulse toward a coalescing spiritualization counters the materialization of the text." "Reading" becomes "gazing." The numerous examples from all writing traditions show, nevertheless, that writers have been concerned not only with the reading but also with the "fascinated" gaze. Generally, the possibilities of a gradual actualization of a latent material cosignification lie within the normal writing system of a culture and are not differentiated as a

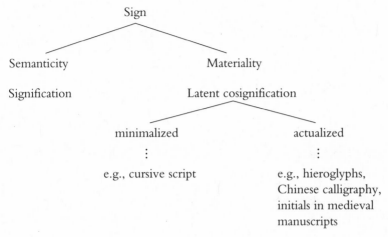

Fig. 6. The cosignification of the material sign

special script. Such differentiation is precisely the case in Egyptian, however. Here, from the special script of hieroglyphs, a cursive script was developed for everyday purposes, in which the cosignification of sign forms was minimalized and semiotic interference mostly nullified. This presents us with a real *digraphic* situation, in which one script developed from the other but removed itself so far from the initial script that it had to be learned separately. Thus it was possible for the "sacred" script of hieroglyphs to cultivate its dysfunctional extravagance, an extravagance in both production and (on account of the high degree of semiotic interference) reception.

Monumentality and Immortality

Up to now, in dealing with the "embodiment" of the sense, we have only spoken about the materiality of the sign. There are an additional two elements for a total of three aspects of the physical. Here we see that, in view of the modalities of the embodiment of communicative sense, we must distinguish oral and written communication as well as inscriptional communication.

Figure 7 illuminates the surprising fact that, with regard to physical presence and specificity, the inscriptional situation is much closer to the oral than to the written. The aestheticized script,

Communication

	Oral	Written	Inscriptional
Materiality of the sign	Voice	Neutral script	Aesthetic script
Sign carrier	Body	Paper, etc.	Monument
Physical situation	Limited by space–time	Unspecified	Limited by space

Fig. 7. The modalities of communication

actualized in its cosignification, takes the place of the voice. The monument takes the place of the body, and the monumental physical situation, limited by space, takes the place of the oral physical situation, restricted by both time and space. This monumental context can more or less be specified and limited in spatial terms (e.g., churches, mausoleums, squares). The three aspects of oral communication—voice, body, and limited situation—are neutralized and minimized in everyday, utilitarian writing. This is made possible by a legible script, easily transported carrier material, and the situation-unspecific, arbitrary receptivity that such material allows. The three aspects of orality are carefully reconstructed by other means in the inscriptional situation.

In considering Egyptian hieroglyphs, we stand before a sensual presence of the greatest imaginable intensity. Hieroglyphic writing is to be found almost exclusively in the context of monumental carriers and important, limited communicational spaces. The Egyptians realized the monumental embodiment of sense through unprecedented expenditure. Behind this is what Paul Eluard has called "le dur désir de durer," or the stubborn quest for permanence, a desire for eternity that seeks its salvation in the sheer persistence and massiveness of its material. We are also in the land of mummification, that is, the inability to imagine the soul without the body, the spirit without the material. By erecting such monuments the Egyptians created, alongside the everyday, a world of stone in which impermanent existence was made permanent and the material basis for eternal life was prepared. This was the "sacred space of permanence" that, as a communicational situation, was open to the divine. In this space one became physically present through monuments and gained speech and voice through hieroglyphs.

Systemic Openness: The World as Text

Idolatry and Direct Signification

There is a reverse side to the idea that spirit cannot be imagined without matter and that everything must be done to preserve the body. Matter cannot be imagined without spirit. Matter therefore *eo ipso* has soul. The concept of "matter" does not exist in Egyptian.* It would never have occurred to the Egyptians to scorn a deity because it was made of bronze or stone. An Egyptian maxim admonishes one to "honor God in his way, who is made of bronze and stone" (Merikare 125, in Volten 1945: 67–69), that is, "God" and not the "image of God." According to Egyptian beliefs, the idol does not represent the body of the god but *is* the body of the god. One can read in another text that "gold is the flesh of the gods" (Schott 1961: 150, 169–70). Matter as a lifeless, meaningless, and arbitrary substance, from which everything, including even gods, can be made, is an invention of the Israelites:

> He plants a cedar and the rain nourishes it.
> Then it becomes fuel for a man;
> he takes a part of it and warms himself,
> he kindles a fire and bakes bread;
> also he makes a god and worships it,
> he makes it a graven image and falls down before it.
> Half of it he burns in the fire;
> over the half he eats flesh,
> he roasts meat and is satisfied;
> also he warms himself and says,
> "Aha, I am warm, I have seen the fire!"
> And the rest of it he makes into a god,
> his idol; and falls down to it and worships it;
> he prays to it and says,
> "Deliver me, for thou art my god!"
> (Isa. 44: 14–17, Revised Standard Version)

In Egypt we find ourselves in the opposite world. It occurred to no one that matter was involved in the use of images. The reason for this lies in the fact that Egypt was a culture of "direct significa-

*Significant in this context is the practice in inscriptions within the sarcophogus chamber of avoiding or mutilating certain hieroglyphs that portrayed living beings. Thus they could not threaten or harm the deceased.

tion," in the sense of Aleida Assmann's distinction (A. Assmann 1980: 57–78). This means that the world reveals the godly or sensual in inexhaustible forms. These are then deciphered by the "fascinated glance" of the observer. Hieroglyphs refer to these forms in their iconical "world reference" and in this way offer themselves not only as reading material but for contemplative observation.[4] If the divine manifests itself in the sensually comprehensible physical forms of the world, then the world reference of the images signifies god reference. The Bible therefore hits the nail on the head when, in the many passages where it fights against graven images, it equates the manufacture of images and the worship of idols. Images are in themselves already idols. Decorative and other harmless purposes are not recognized:

Therefore take good heed to yourselves. Since you saw no form on the day that the Lord spoke to you at Horeb out of the midst of the fire, beware lest you act corruptly by making a graven image for yourselves, in the form of any figure, the likeness of male or female, the likeness of any beast that is on the earth, the likeness of any winged bird that flies in the air, the likeness of anything that creeps on the ground, the likeness of any fish that is in the water under the earth. And beware lest you lift up your eyes to heaven, and when you see the sun and the moon and the stars, all the host of heaven, you be drawn away and worship them and serve them, things which the Lord your God has allotted to all the peoples under the whole heaven.   (Deut. 4: 15–19. Cf. Exod. 20: 4; Deut. 4: 23, 25, 5: 8)

The Israelites also lived in a nondisenchanted world. They therefore had to protect themselves from images. Since Jehovah does not appear in this world in any physically comprehensible manifestations or forms (*t⁽ᵉ⁾munah*), the world reference of images must refer to other gods. Idolatry is therefore equated with the worship of *other* gods.

Crocodilicity: or, The World as Text

The systemic openness of hieroglyphic writing is related to its world reference as well as to the fact that this is a world of direct signification. New signs can constantly be introduced on the basis of both the meaningfulness of the world and the iconicity or world referentiality of the sign. This possibility was restricted until the Late Period by certain valid requirements of legibility. These fetters were broken in the Ptolemaic Age. The result was an explosive increase in the number of signs from about 700 to over 7,000 (see Janssen 1974; *Catalogue* 1983). But this is not all. Most signs took on various meanings, some a dozen or more. The peak of sophistication was reached in inscriptions that use only one sign, repeated again and again with different meanings (see Vernus 1977).*

The language reference of writing is hardly changed by this increase in the number of signs and sign values. The decisive changes are to be found at the level of world reference.[5] We are dealing with a kind of literal allegory, with "allography" or "écriture figurative" (Sauneron 1982). With the introduction of new signs, new "things" are introduced into the writing system. The world reference of the system is strengthened, not by the traditional means of iconical realism, but by the new means of increasing the things that serve as signs. The virtual congruence between the corpus of the *signs* and the corpus of *things* is important. Through this, the world is definable as a corpus of signs and writing as a corpus of things. Writing takes on cosmic traits; the cosmic takes on written traits. Both are codifications of signs: the world as "the hieroglyphics of the gods" (Junge 1984: 272), writing as a kind of pictorial encyclopedia.

There is, however, an important difference in the signification mode of things, that is, the way things are able to take on meaning as soon as they are introduced into the framework of hieroglyphic writing. I would like to call the first, normal mode "direct" and the second and more unusual the "metaphoric." In the direct mode the image of a thing represents either the thing itself (as with an ideogram) or its name in its (consonantal) sound value (as with a phonogram). In the metaphoric mode the image of a thing does not represent the thing itself but rather a quality that this thing embodies in a paradigmatic or emblematic way. The sign of the crocodile, for example, can simply mean "crocodile." This is the direct mode. It can also serve as a determinative in words that mean "greed," "to be greedy," "violence," "to attack," and so on. This, I think, is a completely different mode of representation. The thing,

---

*This intentional encipherment or cryptography of the text is "calligraphy," an aesthetic principle. The main concern is not to protect a particularly sacred text from unauthorized reading but to employ an especially artistic inscription in certain important passages. See Sauneron 1982.

here the crocodile, does not simply represent the word or the concept "crocodile" but a concept of "crocodilicity" as an aggregate of the behavioral qualities of the crocodile transferred to humankind. It is important how the metaphor, applied to the functions of writing, works. Instead of calling a man a "crocodile" on the basis of his greed and aggression, one writes the words for "greed" and "aggression" with the sign of the crocodile.*

The metaphoric mode plays only a supporting role in the classical writing system but it is not entirely uncommon. There are, after all, some twenty signs, all animal images, that are used in the metaphoric mode. The nicest example is the sign of the cow that gives suck to its calf and licks it lovingly at the same time. The word determined in this manner, *ꜣms-jb*, means "to be happy." This motif also plays an important role in the bucolic scenes on tomb walls (see Mathiae 1961; Keel 1980: 55–114). The world functions not only as a reservoir of types with such signs but also as a text that conveys meaning.

The metaphoric mode was considerably enlarged in the later period. Only in late antiquity did it achieve its exclusive monopoly on the memory that was left of the meaning of hieroglyphs. In the fifth or sixth century A.D., the Egyptian priest Horapollon gave a description of hieroglyphs that interprets all signs in the metaphoric mode.[6] Most of the so-called signs have nothing at all to do with real hieroglyphs, but even when he hits the mark, his explanations are false. For example, he connects the picture of the duck with the meaning "son" by pointing out the "sense of family" of the duck, and links the picture of the rabbit with the meaning "to open" by reference to the fact that rabbits never close their eyes.[†] The text of Horapollon is based on and correlates three catalogues: (a) a catalogue of conceptual denotations like "son," "to open," "time"; (b) a catalogue of pictures (of these, approximately 10 percent are true hieroglyphs); and (c) a catalogue of universal knowledge that is roughly equivalent to the bestiary of Physiologus.

---

*Of primary concern are the words *zkn* "to be greedy," *hnt* "to be greedy," and *zd* "to be furious, violent, aggressive." The sparse remarks of Grapow 1924: 95–96, do not in any way do justice to the meaning of the crocodile image in Egyptian metaphoric language.

†What is actually taking place is the simple sound transferal from *zꜣ* "duck" to *zꜣ* "son" and from *wn* "rabbit" to *wn* "open." This mode had been completely forgotten by the time of Horapollon.

These catalogues are usually correlated according to the following scheme: "If you want to express (a), draw (b), because (c)." All of this is pure fantasy, but it possessed for late antiquity enormous natural authority because it coincided exactly with their biological and above all zoological knowledge, a kind of allegorical ethology. The component (c) in Horapollon's scheme corresponded exactly with the worldview whose validity was unquestioned up until the Renaissance. Horapollon's text was in this way able to gain great influence in the sixteenth and seventeenth centuries (see Iversen 1961; Giehlow 1915; Volkmann 1923). This text led to the development of hieroglyphics or emblematics as systems of communication with metaphoric or allegorical images, an "allography." It also established a hieroglyphic worldview that understood the world as a complex of meaningful signs, the worldview of "direct signification." Not until the deciphering of hieroglyphics by Champollion was this thousand-year-old misunderstanding cleared up through the rediscovery of the "direct" mode of signification. At the same time, all the real knowledge that was a part of this writing system was allowed to be forgotten.

JAN-DIRK MÜLLER

The Body of the Book:
The Media Transition from
Manuscript to Print

More Durable than Bronze

"Now I have created your image in marble, if you deign to receive
favorably the verses already begun. Soon I will fix it in gold, in the
Temple of Minerva, that is to say, in the pure hearts of scholars."*
With these words, Viennese professor of rhetoric Johann Alex-
ander Brassican recommended epigrams praising the government
bureaucrats of Lower Austria in 1525. Verses, as hard as marble
statues and eventually as valuable as gold, would recall the secre-
taries and councillors for all time, not only in a temple but everywhere in the hearts of the scholarly world. It is an old argument
that memory preserved in writing is more permanent than any
other monument. The elder Pliny already knew that immortality
depended on the use of papyrus (*Nat. hist.* XIII, 21). The humanist
panegyrists around 1500 believed they had immediate proof: the
rediscovered writings of antiquity preserved the names of kings
and senators, of generals and artists. Was it not reasonable to
promise the same to one's own patron, especially insofar as he was
only willing to support scholarly verses (and their authors) that
immortalized his name?

The argument seemed convincing, and yet one important dif-

*From a leaflet concerning the victory of Charles V over France (1525).

ference escaped notice: the altered communications situation and the change of the medium. The appeal of advertisements like Brassican's depended on a history in which select texts in single manuscripts were brought back to life after the passage of time. But what would happen if suddenly everywhere an army of writers engaged in the business of immortality? What if their texts no longer circulated in small groups as manuscripts, but were suddenly available everywhere in great numbers as printed leaflets? Technical reproduction might have seemed at first a chance to preserve writing for everyone and for all time, but it abolished traditional selection mechanisms that established what is worth knowing and preserving. Written and printed monuments ceased to be monuments capable of recalling memories.

Brassican promises monuments of solid materials, marble and gold, but delivers a few pages of printed paper, a material that is, as we know, perishable and hardly permanent. He promises a precious and desirable object, but his leaflet was of little value, and almost no one held on to it. He promises a work of art that is unique or nearly so, having only a few replicas in a sacred site; but this kind of broadsheet has no particular place. Addressing virtually everyone, it concerns no one in particular. The place in the hearts of the scholarly world that was promised the Austrian bureaucrats was none too certain. Verses of praise and those praised were both fairly soon forgotten.

It is worthwhile to look from today's standpoint at the deep rift in the writing culture during the time of early print. The change wrought by the advent of print in the organization of knowledge and the social function of writing of that time was as drastic as the change wrought by the advent of electronic media today. I will not discuss the complex assumptions and consequences of book printing (see Eisenstein 1979) but will deal instead with a particular problem, the materiality of writing and its medium (marble, paper) and, along with this, the change in attitude toward time and duration and the change in perception of text and tradition. All these concepts are topics of contemporary discussion, yet in an entirely different sense. Classifieds announce the "dematerialized" newspaper of the twenty-first century, and funeral orations are held in public for the book, that cumbersome object of information conveyance. The networking of all pieces of knowledge promises an immense acceleration of progress, that is to say, the irrelevance of anything that is old. Text is only the transitory product of the personal computer, between one proof and another. We cannot yet predict the continuing course of the process that was put in motion with the first technical revolution of writing culture. One should be cautious regarding historical parallels between the advent of printing and that of electronic media, and teleological assumptions proved to be wrong anyway, but the reactions of that time are telling insofar as they reflect certain conditions of modern writing culture in terms of resentments and exaggerated expectations, as well as the difficulty the established cultural system had in adjusting to these conditions.

Reproduction and Aura

Multiplication (*multiplicatio*) was one of the main points in the praise of the new invention (Widmann 1972: 253). But very soon the other side of the coin was discovered, the "overabundance of writing" (*vile der gschrifft*), the fact that everything was printed with little concern for selection and correctness, "for profit alone" (*alleyn vff gewynn*), and as a "great scam" (*groß beschisß*). Books lost value everywhere (*nütz gelten überal*) and along with them the scholars, who were now replaced by "rude people" (*geburen*) (Brant 1968: chap. 103, vv. 77–78, 98–104). According to Brant, selection and refinement of the written tradition are taken away from the only competent faculty, scholars. Ecclesiastical and governmental control of writing grows more and more difficult (Schreiner 1984). If it were true, as the Parisian theologian Guillaume Fichet claimed around 1470, that everything that can be said or thought can be immediately written and preserved for posterity by movable type (Swierk 1972: 81), then the memory capacity of the cultural system would be overstressed and oblivion would be the result. Conrad Gesner asserts in 1545, after almost a hundred years of printing, that books disappear as quickly as they are produced. He demands the establishment of public libraries at least for the valuable old manuscripts, as the apparently unlimited possibilities of reproduction by print lead to arbitrariness and uselessness (Gesner 1966: 3r). The written word loses the "aura" that it possessed in medieval culture as a guarantor of truth, as a vessel of arcane knowledge, even as a component of magical practices.

This trivialization of the written was counteracted from the beginning by the attempt to save the aura of the medium, artificial writing (*artificialiter scribere*). God Himself gave humankind the new invention, because the requirement for writing had surpassed the work capacity of the scribe to the point that science and the handing down of sacred truth were endangered. Now a printer could produce more pages in a single day than could a scribe in a whole year (see Swierk 1972: 81, for further examples). Early on the new art was called "divina ars." The colophon of Justinian's *Institutions* (1468) compares the inventors with the greatest artisans of the Old Testament, who built the tabernacle and the temple furnishings.* What Bezaleel and Hyram contributed to the cult of Jehovah was accomplished by Gutenberg and Fust for the renewal of the Church by Christ. Books are tabernacles of God's truth: "In libris posuisti procul dubio tabernaculum tuum" (Bury 1960: 16). If God is not Himself claimed to be the inventor, print is at least placed among the cultural technologies that humanity owes to mythical heroes (cf. Polidorus Vergilius 1502: xxxvii r/v). And if the product of the press is fleeting and subject to rapid deterioration, at least the more solid quality of the writing material is emphasized: not the brittle reed, stylus, or quill but brazen letters made for longevity (see Swierk 1972: 82, for further examples). In any case, such arguments could not conceal the fact that book printing did not create a new temple as a center of Christianity but instead decentralized the Christian world. Nor could they conceal that ordinary means of control of writing and criteria of relevance were shoved aside or subjected to the needs of the market.

Very early on, print separated itself from traditional centers of writing (bishops' seats, religious convents, and universities). It became a profit-oriented commerce that had to meet the varied and growing demand of a diverse and predominantly urban society with its antagonistic interests. Although at the end of the fifteenth century it was still possible for a bishop of Mainz to oblige the printers of a town like Frankfurt to subject themselves to censorship, in the long run an effective control of all production sites, not to mention those prints that could be exported, was far beyond the

---

*"Moses cannot complete the plan of the tabernacle, nor can Salomon complete the temple, without ingenious craftsmen. Thus, the one who is greater than Salomon (= Christ) creates anew Bezaleel and Hyram (i.e., Gutenberg) wishing to renew the Church" (Heidenheimer 1925: 109).

capabilities of any political institutions of the time. And no matter what was written about the durability of the press in comparison with the pen, its product was no longer the costly treasure that was preserved with care and passed on from generation to generation.

Longevity of the Codex Versus Longevity of the Text

The notorious and curious words of Abbot Johannes Trithemius (1462–1516) in his *Praise of the Scribe* (*De laude scriptorum*, 1494) express how the nature of the written tradition changed along with the material characteristics of the medium. He reminds his Benedictine brethren of their duty to copy sacred books:

> The devotion of the scribe is more valuable than the office of the preacher because the admonition of the preacher disappears in time, but the message of the scribe lasts for many years. The preacher only speaks to those present, whereas the scribe also preaches to those in the future. . . . When the preacher dies, his work is finished; the scribe continues to be a teacher of morality even after his death.   (Trithemius 1973: 58)

These are well-known arguments supported by quotations from Church Fathers and theologians. But are they not rendered obsolete by printing, which reproduces the sacred text much faster and for many more readers? The answer:

> Who is ignorant of the difference between writing [*scriptura*] and printing [*impressura*]? A manuscript, written on parchment, can last a thousand years. How long will print, this thing of paper [*res papirea*] last? It is quite a lot if it can last two hundred years in a volume of paper [*in volumine papireo*]. . . . Actually, no matter how many books are printed, there will never be so many printed that one couldn't find something to copy that hasn't yet been printed. Hardly anyone will have access to all books or be able to buy them. But even if all the books in the world were printed, the devout scribe should never lessen his zeal. He should copy the usable prints and thereby give them longevity, since otherwise they would not last long. In so doing, the scribe grants stability to instable writings [*scripturis mutantibus*]. He gives value to those of little worth and longevity to those subject to deterioration. The devout scribe will always find a task by which he will do a great service. He is not restrained by external conditions like the printer. He is free and rejoices in his freely performed task. He is in no way inferior to the printer, and his zeal must not weaken because the other prints.   (Trithemius 1973: 62, 64)

D. Mertens (1983) has elucidated the background of this strange admonition. Trithemius is concerned with the reform of his order. It is therefore not a contradiction when elsewhere he praises printing and when he even benefits from its potential by giving his *Praise of the Scribe* to the press. He recognizes two main problems: selection and longevity. Not all manuscripts are printed and especially few from the Benedictine tradition (Mertens 1983: 92). Printing therefore does not encompass the entire stock of writing. Whatever is excluded has little chance of being passed on. A sufficient and standard demand must first exist in order for the effort to pay off. The rapid rise and fall of some shops and the number of business failures (see Chrisman 1982) testify to how the market corrects a publisher's bad decisions with brutal efficiency. The considerations that the printer must take into account are summarized by Trithemius as "restrictive conditions" (*constringi sub conditione impressoris*). This he juxtaposes with the "freedom" of the scribe. The opposition between the "seven liberal arts" of the noble and the bound *artes mechanicae* of the artisan earning his living may be the background of this assertion. However, Trithemius also describes two ways in which texts of a past culture are handed down: extraneous conditions, and free and responsible decisions (the latter assuring results of a more durable nature). Above all, the longevity of the text is linked to writing material. "Printing is a matter of paper and deteriorates quickly" (Trithemius 1973: 34). This is obviously a weak argument; it is based on false assumptions concerning the longevity of paper and disregards the possibility of printing on parchment—even if it is true that printing was done primarily on paper, that only the mass production of paper had allowed the development of the new technology, and that only texts of extraordinary subject matter sometimes were done on parchment (Mertens 1983). It is striking, however, that Trithemius is concerned less with the life of the text than with the life of the body of the text, that is, the individual codex. He therefore advocates the copying of prints, including his own *Praise of the Scribe*, onto parchment. This can only be understood in the framework of the manuscript culture. Jean Gerson, chancellor of the Sorbonne, made similar arguments around 1400: "A piece of writing can last not just for a short time, but for 10, 100, or 1,000 years, and this not only by itself [*in se*] but also by the multiplication of the exemplars [*per multiplica-*

tionem exemplariorum] that are copied from the original" (Gerson 1973: 425). Reproduction is the worse alternative because every copy is a variation if not a change of the original. A reduction of the steps of reproduction ensures the integrity of the text. Gerson criticizes the many incapable scribes and the many corruptions of texts. He recommends "drinking" as closely to the "source" of truth as possible, at the "scripta veterum," this being the works of the ancients as well as the written texts. Hence, a text on parchment lasting a thousand years is more trustworthy than a chain of ten texts on paper, copied from each other, but each enduring only a short time (Gerson 1973: 428). Only the sound body of his book can guarantee the author a life after death. Otherwise the costs and labors of writing are lost.

The Book as Body

Writing survives as a physically present object in the body of a book. If medieval culture is performance, the interaction of voice and bodies, as P. Zumthor (1987b) demonstrates, then that culture also had a far more corporeal conception of writing than the age of the early print had. The comparison holds all the more true for the age of the ubiquitously available writing of electronic media. Writing not only is more permanent than speech, but also, strangely enough, has a stronger effect on the senses. This is in any case the opinion of Richard de Bury (1287–1345) in his famous *Philobiblon* (1345). Truth that appears—with Boethius—in thoughts, speech, or writing is most profitable in books:

> For the meaning of the voice [*virtus vocis*] perishes with the sound; truth latent in the mind [*mente latens*] is wisdom that is hid and treasure that is not seen; but truth which shines forth in books desires to manifest itself to every impressionable sense [*omni disciplinabili sensui*]. It commends itself to the sight when it is read, to the hearing when it is heard, and moreover in a manner to the touch, when it suffers itself to be transcribed, bound, corrected, and preserved.   (de Bury 1960: 19)

Others add the sense of taste in the sampling and rumination of what is read. Compared with writing, thoughts lack a discursive partner (*socius*) and oral instruction does not affect the sense of sight. The written word, on the other hand, is the perfect teacher, a living partner, but without the failings of a person such as bad moods, tiredness, or infirmity and death. Always friendly and available to provide information, books "are masters [*magistri*], who instruct us without rod or ferule, without angry words, without clothes or money. If you come to them they are not asleep; if you ask and inquire of them, they do not withdraw themselves; they do not chide if you make mistakes; they do not laugh at you if you are ignorant" (de Bury 1960: 21). Books are the teachers, not their authors. The conversation is held with books, not their authors. In them the author is present. This apparent presence is expressed in pictures of authors common in medieval manuscripts. The metaphor *accessus ad auctorem*, used as a typical medieval formula of introduction, expresses the same concept. That the author is conceived as present is shown in translations of Latin texts into the vernacular. Often the author does not appear as the speaker, as in modern translations, but the translator defers to the one to whom he gives a voice: "Here Master X speaks and says . . ."

The metaphor of tradition or its loss speaks of books in terms of living beings. They, or actually the authors embodied in them, suffer in unworthy captivity, rot in cellars subjected to the bites of moths and roaches. Since the transmission of truth depends on the survival of the codices, they must be protected from decay. Nevertheless, they are mortal: "But because all the appliances of mortal men with the lapse of time suffer the decay of mortality, it is needful to replace the volumes that are worn out with age by fresh successors, that the perpetuity of which the individual is by its nature incapable may be secured to the species" (de Bury 1960: 147). Longevity (*perpetuitas*) means a never-ending chain of mortal individuals—the books—in whom the species survives:

For as the bodies of books [*librorum corpora*], seeing that they are formed of a combination of contrary elements, undergo a continual dissolution of their structure [*suae compositionis*], so by the forethought of the clergy a remedy should be found, by means of which the sacred book paying the debt of nature may obtain a natural heir and may raise up like seed to its dead brother, and thus may be verified that saying of Ecclesiasticus: His father is dead, and he is as if he were not dead; for he hath left one behind him that is like himself.   (de Bury 1960: 147. Cf. Eccles. 30: 4)

To copy the ancients means to produce sons (*propagationes recentium filiorum*), to whom the office of the fathers (*paternum officium*) is transferred. The metaphors don't seem totally convincing: a procreation by clerics, with dark relationships (brother? son?). The understanding of tradition is nonetheless clear. Ecclesiasticus speaks of permanence and change in a traditional society. Such a society is made all the more stable as the elders successfully transmit their knowledge to their sons. The heritage of the past changes constantly because it must be passed on from one individual to another. Yet everything remains basically the same as it was and always has been, because the father lives on in the son and in the son's son. Likewise the author lives on in his descendants, his books (de Bury 1960: 18). Tradition seems to be a chain of generations. Communication with tradition is therefore not a hermeneutic problem because the substance of the old remains present in the descendant.

This concept of tradition begins to break apart in early humanism. It is one of the main points that the Reformation attacks. Of course, it was recognized before this that traditions can be distorted. This is not seen, however, as a historical-philological problem (as in the *ad fontes* principle of the humanists). Whatever changes also degenerates. Poor copies are bastards. Their nobility (Richard de Bury uses *generositas*, the English translation has "purity of race") is ruined, as in a chain of mésalliances, by compilers, revisers, and (worst of all) translators for the laity. Reborn again from generation to generation, they finally degenerate completely (*regeneratione multiplici renascentes degeneramus omnino*). Their true heritage is distorted: "Ah! how often ye pretend that we who are ancient are but lately born, and try to pass us off as sons who are really fathers, calling us who have made you clerks the production of your studies" (de Bury 1960: 46, 47). The place in the chain of generations establishes nobility and the claim to truth: the authority of age.

The Chain of Generations and the Authentic Text

Brother resembles brother and the son the father, but having a family resemblance is not the same as being identical. It is a fact that, in a manuscript culture, one copy will never be exactly the same as another. But this did not present problems as long as the authenticity of truth was granted by the "purity" of the "genetic heritage." Transmission is therefore above all a moral problem.

The permanence of truth depends on the scrupulous scribe and his care and not on a philological reconstruction of a corrupted text or on hermeneutic efforts to regain an obscured meaning. The truth remains the same in the generations and branches of the written text if the scribe is not lazy or a counterfeiter (and that means: an adulterer).

Textual corruption and textual variants, however, could be ignored less and less the more widespread the practice of copying became. The reform movements of the fifteenth century are not the last to criticize variants in sacred texts since they bring forth conflicts about articles of faith, differences in ecclesiastical discipline, and the religious cult. It therefore seemed necessary to Nicholas of Cusa to produce identical missals for all parishes of his diocese. This plan could have hardly been realized in the age of writing and was perhaps, as has been conjectured, based on ties between Cusa and early printers, since now liturgical books no longer needed to be renewed copy for copy but thanks to the new technology could be replaced all at once.

Yet the idea of the book as an individual within a family did not disappear right away. F. Geldner, an expert on early printing, has described an amazing example. In 1482/84, the bishop of Freising ordered liturgical texts to be meticulously proofread by a Bamberg printer. Evidently this was not done by comparing a sample with the written originals and then making the necessary corrections in the master form or transferring them from the sample to each other copy. Instead, it seems that each copy was compared individually with the written original. Only in this way, according to Geldner (1961: 102), do the payments for the proofreading make sense: 91 florins for 91 breviaries on parchment; 206 florins for 206 obsequies; 400 florins for 400 missals, and so on. The enormous sums as well as the exact correspondence between the numbers of copies and the numbers of florins paid support Geldner's thesis. Otherwise, the proofreading of the sample should have been much more expensive than each transferal of the (few) corrections onto the several copies, an operation requiring far less time. This odd investment is due to the old manuscript culture that required such individual proof, copy after copy. The result of a similar procedure, the proofreading of a printed missal "word for word," seemed like a miracle to the bishop of Regensburg: "And see, it was as if by a miracle of God that the text was found to correspond in order and arrangement in each letter, syllable, word, parts of speech [*orationibus*], punctuation [*punctis*], headings, and everything else that is necessary, in every copy [*in omnibus et per omnia*] to the originals of our church" (Geldner 1961: 104). Correspondence in every detail of every copy (!) was discovered where family resemblance was expected. Now an identical text existed beyond its material realizations. These curious cases, if Geldner has correctly interpreted them, show in an exemplary way how written communication can now be centrally controlled and how it detaches itself from a model of interaction between individuals.

The Chain of Generations and the *Bibliotheca Universalis*

Concerning missals, the authoritative text is the result of careful selection and the decisions of the bishop. Such care was never granted in early printing. On the contrary, whatever manuscript happened to be available was chosen for print, and it was therefore left to chance what kinds of texts would experience the greatest distribution. As before, the chain of texts was simply expanded by one link that replaced the preceding one. The original was often destroyed for technical reasons; no matter: it had been replaced (Schottenloher 1931: 94). Humanist scholars and printers eventually opposed this practice (Widmann 1970: xliii). It was no longer sufficient simply to expand the chain; instead, the ever-growing inventory had to be looked through in order to produce the best text from the greatest number of prototypes. For the new philology, the single copies are but steps on the way to the ideal "correct text," which is actually never attainable but must at least be attempted in some way by comparison and combination. Meaning is not eternally present in the materiality of the book but must first be reconstructed beyond the distance of tradition. If writing must now be collected and deciphered as a clue to a dim past, then historical understanding becomes a never-ending task for the future. Gesner discovers that the newer text, insofar as it is the result of careful philological efforts, is often better than the older text (the "father"), in which the past seems to be present in its natural state (Gesner 1966: 4v). Historical perspective is inscribed in the new culture of writing from the beginning, even though reflection on it lags behind for two centuries.

The generation around 1550 realized a loss of tradition, even though printing seemed at first to secure everything that had been transmitted and was worthy of transmission (*quamuis enim ars typographica librorum conseruationi nata uideatur*; Gesner 1966: 3r). The loss of tradition manifests itself in the destruction of manuscripts. Nicolaus Mameranus states in 1550 that everybody stupidly trusts the first, best print, that is, the son who replaces the father, and hence accepts that old manuscripts, once printed, are sold, cut up, scraped clean, and then used for other purposes: "The books are printed," they say; "isn't that enough?" Not at all, if one wants to establish the word of the author in its original state (*pristinam suam et nativam integritatem*), as Mameranus himself says in his edition of Paschasius Radpertus. To reestablish it, all available copies must be collected; "the old exemplars must be preserved with holy zeal, and guarded as a treasure, even if they are printed a thousand times over" (Schottenloher 1931: 93–94).

Tradition is no longer considered as this or that codex, but as a whole. Its preservation requires new institutions. Mameranus demands, as do Conrad Gesner and Conrad Lycosthenes, that libraries be placed under public oversight via the nobility and government. The private availability of books, although a highly praised achievement of print (Lycosthenes 1551: p. b 1r), does not ensure survival (Gesner 1966: 3r). Gesner's endeavors aim beyond the simple preservation of manuscripts. His *Bibliotheca universalis* is no longer concerned with individual books but with the transmission of all writing, and it makes little difference to him if the listed titles are still extant or not since, if they are lost now, they could be rediscovered later. Like the more limited catalogues of Trithemius, his *Bibliotheca* is of an imaginary extension, no longer a stock placed here or there. Its place is the literary public as a whole. Scientific interests are no longer concerned with the individually available manuscript or print but with the abstract unity of text or tradition. The idea of a corporeal presence of books is no longer appropriate to such a concept. Writing finally loses any analogy to face-to-face interaction, such as had always characterized the medieval manuscript culture, even where it was not oriented toward oral forms of communication. Books can come to everyone, but they are no longer individuals in which the absent speaker is embodied. Their longevity is no longer dependent on their material characteristics but on the mechanisms of selection of society's new institutions that keep public and present what is fixed in writing.

Final Comment

The body of the book, in fact a metaphor, was in the manuscript culture a guarantor of the longevity of the word and of the presence of author and meaning. Writing naturally depends on material conditions even after the invention of print. But longevity is guaranteed no longer by the written "monument" itself but rather by the numerous institutions that select the constantly growing reservoir of writings and allow them to become effective. Text and tradition are phenomena beyond the present available stock of books. The author and the meaning he is supposed to intend are sought behind what is written. The ties and analogies to situations involving oral communication are severed. How this process affects modern writing cannot be dealt with here. Today writing seems in any case to be losing its eminent position. The pictures, gestures, and sounds that supplement and replace it do not show a return to the medieval culture of performance (Zumthor 1987b). Technically produced and disseminated, they only simulate the sensual presence that the medieval scribe still experienced in the book.

K. LUDWIG PFEIFFER

Dimensions of Literature: A Speculative Approach

Writing and Writing Systems

In February 1900, when the twentieth century was but a month old, Daniel Paul Schreber, LL.D. and former high court judge, began writing down his *Thoughts of a Neurotic*. He did not count on any complete understanding of his ruminations. He nevertheless hoped to promote an understanding of his text, which was also to be seen as written in the cause of science, through pictures, examples, and comparisons with well-known human "experiential realities" (Schreber 1973 [1903]: 67). Samuel Weber later attempted a psycho-analytic interpretation of Schreber's text oriented on Lacan's phallus concept and its implications (see Weber's Introduction to Schreber 1973: 5–62). Friedrich A. Kittler saw in Schreber's text the unconscious product of both an epochal "writing system" and the "body" as communications system along with its neurophysiological, technologically organized channels of knowledge. He saw it as a paradigm of a literature that no longer speaks of soul and subject but utilizes its refuse as technicized psychophysics (Kittler 1987: 183–205, 298–324).

The ambition of Schreber, the writer, did not stop with writing systems. Schreber complained of the compelling force that writing systems (books and other recordings) had on his life and his physical integrity (1973: 178–79). These systems made him believe that he thought more or less mechanically, in meaningless repetitions ("we already have that," 173). He furthermore decried "thought coercion," a "system of incomplete speech" that suggested to him that fragmentary sentences can only be completed with certain, often meaningless stereotypes, and, in this way, be denied an integration in his body (240–46). Schreber considered this kind of "idiocy," that is, thought coercion as "not thinking" (245), to be "thought forgery" (244). He organized his defenses: playing the piano, reading books and newspapers, memorizing poems (mostly at night), "namely ballads by Schiller, longer passages from plays by Schiller and Goethe, but also opera arias and humorous poems including things from Max and Moritz, the Struwwelpeter, and Spekter's Fables" (246). He asserted that human thought is inexhaustible, that reading always stimulates new thoughts (173). He fought against the "mind torture" (173) of *writing systems* with (literary?) *writing*.

Does "literary" writing subvert or overcome the limits and compulsions of historical writing systems and technical communications media? This contrast, its dual character as both system and activity, has itself become a topic in the history of writing. According to Walter Benjamin, everyone who wants to establish his "literary importance" must destroy what is organic. Nevertheless a "strange biomorphism of letters" can sprout from writing (see Bolz 1985: 2; on handwriting, see Mattenklott 1985: 18, 37). Certainly, a "history of writing," such as Kittler occasionally calls for (1985b: 40), cannot be completely "hermeneutic." And yet, is there really "nothing to understand" in something once it has been written down? Does the fact alone that something "is recorded and is not not recorded, pose a puzzle" (Kittler 1985b: 56)?

Transcending into the Present and the Materiality Imperative

Kittler characterized the writing system that existed in Germany around 1800 as a product of sociopsychological and pedagogical-technical factors. These included the nuclear family, with the mother as the primary educational authority, and universal literacy. He characterized literature as discourse, and authorship, that illusory potential for writers' expression, as a replacement for older, more sensual media (1987: 115–23, 183–85). This is why contemporary thinkers (Hegel, H. W. Schlegel, Hardenberg) enrich their definitions of literature with aspects of spiritualization that, indeed, seem to find their way into their texts. The possibilities of aesthetic, need-oriented speech (Koppe 1977) exhaust themselves, it would seem, in useless assaults on the boundaries of sociotechnological media. In Kittler's perspective, notions that understand writing, reading, and spectating as multidimensional activities are illusionary. Equally illusionary are beliefs that writing, reading, and spectating are cultural technologies, which under different sociopsychological and technological conditions transform "curiosities, wishes, longings, inhibitions, fears, expectations, tensions, dreams, stimuli, lusts, aggravations, aggressions, desires, instincts, etc." (Schenda 1970: 470–71; cf. 475–76), in short, unresolved situations, into significant human "figurations" (Elias 1978). Again, given this perspective, there is a danger of validating old humanistic notions, if one believes in an "ability for literary articulation that is latent and basically always present." This is an ability that, as B. Scheffer (1985: 115) notes in a "writing behind bars," can be awakened whenever "any person, regardless of social background, education, or individual life story, begins to write based on some external motivation." These kinds of notions can be considered mere remnants of anthropomorphic thinking.

And yet, anyone who cannot completely rid himself of such thoughts can still reformulate the questions. To begin with, one could ask: can technologies of cultural-psychic reconcretization be determined in everyday as well as literary forms of "narration"? Do they maintain a society's "vital chains of action" by contributing the necessary amounts of fantasy for their actualization? The bandwidth of such "interpretations" is extremely reduced in the new media because image and image content melt into a pseudorealism that economizes the "effort of imagining." "But imagination is a fundamental faculty of intelligence, and a society that gradually loses its ability to create symbols would at the same time lose its ability to act" (Leroi-Gourhan 1980: 267). If the "core of mankind" (ibid.), reflective-imaginative thought, is no longer activated, then the contribution of the "imagined" that is necessary for the representation of even the most elementary experiences is eventually lost:

The possibility of changing the world in its linguistic representation will remain an incalculable inheritance of humanity even when it is implemented for most of the time in relatively primitive ways. . . . In free narration, the transmission of an event, an experience, an imagined experience, a level of the "elaborated code" is easily reached that is not analytical but rather reflexive, pointing reality in the direction of irreality. (Claessens 1980: 165)

Realities produced along the indirect route to "fiction" are interwoven with everyday, social realities with which they are closely related, but remain separate. If narration, even mythical storytelling, however limited its social value may be, always remains incomplete and in so doing demands an interpretation that transcends basic realities, a "highly profitable division of labor" has established itself in the media. Over 25 years ago, A. Leroi-Gourhan commented on this "narrow elite" that had raised itself to the "institution of intellectual processing" and relegated the masses to "simple receptive institutions" (1980 [1964/65]: 266–67). Writing never really reached many people as a general *cultural* authority. It may in fact be sentenced to death today because the imaginative needs of most people can be satisfied by physical participation in the ceremonies, rituals, and mythograms of the media (see Leroi-Gourhan 1980: 491–93; Morin 1969: 142–43; 1973: 157–60).

However, even today permanent "scenarios" have to be created, where the models of a vital meshing of action and imagination can be feigned or simulated. The problem that is approached with the often exaggerated rivalry between literature and the media converges in the question, how much differentiation and undifferentiation of imagination can a culture take? It may be that highly specialized forms of modern writing have grown into an excess of irrelevant, merely fantastic differentiations. It may be that the media give imagination the chance to gain acceptance through clear but still strongly suggestive images (see Spangenberg 1988). It cannot be discounted that the media's unfavorable, fatiguing, linear-sequential display of information and imagination, itself unable to show the synchronicity of aspects and their multidimensionality, might someday banish writing to the museum of cognitive devices (see Leroi-Gourhan 1980: 493).

But one does not have to trust such prognostications these days. Also, the motivations for current-situation reports, whether euphoric or critical, are all too transparent. In any case, cultures must provide guaranteed situations that grant the imaginative-significant realizations, devoid of risk, of their modalities of action and experience. In other words, they must develop activities and media that allow the extension of the so-called real in linguistic or pictorial productions. When objects, living beings, possess existential value, especially when institutions can independently develop into a socially controlled and promoted "existential self-worth," then a space for the production or "staging" of behavior becomes necessary in which institutions and social life may be transcended—not for some life to come, but for the lived present itself. These central forms of experience and action must be guaranteed a useful significance and permanence in cultural memory, if not in social semantics (see Gehlen 1975: 14–16, 54–57).

To accomplish this always necessitates a variety of media. Still in the nineteenth century, Bentham claimed the possible functional equivalence of bowling, football, and literature. This variety of media (see Heider 1959, e.g., 1, 7, 13, 16, 23), where impulses and realizations compete and become plastic, is characterized by innumerable degrees and layers. Of course, certain changes in the media landscape are especially noticeable to contemporaries. For this reason, the concept of media today sometimes concentrates on the electronic arena. Claims concerning the cognitive range of technological change are risky, however. The lists of existence-determining technological "extensions" of mankind, not only McLuhan's (1964), strike one as arbitrary or scholastic (see Raabe 1986). Walking and flying faster than sound, human interaction and computers, Schiller and *Dallas*, classical music and rock—it seems that nothing connects these. And still the thesis can be presented that the modern media enrich the experience of the old. They may reduce their range, but they guarantee their existence at the same time, since every medium has deficits that must be compensated for.

Whatever. These very different media, guaranteeing margins for a transcendence into the present, are subject to a kind of materiality imperative. Of course they aren't able to shake off the cultural semantics within themselves, be they archaic rites or modern football rituals, ancient dramas or highly reflexive modern novels. If the boundaries of the everyday are to be overcome, even if only "fictionally," then the guarantees must not become too conscious, they must not make use of highly explicit meanings that are only reflexively grounded. These are historically always present in plurality, in conditions of competition and decline (see Gehlen 1975: 44–51). Media that must rely on the evidence of situations that they themselves produce, on a successful blending of reality and imagination, cannot afford to achieve fulfillment through higher degrees of semantization and reflection. This includes the small area of transcending into the present that might be stimulated by "literary" writing. One may grant that the modern novel (Mann, Musil, Proust, etc.) possesses a "clarity of reflection that one would wish for certain philosophers" (Gehlen 1975: 63). But this judgment is partially misleading, because reflection and semantic intensity of what is represented in these novels also converge in the rejection of claims of "mere" thought. They shift to the silent rehabilitation of mute materiality and presence of completely different situations (such as those mistakenly called "physical").

The materiality imperative therefore requires that not only everyday situations but also fictional accomplishments be understandable on their own. Texts and images, where reality and imagination are intertwined, demand a vital presence that cannot be damaged by internally produced reflections. Even if this thesis is only partially valid, it certainly undermines interpretation, that central activity of literary criticism that has for some time been plying its trade. Literary criticism of the eighteenth century, for instance, was not concerned with what would later be called the meaning(s) of works that have come down on the reader's side in reception aesthetics. The criticism of that century was still trying to define the effects, from laughter to horror, from elementary physical reactions to differentiated emotions, of the texts and dramas that are organized into "works." What was important was the definition of the effects that come through despite semantic differences (see, e.g., Zelle 1987). The critical emphasis changed in the nineteenth century. At this time literature, with its discursive spheres of theology, law, history, ethics, and science, all thoroughly disciplined by power politics, was also subjected to semantic explication, to those concepts of those traditions fabricated by social needs of legitimacy. Literary criticism of the twentieth century has continued this trend in different ways, mostly in an increased intellectualization, also including the reader. The intellectual overestimation of literature in many works of the 1960's and 1970's, including those on reception aesthetics, provide ample evidence.

Writing, Media, the Drive Toward Textuality

I am getting ahead of myself. We still seem to think it necessary to pull together an unbelievable medial and cognitive variety under the label of "literature." "Literature," at least in "occidental" cultures, seems to be predominantly tied to the medium of writing. Of course, we can always assume some underlying "pure" orality for past or even recurring situations. In these, what is later called literature acts as an encyclopedia of social conduct and cultural memory. E. A. Havelock interpreted Plato's attacks on poetry (which had in the meantime been written down and were therefore sociopsychologically more difficult to control) in this sense (1963: 13–47). The writing of history and philosophy must take over as educational institutions, a role that written, overly complex literature has failed. Orality erodes with the "literacy" of Homer. The possibility of dramatizing desirable and performable forms of experience in oral situations is gone. Nevertheless, even modern cultures partially subsist on the possibility of recreating oral situations under more difficult conditions. Most written texts were intended to be read aloud up until the eighteenth century and beyond. The written text is compatible, for instance, with sociooral institutions from coffeehouses to secret societies (Havelock 1978: 4; Ong 1982: 157; cf. Galitz 1986). Dickens's frenetic reading tours were motivated by the attempt to prevent or slow down the slide of texts into their inscribed semantics, that is to say, into ideology. Today's chroniclers of those tours are still captivated by "material" phenomena like Dickens's high pulse rates and the listeners' fainting spells. It is difficult to say what similar practices could mean today for a supposedly reader-oriented theory of literature (see Ong 1971: 23–47; 1977: 88–89; 1982: 149, 171). One would have to assume, along with W. J. Ong (1982: 175), that pure orality is empirically and sociopsychologically seldom an ideal for need fulfillment. One would presumably have succumbed to remnants of teleological thinking if one wanted to interpret the stages of the history of writing through writing and print and the pseudoreoralization by the new media as a history of increasing alienation from some original state. The new media do not sweep away the old but often compensate and strengthen the potential they still have (Ong 1977: 17, 82–83; cf. Assmann and Assmann 1983: 278). The more the accelerated development of technologies and media increases or limits creative possibilities, the more differentiated their dissemination and effect become. One always has to count on forms of cultural gradation where cultures play out their ability to reject or conform (see Varagnac et al. 1959: 90).

Such medial-cognitive dislocations (still) focus themselves, as already mentioned, on the diffuse medium of writing, and on what this says in terms of psychophysical implications for writing situations. If it is true that all great writing systems go back to stages of pictorial writing, which gradually dissolves with the fading of the signs without being completely lost (see Földes-Papp 1984: Preface and 50, 64–66), then systems of writing always canalize two currents at once. In their technical manifestations, they function as recording systems, as recordings of what in everyday social terms is defined as "realistic." In their pictorial character—even in the suppressed pictorial character of advanced, abstract writing systems—a "phantasmagoric inspiration" hangs on tooth and nail (Varagnac et al. 1959: 208). If writing intellectualizes cultures and relegates them to such invariance that the Greeks were able to base the primacy of the pure idea on it, then the phantasmagoric remnant prevents body and soul, imagination, thought, and action from completely falling apart, despite Descartes. One can suspect that people have lived and will always live with *and* without writing, despite functionalizations by the primacy of extended, abstract writing systems (Varagnac et al. 1959: 420). The cultural competence of writing may have historically always served needs of power and prestige or something similar.[1] Nevertheless, almost everywhere a general, functionally unpragmatic "requirement for texts" (J. Assmann 1983: 87) comes into being as soon as the social whole is no longer directly discernible. H. M. Bakhtin similarly described the origin of the polyphonic "novel" in late Hellenistic times. If this is the case, the *summae* of the Middle Ages, the encyclopedias of the Enlightenment, the lexicons of the nineteenth century, and the data bases of the present force knowledge into historically hard structures. On the other hand, textual "fascination types," such as acts of martyrs, saints' lives, dream accounts, auto-biographies, and even novels, veer toward areas where physicality and imagination converge in realities, or even better, in places of intense life (see Gehlen 1978: 160; Winnicott 1973: 121–23; Gumbrecht 1983: 162).

The "Discovery of the Mind" and Drama

In Occidental cultures, all areas of written life come under pressure from impulses to rationalize. The literary languages of other cultures that have remained pictorial, like Chinese, can better subvert this pressure. Thus, in the West, the "erotic sphere" (Max Weber) becomes entangled in concepts of honor and values, whose explicit semantization does not have to wait for a *Cortegiano* or the intellectualism of salon cultures to be completed. The decline of natural units of "cognitive, evaluative, and expressive symbolism" (Schluchter) forces the semantization of even those spheres that are supposed to give us some respite from the rational.[2]

The materiality imperative for some discursive and productive practices remains valid nevertheless. Drama originates from the failing fulfillments of archaic rituals. In a constellation where discourses such as philosophy or history have to formulate problems of truth, drama also becomes a theoretical problem for philosophy. Aristotle, significantly called "reader" as a student in the Academy, believed that the quality of a tragedy was independent of its performance.[3] This need not mean much. Reading *can* open up imaginary and fantastic spaces excluded by situational hearing and spectating. Such a need for imagination originates in more complex, "political" situations where the drama has to allow for social semantics without succumbing to them. There is, of course, a lot of talking and debating in Greek dramas. But comedy gets around social semantics, with which it operates, through fantastic images that are effective but do not have to be intellectually convincing. Aeschylus may have attempted to reformulate ethical foundations for a radically changed society in *The Oresteia*, perhaps Greek literature's central dramatic trilogy, which resulted in the first completely written dramatic "text." But he unfurls a sequence of events that reaches from the residues of matriarchal orientation, self-help, and feud to the abstract and therefore "politicized" order of the Polis.

Actions seem to be forced into discourses of legitimacy. "Entirely new risks of human existence" come forth out of a general weakness of primary, familial institutions (Meier 1980: 152–53, *passim*). The adherence to "direct" realities is loosened. "Quite possibly the greatest incarnation of the political that the fifth century found is presented in Aeschylus's *The Eumenides*" (Meier 1980: 154). What does this mean? The pieces stage the semantics and their overthrow, semantics that are required by society to deal with the new situation in the first place. The long discussions about revenge and counterrevenge and the expiation of capital crimes converge in a strategic bypassing of what is semantically and ideologically presented. Athene exits and figuratively enters the path to the Polis through the left parodos. She calls together a human court that is charged with rendering legal decisions and considerations. Their legitimacy does not depend on laws, however, but on the institution of the court, whose members must shine by virtue of their moral qualities, above all the ability to be enraged by injustice. It aims at the Polis not as a defined institution but as the simulated, public, homely concreteness in which it presents itself (cf. generally Claessens 1980: 298–303). The decision on behalf of Orestes is not founded on legal norms. Athene takes sides. She praises the power of sensible persuasion, but the transformation of the Furies, those dark, chthonic powers, into the well-intentioned Eumenides takes place through a "turnaround," a "miracle" (Melchinger 1979), after a moment of speechlessness. This silence marks the spot at which semantics fail and the theater points to a mute persuasive power ("theater of showing," Melchinger 1979). The decision on behalf of Orestes was known to the audience. Nevertheless the drama does not support the rationality of words that could be expected of the Greeks after the "discovery of the mind" (Snell 1960). Political doctrine veers toward "decisionism" in the broadest possible replacement of semantic determination by decisions. Importance and truth part ways in the political process. The Polis must rely on the binding metasemantic medium of citizen friendship. The pieces realize dimensions of the materiality imperative not only because they rely on the eloquence of gestured rituals (Agamemnon allows his shoes to be taken off and so seems to accept his fate), or on a "choreography of horror" in the stunning appearance of the Furies who moan and shriek in shrill tones, or on a projection of diffuse productions in sound, costume, and movement (as with Cassandra or the "royal predatory animal" Clytemnestra), but also because "nothing is only to be read here, letter, book, literature." The meaning shows itself—so Melchinger, waxing poetic—as "brightness that shines from the depths" (Melchinger 1979: 154–55; cf. 74, 79–83, 117–18, 130–31, 138, 145–47; and Meier 1980: 193–97, 209–11, 218). One could call the specific profile that the pieces gain in the presentation not of the political but of the impulses to politicize a Polis myth (Meier 1980: 219; cf. Lyotard 1983: 223). The avoidance of semantic determinations does not relinquish the obligations of a new political framework that promises orientations but does not yet formulate them. Elementary needs and practical interests must be negotiated. They take shape and even transitory definition. But their demands are not met in the semantics of discussion.

Drama and Semantic Overload

Theater cannot rest on these laurels, if that's what they are. The preceding comments have only touched briefly on an analysis of what could commonly be called material-theatrical signs, the inexpressible or unexpressed dimensions of the production. People in theater have always used these to resist the overbearance of semantic-ideological interpretations of drama. In performance theater, the materiality of unintegrable but highly relevant signs takes on a constitutive character. But if one takes a look at the time between Aeschylus and Robert Wilson, then the preceding comments could completely lose any trace of validity they might have possessed. Since the Renaissance, a trend has gained currency that seems to raise literature and drama to regions of refined semantic independence and explicitness. This is accomplished with the combined effect of the spread of the written medium, literary specialization, and social differentiation. Then, in the courtly novel and in poetry, concepts of love were categorized or invented that prevent or don't even allow for a linkage to possibilities of normal events. Possibilities of interpreting the plot in these dramas turn into compulsions. Impulses of action collapse, and their heretofore self-evident, concrete goals (morality, power, etc.) become almost intangible. In this sense *Hamlet* has perhaps become a myth of independent, contradictory (feudal, Christian, "philosophical") semantics.

For this reason Robert Musil, in a "historico-philosophically" radical newspaper article, attested to the bankruptcy of the theater as a present and future medium for human self-production. Theater has not been able to cope with the transfer from its ritual, feudal origins to the bourgeois-capitalistic system. It has lost its "social foundation." A concoction has formed where "operettas and tragedies float about," a brew "that still has a certain redeeming quality but that has taken on a markedly sour taste." Theater must become accustomed to its permanent slide into oblivion. The skill of the actors underscores the realization that their art has more or less declined to "phrase thrashing and gesticulation" (Musil 1978, 9: 1711–12).

The medium of theater has human, subjective action as its system of reference. Such a reference system can only maintain itself given conditions of a minimal differentiation of social systems, such as feudal or special bourgeois constellations. If systemic concepts of social reality gain the upper hand, then theater as a form of social communication is marginalized and has to be kept alive artificially. This thesis can be focused by saying that, after the Renaissance, drama survived on the differentiation, semantization, and problematization of plots (as in the reinterpretation of rise and fall) that have supplied centrally important forms of conflict for the Renaissance only. Like the subjectivization of fate, this could be revitalized temporarily in the type of drama of Schiller or Goethe. Regarding post-Renaissance drama in its totality, however, Coleridge was probably not wrong when he complained about the "tragic dwarves whom an exhausted Nature has apparently deemed necessary to produce since Shakespeare" (quoted in G. Steiner 1962: 102). An intense semantization began with Shakespeare's contemporaries and heirs, since subjective action in the social system threatened to become aimless or pathological. This semantization often took the form of intense moralizations that gave at least the English theater a rather desolate character until the end of the nineteenth century. At most George Bernard Shaw and possibly a few other individuals have temporarily remedied the situation since then (see Pfeiffer 1979). If the pre-Shakespearean drama is characterized by the fact that morality can quietly coexist with an entire spectrum of seemingly contradictory actions, then Shakespeare's characters are increasingly challenged by an overload of competing interpretations of their actions and their futures. These interpretations conflict with the routine, ritualistic attempt to mobilize the mute potential of the self-evident ability to act (see Polanyi 1964: Pt. II, "The Tacit Component"). A negotiation of what lies between three elements—the historically "mute components," the "given" (such as the representation of status), and its exhaustive interpretation forced by power strategies—is not successful. The age of political ideologies and subjective fictions dawns. The exhaustive interpretation of those shapes of action that are at hand but without real differentiation (such as the limited number of conflict possibilities) soon trivializes the interpretations themselves. Hamlet and Troilus already lament "empty" words in politics and in love. Those who follow Shakespeare simply get by for a time by squeezing all they can out of unusual (criminal, perverse, or simply strange) character types. The newer theater, at least since the spectacular shows of the nineteenth century, attempted to remedy this deficiency with the more solid "materialities" of stage technology or with a borrowing of current semantics ("current" according to the motto: Shakespeare, our contemporary). Physiological theories of art remain virulent from Nietzsche to Gehlen, and vent themselves on supposed pulse-quickening, breathtaking, but socially and semantically inconsequential effects of art (Gehlen 1961: 120–26). But a new culture that, as Nietzsche himself remarks, can no longer "excrete" and must constantly support itself with psychologizing, moralizing, and interpreting, that is, with unflinching semantic maneuvers, never again makes use of the physiological in its own right (Nietzsche 1969b: 459).

Shakespeare himself linked the limited possibilities of a physical-material, physiological art to an entirely different materiality, a new "system" of sociopolitical communication. In this way the allegorical figure of Rumour opens the second part of *Henry IV*. The figure allies itself, as is the old custom for figures of vice, with a moral tradition and acknowledges its fact-altering intrigues. Nevertheless Rumour has already *de facto* become a predominant medium, on which the risky management of social and political action depends. Rumour operates in the directness of interactive, oral situations. It destroys their reliability, however, because it saturates them with information from a world that can no longer be secured through interaction.[4] The moral-allegorical figure changes itself into an allegory of places that, morally and otherwise, are no longer overseeable. Messenger reports therefore also lead to confusion. Northumberland requires of the messenger an eyewitness report of a battle. The eye can no longer satisfy this demand. Othello demands eyewitness accounts (ocular proof) with equally disastrous results. What the dramas stage and produce is the crumbling of their own reference system, of the action that is revealed in decisive phases through scenic-physical, material-communicative directness (see 2 Henry IV, Induction 2.1). Richard III uses this system and manipulates it to his own advantage when he takes his place between two bishops after the murders that clear the way to the throne. He seduces his onlookers into acknowledging this "view" of the situation (the Duke of Buckingham, to make completely sure of that, calls him a "Christian prince"). Richard II still unconsciously relied on the power of regal presence and ritual. But his embodiment of regality cannot compete with the more abstract calculation of power that Bolingbroke (Henry IV) stages. The uselessness of the old mute acknowledgments becomes apparent in a crisis: "Yet looks he like a king: behold, his eye, as bright as is the eagle's lightens forth controlling majesty" (3.3). Still in 1 Henry IV Hotspur perceives the world and people from the perspective of a mute knowledge that a unified, cosmological anthropology had made available. He sees himself as a "temperament" that blocks semantic choices and abstract possibilities. For the last truly feudal baron, the old material comparisons between mankind and the world lie in ruins, they have become empty metaphors. His breath is taken away in a fatal entwining of the literal and the merely metaphoric because he can no longer understand and control the gradation of meanings from concrete, present situations to the abstract and enigmatic. Falstaff, on the other hand, recognizes that body language, its inexpressible social semantics, and the failing concretism of a Hotspur must give way to a semantically more subtle, Machiavellian language of power. Since he is denied access to such power himself, he would like to play the body game in a different, more intelligent way than the feudal barons, and by so doing, save it again. The gospel of the stomach and of alcohol are supposed to subvert the separation of body and semantics in a manipulated restaging of their unity. Alcohol is a means that can serve, according to its use, directness as well as social abstractions, honor and similar things (2 Henry IV, 4.3). But this body management does not work anymore. Alcohol, according to the porter in Macbeth (2.3) in another context, provokes the desire but takes away the performance and, with Falstaff, also the abstract and now necessarily more complex cognitive performance. There is no room for Falstaff in a world of immaterial power relationships where body and physical violence are used strategically. Other forms of rationalizing action are required.

Othello and Hamlet are probably destroyed in the end because they cannot control or direct the informational dynamics of their world. These are illuminated in the interpretations of these dramas as semantic being-seeming oppositions. They do not know how to gauge the credibility of what appears as situational reality. Hamlet dies because he consents to a duel, to a play of the body, whose staging he does not understand. His death no longer presents a self-evident meaning but, as Shakespeare criticism shows, provokes a never-ending semantization. Iago incites Othello to the greatest nonsense because Othello no longer differentiates between manipulated sensual certainty and credibility.

Poetry and Muscular Sensibility

It may therefore seem that theater has lost the chance to show the "anthropological-material" potential of human self-production not used up in the semantic abstractions of systems. It may be true that theater overcame this loss under conditions of temporarily advantageous social situations (like Shakespeare's time and certain other periods) through the confrontation of a mute knowledge of action and the rising possibilities of interpretation. It seems that theater was forced by the historical trivialization of (love and conflict) semantics into an increasingly stronger use of technological materialities (stagecraft, etc.) or into constant ideological adaptations. If one looks at it this way, then matters hardly seem better or are maybe even worse for poetry. There, too, it is difficult to understand "texts" as various media in which the division of history into its cultural, political, social, and psychological dimensions and its "subterranean," anthropological-material tendencies (instincts, passions, and the body "distorted" by civilization) is, if not over-done, then at least undermined (Horkheimer and Adorno 1969: 246). A. Leroi-Gourhan, it is true, claims for poetic images an inextinguishable potential for excitement of a muscular, visceral sensibility:

The Beautiful, the Good, and the Sublime will assume increasing intellec-tual value in the following chapters. In fact, when one reads a poem in complete stillness, one may forget that each image produced by words only has meaning insofar as it refers to all the experiences that one has had in real situations and that are comparable to the poetic image insofar as this image is intellectually comprehensible. Every real experience has its first reference in the foundation, the *situation* (as shown by the many meanings of this word), that is, in its relation to time and space as they are physically realized. We must hold on to this concept of the mind if we want to judge the aesthetic or spiritual expressions of a higher level.   (1980: 358; cf. 352)

Jean Baudrillard similarly granted poetry the discourse-breaking forms where things take place without continuity, consequences, and mediations. Poetic words are not infused with meaning. They provoke each other in a "catastrophe of magic" (1987b: 93–94). Baudrillard does not implore the irrational. He steers toward what Barthes called the "rustling of language." This rustling "irrational-izes" semantics without simply dismissing it (Barthes 1984: 94–95). This kind of idea could already have degenerated into the postmod-ern illusion that seemingly is done with meanings and is engaged in a search for new/old forms of fascination.

In any case, the poets themselves, however they may have postured, have often enough lamented the failings of their me-dium. In the sixteenth century, Fulke Greville complained that a kiss cannot be written down or printed, that the written lines are deceptive ("Myra," last line). However: the seemingly self-evident lament is easily uncovered as attitude. The opposition between the "materiality" of the kiss and the writing that destroys it is only illusion. If materiality, however it may be packaged, is to be en-joyed, it requires a touch of semantics. Even sensual materiality is not to be taken for granted. If it comes into play at all, it does so under minimal cultural conditions of a situation that is at least somewhat semantically transparent. But it resists semantic abstraction even though it may act out within its contexts. This writing out has been a necessity since antiquity. Sir Philip Sidney is confronted with this paradox in and through writing. Writing cannot console a troubled heart. The transfer of the pain to ink, however, allows him to discover the particular nature of feminine power that confuses him (*Astrophel and Stella*, 1591, no. 34; cf. nos. 1, 2, 71). Only the written construction of emotion can create the differentiated, relevant modalities of his feelings. The shadow that separates a full life from broken, written communication is not cast between oral interaction and abstract writing. What is natural and unchanged must be caught in rhetorical forms. This does not invalidate the idea of the inexpressible. Love is sketched in a series of building blocks that go from seeing to liking, from the codified interpretation of the Fall to its denunciations and back again.

These kinds of problems accumulate with Petrarch. The professional poet with loose social bonds criticizes the depraved culture of the modern city. This distinguishes him from the *dolce stil novo* that bases its mastery of the art of poetic differentiation on city culture. *Gentilezza* and the secretiveness of love document the specialization of groups that approach love like any other practical or juridical fact.[5] Petrarch enjoys the more or less obsolete privileges of patronage. Patronage does not exactly deliver the coordinates of the writing situation for the *canzoniere*. Petrarch inhabits the peripheries of his reference system—as priest, scholar, intellectual, and court poet, as patriot and as "lover" (see Foster 1984: 141; Ceserani and de Federicis 1979: 269). The *canzoniere* is indebted to a relatively free writing situation. Petrarch plays around with it for decades, constantly scribbling something that has no real basis in an imagined or actual experience (Laura). Writing does not create a simple phantasm of remembering. Writing also does not profess to be the proof for "spiritual credibility and truth" (Friedrich 1964: 194). The combination of writing and stylized remembrance at first "deconstructs" existing, platonizing traditions. The *memoria* is diluted in the process to a *rimembranza* that must create itself in a writing that it consumes (Warning 1982: 197; cf. 187–89). The construction of emotion through writing does not just produce written semantics or fiction. The writer cannot escape a previous "error" even if he believes he understands it. Canzone 129 ("Di pensier in pensier, di monte in monte") illustrates how the montage of stylized remembrances, imagination, reflection, and writing creates approaches to a state of affairs that can *then* be considered to be dimensions of the phenomenon itself (love, emotions).

Petrarch's writing shows the contours of a possible psychological history. Only in this sense is the subject of the *canzoniere* "mankind itself" (Friedrich 1964: 210). However Shakespeare's sonnets are interpreted, the structural requisites of a real history that cannot be ignored, no matter how dark its references and personalities, are more prominently defined. Shakespeare at least stops those traditions where (see Wyatt, Spenser, Sidney, Fulke Greville) the topic of love often functions only as an allegorical, political reference (see Javitch 1978; Norbrook 1984). Shakespeare's writing situation can hardly be reconstructed. Apparently the intensity of self-thematization rises with the assumed severity of psychologically unsolved problems. The poetry has to reassure itself of its own superior productivity through self-thematizations (Leishman 1963). These are often conventional enough (poetry as protection against time, as a guarantor of immortality, etc.), but they also have other effects. It would be useful, first, to examine a tendency of the sonnet form to enact the tilting of "monumental" semantic claims into tautology (Ramsey 1979: 159–60). The expansion of praise semantics to a monumental scale demonstrates to what degree semantics have already been trivialized to "empty" rhetoric (see sonnets, nos. 55, 84, 116). The communications situation is puzzling. The public dimension of the "creative sonnets" (nos. 1–20) is undermined by the intimacy of later situations, above all in the "Dark Lady" sonnets, so that an authorized publication would seem to be impossible. Finally, possible thematic references (friendship, homo- or heterosexuality, historical references) seem to disappear as soon as their historical or psychological consistency is questioned. If the idea were not self-evident, the unrestrained interpretive controversies would make it obvious. Shakespeare plays with the fictitious opposition between plain language, lack of style, and stylistic and rhetorical conventions. The text thereby gains a sort of pseudo-declarative status (see nos. 32, 78, 79, 84, 86). If one accepts conventional meanings (amor theology, conflict between spiritualism and sensualism, between permanence and change), then one is lying. If one expresses a meaning, then one suppresses the differences of the play where meanings are created (no. 105). On the other hand, silence cannot be poetically maintained; thus, it must constantly be staged anew (nos. 23, 24, 85, 101).

Since there is no archetypal mind that "at first in character was done" (no. 59), no original text of the facts and of what is praised, poetry dispenses with the standards by which its declarations can be measured. As a result, the "facts," the erotic, ethical ambivalences, cannot be determined with any certainty because the language produces its own treacherousness (Felperin 1985: 198). A given, whether it be of a sensual or ethical nature, cannot be found. The legibility of the world and of people, the direct path from the eye to the heart, is gone (no. 23). Still, the "Dark Lady" sonnets above all demonstrate how absence of both basic meanings and basic sensuality gain new relevance through clever writing and linguistic s(t)imulation. The unavailable, which is semantically powerless, and the situations between figures that can hardly be called "lovers" claim a kind of urgency of experience. Although not embedded in any specific context, not transferable, and satiated with lies, the situations are nevertheless there (see above all no. 138, with its plays on the word "to lie"). Simulation is a "metamimetic project" (Felperin 1985: 193). The unpresentable requires simulation and play with its models organized culturally and above all in writing. Through this it does not simply become available. The models, however, outline a margin of affective investments. Real interaction no longer suffices for their development and production. The reciprocal relationship between form and meaning, relevance and significance, presence and interpretation becomes apparent in rhythmic, lyric writing. Shakespeare's sonnets, in their carved-out causality of values, trade the damaged semantics of love for moments of idleness, for their own weight, and for the reciprocal dynamics of the situations.

Writing Novels

We have Morin (1969: 144–45) to thank for an anthropologically based concept of simulation. Culturally schematized situations and semantics function as triggers but not as expressions of figurations of perception or conduct that they themselves have produced or s(t)imulated. Such a concept of simulation is neutral vis-à-vis on-tologically motivated differentiations between reality and fiction. This concept distances itself simultaneously from older doctrines about anthropological constants. It may cause literary writing sit-uations to be understood as a catalogue of productions and simula-tions where interpretational margins (*play spaces*) can be negoti-ated. The possibilities of semantic openness that come up short in the interpretive constraints of living situations can also be main-tained (see Iser 1982: 20–21).

Given this background, we can understand literary processes and conformities as dimensions of generalized rhythmizing. They take place in special rhythms and forms in music or poetry. They enable access to an open semantics under limited terms (see the essay on rhythm by H. U. Gumbrecht in this volume). These kinds of processes harden into norms and requirements in rules dictated by poetics and in concepts of literature as formulated by aesthetics and literary theory. They rein in productions by means of cogni-tive, moral, and social bridles. They transform figurations into culturally canonizable and limitable products. This is understand-able but also unpreventable. Nevertheless the much-lamented ero-sion of book culture seems to apply more to "works" forced to conform to notions of classical "meaningfulness" and values than to the wide variety of writing situations and activities (see Iser 1982: 20; 1977: 183). The discussion about the colonization of the unconscious through the mass production in the media of ready-made pictures of reality likewise does not take into account that a literary and highly stylized writing, reading, and spectating was usually present on the borders of social production and never had any significant influence on the social unconscious. Even sophisti-cated literary theories or literary comparisons with the mass media subsist on the generalized sense and humanizing potential of litera-ture. But this was never literature's real province. It was insinuated by interested groups and exploited for the reciprocal effects of social self-glorification. In the meantime, couch potatoes or TV addicts have formed their own group. And yet it is still possible that the oft-predicted society of leisure of the twenty-first century might once again need reading or even the professional reader in order to fill its free time with a variety of status-promoting ac-tivities not to be gleaned from any profession.

However things may turn out, in view of the variety of writing situations an unsolved problematic rest remains. In poetry and in the theater, writing, like everything else, is fettered by the conflict between anthropological and technological materiality, between the production of the semantically unavailable and the limitations of means of communication. It is subject to pressure from social-semantic differentiations. The passages on theater and poetry are meant to indicate that even under the difficult conditions of technical semantic abstraction the chances that these kinds of writing will maintain semantics in virtual materiality don't disappear completely. In reclaiming "poetic" language as a medium that stems social-semantization trends in the interest of creativity, one could refer to the many means of the rhythmizing of theatrical-poetic "discourses." Rhythmization (rhythm in the narrow sense: meter, rhyme, singing, or the physical production of texts) prompts electrical activities of the brain, loosens emotional rigidity, and creates other creative conditions (see Jaynes 1976: 73; Kornhuber 1984: 89–92; Schlaffer 1986: 15). These kinds of arguments, even if they seem simple, are by now neurologically proved. They have apparent limitations when one attempts to apply them to a literary, narrative genre like the novel. Drama and poetry may be threatened by a loss of relevance of the human subject in a system that has become reality. But in the rhythmized allotment of worldly components into subjective action and experience, they conserve modalities of creating reality that have not yet been expunged from the cognitive, anthropomorphic catalogue of human self-interpretations. But the novel, as we have known it since the eighteenth century and occasionally from earlier periods, is under pressure from a social-semantic complexity that is not to be underestimated. This is most often explained by reference to the differentiation of society and its knowledge, and the spread of printing and book sales. Printing, the "splendid invention" that, as Bacon still optimistically announced in the seventeenth century, had contributed so much to the expansion of knowledge (1982: 117), claimed its first victims in the eighteenth century. The printer and novel writer Samuel Richardson was able, in his novels, to engage in the intimate communication that the anonymous society of the city and of printing had destroyed. Richardson fell victim to an early form of phobic neurosis that has been described as a typical disorder of the urban psyche. He did so in the physical proximity of and the simultaneous psychic-social distance between the masses that could hardly meet each other as individuals. He interacted with his family and employees primarily through written notes. He also oversaw his employees through a hidden window (Watt 1957: 201–16; cf. Schlaffer 1986: 21). It is conspicuous how more stable writers, like Defoe and Fielding, place the city at a distance or at least show it in its past, more simple structures as a place where life is mastered. Along with the novel of the city comes the novel of city flight, of avoidance of abstract complexity. Novels must in some way insert themselves into social semantics and systems. If drama subsists on figures that are based on characterological typologies even to the present, then the novel struggles with the problem of representing socio-ideological absorption of persons without completely sacrificing their assumed humanity. This forces the use of manic compensation strategies: the novel of letters as a form of apparent communicative directness, varied authentic fictions (travel reports, diaries), the dialogue with the reader, and so on. Sterne asserts that the "correctly undertaken" writing of a novel is only another name for good conversation (*Tristram Shandy*, II.2; see Nonner 1975: 294–97; Lanham 1973: 25–26). Sterne integrates all semantics in the enjoyment of words. This game has become a highly intellectualized, strenuous matter, however, that perhaps only the fit academic can enjoy or survive in the long run (see Lanham 1973: 37–50, 52–67; Iser 1987).

The novel is not, in the sense of Derrida, a postcard for which the distinction between the written and the unsaid, between picture and meaning, front and back, text and address has become secondary (1979: 17–18). The increased variety of social, religious, and scientific discourses took over many of the possible spaces of imagination in the nineteenth century. This variety forced the failed attempt at "realism," that is, the semantic adaptation to a world taken over by discourse, an intermezzo that promptly fell apart in modernism.

Put another way, the history of the novel can also be outlined differently as the history of novel *writing*: Writing is a search for meaning that is produced by writing. At the end of the search, meaning disappears and reveals a meaningless reality. What remains? What remains is the duality of writing: the path to meaning and the disappearance of meaning. . . . Every attempt ends the same way: with a disintegration of the text in reading, destruction of meaning in writing. The search for meaning reaches a climax in the appearance of a reality that lies beyond meaning, that dissects and destroys it.   (Paz 1982: 27–28)

Flaubert already has to test the scope of this situation. The "lower" (social, semantically occupied) realities of *Mme Bovary* and *Education sentimentale* give way to a "sadistic imagination" (Sainte-Beuve) in *Salammbô* that no longer allows for a differentiation between historical precision and detailed, monumental meaninglessness. If the preceding novels reflect a phase where hallucinations, fantasy, and work are still welded together in a "precise" style, then their synthesis has already disintegrated in *La tentation de Saint-Antoine*. Fantasy and writing are not damaged by the fact that Flaubert's fantasies, like those of Antonius himself—Foucault insists on this—feed off of the arsenal of books and libraries, that desire exhausts itself not in satisfaction but in an endless production of images. *La tentation* rather anticipates Leroi-Gourhan's thesis about the correlation between imagination that is maintained in and mobilized by writing and the vital chains of action of a culture. Only in written images do objects gain an almost physical clarity, do the old theological images reveal a physical-sensual core (see Gendolla 1991: 162–213).

This outline requires a reformulation of the popular theoretical cliché that the novel is an amorphous genre. Novel writing is only very marginally bound to the *genre* of the novel, to the social conditions that are certainly its (bourgeois?) origins, to the completed book and to its status as a cultural-commercial product. Musil pays tribute to what is unavoidable in society and its semantics with his "The Likeness of It Happens." But the program of a *man without qualities* presumes a semantically overloaded, dispersed culture that can no longer stabilize and equalize the ordering of subject and knowledge. At first the main figures seem to get bogged down in endless conversations in which semantics are constantly jumbled together. The path to new knowledge or to old experiences seems equally blocked. The semblance of experience only appears in a "condition of weakness" (Musil 1978, 1: 25) where one stumbles over the sparse temptations of inherited clichés, like romantic love, from case to case. Still the trivialization of experience can become unimportant if it collides with the images of an imagination in the process of *writing* itself. Such instances come to light occasionally in the contacts between Ulrich and Clarisse, and often in Ulrich's and Agathe's living together. It implodes at a garden festival in the unfinished parts where Ulrich practically rapes Diotima, disguised as a Napoleonic colonel, who has been disappointed by Arnheim. Ulrich suddenly sees in her the image of Agathe that he has developed in his diary (5: 1619–20).

So Ulrich writes. Only in writing can one provide the proof that one could live differently. Writing could almost be an answer to the question to which, according to Wittgenstein, there is no answer. But Ulrich does not write a book. A book would prove that one could *not* live differently (4: 1278–79).

Books, including those categorized as literary, have represented just about everything from the Middle Ages to the present. They carried and carry material-economic values that were capable of being raised, not only in the Middle Ages, by a presumption of their spiritual value. Medieval monks as well as intellectuals of later periods performed the penances required by their respective ages with their fatiguing copying and reading of manuscripts and books. Books often enough don't transport any kind of spirit. Their material value may benefit from a material beauty that can even hypnotize the critics of their content (see Le Goff 1986: 18, 92–94; Burckhardt 1966: 181). In the nineteenth century, William Morris undertook the attempt at a material-semantic-economic synthesis in the restoration of medieval genres and the art of producing handmade books. The book as a way of life is not guaranteed any lasting success, even if it may play an even greater role today as an economic factor. According to an initial investigation at Southern Methodist University in Dallas, reported by the University of California, Berkeley, in its *Health Report*, writing down traumatic experiences is at least as helpful as talking about them (vol. 4.2, Feb. 1988, p. 2). We have perhaps returned to Schreber. Maybe novels survive as texts the writing of which develops the paradigm of the model character of problematic, cognitive activities. Maybe they survive because, at least since Musil, they have been impossible to complete. By ridding themselves of the historically manifest embarrassment of having to end, they escape the hold of social semantics whose omnipresence they must at the same time demonstrate. Their trivialization, their oblivion, originates with this omnipresence and the overload of social-cultural semantics. Nobody needs to concern himself with yesterday's ideologies. New/old margins of a transitory production of anthropological potentials or a sensual materiality in the form of an "imagination of the body" could thereby be freed in writing. This would, however, have to occur within the conditions of modern technology. Aldous Huxley banished such a possibility to the horrific vision of his brave new world.

There, the text remained hung up in cultural, ethical semantics. It is an open question how ethical discourses can continue to be cultivated (see Lyotard 1983). It seems, however, that in the "pre-writing" of possible connections between anthropology, technology, and ethics, and in the question of a cost-intensive, synthetic perfection or catastrophe of anthropological potentials, an admittedly small part of the contemporary novel, frequently pronounced dead (Lawrence Durrell, Angela Carter, Stanislaw Lem, etc.), has again escaped our cultural-academic systems of semantics.

The question poses itself for the study of literature, given these horizons, of when and in what way the consistency-affirming "reading-to-the-end" and its stylization in interpretation still yield a sufficiently scholarly form of behavior. Georges Perec, tellingly enough, in 1978 gave his puzzle-like blend of biographical, detective, descriptive, scientific, and other text types the title *Life: A User's Manual* and the subtitle *Novels*.

MARTIN STINGELIN

Comments on a Ball: Nietzsche's Play on the Typewriter

for Stefan Brotbeck

GEN I DIN MASKINE IKKE DUEDE. JEG HAR FAAET
MERE KUGLEUDTALELSER. IGAAR VAR HER JO
CONFIRMATION; JEG SLAP HELSKINDET FRA DEN
JO FOR MIG NOGET ANSTRENGENDE DAG, HVIS
HOVEDGJERNING DOG BLEV UDFÖRT AF MIN
SVOGER FRA JYLLAND.
— Malling Hansen, writing sample

The typewriter "wrested the pen from the hands of writers" (Benjamin 1980 [1928]: 105), probably earlier than Walter Benjamin may have wished. A quarter-century after Nietzsche's play on the typewriter, Herb could write, "The use of a typewriter, even with poetry . . . , has become more and more necessary" (Herb 1907: 12). The Hamburg *Schreibmaschinen-Zeitung*, under the headline "The Dead Letter," paraphrased Madame Clemenceau-Jacquemaire's complaints about typewritten correspondence, which she had published in *Figaro*: only the curt signature at the end gives a personal touch to the otherwise standardized, uncommunicative lines. Typewritten correspondence suppresses the deliberate impulse, the natural gesture, the unconscious movement, and destroys the illu-

EPIGRAPH: "doesn't work in your machine. I've received several comments on the ball. Yesterday was confirmation. I survived the fairly stressful day since the main chores were done by my brother-in-law from Jutland." Nietzsche enclosed this writing sample (excerpt) in his letter to Franz Overbeck in Zurich (Sils-Maria, August 20/21, 1881). It was sent to him by the Danish pastor and deaf-mute teacher Hans Rasmus Johan Malling Hansen along with illustrations and comments from Copenhagen professors concerning the typeball developed by him. Quoted from the original in the manuscript division of the Universitätsbibliothek Basel.

sion of the writer's presence. "Letters without warmth, without life, without movement, from which we try to glean something in vain" (Anonymous 1911b: 219).

At stake is the relationship between text and interpretation. "Playing the literary piano" is how *Scientific American* described the use of the Pratt typewriter (quoted in Martin 1949: 478). The replacement of hermeneutic models of the text as transcendent and static-linear with Roland Barthes's plural concept of a "mobile text structure" (Barthes 1985: 330; cf. 1976) is as much bound to the flexibility of discreet letters that, with the typewriter, gain a new quality for the literary production process as is the disappearance of the author and his thematization (Foucault 1979). I doubt, however, whether the flat discourse of a literary-critical reconstruction of the epistemological break between hand and typewriting can recognize itself as an effect of this same break or whether it is able to reflect upon other shifts in the *hic et nunc* conditions of human existence as conditions of its own possibilities. The blind spot of this (methodological) self-reflection is its actuality. It is impossible for us "to describe our archive [as a system of statements] since we speak within its rules and since it gives what we are able to say, including itself as the object of our discourse, its own manifestations, its own forms of existence and coexistence, its own system of accumulation, of historicity, and disappearance" (Foucault 1986: 189). Given this methodological restriction on discourses "that have stopped being our own" (ibid.), I turn to the dead letters that began to dance on Nietzsche's typewriter—literally and figuratively.

On February 4, 1882, on a month-long visit to Genoa, Paul Rée brought his friend Nietzsche a Christmas present from his mother and sister. The poet and philosopher is said to have shared his "Réealism" with Rée since *Human, All Too Human*. The present was a typewriting machine called a "typeball" from the Danish pastor and deaf-mute teacher Hans Rasmus Johan Malling Hansen. Nietzsche had trouble "making the lines flow"* and wrote that typewriting "IS INITIALLY MORE EXHAUSTING THAN ANY OTHER KIND OF WRITING" (*KGB* III.1, 173). The Malling Hansen ball arrived in Genoa severely damaged by the journey and was "somewhat bent" (E. Pfeiffer 1970: 93). It had to be "repaired" and thus

*Nietzsche, *Briefwechsel* III.2, 229. Hereafter I cite this work as *KGB* and Nietzsche's *Sämtliche Werke* as *KSA*.

for a week was in the shop of the "local mechanic" (*KGB* III.1, 166, 170). When it was returned to Nietzsche, he euphorically reported to his sister on a handwritten postcard: "Hurray, the *machine* has just arrived in my apartment. It's working again perfectly" (ibid., 170). The blocks that had caused it to stick had loosened. Paul Rée wrote to Elisabeth Nietzsche on the day of his arrival that they had been "inexplicably poorly glued. Actually they should have been nailed in place. Consequently the ball was thrown back and forth in the box" (E. Pfeiffer 1970: 93). On March 4, 1882, two weeks after Nietzsche had sent the first typescript to his scribe and corrector, Heinrich Köselitz, he wrote to his sister and mother: "THE MACHINE WAS IN THE SHOP AGAIN" (*KGB* III.1, 175). On March 21 the cotton ribbon, sensitive to humidity, gave up the ghost: "The weather is grey and cloudy, that is, humid: the ribbon is *damp* and *sticky*, so that every letter sticks and the writing is *completely* illegible" (ibid., 188). Three days later the last typescript was sent off to Köselitz.

The typeball that Malling Hansen developed in Copenhagen between 1865 and 1867 was originally intended, as were its two predecessors, the Foucauld typewriter (1839/1850) and the Thurber (1843), as a machine for the blind. The model patented in Germany in 1878 first had 52, then 54, keys for capital letters, numbers, and signs. Malling Hansen gave up the electric carriage movement in 1875 because it considerably increased the cost of the not inexpensive typeball. The type was legible only if one looked at it sideways. (Not until 1888 did Hermann Wagner invent the typebar gear that would revolutionize the typewriter market when it was introduced in the Underwood constructed by his father, Franz Xaver Wagner, in 1898. As if the history of the typewriter were coming to an end along with the intellectual life of its most reflective user, Hermann Scholz wrote in 1923 in his book *The Typewriter and Typewriting*: "No new progress of any significance in the development of the typewriter has been noted since 1888" (Scholz 1923: 14). Nietzsche, who was extremely nearsighted, had "the greatest hopes for the machine" (E. Pfeiffer 1970: 95), which "after a week's practice, eliminates the requirement for the use of the eyes" (*KGB* III.1, 117), as Malling Hansen assured him when he sent the writing sample. In 1879, Nietzsche had had to ask for relief from his university obligations because the deterioration of his sight, recently determined by Professor Schiess, made it "impossible to read or write for more than twenty minutes without pain" (*KGB* II.5, 411). Nietzsche wrote to his sister in St. Aubin from St. Moritz on August 14, 1879, "Is the typewriter in Zurich?" (ibid., 435). Among the available models, his choice was the Malling Hansen, weighing only about six and a half pounds, because, as a portable typewriter, it "must be fleeting and transportable, as I am" (*KGB* III.1, 128). "*This* is the one I want (*not* the American one, which is too heavy)" (ibid., 146). (The Remington Model 7 weighed about 28 pounds; see Martin 1949: 69. The first models were probably not much lighter.) He also did not want one that "everybody else had played around with" (*KGB* III.1, 145). A nearsighted person, whose sight had already deteriorated to ten diopters,* should be able to read the keys and blind script at "a distance of 40 centimeters," so that the typewriter "spares one's eyesight while writing, and more important, while reading." "Barely legible handwriting promotes nearsightedness, especially since it is so small and at the same time so delicate to those who are themselves nearsighted" (Anonymous 1911a: 217). Nietzsche's handwriting was poor because his eyesight forced him to hold his head very near the paper while reading and writing (see Fuchs 1978: 633). These circumstances very early on had an effect on his work. On May 25, 1865, he wrote to Carl von Gersdorff: "Please excuse my hideous writing and my discontent with it. You know how much I upset myself over it and how I can then think of nothing else" (*KGB* I.2, 57). The Malling Hansen typeball was supposed to make it possible "to write, or rather to print, with stenographic speed and still in the normal alphabet, in the darkest night, tossed on ocean waves, driving over a corduroy road, or lying in bed" (Martin 1949: 461). This was the ideal tool for Nietzsche, who wrote to Franz Overbeck on July 13, 1881: "Oh the barbarity of my handwriting that no one can read anymore, not even myself! (Why do I allow my thoughts to be printed? So that *I* can read them" (*KGB* III.1, 105). Half a year later, he took pen in hand once again

*Gottfried Benn asks: "Has anyone ever considered that Nietzsche had fourteen diopters, usually two glasses, and that boys guided him up and down steps?" (Benn 1984: 168).

in order "to handwrite the *last* manuscript (the typewriter arrives in a few months). The manuscript concerns the continuation of *Daybreak* (chapters 6 to 10)" (ibid., 150).

The trial with this typewriter lasted only six weeks (see Kittler 1985a; 1986: 293–310; 1987: 183–210). The text corpus produced on the typewriter includes fifteen "dead letters" (one of which had to be completed by hand) and a folio that is now held in the Goethe- und Schiller Archiv der Nationalen Forschungs- und Gedenkstätte der klassischen deutschen Literatur in Weimar under the catalogue number Mp XVIII 3, assigned by Hans Joachim Mette. The folio comprises 32 pages of typewritten drafts of poems and aphorisms collected under the heading "500 INSCRIPTIONS / ON TABLES AND WALLS. / FOR FOOLS / BY / A FOOL'S HAND." Among these pieces are drafts of the long *Song of the Little Brig "The Angel,"* in the *Idylls from Messina*; drafts of 34 poems in " 'Joke, Cunning, and Revenge': Prelude in German Rhymes"; a draft of the motto to the first edition of *The Gay Science*; and drafts of 27 aphorisms in the second and third books of *The Gay Science*.[1]

The typewriter first affects the role of the author himself. In 1878, Nietzsche wrote in the 156th aphorism of "Mixed Thoughts and Sayings" from *Human, All Too Human*:

The name on the title page. It is the custom nowadays to have the author's name appear in the book, and practically required. This is, however, one main reason that books are so ineffective. If they are good, then they are valued more than the persons, than their quintessence. As soon as the author makes himself known in the title, then the quintessence is diluted by the reader with the personal, the most personal. The purpose of the book is thereby frustrated. It is the ambition of the intellect not to appear individually.   (*KSA* 2, 442–43)

On the draft title page for his typewritten poems and aphorisms (see Fig. 1), Nietzsche uses, in place of a byline with his own name, the metonymy "BY / A FOOL'S HAND," and in correspondence he replaces his own signature with the typed initials "F.N."[2] With these substitutions he makes conspicuous what Benjamin meant when he wrote: "The precision of typographical forms enters directly into the concept of his [the author's] books" (Benjamin 1980: 105). He places himself within a tradition. The first "dead letter" that William A. Burt wrote to his wife from New York, on

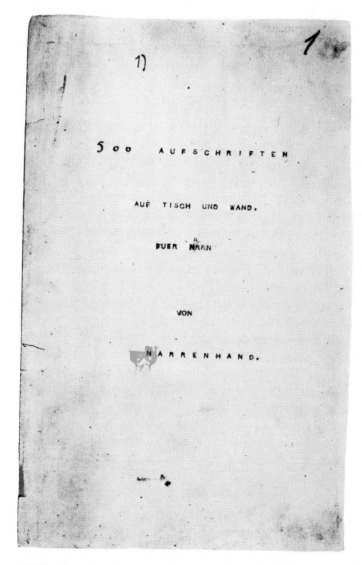

Fig. 1. Title page of Nietzsche's typescript folio "500 INSCRIPTIONS ON
TABLES AND WALLS" (Mp XVIII) (Courtesy Goethe- und Schiller-Archiv,
Nationale Forschungs- und Gedenkstätten der klassischen deutschen Lite-
ratur in Weimar)

March 13, 1830, on his self-constructed "typographer"—on the
first typewriter that "as far as we know, was used for a practical
purpose" (Martin 1949: 12)—was signed in typewriting (see Martin 1949: 14, fig. 13). Also mechanically signed were Charles Thurber's letter to his patent attorneys dated February 3, 1846, typed
on a "mechanical chirographer," a predecessor of the Malling Hansen machine, and Christopher Latham Sholes's letters to Charles
Weller. These four cases, with a nice touch of autoreferentiality,
represent the progress of typewriting, for each letter was typed on
the most current precursor model to the Remington (see Martin
1949: 47–49, figs. 58, 60, 61).

These early users of the typewriter not only violated what
would later become conventions against the use of the typewriter
for personal letters (see Scholz 1923: 92), but denied their letters the
final natural gesture. Jacques Derrida's deconstructionist scheme is
comparatively clumsy. This scheme has it that a proper name
placed in quotes[3] reflects that "neither benefit nor detriment, calculated or not, comes to the holder of the name but only to the name
itself. The name itself is not the holder [of the name] and is therefore *a priori* a lifeless name" (Derrida 1980: 72–73). Typing as a
dissection of one's own name into a series of discrete signs forces a
reflection on the literalness of the name. This reflection predicates
Nietzsche's reflection on "Art and Writing" (*KSA* 9.678), a draft
title for one portion of *The Gay Science*.

It would be worthwhile to analyze how writing instruments are
thematized within the circle of poems formed by the published
versions of 52. "Writing with One's Feet" and 59. "The Pen Is
Stubborn," in "'Joke, Cunning, and Revenge': Prelude in German Rhymes"; the corresponding typewritten drafts of those two
poems in folio Mp XVIII 3; and the following typescript poem not
incorporated in the published cycle:

> THE TYPEBALL IS A THING LIKE ME: MADE OF IRON
> BUT STILL EASILY BENT ON JOURNEYS.
> PATIENCE AND TACT AND DELICATE FINGERS ARE REQUIRED
> TO USE US
>
> (Mp XVIII 3, 19a)

This poem is typed twice. Nietzsche had a difficult time "PRINTING
OUT A LONG SENTENCE" on the "delicate machine" (*KGB* III.1,

172). The opening line is the last verse that can be identified as having been typed on this machine. A year after being forced to give up the use of the typewriter, Nietzsche seems to have encountered the Malling Hansen again in Genoa. He wrote to his sister on April 27, 1883, after his falling-out with Lou von Salomé and Paul Rée:

As for the typewriter, the kinks are out of it now, like everything else that people of weak character get a hold of for a while, whether these are machines or problems or Lou's. My current doctor, from Basel, who cured me of a malaria-like influenza, is amused by the typewriter and wants to cure it. Recently he showed me a verse that he had composed that began: "A typeball is a thing like me of iron."   (*KGB* III.1, 369)

At this point, I would like to concentrate on a new factor in the production of poetry on the typewriter that becomes evident through typing mistakes, failure of the carriage return, and varieties of corrections. The title page of the typescript folio (Fig. 1) shows clearly that as the word "NARRN" ("fool") was typed, the carriage became stuck,[4] causing "A" to be written over the "N." The "N" seems to have been highlighted by hand at a later time. The inserted "A" is written in pencil and mimetically given the character of the type in its outline. This mimetic approximation by hand of the typewritten character can often be seen in Nietzsche's typescripts and is completely atypical for Nietzsche's handwriting. This is easily determined by comparing the handwritten drafts or the continuations of the poetry and aphorism sketches. In Mp XVIII 3, 5, for example (see Fig. 2), Nietzsche adds the double "S" in "STEISS" in the second verse of the fourth epigram. This mimesis is particularly evident in the rhyme of the seventh epigram, where the last four letters in "GENUNG" are added by hand to correspond to the typewritten "JUNG." Typing mistakes, like printing mistakes, necessitate a reflection on the semantic effect of the addition, deletion, or inversion of a letter. The four-line poem draft on Mp XVIII 3, 45 (see Fig. 3), repeated here for the seventh and last time in the folio, bespeaks the possibility of interpreting the literalness of typewriter literature. This is accomplished with a significant deviation from the preceding variants. A missing "N" in *Freund* reveals the history of Nietzsche's interpretive attempts to circumvent literalness after producing his typewritten drafts of poems and

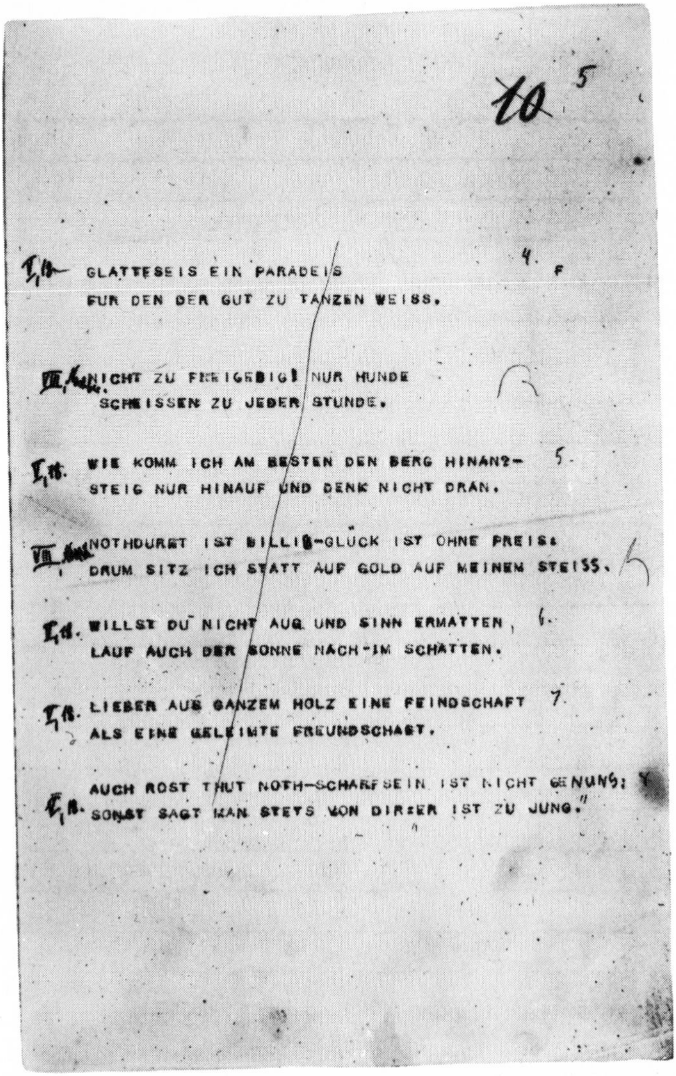
GLATTESEIS EIN PARADEIS
FUR DEN DER GUT ZU TANZEN WEISS.

NICHT ZU FREIGEBIG! NUR HUNDE
SCHEISSEN ZU JEDER STUNDE.

WIE KOMM ICH AM BESTEN DEN BERG HINAN?-
STEIG NUR HINAUF UND DENK NICHT DRAN.

NOTHDURFT IST BILLIG-GLUCK IST OHNE PREIS:
DRUM SITZ ICH STATT AUF GOLD AUF MEINEM STEISS.

WILLST DU NICHT AUG UND SINN ERMATTEN,
LAUF AUCH DER SONNE NACH-IM SCHATTEN.

LIEBER AUS GANZEM HOLZ EINE FEINDSCHAFT
ALS EINE GELEIMTE FREUNDSCHAFT.

AUCH ROST THUT NOTH-SCHARFSEIN IST NICHT GENUNG:
SONST SAGT MAN STETS VON DIR: ER IST ZU JUNG."

Fig. 2. A page of epigrams from typescript folio Mp XVIII 3, with handwritten corrections by Nietzsche (Courtesy Goethe- und Schiller-Archiv, Nationale Forschungs- und Gedenkstätten der klassischen deutschen Literatur in Weimar)

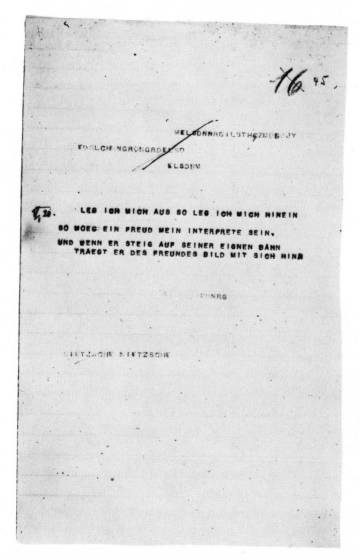

Fig. 3. Draft of the poem "WHEN I INTERPRET MYSELF," from typescript folio Mp XVIII 3, with handwritten corrections by Nietzsche (Courtesy Goethe- und Schiller-Archiv, Nationale Forschungs- und Gedenkstätten der klassischen deutschen Literatur in Weimar)

aphorisms. In the semantic effect of its absence, this "N" reflects on literalness and differentiality as requirements for the possibility of speech as something meaningful:

> WHEN I INTERPRET MYSELF, I GET WRAPPED UP IN MYSELF.
> THUS MAY A FREUD BE MY INTERPRETER.
> AND WHEN HE ENTERS ON HIS OWN PATH
> HE CARRIES THE IMAGE OF A FRIEND WITH HIM.
>
> (Mp XVIII 3, 45)

The production aesthetic of this typewriter literature is barely correctly identified when, as Nietzsche says in a draft of a different poem (34. "Seneca et hoc genus omne," in "Joke, Cunning, and Revenge"),

> IT WRITES AND WRITES ITS UNBEAR-
> ABLE NONSENSE:
> AS IF IT WERE REQUIRED PRIMUM (V)SCRIBERE
> DEINDE PHILOSOPHARI.
>
> (Mp XVIII 3, 21)

Typewriter poetry falls back on the uncertainty of the meaning of its possibilities. Also on Mp XVIII 3, 45 (see Fig. 3), above the four-line poem, are these lines:

> MELSDNDRGILSTHCZMOSMJY
> EDSLCHMNGRONGRDELSO
> ELSDNM

Nietzsche's works, however, recognize the literalness in this se-quence.* The "distinctness of the letters" has an effect on more than

---

*This is so even if, at least initially through titling and accommodation to another context, interpretive attempts by the author can be observed. In this way, what can be read in the draft version of "Seneca et hoc genus omne" as a reflection on the production aesthetic of typewriter literature can be seen in the published version (no. 34 in "'Joke, Cunning, and Revenge': Preface in German Rhymes") to be aimed at a distinct group of philosophers. The draft "WHEN I INTERPRET MYSELF," a later version of which is included in the "Prelude in German Rhymes" under the less tendentious title "Interpretation," is titled "E.R." in M III.1, Febru-ary 1882. This abbreviation is spelled out in Nietzsche's correspondence with Franz Overbeck from this time: "[Erwin] Rohde wrote: I don't believe that his image of me is correct. Still I'm relatively pleased that it isn't worse. But he is incapable of learning anything from me. He has no empathy for my passion and suffering" (*KGB* III.1, 180).

just the "pithiness of the sayings," for which Köselitz thanked Nietzsche on February 19, 1882, from Venice:

Dear Professor,

I would like to thank you most kindly for your generous writing sample. I was very surprised by the distinctness of the letters, but more so by the pithiness of the sayings. . . .—I would like to see how the typewriter is manipulated. I would think that it takes much practice before the lines flow smoothly. Perhaps you will even acquire a new way of expressing yourself with this instrument. At least this could happen to me. I do not deny that my "thoughts" in music and words often depend on the quality of the quill and paper. This is perhaps the most appropriate judgement of my "thoughts." (*KGB* III.2, 229)

Nietzsche answered: "YOU ARE RIGHT—OUR WRITING INSTRU-MENTS WORK ALONG WITH OUR THOUGHTS" (*KGB* III.1, 172). The typewriter actually does mark a decisive break in Nietzsche's works. His reflection on language comes explicitly to an end with the lingui-theoretical writings of the early 1870's. This reflection concentrates above all on the "proto leap" of language and is, at least in the Basel Rhetoric Lectures of 1872/73, still weighed down by metaphysical aporias that are taken from Gustav Gerber's book *Language as Art* (see Stingelin 1988). In at least a fifth of the seven paragraphs of the Rhetoric Lectures published in 1912, Nietzsche takes his premise virtually verbatim from Gerber's book: "All words are from the beginning in themselves tropes in regard to their meaning" (Nietzsche 1912: 249).[5] Nietzsche's detour via rhetoric does not end there. His thinking about an original difference as an inverted figure of metaphysical presence is reciprocally bound in its argumentation to a metaphorical use of the metaphor in a never-ending regression (see Lacoue-Labarthe 1986: 90–91). This thinking about an original difference or chasm is replaced by Nietzsche's wordplay as a poetic formulation of poetological information concerning how this wordplay comes into being. In the distortion that it creates, the wordplay reflects, predominantly as paronomasia, on the literalness/differentiality as a condition of itself and thereby on the possibility of language. This is the implicit continuation of Nietzsche's reflection on language that has rid itself of its metaphysical aporias and is lost on a philosophical writing that emphasizes what is already explained. The typewriter stands at the brink of these two forms of language reflection. Here the letter speaks. If Nietzsche's wordplay tends before the use of the typewriter toward illustration, then the wordplay later becomes constitutive for his texts. The author's name falls with the text itself for the sake of a new relationship between text and interpretation and a new concept of authorship. On the same page as the contingent exclusion of a letter and the draft poem for "Interpretation" (see Fig. 3), the attempt is made to secure the author's name through iteration of the identity with its carrier. "NIETZSCHE NIETZSCHE"? The transparent blue trace of the impression of an aniline-soaked cotton ribbon on paper in small-octavo format.

VIVIAN SOBCHACK

The Scene of the Screen: Envisioning Cinematic and Electronic "Presence"

It is obvious that cinematic and electronic technologies of representation have had enormous impact upon our means of signification during the past century. Less obvious, however, is the similar impact these technologies have had upon the historically particular significance or "sense" we have and make of those temporal and spatial coordinates that radically inform and orient our social, individual, and bodily existences. At this point in time in the United States, whether or not we go to the movies, watch television or music videos, own a video tape recorder/player, allow our children to play video and computer games, or write our academic papers on personal computers, we are all part of a moving-image culture and we live cinematic and electronic lives. Indeed, it is not an exaggeration to claim that none of us can escape daily encounters— both direct and indirect—with the *objective* phenomena of motion picture, televisual, and computer technologies and the networks of communication and texts they produce. Nor is it an extravagance to suggest that, in the most profound, socially pervasive, and yet personal way, these objective encounters transform us as *subjects*.

NOTE: A much shorter version of this paper was published in *Post Script: Essays in Film and the Humanities* 10, no. 1 (Fall 1990): 50–59, under the title "Toward a Phenomenology of Cinematic and Electronic Presence: The Scene of the Screen."

That is, although relatively novel as "materialities" of human communication, cinematic and electronic media have not only historically *symbolized* but also historically *constituted* a radical alteration of the forms of our culture's previous temporal and spatial consciousness and of our bodily sense of existential "presence" to the world, to ourselves, and to others.

This different sense of *subjective* and *material* "presence" both signified and supported by cinematic and electronic media emerges within and co-constitutes *objective* and *material* practices of representation and social existence. Thus, while cooperative in creating the moving-image culture or "life-world" we now inhabit, cinematic and electronic technologies are quite different from each other in their concrete "materiality" and particular existential significance. Each offers our lived-bodies radically different ways of "being-in-the world." Each implicates us in different structures of material investment, and—because each has a particular affinity with different cultural functions, forms, and contents—each stimulates us through differing modes of representation to different aesthetic responses and ethical responsibilities. In sum, just as the photograph did in the last century, so in this one, cinematic and electronic screens differently demand and shape our "presence" to the world and our representation in it. Each differently and objectively alters our subjectivity while each invites our complicity in formulating space, time, and bodily investment as significant personal and social experience.

These preliminary remarks are grounded in the belief that, during the last century, historical changes in our contemporary "sense" of temporality, spatiality, and existential and embodied presence cannot be considered less than a consequence of correspondent changes in our technologies of representation. However, they also must be considered something more, for as Martin Heidegger reminds us, "The essence of technology is nothing technological" (Heidegger 1977: 317). That is, technology never comes to its particular material specificity and function in a neutral context for neutral effect. Rather, it is always historically informed not only by its materiality but also by its political, economic, and social context, and thus always both co-constitutes and expresses cultural values. Correlatively, technology is never merely "used," never merely instrumental. It is always also "incorporated" and "lived" by the human beings who engage it within a structure of meanings and metaphors in which subject-object relations are cooperative, co-constitutive, dynamic, and reversible. It is no accident, for example, that in our now dominantly electronic (and only secondarily cinematic) culture, many human beings describe and understand their minds and bodies in terms of computer systems and programs (even as they still describe and understand their lives as movies). Nor is it trivial that computers are often described and understood in terms of human minds and/or bodies (for example, as intelligent, or as susceptible to viral infection)—and that these new "life forms" have become the cybernetic heroes of our most popular moving image fictions (for example, *Robocop* or *Terminator II*).* In this sense, a qualitatively new techno-logic can begin to alter our perceptual orientation in and toward the world, ourselves, and others. And as it becomes culturally pervasive, it can come to profoundly inform and affect the socio-logic, psycho-logic, and even the bio-logic by which we daily live our lives.

This power to alter our perceptions is doubly true of technologies of representation. A technological artifact like the automobile (whose technological function is not representation but transportation) has profoundly changed the temporal and spatial shape and meaning of our life-world and our own bodily and symbolic sense of ourselves.† However, representational technologies of photography, the motion picture, video, and computer inform us twice over: first, like the automobile, through the specific material conditions by which they latently engage our senses at the bodily level of what might be called our *microperception*, and then again through their explicit representational function by which they engage our senses textually at the hermeneutic level of what

*__Robocop__ (1987) was directed by Paul Verhoeven; *Terminator II: Judgment Day* (1991) by James Cameron.

†Reference here is not only to the way in which automotive transportation has changed our lived sense of distance and space, the rhythms of our temporality, and the hard currency that creates and expresses our cultural values relative to such things as class and style, but also to the way in which it has changed the very sense we have of our bodies. The vernacular expression of regret at "being without wheels" is profound, and ontologically speaks to our very real incorporation of the automobile as well as its incorporation of us.

might be called our *macroperception*.* Most theorists and critics of
the cinematic and electronic have been drawn to macroperceptual
analysis, to descriptions and interpretations of the hermeneutic-
cultural contexts that inform and shape both the materiality of the
technologies and their textual representations.† Nonetheless, "all
such contexts find their fulfillment *only* within the range of microperceptual possibility" (Ihde 1990: 29; my emphasis). We cannot
reflect upon and analyze either technologies or texts without having, at some point, engaged them *immediately*—that is, through our
perceptive sensorium, through the materiality (or *immanent mediation*) of our own bodies. Thus, as philosopher of technology Don
Ihde puts it, while "there is no microperception (sensory-bodily)
without its location within a field of macroperception," there can
be "no macroperception without its microperceptual foci" (ibid.).
It is important to note, however, that since perception is constituted and organized as a bodily and sensory *gestalt* that is always
already meaningful, a microperceptual focus is not the same as a
physiological or anatomical focus. The perceiving and sensing
body is always also a *lived-body*—immersed in and making social
meaning as well as physical sense.

The aim of this essay, then, is to figure certain microperceptual
aspects of our engagement with the technologies of cinematic and
electronic representation and to suggest some ways in which our
microperceptual experience of their respective material conditions

---

*These terms are derived from Ihde 1990: 29. Ihde distinguishes two senses of
perception: "What is usually taken as sensory perception (what is immediate and
focused bodily in actual seeing, hearing, etc.), I shall call microperception. But
there is also what might be called a cultural, or hermeneutic, perception, which I
shall call macroperception. Both belong equally to the lifeworld. And both dimensions of perception are closely linked and intertwined."

†Two types of theory that are, to some degree, attempts at microperceptual
analysis are, first, psychoanalytic accounts of the processes of cinematic identification in which cinematic technology is deconstructed to reveal its inherent "illu-
sionism" and its retrogressive duplication of infantile and/or dream states and,
second, neo-Marxist accounts of both photography's and cinema's optical dependence upon a system of "perspective" based on an ideology of the individual
subject and its appropriation of the "natural" world. One could argue, however, as
I do here, that these types of theory are not microperceptual *enough*. Although
both focus on the "technological" construction of subjectivity, they do so abstractly. That is, neither deals with the technologically constructed temporality
and spatiality that *ground* subjectivity in a sensible and sense-making *body*.

informs and transforms our temporal and spatial sense of ourselves and our cultural contexts of meaning. Insofar as the cinematic and the electronic have each been *objectively constituted* as a new and discrete techno-logic, each also has been *subjectively incorporated*, enabling a new perceptual mode of existential and embodied "presence." In sum, as they have mediated our engagement with the world, with others, and with ourselves, cinematic and electronic technologies have transformed us so that we currently see, sense, and make sense of ourselves as quite other than we were before them.

It should be evident at this point that the co-constitutive, reversible, and dynamic relations between objective material technologies and embodied human subjects invite a phenomenological investigation. Existential phenomenology, to use Ihde's characterization, is a "philosophical style that emphasizes a certain interpretation of human *experience* and that, in particular, concerns *perception* and *bodily* activity" (1990: 21). Often misunderstood as ungrounded "subjective" analysis, existential phenomenology is instead concerned with describing, thematizing, and interpreting the structures of lived spatiality, temporality, and meaning that are co-constituted dynamically as embodied human subjects perceptually engage an objective material world. It is focused, therefore, on the *relations between* the subjective and objective aspects of material, social, and personal existence and sees these relations as constitutive of the meaning and value of the phenomena under investigation.*

Existential phenomenology, then, attempts to describe, thematize, and interpret the *experiential* and *perceptual field* in which human beings play out a particular and meaningful structure of spatial, temporal, and bodily existence. Unlike the foundational, Husserlian transcendental phenomenology from which it emerged, existential phenomenology rejects the goal of arriving at universal and "essential" description, and "settles" for a historicized and "qualified" description as the only kind of description that is existentially possible or, indeed, desirable. It is precisely *because* rather than *in spite of* its qualifications that such a description is existentially meaningful—meaningful, that is, to human beings who are

*For the history, philosophy, and method of phenomenology, see Spiegelberg 1965; Carr 1967; and Ihde 1979.

themselves particular, finite, and partial, and thus always in culture and history, always open to the world and further elaboration. Specifically, Maurice Merleau-Ponty's existential phenomenology departs from the transcendental phenomenology most associated with Edmund Husserl in that it stresses the *embodied* nature of human consciousness and views bodily existence as the original and originating *material premise* of sense and signification. We sit in a movie theater, before a television set, or in front of a computer terminal not only as *conscious* beings but also as *carnal* beings. Our vision is not abstracted from our bodies or from our other modes of perceptual access to the world. Nor does what we see merely touch the surface of our eyes. Seeing images mediated and made visible by technological vision enables us not only to see technological images but also to see technologically. As Ihde emphasizes, "the concreteness of [technological] 'hardware' in the broadest sense connects with the equal concreteness of our bodily existence," and, in this regard, "the term 'existential' in context refers to perceptual and bodily experience, to a kind of 'phenomenological materiality'" (1990: 26).

This correspondent and objective materiality of both human subjects and worldly objects not only suggests some commensurability and possibilities of exchange between them, but also suggests that any phenomenological analysis of the existential relation between human subjects and technologies of representation must be semiological and historical even at the microperceptual level. Description must attend both to the particular materiality and modalities through which meanings are signified and to the cultural and historical situations in which materiality and meaning come to cohere in the praxis of everyday life. Like human vision, the materiality and modalities of cinematic and electronic technologies of representation are not abstractions. They are concrete and situated and institutionalized. They inform and share in the spatiotemporal structures of a wide range of interrelated cultural phenomena. Thus, in its attention to the broadly defined "material conditions" and "relations" of production (specifically, the conditions for and production of existential meaning), existential phenomenology is not incompatible with certain aspects of Marxist analysis.

In this context, we might turn to Fredric Jameson's useful discussion of three crucial and expansive historical "moments" marked by "a technological revolution within capital itself" and the particular and dominant "cultural logic" that correspondently emerges in each of them (1984: 77). Historically situating these three "moments" in the 1840's, 1890's, and 1940's, Jameson correlates the three major technological changes that revolutionized the structure of capital—by changing market capitalism to monopoly capitalism and this to multinational capitalism—with the emergence and domination of three new "cultural logics": those axiological norms and forms of representation identified respectively as realism, modernism, and postmodernism. Extrapolating from Jameson, we can also locate within this conceptual and historical framework three correspondent technologies, forms, and institutions of visual (and aural) representation: respectively, the photographic, the cinematic, and the electronic. Each, we might argue, has been critically complicit not only in a specific "*technological* revolution within capital*," but also in a specific and radical *perceptual* revolution within the culture and the subject. That is, each has been co-constitutive of the very temporal and spatial structure of the "cultural logics" Jameson identifies as realism, modernism, and postmodernism. Writing about the nature of cultural transformation, phenomenological historian Stephen Kern suggests that some major cultural changes can be seen as "*directly* inspired by new technology," while others occur relatively independently of technology, and still others emerge from the new technological "metaphors and analogies" that *indirectly* alter the structures of perceptual life and thought (Kern 1983: 6–7). Implicated in and informing each historically specific "technological revolution in capital" and transformation of "cultural logic," the technologically discrete nature and phenomenological impact of new "materialities" of representation co-constitute a complex cultural gestalt. In this regard, the technological "nature" of the photographic, the cinematic, and the electronic is graspable always and only in a qualified manner—that is, less as an "essence" than as a "theme."

Although I wish to emphasize the technologies of cinematic and electronic representation, those two "materialities" that constitute our current *moving*-image culture, something must first be said of that culture's grounding in the context and phenomenology of the *photographic*. The photographic is privileged in the "moment" of market capitalism—located by Jameson in the 1840's, and cooperatively informed and driven by the technological innovations of steam-powered mechanization that allowed for industrial expansion and the cultural logic of "realism." Not only did industrial expansion give rise to other forms of expansion, but expansion itself was historically unique in its unprecedented *visibility*. As Jean-Louis Comolli points out:

The second half of the nineteenth century lives in a sort of frenzy of the visible. . . . [This is] the effect of the social multiplication of images. . . . [It is] the effect also, however, of something of a geographical extension of the field of the visible and the representable: by journies, explorations, colonisations, the whole world becomes visible at the same time that it becomes appropriatable.   (Comolli 1980: 122–23)

Thus, while the cultural logic of "realism" has been seen as primarily represented by literature (most specifically, the bourgeois novel), it is, perhaps, even more intimately bound to the mechanically achieved, empirical, and representational "evidence" of the world constituted by photography.

Until very recently, the photographic has been popularly and phenomenologically perceived as existing in a state of testimonial verisimilitude—its film emulsions analogically marked with (and objectively "capturing") material traces of the world's concrete and "real" existence.* Photography produced images of the world with a perfection previously rivaled only by the human eye. Thus, as Comolli suggests, with the advent of photography, the human eye loses its "immemorial privilege" and is devalued in relation to "the mechanical eye of the photographic machine," which "now sees *in its place*" (1980: 123). This replacement of human with mechanical vision had its compensations however—among them, the material

---

*The very recent erosion of "faith" in the photographic as "evidence" of the real in popular consciousness has been a result of the development of the *seamless electronic manipulation* of even the tiniest "bits" of the photographic image. While airbrushing and other forms of image manipulation have been around for a long while, they have left a discernible "trace" on the image; such is not the case with digital computer alterations of the photographic image. For an overview, see "Ask It No Questions: The Camera Can Lie," *New York Times*, Aug. 12, 1990, sec. 2, pp. 1, 29.

control, containment, and actual possession of time and experience.* Abstracting visual experience from a temporal flow, the
photographic chemically and metaphorically "fixes" its ostensible
subject as an *object* for vision, and concretely reproduces it in a
material form that can be possessed, circulated, and saved, in a form
that can over time accrue an increasing rate of interest, become
more *valuable* in a variety of ways. Thus, identifying the photograph as a fetish object, Comolli links it with gold, and aptly calls it
"the money of the 'real' "—of "life"—the photograph's materiality
assuring the possibility of its "convenient circulation and appropriation" (1980: 142).

In his phenomenological description of human vision Merleau-
Ponty tells us, "To see is *to have at a distance*" (1964: 166). This
subjective activity of *visual* possession is objectified and literalized
by the materiality of photography, which makes possible its *visible*
possession. What you see is what you get. Indeed, this structure of
objectification and empirical possession is doubled, even tripled.
Not only does the photograph materially "capture" traces of the
"real world," not only can the photograph itself be possessed concretely, but the photograph's culturally defined semiotic status as a
mechanical reproduction (rather than a linguistic representation)
also allows an unprecedentedly literal and material, and perhaps
uniquely complacent, form—and ethics—of self-possession. Family albums serve as "memory banks" that authenticate self, other,
and experience as empirically "real" by virtue of the photograph's
material existence as an object and possession with special power.†

In regard to the materiality of the photograph's authenticating
power, it is instructive to recall one of a number of particularly

*Most media theorists point out that photographic (and later cinematic) optics
are structured according to a norm of perception based upon Renaissance perspective, which represented the visible as originating in and organized by an individual, centered subject. This form of representation is *naturalized* by photography
and the cinema. Comolli says: "The mechanical eye, the photographic lens . . .
functions . . . as a guarantor of the identity of the visible with the normality of
vision . . . with the norm of visual perception" (1990: 123–24).

†It must be noted that the term "memory bank" is analogically derived in this
context from electronic (not photographic) culture. It nonetheless serves us as a
way of reading backward that recognizes a literal as well as metaphorical *economy*
of representation and suggests that attempts to understand the photographic in its
"originality" are pervasively informed by our contemporary electronic consciousness.

relevant ironies in *Blade Runner* (Ridley Scott, 1982), a science fiction film focusing on the ambiguous ontological status of a group of genetically manufactured "replicants." At a certain moment, Rachel, the film's putative heroine and the latest replicant prototype, disavows the revelation of her own manufactured status by pointing to a series of keepsake photographs that give "proof" to her mother's existence, to her own existence as a little girl, to her subjective memory. Upon being told that both her memory and their material extroversion "belong to someone else," she is both distraught and ontologically re-signed as someone with no "real" life, no "real" history—although she still remembers what she remembers and the photographs still sit on her piano. Indeed, the photographs are suddenly foregrounded (for the human spectator as well as the narrative's replicant) as utterly suspect. That is, when interrogated, the photographs simultaneously both reveal and lose that great material and circulatory value they commonly hold for *all* of us as the "money of the 'real.'"

The structures of objectification and material possession that constitute the photographic as both a "real" trace of personal experience and a concrete extroversion of experience that can "belong to someone else" give specific form to its temporal existence. In capturing aspects of "life itself" in a "real" object that can be possessed, copied, circulated, and saved as the "currency" of experience, the appropriable materiality and static form of photography accomplish a palpable intervention in what was popularly perceived in the mid–nineteenth century to be time's linear, orderly, and teleological flow from past to present to future. The photograph freezes and preserves the homogeneous and irreversible *momentum* of this temporal stream into the abstracted, atomized, and secured space of a *moment*. But at a cost. A moment cannot be inhabited. It cannot entertain in the abstraction of its visible space, its single and static *point* of view, the presence of a lived-body—and so it does not really invite the spectator *into* the scene (although it may invite contemplation *of* the scene). In its conquest of time, the photographic constructs a space to hold and to look at, a "thin" insubstantial space that keeps the lived-body out even as it may imaginatively catalyze—in the parallel but temporalized space of memory or desire—an animated drama.

The radical difference between the transcendental, posited moment of the photograph and the existential momentum of the cinema, between the scene to be contemplated and the scene to be lived, is foregrounded in the remarkable short film *La jetée* (Chris Marker, 1962).* A study of desire, memory, and time, *La jetée* is presented completely through the use of still photographs—except for one extraordinarily brief but utterly compelling sequence in which the woman who is the object of the hero's desire, lying in bed and looking toward the camera, blinks her eyes. The space between the camera's (and the spectator's) gaze and the woman becomes suddenly habitable, informed with the real possibility of bodily movement and engagement, informed with a lived temporality rather than an eternal timelessness. What, in the film, has previously been a mounting accumulation of nostalgic moments achieves substantial and present presence in its sudden accession to momentum and the consequent possibility of effective action.

As did André Bazin (1967), we might think of photography, then, as primarily a form of mummification (although, unlike Bazin, I shall argue that cinema is not). While it testifies to and preserves a sense of the world and experience's real presence, it does not preserve their present. The photographic—unlike the cinematic and the electronic—functions neither as a coming-into-being (a presence always presently constituting itself) nor as being-in-itself (an absolute presence). Rather, it functions to fix a being-that-has-been (a presence in the present that is always past). Paradoxically, as it objectifies and preserves in its acts of possession, the photographic has something to do with loss, with pastness, and with death, its meanings and value intimately bound within the structure and investments of nostalgia.

Although dependent upon the photographic, the cinematic has

*For readers unfamiliar with the film, *La jetée* is a narrative about time, memory, and desire articulated in a recursive structure. A survivor of World War III has a recurrent memory of a woman's face and a scene at Orly airport where, as a child, he has seen a man killed. Because of his vivid memory, his post-apocalyptic culture—underground, with minimal power and without hope—attempts experiments to send him back into his vivid past so that he can, perhaps, eventually time-travel to the future. This achieved, aware he has no future in his own present, the protagonist, with the assistance of those in the future, ultimately returns to his past and the woman he loves. But his return to the scene of his original childhood memory at Orly reveals, first, that he (as an adult) has been pursued by people from his own present and, second, that his original memory was, in fact, the vision of his own adult death.

something more to do with life, with the accumulation—not the loss—of experience. Cinematic technology *animates* the photographic and reconstitutes its visibility and verisimilitude in a difference not of degree but of kind. The *moving picture* is a visible representation not of activity finished or past, but of activity coming-into-being—and its materiality came to be in the 1890's, the second of Jameson's transformative moments of "technological revolution within capital itself." During this moment, the internal combustion engine and electric power literally reenergized market capitalism into the highly controlled yet expansive structure of monopoly capitalism. Correlatively, the new cultural logic of "modernism" emerged, restructuring and eventually dominating the logic of realism to represent more adequately the new perceptual experience of an age marked by the strange autonomy and energetic fluidity of, among other mechanical phenomena, the motion picture. The motion picture, while photographically verisimilar, fragments, reorders, and synthesizes time and space as animation in a completely new "cinematic" mode that finds no necessity in the objective teleo-logic of realism. Thus, although modernism has found its most remarked expression in the painting and photography of the futurists (who attempted to represent motion and speed in a static form) and the cubists (who privileged multiple perspectives and simultaneity), and in the novels of James Joyce, we can see in the cinema modernism's fullest representation.*

Philosopher Arthur Danto tells us, "With the movies, we do not just see *that* they move, we see them *moving*: and this is because the pictures themselves move" (1979: 17). While still objectifying the subjectivity of the visual into the visible, the cinematic qualitatively transforms the photographic through a materiality that not only claims the world and others as objects for vision but also signifies its own bodily agency, intentionality, and subjectivity. Neither abstract nor static, the cinematic brings the *existential activity* of vision into visibility in what is phenomenologically experienced as an *intentional stream* of moving images—its continuous and autonomous visual production and meaningful organization of these images testifying to the objective world and, further, to an anonymous, mobile, embodied, and ethically invested *subject* of

*James Joyce, in 1909, was "instrumental in introducing the first motion picture theater in Dublin" (see Kern 1983: 76–77).

worldly space. This subject (however physically anonymous) is able to inscribe visual and bodily changes of situation, to dream, hallucinate, imagine, and re-member its habitation and experience of the world. And, as is the case with human beings, this subject's potential mobility and experience are both open-ended and bound by the existential finitude and bodily limits of its particular vision and historical coherence (that is, its narrative).

Here, again, *La jetée* is exemplary. Despite the fact that the film is made up of what strike us as a series of discrete and still photographs rather than the "live" and animated action of human actors, even as it foregrounds the transcendental and atemporal non-becoming of the photograph, *La jetée* nonetheless phenomenologically *projects* as a temporal flow and an existential becoming. That is, *as a whole*, the film organizes, synthesizes, and enunciates the discrete photographic images into animated and intentional coherence and, indeed, makes this temporal synthesis and animation its explicit narrative theme. What *La jetée* allegorizes in its explicit narrative, however, is the transformation of the moment to momentum that constitutes the ontology of the cinematic, and the latent background of every film.

While the technology of the cinematic is grounded, in part, in the technology of the photographic, we need to remember that "the essence of technology is nothing technological." The fact that the technology of the cinematic *necessarily* depends upon the discrete and still photograph moving intermittently (rather than continuously) through the shutters of both camera and projector does not *sufficiently* account for the materiality of the cinematic as we experience it. Unlike the photograph, a film is semiotically engaged in experience not merely as a mechanical objectification—or material *reproduction*—that is, not merely as an object for vision. Rather, the moving picture, however mechanical and photographic its origin, is semiotically experienced as also subjective and intentional, as *presenting representation* of the objective world. Thus perceived as the subject of its own vision as well as an object for our vision, a moving picture is not precisely a *thing* that (like a photograph) can be easily controlled, contained, or materially possessed. Up until very recently in what has now become a dominantly electronic culture, the spectator could share in and thereby, to a degree, interpretively alter a film's presentation and representation of embodied and enworlded experience, but could not control or contain its autonomous and ephemeral flow and rhythm, or materially possess its animated experience. Now, of course, with the advent of videotape and VCRs, the spectator can alter the film's temporality and easily possess, at least, its inanimate "body." However, the ability to control the autonomy and flow of the cinematic experience through "fast forwarding," "replaying," and "freezing"* and the ability to possess the film's body and animate it at will at home are functions of the materiality and technological ontology of the electronic—a materiality that increasingly dominates, appropriates, and transforms the cinematic.

In its pre-electronic state and original materiality, however, the cinematic mechanically projected and made visible for the very first time not just the objective world but the very structure and process of subjective, embodied vision—hitherto only directly available to human beings as that invisible and private structure we each experience as "my own." That is, the materiality of the cinematic gives us concrete and empirical insight and makes objectively visible the reversible, dialectical, and social nature of our own subjective vision. Speaking of human vision, Merleau-Ponty tells us: "As soon as we see other seers . . . henceforth, through other eyes we are for ourselves fully visible. . . . For the first time, the seeing that I am is for me really visible; for the first time I appear to myself completely turned inside out under my own eyes" (1968: 143–44). The cinematic uniquely allows this philosophical turning, this objective insight into the subjective structure of vision, into oneself as both viewing subject and visible object, and, remarkably, into others as the same.

Again, the paradoxical status of the "more human than human" replicants in *Blade Runner* is instructive. Speaking to the biotechnologist who genetically produced and quite literally manufactured his eyes, replicant Roy Baty says with an ironic concreteness that resonates through the viewing audience even if its implications are not fully understood, "If you could only see what I've seen with your eyes." The perceptive and expressive materiality of the cinematic through which we engage this ironic articulation of the

---

*In the traditional cinema, an image can be "frozen" only by replicating it many times so that it can continue moving through the projector to appear frozen on the screen.

"impossible" desire for intersubjectivity is the very materiality through which this desire is visibly and objectively fulfilled.* Thus, rather than merely replacing human vision with mechanical vision, the cinematic mechanically functions to bring to visibility the reversible structure of human vision (the system visual/visible)—a lived-system that necessarily entails not only an enworlded object but always also an embodied and perceiving subject.

Indeed, through its motor and organizational agency (achieved by the spatial immediacy of the mobile camera and the reflective and temporalizing editorial re-membering of that primary spatial experience), the cinematic inscribes and provokes a sense of existential "presence" that is as synthetically centered as it is also mobile, split, and decentering. The cinematic subject (both film and spectator) is perceived as at once introverted and extroverted, as existing in the world as both subject and object. Thus, the cinematic does not evoke the same sense of self-possession as that generated by the photographic. The cinematic subject is sensed as never completely self-possessed, for it is always partially and visibly given over to the vision of others at the same time that it visually appropriates only part of what it sees and, indeed, also cannot entirely see itself. Further, the very mobility of its vision structures the cinematic subject as always in the act of displacing itself in time, space, and the world—and thus, despite its existence as embodied and centered, as always eluding its own (as well as our) containment.

The cinematic's visible inscription of the dual, reversible, and animated structure of embodied and mobile vision radically transforms the temporal and spatial structure of the photographic. Consonant with what Jameson calls the "high-modernist thematics of time and temporality," the cinematic thickens the photographic with "the elegaic mysteries of *durée* and of memory" (Jameson 1984: 64). While its visible structure of "unfolding" does not challenge the dominant realist perception of objective time as an irreversibly directed stream (even flashbacks are contained by the film's vision in a forwardly directed momentum of experience), the cinematic makes time visibly *heterogeneous*. That is, we visibly perceive time as differently structured in its subjective and objec-

*For a complete and lengthy argument supporting this assertion, see Sobchack 1992.

tive modes, and we understand that these two structures *simulta-neously* exist in a demonstrable state of *discontinuity* as they are, nonetheless, actively and constantly *synthesized* in a specific lived-body experience (i.e., a personal, concrete, and spatialized history and a particularly temporalized narrative).

Cinema's animated presentation of representation constitutes its "presence" as always presently engaged in the experiential process of signifying and coming-into-being. Thus the significant value of the "streaming forward" that informs the cinematic with its spe-cific form of temporality (and differentiates it from the atem-porality of the photographic) is intimately bound to a structure not of possession, loss, pastness, and nostalgia, but of accumulation, ephemerality, and anticipation—to a "presence" in the present in-formed by its connection to a collective past and to a future. Visu-ally (and aurally) presenting the subjective temporality of memory, desire, and mood through flashbacks, flash forwards, freeze fram-ing, pixilation, reverse motion, slow motion, and fast motion, and the editorial expansion and contraction of experience, the cinema's visible (and audible) activity of *retension* and *protension* constructs a subjective temporality different from the irreversible direction and momentum of objective time, yet simultaneous with it. In so thickening the present, this temporal simultaneity also extends cinematic presence spatially—not only by embracing a multiplicity of situations in such visual/visible cinematic articulations as double exposure, superimposition, montage, parallel editing, but also pri-mally, by expanding the space in every image between that Here where the enabling and embodied cinematic eye is situated and that There where its gaze locates itself in its object.

The cinema's existence as simultaneously presentational and representational, viewing subject and visible object, present pres-ence informed by both past and future, continuous becoming that synthesizes temporal heterogeneity as the conscious coherence of embodied experience, transforms the thin abstracted space of the photographic into a thickened and concrete *world*. We might re-member here the animated blinking of a woman's eyes in *La jetée* and how this visible motion transforms the photographic into the cinematic, the flat surface of a picture into the lived space of a lover's bedroom. In its capacity for movement, the cinema's em-bodied agency (the camera) thus constitutes visual/visible space as always also motor and tactile space—a space that is deep and textural, that can be materially inhabited, that provides not merely a ground for the visual/visible but also its particular *situation*. Indeed, although it is a favored term among film theorists, there is no such abstraction as *point of view* in the cinema. Rather, there are concrete *situations of viewing*—specific and mobile engagements of embodied, enworlded, and situated subjects/objects whose visual/visible activity prospects and articulates a shifting field of vision from a world whose horizons always exceed it. The space of the cinematic, in-formed by cinematic time, is also experienced as heterogeneous—both discontiguous and contiguous, lived from within and without. Cinematic presence is multiply located—simultaneously displacing itself in the There of past and future situations yet orienting these displacements from the Here where the body at present is. That is, as the multiplicity and discontinuity of time are synthesized and centered and cohere as the *experience* of a specific lived-body, so are multiple and discontiguous spaces synopsized and located in the spatial *synthesis* of a particular *material* body. Articulated as separate shots and scenes, discontiguous spaces and discontinuous times are synthetically gathered together in a coherence that is the cinematic lived-body: the camera its perceptive organ, the projector its expressive organ, the screen its discrete and material center. In sum, the cinematic exists as a visible performance of the perceptive and expressive structure of lived-body experience.

Not so the electronic, whose materiality and various forms and contents engage its spectators and "users" in a phenomenological structure of sensual and psychological experience that seems to belong to *no-body*. Born in the U.S.A. with the nuclear age, the electronic emerged in the 1940's as the third "technological revolution within capital itself," and, according to Jameson, involved the unprecedented and "prodigious expansion of capital into hitherto uncommodified areas," including "a new and historically original penetration and colonization of Nature and the Unconscious" (1984: 78). Since that time, electronic technology has "saturated all forms of experience and become an inescapable environment, a 'technosphere'" (Landon 1987: 27). This expansive and totalizing incorporation of Nature by industrialized culture, and the specular production and commodification of the Unconscious (globally transmitted as visible and marketable "desire"), restructures capitalism as multinational. Correlatively, a new cultural logic identified as "postmodernism" begins to dominate modernism, and to alter our sense of existential presence.

A function of technological pervasion and dispersion, this new electronic sense of presence is intimately bound up in a centerless, network-like structure of instant stimulation and desire, rather than in a nostalgia for the past or anticipation of a future. Television, video cassettes, video tape recorder/players, video games, and personal computers all form an encompassing electronic representational system whose various forms "interface" to constitute an alternative and absolute world that uniquely incorporates the spectator/user in a spatially decentered, weakly temporalized, and quasi-disembodied state. Digital electronic technology atomizes and abstractly schematizes the analogic quality of the photographic and cinematic into discrete pixels and bits of information that are then transmitted serially, each bit discontinuous, discontiguous, and absolute—each bit being-in-itself even as it is part of a system.*

Once again we can turn to *Blade Runner* to provide illustration of how the electronic is neither photographic nor cinematic. Tracking Leon, one of the rebellious replicants, the human protagonist Deckard finds his empty rooms and discovers a photograph that seems, itself, to reveal nothing but an empty room. Using a science fictional device, Deckard directs its electronic eye to zoom in, close up, isolate, and enlarge to impossible detail various portions of the photograph. On the one hand, it might seem that Deckard is functioning like a photographer working in his darkroom to make, through optical discovery, past experience significantly visible. (Indeed, this sequence of the film recalls the photographic blow-ups of an ambiguously "revealed" murder in Michelangelo Antonioni's 1966 classic, *Blow-up*.) On the other hand, Deckard can be and has been likened to a film director, using the electronic eye to probe photographic space intentionally and to animate a discov-

---

*It is important to point out that although all moving images follow each other serially, each cinematic image (or frame) is projected analogically rather than digitally. That is, the image is projected *as a whole*. Electronic images, however, are transmitted digitally, each bit of what appears as a single image sent and received as a discrete piece of information.

ered narrative. Deckard's electronic eye, however, is neither photographic nor cinematic. While it constitutes a series of moving images from the static singularity of Leon's photograph and reveals to Deckard the stuff of which narrative can be made, it does so serially and in static, discrete "bits." The moving images do not move themselves, and they reveal no animated and intentional vision to us or to Deckard. Transmitted to what looks like a television screen, the moving images no longer quite retain the concrete and material "thingness" of the photograph, but they also do not achieve the subjective animation of the intentional and prospective vision objectively projected by the cinema. They exist less as Leon's experience than as Deckard's information.

Indeed, the electronic is phenomenologically experienced not as a discrete, intentional, and bodily centered projection in space but rather as simultaneous, dispersed, and insubstantial transmission across a network.* Thus, the "presence" of electronic representation is at one remove from previous representational connections between signification and referentiality. Electronic presence asserts neither an objective possession of the world and self (as does the photographic) nor a centered and subjective spatiotemporal engagement with the world and others accumulated and projected as conscious and embodied experience (as does the cinematic). Digital and schematic, abstracted both from *reproducing* the empirical objectivity of Nature that informs the photographic and from *presenting* a representation of individual subjectivity and the Unconscious that informs the cinematic, the electronic constructs a metaworld where ethical investment and value are located in *representation-in-itself.* That is, the electronic semiotically constitutes a system of *simulation*—a system that constitutes "copies" lacking an "original" origin. And, when there is no longer a phenomenologically perceived connection between signification and an "original" or "real," when, as Guy Debord tells us, "everything that was lived directly has moved away into a representation" (1983: n.p.), referentiality becomes *intertextuality*.

*"Network" was a term that came into common parlance as it described the electronic transmission of television images. Now, we speak of our social relations as "networking." In spatial terms, however, a "network" suggests the most flimsy, the least substantial, of grounds. A "network" is constituted more as a lattice between nodal points than as grounded and physical presence.

Living in a schematized and intertextual metaworld far removed from reference to a real world liberates the spectator/user
from what might be termed the latter's moral and physical gravity.
The materiality of the electronic digitizes *durée* and situation so that
narrative, history, and a centered (and central) investment in the
human lived-body become atomized and dispersed across a system
that constitutes temporality not as the flow of conscious experience
but as a transmission of random information. The primary value of
electronic temporality is the bit or *instant*—which (thanks to television and videotape) can be selected, combined, and instantly re-
played and rerun to such a degree that the previously irreversible
direction and stream of objective time seems overcome in the
creation of a recursive temporal network. On the one hand, the
temporal cohesion of history and narrative gives way to the temporal discretion of chronicle and episode, to music videos, to the
kinds of narratives that find both causality and intentional agency
incomprehensible and comic. On the other hand, temporality is
dispersed and finds resolution as part of a recursive, if chaotic,
structure of coincidence. Indeed, objective time in postmodern
electronic culture is perceived as phenomenologically discontinuous as was subjective time in modernist cinematic culture. Temporality is constituted paradoxically as a *homogeneous* experience of
discontinuity in which the temporal distinctions between objective
and subjective experience (marked by the cinematic) disappear and
time seems to turn back in on itself recursively in a structure of
equivalence and reversibility. The temporal move is from *Remembrance of Things Past*, a modernist re-membering of experience, to
the recursive postmodernism of a *Back to the Future*.

Again "science fiction" film is illuminating.* While the *Back to
the Future* films are certainly apposite, Alex Cox's postmodern,
parodic, and deadpan *Repo Man* (1984) more clearly manifests the
phenomenologically experienced homogeneity of postmodern discontinuity. The film is constructed as both a picaresque, episodic,

---

*It is no accident that all the films used illustratively here can be identified with
the generic conventions and thematics of science fiction. Of all genres, science
fiction has been most concerned with poetically mapping the new spatiality,
temporality, and subjectivities informed and/or constituted by new technologies.
As well, science-fiction cinema, in its particular materiality, has made these new
poetic maps concretely visible. For elaboration of this mapping, see chap. 4,
"Postfuturism," of Sobchack 1987.

loose, and irresolute tale about an affectless young man involved with car repossessors, aliens from outer space, Los Angeles punks, government agents, and others, and a tightly bound system of coincidences. Individual scenes are connected not through narrative causality but through the connection of literally material signifiers. A dangling dashboard ornament, for example, provides the acausal and material motivation between two of the film's otherwise disparate episodes. However, the film also re-solves its acausal structure through a narrative recursivity that links all the characters and events together in what one character calls both the "cosmic unconsciousness" and a "lattice of coincidence." Emplotment in *Repo Man* becomes diffused across a vast relational network. It is no accident that the car culture of Los Angeles figures in *Repo Man* to separate and segment experience into discrete and chaotic bits (as if it were metaphysically lived only through the window of an automobile)—while the "lattice of coincidence," the "network" of the Los Angeles freeway system, reconnects experience at another and less human order of magnitude.

The postmodern and electronic "instant," in its break from the temporal structures of retension and protension, constitutes a form of absolute presence (one abstracted from the continuity that gives meaning to the system past/present/future) and changes the nature of the space it occupies. Without the temporal emphases of historical consciousness and personal history, space becomes abstract, ungrounded, and flat—a site for play and display rather than an invested situation in which action "counts" rather than computes. Such a superficial space can no longer hold the spectator/user's interest, but has to stimulate it constantly in the same way a video game does. Its flatness—a function of its lack of temporal thickness and bodily investment—has to attract spectator interest at the surface. Thus, electronic space constructs objective and superficial equivalents to depth, texture, and invested bodily movement. Saturation of color and hyperbolic attention to detail replace depth and texture at the surface of the image, while constant action and "busyness" replace the gravity that grounds and orients the movement of the lived-body with a purely spectacular, kinetically exciting, often dizzying sense of bodily freedom (and freedom from the body). In an important sense, electronic space disembodies.

What I am suggesting is that, ungrounded and uninvested as it is, electronic presence has neither a point of view nor a visual situation, such as we experience, respectively, with the photograph and the cinema. Rather, electronic presence randomly disperses its being *across* a network, its kinetic gestures describing and lighting on the surface of the screen rather than inscribing it with bodily dimension (a function of centered and intentional projection). Images on television screens and computer terminals seem neither projected nor deep. Phenomenologically they seem, rather, somehow just there as they confront us.

The two-dimensional, binary superficiality of electronic space at once disorients and liberates the activity of consciousness from the gravitational pull and orientation of its hitherto embodied and grounded existence. All surface, electronic space cannot be inhabited. It denies or prosthetically transforms the spectator's physical body so that subjectivity and affect free-float or free-fall or free-flow across a horizontal/vertical grid. Subjectivity is at once decentered and completely extroverted—again erasing the modernist (and cinematic) dialectic between inside and outside and its synthesis of discontinuous time and discontiguous space as conscious and embodied experience. As Jameson explains:

> The liberation . . . from the older *anomie* of the centered subject may also mean, not merely a liberation from anxiety, but a liberation from every other kind of feeling as well, since there is no longer a self present to do the feeling. This is not to say that the cultural products of the postmodern era are utterly devoid of feeling, but rather that such feelings—which it might be better and more accurate to call "intensities"—are now free-floating and impersonal, and tend to be dominated by a peculiar kind of euphoria. (Jameson 1984: 64)

Brought to visibility by the electronic, this kind of euphoric "presence" is not only peculiar. At the risk of sounding reactionary, I would like to suggest that it is also dangerous. Its lack of specific interest and grounded investment in the human body and enworlded action, its saturation with the present instant, could well cost us all a future.

Phenomenological analysis does not end with the "thick" description and thematization (or qualified reduction) of the phenomenon under investigation. It aims also for an interpretation of the phenomenon that discloses, however partially, the lived meaning, significance, and non-neutral value it has for those who engage it. In terms of contemporary moving-image culture, the material differences between cinematic and electronic representation emerge as significant differences in their meaning and value. Cinema is an objective phenomenon that comes—and becomes—before us in a structure that implicates both a sensible body and a sensual and sense-making subject. In its visual address and movement, it allows us to see what seems a visual impossibility: that we are at once intentional subjects and material objects in the world, the seer and the seen. It affirms both embodied being and the world. It also shows us that, sharing materiality and the world, we are intersubjective beings.

Now, however, it is the electronic and not the cinematic that dominates the form of our cultural representations. And, unlike cinematic representation, electronic representation by its very structure phenomenologically denies the human body its fleshly presence and the world its dimension. However significant and positive its values in some regards, the electronic trivializes the human body. Indeed, at this historical moment in our particular society and culture, the lived-body is in crisis. Its struggle to assert its gravity, its differential existence and situation, its vulnerability and mortality, its vital and social investment in a concrete life-world inhabited by others is now marked in hysterical and hyperbolic responses to the disembodying effects of electronic representation. On the one hand, contemporary moving images show us the human body relentlessly and fatally interrogated, "riddled with holes" and "blown away," unable to maintain its material integrity or gravity. If the Terminator doesn't finish it off, then electronic smart bombs will. On the other hand, the current popular obsession with physical fitness manifests the wish to transform the human body into something else—a lean, mean, and immortal "machine," a cyborg that can physically interface with the electronic network and maintain material presence in the current digitized life-world of the subject. (It is no accident that body builder Arnold Schwarzenegger played the cyborg Terminator.)

Within the context of this material and technological crisis of the flesh, one can only hope that the hysteria and hyperbole surrounding it is strategic—and that through it the lived-body has, in fact, managed to reclaim our attention to forcefully argue for its existence and against its simulation. For there are other subjects of electronic culture out there who prefer the simulated body and a virtual world. Indeed, they actually believe the body (contemptuously called "meat" or "wetware") is best lived only as an image or as information, and that the only hope for negotiating one's presence in our electronic life-world is to exist on a screen or to digitize and "download" one's consciousness into the neural nets of a solely electronic existence. Such an insubstantial electronic presence can ignore AIDS, homelessness, hunger, torture, and all the other ills the flesh is heir to outside the image and the datascape. Devaluing the physically lived body and the concrete materiality of the world, electronic presence suggests that we are all in imminent danger of becoming merely ghosts in the machine.

MONIKA ELSNER, THOMAS MÜLLER,
AND PETER M. SPANGENBERG

The Early History of
German Television: The Slow
Development of a Fast Medium

Media and the History of Mentality

The "regular television program service," which was established in March 1935 under time pressure and with great pride in National Socialist Germany, was of only moderate interest to Berliners. People certainly visited the public television rooms, but the beginning of the television program service was, in the minds of its few viewers, not as much of a breakthrough as was the installation of public radio at the end of 1923. Television only gradually established itself on the horizon of people's awareness, and only the broadcast of a mass event, the Olympics of 1936, introduced the new medium to a broader public. Thus, for its contemporaries, television was connected from the beginning with a program event.

Reconstruction of the historical communication conditions of the television medium is based on a series of questions that converge around interest in *the transformation of forms of communication*.

NOTE: This article was written in connection with our joint work at the University of Siegen on Project A5; *Vor- und Frühgeschichte des Fernsehens* (project director: Professor Hans Ulrich Gumbrecht) within the framework of the special research field 240: *Ästhetik, Pragmatik und Geschichte der Bildschirmmedien-Schwerpunkt: Das Fernsehen in der Bundesrepublik Deutschland*.

With this project, the need arises to expand the established fields of research and the range of questions asked by media research and literary studies. Much too often, media research and the historiography of technical communication media amount to nothing more than strings of facts obviously bound to a theoretically naive, positivistic ideal of historical objectivity. In contrast, we shall try to merge elements of technological, program, and media history into the overall perspective of the history of mentalities and discourse. If the concept of media is not restricted to the technological communication media of the twentieth century (as unfortunately often happens), then new horizons open on the very slow transition between, and coexistence of, a handwriting culture and the medium of printing (see Gumbrecht 1988a). Only in the middle of the nineteenth century did these *longue-durée-structures* undergo a very rapid acceleration of change. The developing communication technologies and forms of reception changed the entire communication system of the society so radically that an analysis of different sections is only possible against the background of the whole development (Kittler 1987: 271–78). Since rapid print media, radio, and film fulfill central communicative functions, the question of whether this means the end of literature has to be asked, or at least we must consider whether, in this new media context, the *institution* of literature has kept more than its name. Because of the shift in paradigms from a *history of the change of* (literary) *forms and genres* toward *media history as a history of the materiality of communicative forms*, the question arises of whether or not modern societies can be predominantly described as communication systems, a question answered by sociological systems theory in the affirmative. Because media research selects as a central subject the material preconditions of communication (the meaning and sensory nature of communication), along with the knowledge structures and distribution processes of such societies, its contribution to the history of mentality in the twentieth century is by no means merely peripheral.

By way of examples from the early history of television in Germany we want to show that media history conceived as such cannot be limited to individual media (radio, film, and record player versus printing, newspapers, magazines, and typewriters) or to the isolated contemplation of the technological or program history of radio or television. Thus, in order to explain the fact that television did not have immediate success in Germany, it is necessary to look at the development of technological possibilities, but just as important to know the expectations and needs of the audience, the nature of the media system in which television had to assert itself, and the communication opportunities in Berlin during the 1930's. In order to explain the image that those National Socialists responsible for television wanted to create, the findings of a program history that is ideologically critical have to be consulted, and the (in our view) mythical elements of the historiography of technology are also informative.

The expression "identity problems of early television" refers to the historical difficulties of assigning a place and function for this medium in the established media and communication system. If a general suspicion of television does not predominate, then one looks for an identity of the *product*, the television show, as distinct from the products of radio and film. In Germany, its communicative possibilities only rarely received attention in terms of the definition of the "television specifics" of television, and mostly in early technological utopias (see Bischoff 1984: 72–74). Not the product, but a new pragmatism of *communicative achievements* determines the identity of television today, precisely because it is accompanied by a new division in the communicative functions of the media system.

Because our interest in knowledge about this kind of history of communicative forms is incompatible with an aesthetically evaluative viewpoint (which by no means excludes partiality), we want to avoid here the old European lament about the "decline," or the growing functional disability, of literature, and rather reconstruct a particular historical situation in which these laments also belonged to the intellectual routine. A relevant context for discussion of our reconstruction are the theses about *the transformation of perception through the technical media*. One must ask what kind of effect television, as the dominant communication medium of the past decades, had on perception structures. Today we unhesitatingly connect the illusionary worlds of staged immediacy, the aesthetics of sensory surprise, and the acceleration of perception with the medium of television, even though media historians use the example of the film medium to describe the genesis of this new way of seeing (see Virilio 1984b: 41–69). Creation of, and access to, worlds through communication cannot, therefore, be limited to the products of one medium. The question arises, from a historical viewpoint, whether early television in Nazi Germany also participated, through the "new way of seeing," in this change in the experience of space and time.

Early Tele-Vision-Utopias: The Expansion of the Horizon of Visual Perception

The old dream of mankind, to be able to see what happens in the distance, to be able to see at a distance, received an enormous boost in the second half of the nineteenth century. In a time of rapid technical and social change, people fantasized about the quick fulfillment of old utopias, and at the same time a whole host of natural science experiments and technical discoveries dealt with the problem of the long-distance transmission of pictures. Technical projects that were devised at the end of the nineteenth century mainly offered solutions for the long-distance transmission of static pictures; for the time being they were, therefore, picture telegraphs, which were called "electrical telescopes," "telectroscopes," or "telephotographs" (see H. Riedel 1985: 15–25).

The need for long-distance transmission of moving pictures seems to have arisen with the invention of the cinematograph, and with the popularity of the motion picture film. The period between about 1875 and 1925 could be called a phase of speculation about television, in which the dominant obsession of both technicians and an interested amateur audience was to be able to *artificially enhance the abilities of the human sense organs*, and to enlarge the horizon of visual perception. The German word *Fernsehen* has its origins in the semantics of the old utopia: seeing at a distance, seeing what is happening in the distance; technical experts, as well as journalists who wrote for a popular audience, used the word *Fernsehen* in this sense first. The discourse of technical knowledge and the discourse of popular utopian fantasy produced a discourse symbiosis, in which the semantics of the old utopia and the numerous projects for its technical realization, or technical projects for picture transmission in general, were speculatively combined with each other; "seeing by electricity," "distant electric vision," was viewed as (another) technical miracle, whose realization seemed to have moved closer in time. The invention of the telephone made it possible to transmit the sound of the human voice and other sounds over distances that would have been completely impossible for natural hearing. In 1926, the British television pioneer John Logie Baird claimed, in an advertisement for his mechanical television apparatus (the "televisor"), that in 1876 some visionaries had already announced that, after hearing by telephone, seeing by telephone would follow naturally (Briggs 1977: 47; see also 40–65).

In his novel *Le vingtième siècle*, published in 1892, the French *author* Albert Robida described the future use of a new invention, which enhanced the technology of the telephone with a component that infinitely enlarged the human eye's natural sight:

Among the exceptional inventions, about which the 20th century boasts, the telephonoscope can be called one of the most surprising. With the telephonoscope, one sees and hears. Dialogue and music are transmitted in the manner of a common telephone, but at the same time the scene itself appears, with its lighting, its decorations, and its actors, on a crystal disc with the clarity of direct visibility. One really attends the performance with eyes and ears. The illusion is perfect! . . . Thus one could (what a wonder!) become a witness in Paris of an event that took place a thousand miles away from Europe.   (Cited in H. Riedel 1985: 13)

In 1911, the Russian *engineer* Boris Rosing depicted, in the French newspaper *Excelsior*, a similar picture of the future with regard to the enhancement, through technology, of the human eye's ability to see:

The area of application of the telephone does not go beyond human conversation. With telescopy, man will not only correspond with other human beings but also with nature itself. Equipped with the "electrical eye," we will go deeply into that which until now no human being ever reached. We will see what up to now no human being ever saw. . . . In everyday life, it will make contact among all members of human society easier.   (Cited in H. Riedel 1985: 13)

In Robida's novel a further use of television was presented: an illustration shows the vision of a bourgeois sitting on a sofa watching with enjoyment ballet dancers at very close quarters on his round screen, which is as big as the wall. The sound of the performance apparently comes from a kind of phonograph, which sits on the table in front of him. Thus, in the early technical utopias of the late nineteenth century, television was already imagined in *connection with technical inventions that were already known*, such as, for example, the telephone and the phonograph/gramophone. Ideas such as these about media combinations were to gain new popularity during the 1920's and 1930's.

Fascination with Technology and New Horizons of Communication: Radio and Gramophone

The phonograph or record player, the tape recorder, and the radio are things we take so much for granted today that it is difficult to understand the mental shock that the preservation of voice, music, and sounds of any kind must have produced in contemporaries (see Kittler 1987: 235–70). The dominant role of writing as a storage medium was broken, and the phonograph permitted the preservation of voice, a part of corporeality that had always been thought of as especially fleeting and transitory. With the introduction of radio, with the possibility of participating in an event "directly," the overwhelming impression created by the phonograph was repeated once again (even though on a different level of complexity). While the basic mechanical principle of the phonograph had been quite easy to understand, a specialized knowledge of radio was necessary in order to understand its functioning. The crystal set and the tube receiver were the first complex electrical appliances in people's private sphere, if not the very first electrical appliance with which they had close contact. Until then, electricity had been predominantly viewed as an energy source for light bulbs. In the home of the 1930's, *Lichtnetz* (light-net) was still the most widely used name for the electric wiring.

The technical operation of the first crystal set, and later of the tube receiver, was relatively easy to learn, and with this knowledge a completely *new horizon of communication* was opened. Enthusiasm about the expansion of the horizon was so great that many technical hobbyists were not in the least interested in what they heard. On the one hand, the worker-radio movement of the Weimar Republic was characterized by fascination with a technology that opened a myriad of communication *opportunities* to anyone who had a knowledge of the subject; and on the other hand, this fascination kept alive the optimism to realize new political opportunities in a self-determined communication medium (see Dahl 1978).

Experiences with radio shaped potential television viewers' expectations. Similar rapid progress, as well as the participation of the technically minded hobbyists in the television's development, was also expected. To some extent there was already, very early on, no lack of attempts to make television technology available for the hobbyists. A popular technical book for the "amateur radio enthusiast" with the title *Bildfunk: Anleitung zum Selbstbau eines Bildempfängers* (Radio photography: instructions for building a picture receiver, by Rudolf Hell) had been published already in 1927. After the introduction of television to a larger audience at the Berlin Broadcasting Exhibitions of 1928 and 1929, a general euphoria about the pending inauguration of "television-broadcasting" spread very quickly. A didactic technical book by Wilhelm Schrage with the title *Television*, regarding "how it works and how the radio listener can participate in it," was published in 1930. An accompanying notice from the publisher said:

Television! Millions of people are waiting for television. . . . Television, long-distance cinema at home, that's what one wants to get immediately, along with radio and telephone. If only it were already safe enough and cheap enough to operate. . . . Probably a new hobbyist movement will start and contribute quite a bit to the development of the technical abilities of our people, to the dissemination of technical knowledge and understanding.   (Cited in H. Riedel 1985: 57)

The complexity of the knowledge required by the subject, the danger of handling high voltage, and the high price of the television set components were crucial obstacles that stood in the way of a technical television hobbyist movement. Nevertheless, the idea persisted until the late 1930's, proof of how much the experience with radio had influenced popular expectations for television broadcasting. A complete television receiver kit with a round 5-inch cathode-ray tube could still be acquired in the U.S.A. in 1937 (see *Radio News*, May 1937, Special Television Number).

In 1935, the "coordinated" *Reichsverband Deutscher Rundfunkteilnehmer* (Reich Association of German Radio Subscribers) appealed to its members:

Join together everywhere and build television communities! Your organized will must ensure that practical machine-building and station-building follow these reception communities immediately! Work for the introduction of television, and you will work for the final victory of the National Socialist idea! Carry the picture of the *Führer* into all German hearts! Announce it to everyone on the other side of the German borders! Fight so that Germany becomes the first country on earth in which all national comrades can watch television!   (Cited in Dahl 1983: 199)

The demand to build and operate their own transmitting installations proves, at least, that this appeal, which was loyal to the party line, was not dulled by any kind of technical knowledge. In contrast to the steady and rapid development of the related media radio and film, the progress of television was characterized by considerably more technical dead ends and repeated, boring research on the details. The basic principle of long-distance transmission of pictures by scanning pictures into dots of different shades (already known from the printing medium) was agreed upon relatively early. However, it remained to be determined whether the production of these scans and their reproduction at the receiver end should be effected through electromechanical or through entirely electrical means. This choice was difficult because, for a long time, it was not clear which process would bring the better results, since in the early 1930's, neither way could show really convincing results. That explains the existence of both technologies in early laboratory equipment and experimental broadcasts.

Further basic difficulties involved, for example, the need for a transmitter with a wide frequency band in order to be able to transmit synchronous picture and sound signals or were caused by the insufficient capacity of individual components, such as those for image resolution—line number, repetition frequency, and the number of picture dots. Even though Braun's innovative tube proved to be a useful screen (called a "picture writer" in popular articles), it raised numerous problems that remained to be solved in order to make this breakthrough attractive for practical application. Only interlaced scanning, for example, prevented the flickering of images; and one had to switch over from a Braun tube filled with gas to a high-vacuum tube in order to prevent the picture from continuing to glow for a few seconds, a condition that would have only allowed the transmission of slow picture changes and movements.

Such complex problems involving the details of television technology constantly arose, and were too much for even the technically ambitious amateur. Consequently, the popular technical fascination that accompanied radio in the first phases of its developmental history failed to materialize, and an exertion of influence on the television movement by "hobbyists" in any country was out of the question. The greater technical *complexity* and component costs central to television development necessitated from the start that it was a field for specialists. The television receiver, as well as the transmitter, were always *industrial products*, and from the start the production and distribution of programs required major financial, technical, and organizational expenditures.

The German electrical industry seems to have been aware of the significance of the *productivity* criterion for the introduction of a new media product on the market. In 1935 (the year of the official opening of a program operation), the industry was not ready for the planned mass production of television sets, despite announcements to the contrary. In the spring of 1935 Telefunken, for example, appeared rather restrained in its announcements, which were meant for radio stores:

One demands clear and undistorted pictures from film. From radio one demands the highest transmission quality. Thus, in both areas a certain quality concept has been developed in the mind of the public, which has to be included in developmental work on television. In contrast to the beginnings of film and radio development, toward which the public had an uncritical attitude, the public already approaches television with certain ideas regarding quality and capability. . . . The more thorough the examinations and tests that are carried out in the field of television, the more surely one averts the danger that the hasty mass production of television receivers will discredit the idea of television, to which a great future is open.[1]

Functional Utopias of Television

The closer the time came for a practical application of the new technology of television in the consciousness of the interested 1920's public, the more extensively formulated the first heterogeneous expectations for the new technology became. When, in the middle of the 1920's, John Logie Baird in England and Dénes von Mihály and August Karolus in Germany first tried to demonstrate the feasibility of television with public demonstrations, they caused a sensation among the already attentive public: the daily press celebrated the working laboratory experiments as a technical sensation, and awakened great expectations with regard to a pending integration of television into daily life, in which, because people were thinking along the lines of radio, the remaining developmental time period was badly underestimated.

For example, an illustrated article—"Die Welt in 40 Jahren: Ein Blick in die Zukunft" (The world in 40 years: A View into the Future)—appeared in the January 3, 1926, edition of the widely circulated *Berliner Illustrirte Zeitung*, only a short time after the first television demonstration by John Logie Baird in London. In the article, along with a vision of dense urban air traffic, the daily use of, above all, a television set is imagined:

Would not social life be considerably restricted, if people sitting in their homes are not only able to speak to each other and hear music or lectures, but can also see each other and any theater performance, indeed, exhibitions and any other performances on their television from the easy chair?

In this article, the telephone and the radio are already taken for granted as elements of a modern home, to which the newest element, the television set, can now be added in order to complete the ensemble of modern technical communication media. That its use will have social effects, that it could perhaps reduce social life, is already foreseen, but it is apparently not known exactly how such a television would function or what kind of pictures it would deliver into the home. There's no other way to explain the general vagueness of the description and, at the same time, the clarity of certain expressions in the text; thus it says, for example, that, with the television, people could see "each other" and also "any theater performance." Can television "look at" whatever it wants to look at? Who is controlling it and its pictures? The unbridled imagination in this text is still considerably influenced by the old *vision of seeing at distance*, and still very far from the *idea of the medium television* with which we are familiar today: a fixed offering of programs, which we are always in charge of through home reception.

One year later, on January 30, 1927, the same *Berliner Illustrirte Zeitung* published an article with the title "From Fantasy to Reality," in which the speed of technical progress was emphasized, and a "gigantic change of all philosophies of life" was announced. It stated succinctly, and as if it were the most natural thing in the world, "Yesterday television was still a utopian fairytale, today it has been invented, and tomorrow it will be practically applied."

A large-sized illustration, which appeared in the *Berliner Illustrirte Zeitung* on January 8, 1928, may clarify how much ideas about "practical application" were still shaped by utopias, conceived in a free-floating fantasy: a full-page drawing shows a man lying in his bed, with a fragmented dashboard in front of him—he seems to steer some technical apparatus and, at the same time, to look at a mountain panorama, which is seen from a bird's-eye view on a kind of projection screen. The caption deciphers the illustration for us:

Marvels that we might still experience: viewing the world from bed through television. The apparatus above the bed serves to operate, by remote control, an airplane that carries the filming apparatus and provides, via radio transmission, views of the area above which the airplane soars. With the map in front of the viewer, he or she can control where the airplane is located.

Among the public, the popular fascination with flying and the fascination with seeing at distance were fantastically combined, and fantasy, totally carefree, overtook the speed of the technical progress: two advanced technologies—one (the airplane) already almost perfected to the point of being commonplace, the other shortly before its breakthrough—were merged in a utopian synthesis that suggested a practical, applicable "role in life" for the embryonic technology. At the same time, it also produced an illusionary horizon of expectations, and thereby determined the reception/evaluation of its real technical application in such a way that disappointment was preordained.

The great euphoria of the Berlin press after the first demonstrations of television receivers, still on the level of laboratory apparatus at the Berlin Broadcasting Exhibitions of 1928 and 1929, raised enormous expectations concerning the imminent realization, and the quality, of television. Like John Logie Baird[2] in England, Dénes von Mihály in Germany had announced a satisfactory and inexpensive "national television." If they allowed themselves to get carried away into really euphoric enthusiasm in the face of such small-format flickering pictures, the visitors, who could only see silent pictures of simple moving objects through a magnifying glass on a mechanically scanned 4 × 4 centimeter picture screen, might have recalled the simplicity of the first crystal radio sets and the rapid development of radio broadcasting. For example, journalist Egon Larsen, after a public demonstration of television, wrote in his article "Television in Sight!":

Here in this ordinary, small, raised ground-floor apartment on the Kant-strasse, the wonder is about to happen, which, for a thousand and one nights, has been the eternal desire of mankind: television, seeing spatially distant objects and events at the moment they occur. Is it really true that the human mind has solved even this secret and burst the bonds of space the same way film and recording have loosened the bonds of time for us mortals?   (Larsen 1929: 9)

Because of the technically more complex problems that had to be solved in order to manage the recording, transmission, and recep-tion of an audiovisual television program, the technicians at the Berlin Broadcasting Exhibitions of the following years couldn't offer a noticeably higher quality of television pictures. The public obviously felt disappointed in its expectations, and increasingly reacted with a lack of interest to presentations of new technology. After the waning of the first sensation-seeking curiosity, the com-plicated high-tech aspect of television could only generate a purely technical fascination among educated specialists. Ultimately, the electronic amateurs and potential consumers *had* to ask about its use value; the everyday *usefulness* of television technology became the crucial criterion.

What had been euphoria at the outset turned into disillusion-ment with, or even angry criticism of, television. For example, an editor with the initials "W. Schr." wrote an article in the *Berliner Tageblatt* on January 28, 1931, entitled "The Scandal About Televi-sion," in which he insistently criticized that the Reich Broadcasting Company (the Reichs-Rundfunk-Gesellschaft, or RRG), kept on financing further television experiments with public money. He wrote:

It was not long ago when one heard almost daily about some kind of "completely revolutionary" television invention, whose introduction would occur in only a few weeks. But the weeks became months, and the months became years, and then everything became quiet. . . . In any case, the German Reichspost has, over the years, spent 2,000,000 Marks for television experiments. . . . Two larger specialized companies have also put a lot of money into television. But all the persons involved (who are partially responsible for the many false ideas that now predominate among the public) have to admit that it may take a while before we can watch faultless television.   (Cited in Lerg 1967: 353)

Finally, the author turned against the experimental transmissions of television pictures by the Post Office, which were carried out at particular times on sound radio frequencies, but which could only be picked up by radio receivers as a "humming." In the interest of radio listeners, such experimental transmissions would have to stop during the main transmitting time, because the simple "humming" of television transmission only disturbed and interrupted radio reception.

During the 1920's, popular discourse about television and the discourse by the technical experts about "transmission processes for making moving pictures visible" (*Fernsichtbarmachung*) started to become clearly differentiated.[3] Even after successful demonstrations of television technology during the broadcasting exhibitions at the end of the 1920's, the technical specialists (with the exception of Mihály) still made reserved and skeptical comments about the future of television. Contravening the general euphoria of the daily press, the technicians dampened expectations, and emphasized the incompleteness of the achievements and the difficulty of the problems that still had to be solved; they refused to commit themselves to deadlines for the realization of television, and they talked about an uncertain future for "actual" television.

In Germany around 1930 the fully differentiated discourse of the technical experts and the popular discourse of the amateurs met and clashed in institutionalized form: in 1929 the General German Television Association was founded in Berlin, to which belonged technicians who had a part in the development of television and leading figures in the radio administration and the Reichspost, as well as an interested circle of journalists and amateurs. This club wanted to devote itself to the promotion of television, and toward this end it published the journal *Fernsehen* (Television). Both the down-to-earth discourse of the experts and the speculative popular discourse about the possibilities of developing television were represented in articles in this periodical, and they were also partly mixed with each other. The fact that, during 1930 for example, the appearance of skeptical articles increased remarkably in a journal that was supposed to promote television was probably also a symptom of the increasing lack of interest on the part of the general public in an as yet experimental medium. Characteristic of the spreading skepticism among the disappointed public is an article by journalist Eduard Rhein with the title "It Is a Long Way Off . . . ," which came out in September 1930 in *Fernsehen*:

There we are standing—we, who look up to the new coming miracle with wide eyes—quite disappointed, perhaps angry. What the daily press shouted at us with sensational slogans were phrases. The hope created in us,—phrases. It is nothing. Two years passed between the first and the last disappointment. Whatever progress is recorded, proved with differentials, integrals, slide-rules, curves: *we can't see it.*   (Rhein 1930: 415)

The solution of technical problems remained uninteresting as long as only technical knowledge was accumulated, knowledge that might be a step toward solutions, without being of such quality that one could already talk about the apparent accomplishment of the new technology. But, after moving from the euphoria of fantastic promise to a state of disillusionment, the amateur audience finally demanded visible results and achievements, and, with the pragmatism of common sense, the question of the specific capabilities of the new technology became the center of attention: What *new things* does television offer us?

In the article mentioned above, Eduard Rhein also recommended patience to the *Verein zur Förderung des Fernsehens* (Association for Television Promotion): "Television is fostered when one simply tries to prevent television from becoming discredited before it is here. Television is also promoted when one honestly admits: technology is not yet ready, you still have to wait a couple of years!" (ibid., 414).

Media Competition

The difficulties of television in finding its place as a new medium cannot be explained merely in terms of the technical problems that repeatedly disappointed the expectations of the public. Rather, one must remember that television had to assert itself within an already established *system of technical communication media, with allocated responsibilities*. Photography not only delivered a very high picture quality, but was already a very quick, topical medium, whose capabilities were further enhanced through the facsimile or wirephoto. In the printed media, photographs made possible a new quality of information that was so successful with the audience that a new visual type of newspaper, the magazine, was born. The wax cylinder of Edison's early phonograph was developed into the record, and with the phonograph, radio had an uncomplicated storage medium at its disposal. Film had developed from a fun-fair attraction into an acceptable art form, and—even though many people had not only misjudged sound film but rejected it for aesthetic reasons—by 1932 it replaced the silent movie. By the mid-1920's, radio was considered, by politicians of every political shade as well as by artists, to be the most important medium for the formation of opinion and for the education of the masses. Intellectual and political control of this medium stood at the center of debate.

During this period, the radio and the airplane were held responsible for a paradoxical change in the experience of space. The spectator was overwhelmed by the world. The sphere of experience now available found its new limits in the speed of the flying machines or in the spreading properties of the radio wavelengths. The possibility of being present, either physically by means of rapid transportation or electronically by means of the "ear on the world," the radio set, broadened the potential horizon of experience, but at the same time people experienced an implosion of the global space. The railroad, automobile, large passenger steamers, and, as a central emblem of faster transportation, the airplane perfected the spatial control of nature, and film was ready, as a further media substitute, for their particular experience of space.

In large metropolitan cities, new forms of cultural experience were created; movie palaces, modern theaters as "illusion machines," cabaret and variety stages, as well as huge halls for events and places for a culture of popular entertainment, all influenced a new style of (cultural) perception: the heightening of illusions, "accelerated perception," and the mechanization of sensual experience (see Hickethier 1986) created a new dimension of reality, which was experienced as an intensification of life. Large cities, like

Berlin, attracted a mass public with huge sporting spectacles (the famous six-day bike races at the *Sportpalast*) and lavish revues. In Weimar Germany, mass marches and demonstrations by every political organization supplemented a collective body's experience of itself and of others. Television had to succeed in the context of the abundant offerings of new communication forms and entertainment media. But against the established competition, the "visible" results of the new medium were too meager.

In the 1930's, radio experienced another tremendous increase in the number of listeners. Its technical development had left the do-it-yourself stage behind, and commercially produced sets allowed such worldwide reception that the National Socialists in Germany regulated the sale of shortwave sets. Through communal reception, and through the production of inexpensive and poor-quality sets, the world of the German radio listener was supposed to be brought onto the "co-ordinated" information horizon of the national comrades. The mass production of the German small receiver, and of the *People's Receiver 301*, was promoted by the state— a reminder of January 30, 1933, the day on which Hitler had become the Reich chancellor.

Different ideas for *media combinations*, which continually appeared in technicians' discussions as well as in the popular discourse about television, are also an indication of how difficult it was for television to find its place in the established communication and media system. Television could be conceived of, not as an alternative to the existing technical communication media, but as a useful addition to radio, cinema, and the telephone. And in the popular discourse, fantasies of future *media syntheses* outdid the known media/technologies.

When television was introduced for the first time, at the Broadcasting Exhibition of 1928, it was presented at the stand of Telefunken GmbH together with the so-called "synchronically running cinema" (*Gleichlaufkino*), a technique that provided coordinated, synchronously running film projectors at different places as a visual illustration for synchronously transmitted radio programs (see Goebel 1978). And, in a report on the Broadcasting Exhibition of 1928, a Berlin journalist evaluated the television receiver, which was introduced by Mihály, as follows: "A small appliance for home use, similar to the one which we might soon connect with our radio receivers. Sound film, radio, and television might be a unit even earlier than we dare to hope. Then broadcasting will bring the talking, singing live picture, stimulated by music, on the airwaves into the home for us" (cited in Riedel 1985: 38–39). In "Looking Back on the Broadcasting Exhibition of 1929," the renowned Berlin television magazine *Funkstunde* (Broadcast Hour) wrote about television, "The basics exist, which allow us to expect a really usable extension on the optical side of the radio, which until now has been exclusively acoustic" (Sept. 13, 1929, p. 1243).

When, at the end of the 1920's, television experiments were still experienced as exciting sensations and were, to the Berlin press, worth publishing extra pages for, the first successful broadcast test programs of television (which were recognizable for most of the listeners only as "noisy rattling" in the radio loudspeaker) were immediately connected in speculative terms with the known media.[4]

During the early 1930's, *Fernsehen*, the magazine of the General German Television Association, carried intense debates about the size and purpose of visual programming broadcast inside the radio program. The "supplementing of radio by television or distant cinema" was supposed to force "the most economical use of television within the existing broadcasting program," out of "consideration for the other radio participants," or the "mere listeners." This position was relatively strongly represented (see Thun 1930 and Weitz 1930). Others criticized the Reichspost's experiments with television programs over broadcasting frequencies and during the radio broadcasts:

It is impossible to broadcast television and sound programs alternately over the same transmitter. It is preposterous to cut hours out of the already overcrowded daily program, to fill them, for the listener without television, with the "wawawa" of television, just as it was a torture to insert the painful tooting of picture broadcasting into the hours of dance music.   (Rhein 1930: 415; see also his n. 19)

Rhein's proposed alternative amounted, incidentally, to the creation of a kind of "hybrid-program: television and sound broadcasting must run simultaneously, and the programs must be designed in such a way that things are understandable for nonviewers, so that it can be an experience even for them" (ibid). An independent media identity for television was obviously still a long way

off; in the early 1930's, television was not even technically emanci-
pated from radio. Terms like "(wireless) distant-movie-theater,"
"(wireless) home-movie-theater," "television-broadcast," "sound-
picture receiver," "tele-visio-speaking," "television-newsreel," and
"television-film-theater" all document that there was a time when
the word "television" was not able to produce an idea of a concise
signifier in peoples' consciousnesses.

For a long time the size of the familiar cinema screen determined the audience's ideas and expectations about the optical dimensions and quality of the television of the future. Throughout
the 1930's in Germany, there were numerous technical models
(notably those by Karolus) and media projects for large-screen
television projectors in cinema halls, which made it possible to
supplement the cinema program, and which were supposed to
offer "daily television news" as a more current kind of newsreel.
The large-screen television experiments were also promoted for
political reasons: they corresponded with the goal of strengthening
the effect of National Socialist propaganda through regimenting
communal reception.[5]

Someday, after the perfection of television transmissions, the picture
palaces will achieve an enormous increase in their daily relevance. More
and more, movie theaters will become the assembly point for the large
events of our national community. If today the masses gather at political
mass rallies on the streets and squares of the German regions [*Gau*], join
together in a collective experience in front of the loudspeakers, then, in
the future, those same masses (their possibilities for experience enhanced
by the wonder of television) will gather in front of transmissions of the
current television shows in the picture palaces.[6]

Large-screen-television viewing rooms were also available in Berlin, but they obviously did not meet a communication need and
they did not spread, probably because of the public's lack of interest
and the high production costs. Over and against the technically
realizable models of media combinations, there were also, in the
1930's, technological utopias that imagined media synthesis of
which all known technologies were components, which syntheses
were merged into the metamedium of the future. For example, in
1930 Frank Warschauer published an article with scientific pretensions entitled "The Future of Technologization," in which he

sketched a visionary panorama of the future media combination of theater, opera, radio, record, sound film, television, and picture record (an audiovisual storage medium analogous to the record). His plan culminated in the idea for a distant stage, on which technically perfect, three-dimensional, colorful visual-acoustic performances would be reproduced, for example, in a way that would give the viewer the impression of attending an evening of opera (see Warschauer 1930: 425). On the one hand, television technology is at the center of Warschauer's utopia, because it assumes the role of a transmission medium that is considered to be unlimited: "This technology of television and the transmission of color film will make possible the distribution of corresponding representations which will play everywhere with phantom-like clarity and, what is probably more important, it will above all allow people to view and experience, at the very same time, each event happening somewhere else on earth" (ibid., 418). On the other hand, television, as a completed step on the way to a synthesis of technology and art forms, is already outdone by utopia. It is remarkable that many technical utopias of the late nineteenth century as well as of the 1930's—whatever fantastic power of imagination they might release—continuously hold to the idea of a completely manageable technology controlled by the will of a human subject. Communication media (like television, for example) are often introduced not only as an extension of the human sense organs but also as a multiplier of possibilities for interaction for people who seem to be able to control such "media" like an external objectivation of their autonomous will power.*

But more "pragmatic" applications, such as the remote control of ships and passenger airplanes, or medical examination from a distance, were also among the applications that could be imagined from the beginning until the middle of the 1930's. Along with electricity, skyscrapers, and private airplanes as common as cars, one saw the television monitoring of workers and production processes as part of future society; in 1926, this vision's filmed version,

*"Radio is the human ear and mouth extended to infinity" (Warschauer 1930: 435). "In contrast, television wants, ultimately, to extend the range of the eye, in other words, to make possible that which is not possible even with the aid of the best telescopes" (Reiser 1930: 299). Cf. the visions of the future mentioned in the *Berliner Illustrirte Zeitung* of Jan. 8, 1928.

Metropolis, already anticipated these possibilities. Technical visions of the future remained surprisingly constant. The following futurist vision from 1938 makes clear just how much cinema dominated as a visual medium and as a form of reception:

In the small cinema projection room [of the airplane], three-dimensional color-sound-films are shown on the screen, which are actually inserted into the playback unit in the entertainment department of the central airport. The shows are interrupted for the spoken and moving newspaper of the *Zeitspiegel*, whose departments transmit each important political, cultural, economic, or sporting event to the interested offices [as the large news offices did earlier with their telegrams], which in turn forward sound and picture to the mass audience, whether it is in the large television cinemas of the cities, or in the small television cinemas of airplanes, ships, trains, buses, and cars.   (Büscher 1938: 9–10)

The enthusiasm for the potentials of technology dominated in these utopias, which inquired neither as to the need for these possibilities nor as to their economic feasibility. At the same time, there were also, at the end of the 1930's, applications of television technology that were technically and economically realistic, but that were not carried out. The best example of this is the constantly recurring idea of the picture telephone. In Berlin, Leipzig, and Munich, special telephone booths were equipped by the post office with television cameras; and, in an advertisement film titled *Wer fuhr IIA 2992?* (1939, Bundesarchiv Koblenz), a car thief who failed to stop after an accident was convicted with evidence from a picture telephone. But telephone customers hardly used this new equipment, and therefore the service was discontinued because of lack of need. Not every technical advance had public appeal.

From 1930 to 1934, interest in television seemed to wane. The general public listened to the radio; went to the cinema; was enthusiastic about revues, cabaret, and theater; streamed in the thousands to sport spectacles, to the six-day races, and to political meetings. And every summer, at the Broadcasting Exhibition in Berlin, the innovations in television technology that were on display might be glanced at in order to find out that the "tube" still wasn't "ready." The technicians worked in their laboratories searching for the solutions to numerous problems, and, unmolested by utopian fantasies, accumulated, in the course of a few years, some remarkable technical knowledge. For example, the optical-mechanical phase of recording and reception technology was superseded by the introduction of the electrical process; the wireless transmission of a synchronized picture and sound signal was successfully tested; and the first functional television receivers were manufactured. But such technical innovations were first perceived and discussed—without causing a sensation—only by a circle of specialized experts. The discourse of the technical specialists and the popular discourse on television had passed the point of intersection crossed earlier in the 1930's, and continued to develop separately, in fully differentiated contexts.

Staging of a Technological Myth

In February 1935, television was in the headlines again. In Great Britain, the government's Television Committee had presented a final report on January 31, 1935. After half a year's work and the inquiries of numerous experts, the committee concluded that it was time to begin general television broadcasts, and the inauguration of a regular program service for London was recommended to the BBC. The news of this was immediately taken up by the European press, as well as that of the U.S.A., and was the basis of numerous sensational articles. Among National Socialist authorities, such press reports caused an outbreak of panic because it was part of the National Socialist ideology to emphasize the world leadership of Germany's natural sciences and technology. The forthcoming inauguration of a television program service in Great Britain was taken as a challenge to the Nazi leadership's claims of the superiority of German technology. Television technology had become a political issue in Germany.

The Nazi officials of the Reich Broadcasting Company (RRG) and the Reichspost were driven by their political and personal ambitions to beat the British, and to be the first nation on earth to regularly transmit a television program. They also had to fear the risk of disgrace in front of the world (and in front of the Nazi leadership). That is why they tried hurriedly *to bring about and to present a technical event*, for which the prerequisites of sufficient testing and technical maturity didn't exist.

On March 22, 1935, between 80 and 100 invited guests (officials

of the RRG and the Post Office, technicians and representatives of
the electronical industry, some journalists and some low-ranking
Nazi party officials who were representing their ministers) gathered in the Berliner Funkhaus in order to participate in a television
demonstration lasting for an hour and a half, and to listen to several ceremonial speeches. This event later was to be recalled as
the opening of the "first television program service on earth."
Reich Program Director (Reichssendeleiter) Hadamovsky, given
the honor of making the ceremonial opening speech in the absence
of the leading VIPs, tried very hard to lend historical and national
importance to the event:

Today, National Socialist broadcasting, in cooperation with the Reichspost and industry, starts regular television broadcasting, as the first broadcasting system on earth. One of the boldest dreams of mankind has
become reality. . . . In this moment, on German soil, we are making
cultural progress that will someday be considered the culmination of
many individual technical developments of the past decades. While we are
now breathlessly listening and watching here in the hall, a time of a new,
incomprehensible wonder has begun.[7]

The event of the epoch was hardly recognized; even the German
and Berlin press only reported it in passing; as, for example, on
page 12 of the *Frankfurter Zeitung* from March 24, 1935, under the
category "World News." But it seems that word of the "epochal
event" of the now realized "television wonder" did not go completely unheard, because only a few days after March 22, 1935, the
RRG apparently saw itself forced to publish a quite sober press
release, in which it was clarified that all the press reports about the
presentation of a "television-national-receiver" at the forthcoming
broadcast exhibition were a misunderstanding. Once again, in a
detailed press release, the background and the significance of the
celebrated event, which now was called "the opening of a *television-
test program* for Berlin," were clarified in a very matter-of-fact tone.
That adequately described the character of the whole occurrence,
because it was certainly not more than the extension, three times a
week for two hours, of experiments with television technology
that had taken place under laboratory conditions up to now, and
that were now being regularly carried out on a larger scale, and this

before the eyes of a larger circle of interested and prominent amateurs (journalists, party functionaries, etc.). For an expanded laboratory audience such as this, a test program was transmitted—and
frequently repeated as well—which consisted for the most part, in
excerpts from UFA feature-films and newsreels. This was accompanied by short announcements and spoken contributions, which
were still produced by using a mechanically based Nipkow-disk
involving a dark "scanning room" about one square meter in size.
Between August 1935 and January 1936, even the operation of this
modest experimental television program had to be stopped because
of a fire and resulting technical difficulties. But regardless, in Germany it was proudly presented, and is still presented, as the first
regular program service in the world.

In the mid-1930's, National Socialist propaganda was interested
only in pioneering technical achievement; in the following years
this was repeatedly *staged* for an audience whose enthusiasm for
television had already subsided a long time before. The technical
innovation, the "miracle of television," was claimed as a national
engineering feat and dramatized as a great achievement of technology and the natural sciences.

A *national technological myth* was created and was eagerly popu-
larized. It was connected with the name of the German Paul Nipkow, whose 1884 patent for an "electrical telescope" was of some
importance for the development of electro-mechanical laboratory
equipment in the 1920's and early 1930's. One week after the
opening of the so-called first regular program operation in the
world, the Berlin station was renamed " 'Paul Nipkow' Television,
Berlin." The old gentleman, who was still alive but a bit senile, was
overwhelmed with honors, and was photographed a thousand
times next to each new television model so that his picture and his
name could be held up in innumerable articles about the miracle of
German television and about the superiority of German scientists
and technicians. Although television technology was obviously an
international development, and was presented as such in Germany
before 1933, although television laboratory experiments in the
U.S.A. and England had reached at least a similar standard, and
although, as of 1936 (when television technology entered its electronic phase) the patent of Nipkow had been old hat for a long

time, the national technology myth about the German "father of television," Paul Nipkow, was told often and kept alive between 1935 and 1945.*

Aside from its suitability for Nazi propaganda, the attractiveness of this myth probably lies in the fact that the mechanical principle of Nipkow's rotary scanning disk could still be explained to a wide audience, while such an audience was not capable of comprehending a higher technical level of complexity such as that of the electronic high-technology television of 1936. But in the 1930's, there was clearly still the public demand that any technology that was supposed to come into the home be basically understandable by amateurs. The popularity of the Nipkow myth may have been just as great as the fear of having an unfathomable and uncontrollable appliance at home. Thus, perhaps, the constant return to the metaphor of the human eye in order to explain the functioning of television is motivated by the repression of human fear of an incomprehensible technology.[8]

It is interesting that the Nipkow myth was also revived at the beginning of German postwar television in Hamburg on December 25, 1952, and was kept alive in the 1950's by television magazines like *Hör zu*, though it had been modified. The touching story was told of the poor student Nipkow, who thought of his patent on a Christmas eve (!) far away from his family (!), in order to provide future generations with the technical ability to bring physically separated family members closer together with the help of television. The German television myth of the 1950's was not, like that of the 1930's, exclusively nationalistic; rather it had switched to the motto "technology and *Gemütlichkeit*," and was suitable for dressing up the idyll of the new television family.

Television as a Substitute?—The Olympic Games of 1936

A larger audience in Berlin and Leipzig only became aware of television with the Olympics of 1936; about 150,000 Berliners

---

*Until today the myth of the inventor-genius Paul Nipkow, the "father of television," has been uncritically continued in the Federal Republic of Germany in numerous, predominantly technical publications. See, e.g., as one of many publications, Hardorn and Cortesi 1986, 2: 164–67.

could watch a daily television program of up to eight hours in 28 so-called "television rooms," public rooms for about 30 to 50 viewers. The television program was composed of live transmissions from the Olympic stadium and of inserted film reports and announcements from the studio. In the press, this "great technical feat," and especially the new electronic iconoscope camera (developed for the most part by RCA's Vladimir Zworykin in the U.S.A.), was also celebrated as new proof of the achievement of German technology.[9] The rudimentary television audience was not considered worth mentioning; rather, it was perceived as an extension of the audience in the stadium. Viewing the television was thought of not as a specific or perhaps privileged form of vision, but rather as a substitute for being there in the stadium, which was preferred as the better form of seeing and experiencing. In this way, television was, during the Olympic Games, an appendage of the stadium, rather than a medium that was important in its own right.

An episode reported by Walter Bruch, an engineer and cameraman in the stadium in 1936, might clarify this. The television technicians quarreled with the officials about the placing of the iconoscope camera (which, because of its size, was also called a "television cannon") in the stadium: "The main thing for them [the officials] was that we didn't disturb anything" (Bruch 1967: 60–61). Despite all the pride in the new technology, the television people had to submit to overriding considerations: the political leaders of the National Socialist state attached great importance to the staging of the Olympic Games as a perfect *live* mass spectacle.[10] And although the transmissions of the Olympic Games were a first high point in the history of German television and made the new medium popular to a certain extent, this assessment of television as a surrogate for the viewer's physical presence in the stadium persisted for years to come. The following examples may speak for the continuity (even among television people) of such attitudes. "While a hundred thousand people were granted the privilege of experiencing the event of the Olympic Games in the area around the stadium, the new television increased still further the circle of those who experienced it."[11] Writing retrospectively in 1940 about this achievement, C.-H. Boese stated proudly in 'That's How We Started!': ". . . to have presented to many thousands of less well-off national comrades—who were not in the position to buy the expensive tickets to the Olympic events—the athletic competitions on the Olympic tracks, the exciting competitions from the swimming stadium, etc., in the television rooms with live transmissions" (Boese 1940: 16).

What had been anticipated very early on in England and the U.S.A. as being distinctive about the new technology and the new medium, namely the particular new reception situation of home viewing, was hardly recognized in Germany, or, for political reasons, was not promoted. Instead, forms of collective reception, which were supposed to take on a surrogate function for physical participation in mass assemblies, were obviously favored.

Only since the end of the 1950's has television—especially the transmission of sporting events (supported by more refined camera and directing techniques)—been intended to transmit to the viewers at home media viewing experiences that could be experienced (then, and increasingly so, up to today) as "privileged" seeing: even closer and more intense, "as if one were there in the stands oneself"; even in the 1950's, this was a spectacular promise of experience in television set advertisements. By contrast, even the spectator in the last row of the Berlin Olympic stadium in 1936 felt closer to the event than the television audience at that time, which watched the athletes on the (few) large image-projection screens or on the screens in the television rooms. In addition to the purely technologically oriented explanations of each of the different historical stages of development, symptoms of *other habits of seeing* should not be underestimated when reconstructing the less than spectacular early history of the medium (in terms of resistance at the level of the history of *mentality*): in the 1930's, seeing could only be experienced as physical participation, since the physical dimensions of experience were essential for the idea and experience of communication.

Technology Without Media Identity

Aside from the high points of earlier television history, such as the live transmission of the Olympic Games of 1936, the everyday transmission of the "first television program service" in the world was uninteresting, and attracted only a little public attention. In order to "summon a people to watch,"[12] television, which was placed *between* radio and film on the stage of Berlin media competition and took elements from each without being able to offer anything decidedly new, had to overcome the obstacle to making "visible" the attractiveness of its "home reception," as well as the distinction between its programs and those of other media. Since the new "medium between two stools" lived off elements that were already available, but was still far from organizing its "achievements of adaptation" of the heterogeneous elements of other media (within the bounds of its own reception situation) into a new form of appearance and effectiveness, its media identity remained in the background for a long time. Because of its hasty beginnings, television in Germany first had a merely *technically determined identity*, while in the U.S.A. (despite higher technical achievements), the developmental stage of television was until the late 1930's still seen by those responsible as having the status of "laboratory tests." When the new communication medium finally was presented to the American public, it was done so as a finished product, *ready for commercialization*, when all the perspectives of technical maturity, of commercialized usability, and of exact program ideas were already available.[13] In 1935, there simply could not have been talk about a clear idea of the medium and a communication situation embodied by "television." While in the U.S.A., television was, until its inauguration in 1941, conceived of as a private entertainment medium for the living room, a medium that was, through commercial licensing, to be expanded across the entire nation,[14] in Berlin during the 1930's, the media innovation was dramatized as a "technical innovation of German [!] spirit," but this without exercising any great power of fascination over the audience in the capital. Interest in forms of medium-specific program planning disappeared behind a vague vision of the future, which seemed, rather, to keep alive the possibility of "implanting the picture of the Führer deeply and inextinguishably in the hearts of all Germans."[15] Further, as long as programming remained a "minor matter" (planning regarding content, as well as the search for distinctive laws of programming, came off badly, even in the years after the beginning of transmission), public interest was characterized by a patient, albeit curious, skepticism.

In 1937, the program planners filled the main part of almost every evening with abridged versions of feature films, which the film industry, on the instruction of the Reich propaganda minister, had to put at the disposal of the "home-cinema," television. From the beginning, the proximity and the inevitably disadvantageous comparison of a "home cinema" with the popular film palaces of the 1930's not only created high expectations among viewers who were used to the picture quality (and visual intensity) of film, but also hindered the "medium identity" of television: "What is more obvious than to think in terms of film or, more exactly, of home cinema. Everything encourages the spectator to this: the darkened room [satisfactory picture quality could be reached only in a darkened room, the authors]; the light surface, on which the picture is formed; the newsreel, which rolls daily; the scenes, etc." (Wagenführ 1938). At the same time, any image of "home reception" also had to remain confusing and unattractive, in view of the program's lack of identity:

Their remarks were matter-of-fact and unkind; they complained about the smallness and the flickering of the picture, the dye (beige or blueish-white), the noticeable disturbances, the "primitive" program that was still too simple in content, variety, and length. Comparisons with film were drawn too hastily; the sense of participating in a "miracle" soon vanished; then the question arose: "And what is on the program tomorrow?" (Wagenführ 1983)

To the extent that the promotion of the "feasibility" of television as a "technical miracle" was less and less satisfying, and in order to raise the interest of the audience, more and more the "proof of the need for television" (Thun 1932: 135) had to be questioned against the background of an established media scene. But if a question about the services that television had to offer was asked, then it became clear that, at least potentially, it could do many things faster than radio and cinema but not, in fact, anything really new. Radio and cinema had already opened up the entire world as a potential horizon of experience. The newsreel, along with live radio reports, met the demand to be a "contemporary and important portrait of current events" (*Frankfurter Zeitung*, July 27, 1935, pp. 1–2). Thus, the only thing that remained for television was the further intensification of the spectator's participation through media. With television, a stage was reached where questions had to be asked about the cost-profit ratio of new communications media, and they could not catch on merely because of fascination with technology.

As can be seen against the background of resistance (at the level of the history of mentality) in Germany during the 1930's, the dilemma of television lay in the fact that the additional value of this new technical medium, and the demonstration of its purpose and its profile with regard to content, were only selectively or un-systematically thought of in terms of the context of its private-reception situation. According to Carl Haensel, television also remained "co-ordinated" in National Socialist Germany: "Importance was not attached to its intimacy, but rather to community reception. The television rooms were nothing more than electrically operated film theaters, basically unnecessary in this respect, and that's why they were closed at the beginning of the war" (Haensel 1952: 95). The new "broadcast-television" was apparently in the ambivalent situation where, on the one hand, its purpose for "home use" was already recognized (Thun 1932: 134), while on the other hand—or perhaps, because of that—the new medium couldn't find its place within the communication and media system of the 1930's. According to numerous contemporary reports, the reception situation of home viewing—"in the darkened room"—without the psychological conditions of community experience, communal laughter, or emotion, and in view of a smaller or even flickering picture surface, must have been hardly attractive. It is clear from a 1939 article (in which it is predicted that future program planning will be divided into winter and summer seasons), that in the 1930's, the idea of television as "domestic art" still must have offered rather greater disadvantages than advantages: "On a nice Sunday afternoon, one likes to listen to radio music on the balcony, but only reluctantly does one go from the warmth and the light into the room, in order to watch pictures in the oppressing mugginess of the closed room" (Wagenführ 1983: 23). Without the compensation of the particular visual and experiential intensity comparable to that of the cinema, the reception conditions for the body, which (without any contact with a larger audience) was taken out of the interaction in the darkness, could only be experienced as being unattractive; the television transmissions must have seemed mere "pictures" of a four-wall peepshow box without any *quality of experience*. The positive reception of mass experiences that is evident in numerous pictures of live mass-events during the 1930's verifies a fascination of the time, the wish to abandon oneself to the physical dynamics and the momentum of the crowd. This disposition to let oneself be carried along by "events" (which could be organized and intensified by the National Socialists) caught up sports as mass spectacle in its undertow. This implies a communicative disposition, "wanting to be near where the action is," wanting to "be there," which seems to have been characteristic of the 1930's.[16] The desire for *physical participation with spatial proximity*— even away from the action and without a good view—"brings the masses close to the events." An example of this fascination is the "Journey of Tens of Thousands to the [Max] Schmeling Fight" (headline in the *Frankfurter Zeitung* of March 10, 1935), which attracted to the "fight city" (Hamburg) even those who didn't have a ticket:

Overnight, the big city at the mouth of the Elbe became a gigantic magnet. It seemed that more people than could actually be held by the Hanseatenhalle came. Two young people, who collected the money for the train ticket at the last minute, sat in a special train from Berlin. They didn't have a penny more in their pockets, and they certainly didn't hope that the waves would wash two free tickets ashore to them as flotsam and jetsam on the Alster. The most important thing was that they wanted to have been in the fight city, which, in the course of a few days, had become a world center, as New York once was during such an event.

Against the background of this frame of mind, the presentation of a home medium, the mediated experience of physical presence, could not have exerted any real attraction. As long as the desire to be seen and to participate in the body of the crowd was of any significance, what could be transmitted "live" on television could only be experienced as a *surrogate for being present*. "Millions of people want to see, to see, to see: the pleasure of watching propels the masses in the vicinity of the events. One wants to be there. But everybody can't always be everywhere" (*Berliner Illustrirte Zeitung*, no. 1 [1937]: 26). In being a substitute, best done by visual means, for still-dominant physical participation, and in characterizing the experience of seeing in terms of a close connection between seeing and being there, television transmissions from the packed Berlin stadium of the Olympic Games of 1936 could help television to a breakthrough (of topical interest), after which it had to decline again. Furthermore, participation in sport spectacles as well as in theater, revue, and cinema presentations, which offered the social reception form of "being there," remained superior to the idea of home reception. Compared with the programs offered by the popular medium radio, given the popularity of the rising new medium sound film, and with the wealth of cultural and entertainment programs that were offered "live" every evening in Berlin, the "tube" could only disappoint the Berlin audience of the mid-1930's. Descriptions of the pleasure of going out and of physical presence at live performances of revue and cabaret, for instance, are still for us today precisely what constitutes the nostalgic quality of this epoch, which seems, for many habitual home viewers of the 1990's, to be lost forever. Indeed, private reception (analogous to radio reception with the *Volksempfänger*) was already *viewed*, toward the end of the 1930's, as the natural reception situation for the new medium, but was thought of as being feasible only in the remote future. The television people also foresaw a future for the new medium in home reception, but they were able to apply this only selectively as a trump or even a prospect for television compared with other media.

This is why, in Germany during the 1930's, a sufficient number of home receivers remained even harder to imagine than the installation of further public television rooms or other forms of public reception, such as, for instance, large-screen television in the cinemas. Although until 1939 the technicians regarded a living-room medium as too expensive, the Nazis had practically no idea, apart from their interest in making a mark for themselves as technically superior, of what to do with this medium: "In television broadcasting, if a picture is not the way one imagined it to be, one cannot cut out or copy in something later. After it has slipped into the iconoscope, it races as fast as a thought through the air and into the receiver's television picture; and then nobody can remove the less successful parts with scissors or retouching."[17] In the age of perfect staging of mass spectacles whose meaning as experience should correspond with the meaning intended by the rulers, such spontaneity was not wanted. In the media system of the Third Reich, television was not needed, either as a direct propaganda instrument like radio or as an offering of entertainment and escape like the UfA productions.

As long as the identity of the medium was not recognized in

terms of its private *reception situation* (which has been familiar to us since the 1950's), television had to legitimate itself all the more forcefully in terms of the specific quality of its *products*, which, as "works," had to stand out from other media products; it had to legitimate itself in a system of "art" classification. By 1935, the displacement of silent pictures through the technical realization of sound film and the devaluation of the quality of experience through media (for instance, the devaluation of "music as an event" to which one had to be devoted, in contrast to radio music, which was permanently available at home) had created a further obstacle. The "dangers of television," in a typically European, culturally pessimistic perspective, were seen as embedded in technical progress that automatically caused "a decline in artistic achievement" (Schücking 1935: 13). Therefore, from the beginning of its development in Germany, television had to reckon with a defensive attitude that tried "to protect and to preserve" existing "art forms" against the new technical development, against the flourishing form of radio-drama, or against, for instance, cinema and theater, which were not intended to be "always available for everybody at any time" (ibid.). Thus, in addition, television came under a specifically "artistic" pressure, which the programming people of German television could not relate to at all. In the developing national discourse about "artistic media identity," all hopes for product identity were placed on the "television play"; but, for a long time, that remained only an experiment. According to Kurt Wagenführ, the "first German television show was only a variety afternoon" (Wagenführ 1985: 297).

The first German television play, thought of as a floor show and earlier probably called "cabaret," provided singing and music, and whoever saw this promising venture for the first time probably no longer wanted to be astonished by the new miracle, which hardly surprises us anymore because we already know sound film and seldom consider the knowledge that was necessary in order to master this technical process and to lead to this result.   (Anonymous 1935: 298)

Kinds of Television Reception

As long as people still were not convinced of the special reception situation of the television transmitter and still had to wait for an "artistic" formulation of the program, the entire media identity of television had to rest on current events, direct live-transmission, and the so-called "direction of the moment," which, at best, dramatized a presentation of a *future quality of shared experience*. Before the institutionalization of the new medium in everyday life, an improvement was expected in the achievements of the technicians and program producers, rather than a change in the recipients' attitude toward the new medium, for which people were not yet ready because of their lack of the necessary experience. Therefore, reporting from the 1936 party convention in Nuremberg, which attracted a specially established flight service between Nuremberg and Berlin, was supposed, despite the time delay, to look more vividly "live." It was the pride of the television people at that time, "since the uniqueness, the fact that it couldn't be corrected, caused the 'excitement' and the enthusiasm" (Wagenführ 1983: 16). The excitement is evident in this advance description: "Radio, press, and film are eager to report on the great days in Nuremberg, in detail and as quickly as possible, to all those who can't be there. They are accompanied by television, the miracle of technology."[18] Regardless of the dominance of physical participation and collective reception that were characteristic of this epoch, there are also, at the same time, though typologically some twenty years ahead, other reception concepts, such as those that (in retrospect) would only become dominant in the 1950's, and would then contribute to the institutionalization of television. The following instance of reception of the transmission of the Nuremberg party rally in 1937 impressively demonstrates how the connection of "natural" and "technical" perception was already merging together into a new quality of media experience:

Isn't it a miracle! One sits in one of the television rooms in Berlin and stares in doubt and disbelief at the flashing picture screen of the receiver. . . . But then the eye becomes accustomed—exactly the way eye and ear have to become accustomed in the theater, in order to hear the voices and to see the actors—and one recognizes marching columns, faces appear, a flag is flapping, people are talking. One picture fades out, and a new one appears, and now the eye attaches itself firmly to the luminous figures. One forgets its corporeality; one detaches oneself from earth-boundedness, and one is there. . . . Much more than one would know, one thinks: now I am in Nuremberg. And only later, when two hours had passed without noticing, one rationally realizes that one had seen an event at a distance of over 400 kilometers. But it wasn't just seeing, it was intensive experience through distance. . . .

More than eye and ear, here all senses are involved, and one thinks one breathes the air in Nuremberg, thinks one recognizes the blue of the late summer sky, one feels among the lucky people, and is filled with their enthusiasm. And it happens that a suppressed triumphant cheer breaks in the tense silence, the cheer of a television viewer who got so carried away that he forgot the distance and felt only the vital closeness.[19]

Even though the attractiveness of television might have been increased through the live transmission of such events, we still cannot consider a *general* enthusiasm for a new experience of such media participation as "typical" or symptomatic, as it is described here by Ludwig Kapeller, the editor-in-chief of the program magazine *Hier Berlin!* But it is certain that the function and "nature of television" are increasingly conceived in terms of a live service and direct transmission from the location of the event. In 1939, Kurt Wagenführ reported on the topical program service of the Broadcasting Exhibition, through which, under the motto "Sports and Microphone," Harbig's world record was also transmitted from the Olympic stadium:

During the so-called eight days, it became obvious what television could someday mean. . . . Television is always most convincing when it marches in step with events. Whoever experienced those days, suddenly noticed that the word of the radio reporter lags behind the events, because it first has to interpret the event. No matter how small the tension—we suddenly became aware of it.   (Wagenführ 1983: 25)

Nevertheless, this temporal optimization of television remains only moderate compared with other reporting media, and the limited advantage of being slightly faster and therefore more current than film is rather farfetched,[20] and appears like an alternative argument for *product* identity, an argument that might help to sweep the issue of television's particular *reception* situation under the rug. Unfortunately, in order to secure the continued interest of a mass audience for television on the basis of this argument alone, television in the 1930's could offer only a few highlights, even in the case of current events with "relatively" small live delays.

In 1938, there was little evidence of a changing attitude toward "home viewing." Nevertheless, quotes like the following from a German television history can be seen in retrospect to have been symptomatic of a change in recipients' attitudes, which could only then constitute the specific identity of the new communication situation. Thus, for instance, Kurt Wagenführ, who, as an owner of a home set, was already sensitized to the new communication situation, verifies, in *his* observations of guests in front of the television receiver, "how fast the first audience tried to fit the television program into their life":

Television's breakthrough into domesticity is powerful and sometimes almost stunning. It is immediate, it starts when the receiver is put into operation; natural defense-mechanisms against it seem to become noticeable; these aren't due to a rejection, but to a shock that has to subside. Nobody likes to lose one's balance. But, most of the time, this feeling passes very quickly, indeed, in many cases that I was able to observe, too quickly. Not to the detriment of the program people, but to the detriment of the viewer.   (Wagenführ 1938)

Despite the dominance of a public sphere that hindered the establishment of private forms of communication and reception, one could recognize very early the involvement of those viewers who already had the opportunity of regular private television viewing in new kinds of reception—after the threshold "breakthrough to domesticity" was passed. The media identity of television, which has led since the 1950's to a new mediated experience through the *coupling* of current events, the private reception situation, and a new quality of picture resolution, could not, in terms of the interaction of those individual elements, have been experienced during the 1930's. Notwithstanding constant complaints about the poor picture quality of the medium, the observation was made as early as the 1930's that the television eye was "more potent than the human eye" (the comparison of the television camera with the human eye refers to the experience of both the extension of and the still-felt proximity to natural sight). But in the early phase of television, one was confronted only "unintentionally" and without any lasting effect with a *different quality of seeing* as compared to film. For instance, at the end of the "nonpublic propaganda transmission" of April 30, 1935, which was planned "for the first television transmission vehicle on earth" to be a dress rehearsal for the celebration of May 1 (Labor Day): "I believe that the nicest thing was the nonformality here at the end, especially when several gentlemen suddenly behaved in a quite relaxed way, so that, actually, we didn't have the impression that a film was being shown to us, but rather, that we were seeing at a distance, and watching them, without their having the slightest ideas of this" (cited in *Fernseh-Informationen*, no. 7 [1985]: 208). This kind of observation became an obsession for a broader audience only in the 1950's. Only then could the television viewer's new privileged quality of seeing establish itself on a broader basis, in connection with a private reception situation that was "freed" from the risks of human interaction and participation; as, for instance, at the first great postwar television event, the transmission of the coronation celebrations of Elizabeth II, in 1953:

One example of the extent of observation of moments previously inaccessible to the eye shall be mentioned here, because it demonstrates so convincingly what television is. Millions of people watched as, at the homage of her husband, tears filled the eyes of the English queen during the course of the coronation. These were true tears, in comparison with the ones of glycerine mentioned above. But the same millions would also have been witnesses to any sudden feeling of faintness that might have overtaken the queen. Despite the inevitable technical difficulties, everyone who followed the course of the English coronation had the strange feeling of knowing personally the person who now personifies the queen. In any case, this extreme example demonstrates how the television camera breaks through any formality, any official ceremony, and picks out the person under the mask or the costume.   (Eckert 1953: 70)

Therefore, television in 1953 meant not only a "surrogate for being there" in a "dark, small room," one even began to experience it as a *new, privileged* way of seeing, since it moved the viewers into an "otherwise probably inaccessible area of life" (Eckert 1953: 39) and provided them with views that weren't possible even for those who were present at the coronation celebrations. With the beginning of a new period of "the staged illusion of immediacy"[21] in the history of television, one could even experience a "form of immediacy" at such a ritualized process as the British coronation ceremony, an immediacy that was experienced all the more intensely when the prominent figures and the people acting in public weren't as conscious as today of the fact that the television camera was observing them up close, and was always present. In the same way, not only have television viewers become, since the 1950's, "through many programs, used to the fact that television allows them 'to be present'" (Eckert 1953: 8), but also, despite all the loss of corporeality and human interaction, the television set has since become an even "better way of being present in the world."

(Translated by Gertrud Rath-Montgomery)

SOUNDS, COLORS, AND THEIR NONSEMANTIC FUNCTIONS

ALBRECHT RIETHMÜLLER

"The Matter of Music Is Sound and Body-Motion"

The statement that sound and body-motion form the matter of music does not come from a musicologist or music theoretician who, in preparation for a seminar entitled "Materialities of Communication," desperately attempts to link an aspect of music to the subject of the seminar. The statement comes from Aristides Quintilianus, author of the Greek *De musica*, three books written between the first and fourth centuries A. D.[*] The statement may seem surprising insofar as we have become accustomed to view music as the most nonphysical, nonmaterialistic of the arts. Even its material (that is, its elements: tone and sound) seems to be nonmaterialistic.

I

We will acquaint ourselves methodologically with the virtues or vices of a commentator of antiquity and look at the elements of Aristides Quintilianus's statement one at a time. Each of its four, or more precisely five, main words provides matter for practically endless discussions, insofar as these concern basic concepts in the areas of music and beyond. In speaking of the matter (Grk. *hylē*, Lat. *materia*) of music, one is forced in translation to choose between two divergent aspects of "materiality" in music: its matter

---

[*]Aristides Quintilianus 1963: 5 (*De musica* I.4): "hylē mousikēs phōnē kai kinēsis sōmatos"; translation by Meibom 1652: "Materia Musices vox est, & motus corporis."

and its material. The way in which Aristides handles and determines the matter of music brings to mind the Aristotelian distinction of matter and form, with which all that is constructed, including music, can be investigated. The first conclusion would then be negative: sound and body-motion do not belong to the formal aspect of music. The next question is whether music or its elements, tone and sound, possess a material foundation. Here in the course of history, above all in artistic and aesthetic areas, things become rather confused. The opposition of matter and form refers in dramas or novels, without ever really denying its Aristotelian origin, more to the modern opposition of content and form. (This often includes a redefinition of the matter that is subordinate to form as the form that is subordinate to content.) The matter of a drama or a story—the *sujet*, or, in Aristotelian language, the story (Grk. *mythos*)—is for Hegel the lowest component of what he calls content. It is difficult to say whether this use of the term "matter," common in aesthetic literature to the middle of the nineteenth century, is based on a metaphorical sense. The real difficulty lies in the fact that there is rarely any clear distinction in the use of the terms "matter" and "material" in any aesthetic discussions, especially in relationship to music. The emphasis that so-called musical material has received in the past few decades has led to a rather imprecise usage that no longer requires a distinction between the two terms. T. W. Adorno is at least partially to blame for the almost fetishistic discussions about the (historical) "condition of musical material." Both tones (that is the material of music) and any kind of (mostly historically stratified) materials of which a composer might make use (mostly forms, or components of forms, of music) are counted as musical material.

Although philosophical commentaries about material have been numerous and continuous, it is not surprising that there is little mention of material (either the noun *hylē* or the corresponding adjective *hylikon*) in ancient Greek musical treatises. Aristoxenus, a pupil of Aristotle's and in a certain sense the forefather of musicology, never uses these words. If he, the music expert so well versed in the terminology of the peripatetic father of terminology, proceeds in this manner, then this fact alone gives cause for thought. In his considerations of what is high and what low, Aristotle states that mankind is the best example of the fact that the high corresponds to the feminine and the low to the masculine. He further notes that humans alone are capable of using *logos* (reason, language, etc.) and that voice or sound (Grk. *phōnē*, Lat. *vox*)— according to Aristotle the voice or the sound of something alive— is the matter of *logos*.* There can be no doubt that this voice/sound defines that part of sound production that remains removed from mental control. It describes that sound or tone field that must do without more precise semantic-logical (linguistically logical) possibilities. This is remotely reminiscent of the semiotic difference between phonetics and semantics as well as the phonetic differentiation between phoneme and morpheme. *Phōnē* (voice or sound) and *logos* seem to be related as are material and form, body and mind.

The mathematician and astronomer Claudius Ptolemy, who wrote the most complete and perhaps most impressive work on music theory that is extant from antiquity, talks about *hylē* at the beginning of his *Harmonika*. Familiar with both Aristotelian and Stoic philosophy, he begins by differentiating two categories of harmony: namely, hearing (*akoē*) and reason (*logos*). The category of hearing includes matter (*hylē*) and condition (*pathos*). The category of reason includes form (*eidos*) and cause (*aītion*) (Ptolemy 1930: 3 [*Harmonika* I.1]). Unlike sensual perception (*aisthēsis*), *logos* is simple and homogenous. Sensual perception always proceeds with a richly heterogenous and flowing matter (Ptolemy 1930: 3 [*Harmonika* I.1]: "tēn d' aisthēsin meth' hylēs pantote polymigoos te kai rheustēs"). According to Ingemar Düring, Ptolemy significantly relates the Aristotelian opposition of material and form to the Pythagorean opposition of perception and reason.† Of course, Ptolemy does not elaborate on what the matter of music consists in or of what matter in music and harmony is made.‡ Only briefly and

---

*Jan 1895: 7 (*De generatione animalium* V.7): "tou de logou hylen einai ten phonēn." Cf. Aristotle 1956: 47 (*De anima* II.8.420b, 5).

†Düring 1934: 142. He also refers to the Stoic opposition of condition and cause (*pathos* and *aition*) as well as the Platonic opposition of the intelligible and sensible (*noēton* and *aisthēton*).

‡Except Ptolemy 1930: 17 (*Harmonika* I.8), where he questions the permanence of matter and forms ("en tais hylais kai tois schēmasi aparallaxian"). This question is raised in sound experiments in which no reliable measurement can be made, at least not of the reliability that he believes is achievable with his string "canon."

in an Aristotelian manner does he take up the question of matter, when he mentions the teaching of principals (*archai*).* Porphyry, in his commentary on Ptolemy's *Harmonika*, broadly defines the two categories of harmony, but he goes no further in the general aspects of the material-form problem, not allowing any glimpse of specific musical perspective (Porphyry 1932: 11 [*Comm. in Ptol. Harm.* I.1]).

All this points to the fact that Aristides tries to formulate a theoretical principle of music with the term "matter of music" rather than an aesthetic conviction. He does not inquire, as we might today, into a musical materiality or musical materialities in the context of the content and meaning of music. This has to do with the old concept of music as a sphere of knowledge and application. If music is defined as both a science (Grk. *epistēmē*, Lat. *scientia*) and an art (Grk. *technē*, Lat. *ars*), then the term "music" (*mousikē*) is defined first as the theory of music and only secondarily as the resulting sound of music that we identify with the term music today. Without being able to go into the specifics of the Greek term *mousikē*, I will still assert that this is an important fact. It implies a shifted perspective in light of what must be seen as the object or the reality of "music" and therefore also as its materiality.

II

The matter of music is sound, Aristides tells us. "Tone" can also be used as a word for sound, but is this usage really as appropriate as everyday life would seem to imply? "Tone" (referring to a particular music as well as to music in general) had and still has an entire range of nuances of meaning. The term "sound" has found its way into slogans of pop culture as well as into certain circles of experts: music should have a "powerful sound." The vagueness of what is meant by this serves the purposes of propaganda or advertisement, the newest kid on the block reared by two prolific parents: psychology and rhetoric. It is questionable, of course, whether such phrases are only products of contemporary times and their criticality. The phrase "good breeding," which was fashionable for a time, was probably likewise tainted. [Translator's note: the original German plays on the word *Ton* in the phrases *der* "*gute Ton*," *den Ton angeben*, and *getönt*.]

*Ptolemy 1930: 92 (*Harmonika* III.3) refers to matter, motion, and form (*hylē*, *kinēsis*, and *eidos*). Cf. Ptolemy 1930: 95 (*Harmonika* III.4).

Aristides uses the word *phōnē*, the root for composites and neologisms such as "phone," "phonetic," "phonology," and so on. The main definitions are voice and sound (Lat. *vox* and *sonus*), secondarily tone, vowel, any articulated noise, the ability to speak, discourse, and language in general. In most cases *phōnē* or *vox* is translated into modern languages as "voice" (Fr. *voix*, It. *voce*) although it would often be better to use the word "sound." The situation is complicated because neither in music nor in other disciplines such as linguistics, physiology, physics, or other fields relating to the audible has a precise distinction between sound and tone been established. This problem attends the French *son* and *ton* and the Italian *suono* and *tuono*, even though the terms are shaded slightly differently. It can even happen that these words are defined differently in different fields, for example, music theory and physics. In physics, the German *Ton* can mean a sine tone, and *Klang* can mean a single tone with its harmonic overtones. In music, *Ton* can mean a single tone,* and *Klang* can mean the consonance of more than one tone or (written) "voice." It seems to have been the same in Greek and Latin, despite the differences of the factual evidence. The musical, and more generally the acoustic, elements seem to be so elementary that a general concurrence never arose, irrespective of the never-ending changes of meaning the words have undergone in the past 2,500 years.

If one wants to understand why Aristides used the term *phōnē*, then it might be advantageous to take a look at related and competing Greek terms. This examination aims a spotlight not only at musical elements but also at linguistic or phonetic elements, insofar as both fields are still one and the same, that is, before they become specific as to tone (sound) and word, song (melody) and language. For about a thousand years, three terms remained primary in Greek writings on music, grammar, and natural philosophy to describe acoustic elements without any noticeable change in their interrelationship. These are *psophos* (Lat. *sonus*), the most general acoustic category in the sense of sound, noise, and tone; *phōnē* (Lat. *vox*, *sonus*), a special category of music and language in the meanings of

---

*Greek *tonos* and Latin *tonus* are not equivalent to *Ton* (as a single tone), but have two limited basic meanings: whole tone (a ratio of 9:8, an interval) and key. Only later, maybe by way of the characteristic of a certain tone as a key, could one have spoken of tone as a realized sound or an aesthetic experience, as in the tone of a song or poem.

voice, sound, and so forth; and *phthongos* (Lat. *sonus musicus*), along with its grammatical meaning (in phonology), the individual musical tone or note. Since any further terminological investigation would lead to a jumble of words, it may be most prudent to assume that Aristides saw the matter of music in this *phōnē*. In doing so, it must be remembered that the main difference between *phōnē* and the musical tone is that the first assumes continuity whereas the latter, as a tone point, is conceived as discrete. Aristoxenus (1955: 15) speaks of two kinds of movement of the *phōnē*: one that is continuous, on which (normal) speaking is based and where the tone levels constantly change, and one that is discrete or intervallic (diastematic), on which singing is based, where distinct tone levels follow one another seamlessly. It is this discontinuity of the progression of tone levels that makes the category of the musical tone (*phthongos*) possible.*

The question of whether sound or the *phōnē* is material or immaterial has been answered differently by competing schools of philosophy. It is not surprising that the Stoics, who wanted to prove the corporeality of so many things, supported the materiality of sound. According to the material conception of *pneuma* (Lat. *spiritus*), they assumed that sound has breadth and is not a tone point analogous to a dimensionless geometric point, as many had thought and as we today are inclined to think. (This is evident in the term *punctus contra punctum*). The Stoics, not satisfied with the one-dimensionality in time of the tone (sound), which Hegel later constructed in his aesthetics, insisted on two-dimensionality in terms of breadth. They even imagined a third dimension insofar as the tone can be understood as a body (Grk. *sōma*). They would have the fewest problems in taking part in a discussion on the "materialities of communication," especially in regards to music. It would even seem that this topic has a Stoic background.

III

The matter of music, as Aristides states, is not only *phōnē* but also body-motion. No one since music has been a topic for thought would have disputed that music is concerned with motion. Noth-

---

*The critique that a glissando falls out of music or singing would be splitting hairs.

ing can be made to produce sound without some preceding motion. It is worthwhile, of course, to distinguish between types of motion, as was done in antiquity, mainly by Aristotle. One must distinguish between the general terms for motion (*kinēsis*, Lat. *motio*), transfer (*metabolē*, Lat. *transpositio*), change (*alloiōsis*, Lat. *alteratio*), and locomotion (*phorā*, Lat. *locomotio*), that motion that a body executes. It is worth noting that some of these terms describing motion have become musical terms, such as "transposition" and "alteration," not to mention "modulation," also a relevant term. Augustine says that *modulatio* is nothing more than motion (Augustine 1947: 30 [*De musica* I.3]: "Ergo scientiam modulandi jam probabile est esse scientiam bene movendi"). In another passage, deservedly a *locus classicus*, Aristotle insists that locomotion is necessary to produce any sound at all (Aristotle 1956: 44 [*De anima* II.8.419b, 13]: "plēgē d' ou ginetai aneu phorās"). Since then the emphasis on locomotion has often been downplayed; that is, *locomotio* has been changed back to the simple *motio*.

The relationship of music and motion is certainly an almost endless topic. The important point in Aristides is that he is not satisfied with stating that motion is the matter of music but adds that this is body-motion. "Body" can refer to at least three things: first, to every real (that is, without transferred meaning) body that participates in making sound; second, to the planets or stars, insofar as they not only are a paradigm for the motion of all bodies but also embody the harmony of the spheres; and third, to the human body, insofar as it participates in musical processes or the production of sonic phenomena. These views can be summarized as follows:

1. If one wants to produce a sound, one needs various things, that is, various bodies. Aristotle synthesizes an old (Pythagorean) notion when he states that a stroke of one thing against another is necessary to produce sound (Aristotle 1956: 44 [*De anima* II.8.419b, 9]: "ginetai d' ho kat' energeian psophos aei tinos pros ti kai en tini"). There can be no doubt that what is doing the striking, for example, the plectrum with which a stringed instrument is struck, and what is struck, for example, the stringed instrument itself, are both solid bodies. (Of course, the point is less unequivocal since the string vibrates and the body of the instrument resonates). A third body that is not solid is posited as the medium through which the

striking takes place. This is normally air, but water would also be a possibility, and difficulties are only encountered in a vacuum. Since the whole process can be looked at another way—namely, one can say that the sound must be transferred so as to strike a receiver, usually an ear—another body dimension is uncovered. The scheme of bodily generation of sound can also be applied to sound production by certain animals and to the instrument of the human voice; in these contexts it must be established that the sound source is physical and the receiver (the ear) physiological.

2. This same scheme was also used for certain bodies in motion, namely the planets. The goal of Aristides's music theory, the harmony of the world, is found in his third book, and his notion of body-motion in the matter of music would be misunderstood if one did not include it in this higher level. Even Aristotle, who radically criticized the old Pythagorean assumption of a sonorous universe, rejected its existence with arguments that used the scheme of bodies, (loco)motion, and striking (Aristotle 1956: n.p. [*De caelo* II.9.290b, 11ff).

3. If more than one solid-bodied instrument plays a role in producing sound, whether these are lifeless bodies or instead parts, appendages, and "organs" of a living human body, including the organs of the voice, then the human body plays a particular role in music and its material foundation. Here sound production is explained in physical-physiological terms in that a natural voice body replaces an artificial sound body. The human voice has to share its claim to naturalness of sound production with such things as thunder, the harmony of the spheres, and certain animal voices. It is reserved for mankind, however, to give form to the matter of sound, to make it a carrier for *logos*, whereby this form can appear as either language or as music. (Hearing, as mentioned, also plays a role.) Rhythm or what is rhythmic, in all its anthropological limitations and musical representations, proves itself to be an important link between body (as matter) and music. Aristides sees rhythm as determined in three ways (Aristides Quintilianus 1963: 31 [*De musica* I.13]). One can first speak about rhythm in terms of immovable bodies; for example, a statue can be eurhythmic (well-proportioned). Second, one can speak about rhythm in terms of all that moves by saying that someone moves eurhythmically (well composedly). Third, in its essential meaning, one speaks of rhythm

in the *phōnē*. Aristides links his general definition to this essential usage of the word. Rhythm is a system of *chronoi* (time elements or "times") that are arranged in some order.

This concept of rhythm as it relates to *phōnē* is valid for music as well as for poetry, insofar as one remembers that antiquity did not yet have a special system of purely musical rhythms. This only came into being in the later Middle Ages in a successive detachment from verse metrics. Music always had its own essential system in the pitch level, something that it could claim for its own; not in rhythmic arrangement, something that it shares with language. Given the elementary importance and meaning of rhythm, the core of Greek music or music theory seems to have been a harmony based on relationships (*logoi*). This is true not only because the so-called rules of harmony could be applied to virtually all things, but also, indeed primarily, because the Greek tonal system was based on distinct pitches and the cosmos of consonances. This harmony is first realized in music through *melos*. In certain respects, *melos* and "music" can be seen as synonymous. The basis of the tonal system cannot be overlooked when the components of a complete or whole *melos* are pointed out by Aristides:

In order to produce something that is complete in singing [*ōdē*], one must consider melody [*melōdia*], rhythm, and linguistic expression [*lexis*]. This means the sound [*phōnē*] according to its quality in regards to melody, the movement of the sound in regards to rhythm, and how it is arranged in regards to the linguistic expression of the meter. What happens when the whole *melos* is brought together is the motion of sound and body, including times [*chronoi*], and the rhythms created from them. (Aristides Quintilianus 1963: 5 [*De musica* I.4])

It seems clear that Aristides is assuming at least two kinds of motion. Even in his own, ethically motivated definition of *mousikē*, he insists on the motion of sound on the one hand and motion of the body on the other: "Music is the understanding [*gnōsis*] of what is fitting in bodies and motions" (Aristides Quintilianus 1963: 4 [*De musica* I.4]: "gnōsis tou prepontos en sōmasi kai kinēsesin"; *or*: "gnōsis tou prepontos en phōnais te kai sōmatikais kinēsesin"). Since the text in this passage is somewhat corrupt, it could also read: "Music is the understanding of what is fitting in sounds [*phōnai*] and body-motions." Even though the ethical perspective may suggest it, one is not forced to bring the oft-cited breadth of this definition into accord with the Greek concept of music that includes music and dance, and even gymnastics and sports. Even if one stays with the "purely musical," the attempt to include the material or matter-body aspect of the acoustical medium that is music presents itself immediately. An important dimension of the materiality of music, even for antiquity, remains excluded, namely the recording of sound in musical notation. This aspect must be dealt with separately.

ANDREAS BALLSTAEDT

"Dissonance" in Music

❖

Dissonantia (Lat.): a bad tone, a mistone.
— J. G. Walther (1732)

Since consonation is nothing absolute,
. . . it cannot be said with certainty where
the consonation of two tones ends and
the dissonation of two tones begins.
— J. G. Sulzer (1792)

Dissonance is the same as expression.
— T. W. Adorno (1970)

"Dissonance" is a central term in music. This seems natural when one considers the etymology of the word: Latin *dissonare* means, quite literally, nothing more than "sounding apart." The strong connection between the term and music and the linkage to its alter ego, consonance, can easily lead to the opinion that the concept, clearly defined by this dichotomy, is unproblematic. The concept can be easily explained, even if not in and of itself. The participants in the 1989 meeting in Dubrovnik had the hope or at least the suspicion that all dissonances, paradoxes, and breakdowns were more comprehensible and clear in music than in other fields since the category "dissonance" had in music its rightful place and genuine application. This hope is deceptive, however, as is shown by the three quotes that introduce this paper. What sounds apart in music and why it is perceived or described as such, how it is established, evaluated, and interpreted, was based in Western culture (the following must limit itself to this area) on historical change. This historical change makes it difficult if not impossible to clearly define the category of musical dissonance. Even the suspicion that "dissonance" has a genuine musical foundation is deceptive since the ancient Greek word *diaphonīa* could describe a conflict of opinions and positions as well as denote a musical situation. This secondary, nonmusical level of meaning is still retained in modern English, whereas in German the musical application is predominant.

In a kind of steeplechase through musical history, theory, and terminology, I will attempt to come to grips with a basic musical framework of "dissonance." This is undertaken without claim to completeness, of course, but in the hope of illuminating divergent ideas, concepts, and interpretations formed over the course of hundreds of years.

I

"Dissonance" has two meanings. The first is a musical definition; the second is a musical fact. We are faced with two perspectives, one concerned primarily with music theory and the other, which is more practical, concerned primarily with composition. We are confronted not only with decisive historical changes but also with the problem that the relationship between the two meanings is full of tension. Not everything that has been defined as dissonance in music theory has been treated as such in the practice of composition (see Dahlhaus 1962). Both aspects will be discussed very briefly and certainly in a very simplified manner in an attempt to find the lowest common denominator of historical thought on dissonance.*

"Dissonance" describes a group of intervals, either as harmonies or progressions, that stands in contrast to a group of consonances; the latter are seen as musically constitutive, whereas dissonances are seen as derived. It is inconsequential here whether the differences between the two groups are mathematical, psychological, or physiological-physical. Having its origin in ancient music theory, mathematics dominated the discussion of consonance and dissonance well into the eighteenth century, as can be seen in the physicalistic proofs of harmonic series as its transformation. From this mathematical perspective, the intervals regarded as consonant were also the most simple and basic numeric ratios. This idea is still an undercurrent in the critique of the so-called unnaturalness of New Music since the Viennese School. Even the psychological and

---

*For the following, see Cohen 1971; Dahlhaus 1962, 1967; Riemann 1901; Voigt 1985; and Winckel, Wellek, Dahlhaus 1958 and the references listed there.

physiological-physical arguments of the nineteenth and twentieth centuries remained indebted at least in their terminology to this traditional conceptual dichotomy. This is so in spite of the fact that these arguments relativized the strict and exclusive division into two interval groups with the help of fusion degree (Carl Stumpf), beat phenomenon (Hermann von Helmholtz), and difference tone theory (Felix Krueger) by describing the differences between consonance and dissonance as gradual rather than qualitative.

The assessment of individual intervals and their membership in one of the two groups has undergone considerable historical change, as the following examples show. Pythagoras only considered the octave (1:2), the twelfth (1:3), the double octave (1:4), the fifth (2:3), and the fourth (3:4) as consonances since these intervals are based on the proportions of the whole numbers from one to four (tetractys). On the other hand, Gioseffo Zarlino, proponent of mean-tone temperament, where the major thirds were intoned as pure (4:5), based his determination of consonance in his *Istitutioni harmoniche* (1558) on the numbers one to six (senario). He "naturally" arrived at a considerably greater number of consonances, but he could not legitimize the minor sixth (5:8), which he wanted to see treated as a consonance in contrapunctual composition, except as a compounded and therefore derived interval (a fourth plus a minor third). Another example of the change in categorization is the "history" of the third (and similarly the sixth), which could be described as the history of its emancipation as consonance. In the Middle Ages, only the octaves, fourths, and fifths counted as consonances. In the thirteenth century, however, the third was first described, depending on the author, as an imperfect consonance (*consonantia imperfecta*) or as an imperfect dissonance (*dissonantia imperfecta*). Along with the sixth, it then achieved some sort of middle position between the *consonatiae perfectae* (octaves, fourths, fifths) and the *dissonantiae* (seconds, tritones, and sevenths). In the last third of the fifteenth century, the third lost its imperfection, which had previously forced it to be resolved into a perfect harmony insofar as it was accepted as capable of finality and was therefore an independent sonority. Since the development of major-minor tonal thought, that is, at least since the seventeenth century, both thirds and sixths have been recognized as consonances. The third even became the main interval, which determines the mode.

Dissonance played a role not only as a category in concepts of music theory but also as a compositional phenomenon in musical works themselves. Two examples will show that music theory and the practice of composition do not always have to coincide. Johannes Tinctoris, in his *Liber de arte contrapuncti* (1477), counted the fourth as a perfect consonance on the basis of mathematics. It was categorized, however, as dissonant in contrapuntal structure when it lay directly above the bottom part. If the same interval resulted between two upper parts and a grounding fifth, however, it was considered consonant. The term "consonantia imperfecta" exemplifies the dichotomy between the theory of music and the actual practice of composition. The stylistic function of the interval is addressed with "consonantia." Thirds and sixths could be placed in a series in the middle of a musical line just like "real" consonances and were only required to be resolved in a perfect consonance at the end of a line. The deficient musical disposition, theoretically and mathematically based, is addressed with "imperfecta." In the practice of composition, however, the history of dissonance until the advent of our own century has been the history of its permanent legitimacy as exception or deviation, according to the background of the compositorial norms of the times. This history begins with Franco von Köln's treatise *Ars cantus mensurabilis* (ca. 1280). Here he establishes the rule that consonances in a polyphonic texture should only be placed on strong beats and dissonances only on weak beats. This rule allowed sounds not only to be placed next to each other but also to be bound to each other. The further development of composition until the so-called classical vocal polyphony of the sixteenth century shows that the handling of dissonances was subject to increasingly strict rules (preparation and resolution, etc.). In the age of harmonic thought, dissonance was either understood as characteristic (e.g., the seventh in the dominant seventh chord or the sixth in the subdominant six-five chord) in that it encouraged harmonic continuation, or as a melodic accentuation (suspension, auxiliary note, passing note). This changed nothing regarding the principal need for resolution that viewed dissonance as the exception to the rule. Even the apparent exceptions are related to the appropriate system of compositorial norms and thereby receive their individuality. Thus Ludwig van Beethoven begins his *First Symphony* (1799/1800) not with the tonic, as everyone would have expected, but with a dominant seventh chord, regarded at that

time as dissonant. Richard Wagner veils the actual key in his over-
ture to *Tristan and Isolde* (1857–59) for a long time by a clever
harmonic game of hide-and-seek with suspended and transitional
dissonances.

"Emancipation of the dissonance" (Schoenberg 1975: 216) and
equality in the cosmos of musical harmony began with Arnold
Schoenberg's abandonment of harmonic tonality in the last movement of his *Second String Quartet* (1907–8) and in certain songs from
his cycle *Fifteen Songs of the Hanging Gardens* (1908–9). These are
regarded as the first compositions without a tonal center. The
"Method of Composing with Twelve Tones Which Are Related
Only with One Another" (Schoenberg 1975: 218), put in place after
a phase of free, atonal composition, was simply a new order that
fixed the compositional use of dissonance. Dissonance was up until
this point only regarded as the exception to the rule. Now it was
accepted as equal in the system of rules:

Dissonances are not used here as in many other contemporary compositions as an addition to make consonances "more spicy." For the appearance of such dissonant tones there is no conceivable rule, no logic, and
no other justification than the dictatorship of taste. If dissonances other
than the catalogued ones are admitted at all in music, it seems that the way
of referring them all to the order of the basic set is the most logical and
controllable procedure toward this end.   (Schoenberg 1975: 247)

There was a turnaround of previous circumstances, an implicit
prohibition on consonance, if a composition was to avoid everything that could even appear to evoke tonal centralization (e.g.,
tone repetitions, doubling an octave, etc.). "It seemed in the first
stages immensely important to avoid a similarity with tonality.
The feeling was correct that these free combinations of simultaneously sounding tones—those 'chords'—would fit into a tonality" (ibid., 246). (As an aside, it would be worth considering
whether the term "dissonance," on the basis of its value, is at all
proper given the intended equality of all twelve tones.)

The decisive commonality of the two perspectives of dissonance in the West is that both concern a completely intra-musical
category. Dissonances are always defined within an established
system of compositional or music theoretical norms and are always
an intra-musical conflict. Changes, and there have been many, are

ultimately only modifications within the system and tradition. Even Schoenberg's break with tradition is only illusory, since the Viennese School saw in free atonality and the twelve-tone technique nothing more than a necessary continuation of musical-compositional developments of the nineteenth century.

II

Detailed examination and additional examples would now both support and complicate the previous discussion. There would be no change in the assessment that the category of musical dissonance in the West is an intra-musical phenomenon and problem. Considerable problems arise with this apparent and initially banal insight when one confronts several works of a composer who, despite the unreliability and imprecision of labels, can be counted along with Schoenberg as one of the founders of New Music: Charles E. Ives.* His attitude toward composition was indebted in many ways to the European tradition, particularly his emphatic concept of music and his pathos of progress, which are displayed, for example, when he writes in his *Memos*:

I am fully convinced (that), if music be not allowed to grow, if it's denied the privilege of evolution that all other arts and life have, if (in the) natural processes of ear and mind it is not allowed (to) grow bigger by finding possibilities that nature has for music, more and wider scales, new combinations of tone, new keys and more keys and beats, and phrases together—if it just sticks (as it does today) to one key, one single and easy rhythm, and the rules made to boss them—then music, before many years, cannot be composed—everything will be used up—endless repetitions of static melodies, harmonies, resolutions, and metres—and music as a creative art will die—for to compose will be but to manufacture conventionalized MUSH—and that's about what student composers are being taught to do.   (Ives 1972: 48)

On the other hand, Ives broke with the European tradition, as is already apparent in the preceding passage, when he approached composition with his passion for experimentation, unabashedness,

---

*The following exegesis is not of Ives's work as a whole but only of one aspect of it that can act as a contrastive position in the accompanying context. For an introduction to Ives's aesthetic views and his music, see Burkholder 1985 and Rathert 1989, which also contains the most important references.

and openness that simply nullified many traditional European conventions, norms, and predilections. It is therefore not surprising that after World War II his works were above all received in their assumed role as emissaries of New Music: polytonality, atonality, polyrhythms, quarter-tone composition, space composition, open forms, and so on. He made all this musically productive in his compositions without succumbing to the tendency toward the systematization and consistent application of his European colleagues. He actually had no knowledge of the developments in Europe. Thus Ives was not subjected to legitimacy problems of musical history, and in his work the most advanced and the most traditional compositions stand side by side. European composers, on the other hand, once they attained to the contemporary level of composition, could only fall behind at the cost of their artistic integrity.

Like the music of the Viennese School, some of Ives's works traverse the listening habits developed from nineteenth-century European music in a radical way, for example, the second movement of his *Fourth Symphony* (1910–16) or his orchestral piece *Fourth of July* (1911–13). The most characteristic part of his music comes from one of his most significant compositional principles: quoting* pre-existing musical materials that originate from very different uses. These include music from street festivals and rural dances, patriotic songs and martial music, religious music (hymns), and European art music. This musical material is reworked and rearranged, stratified, contrasted, and mixed. The resultant aural sensation is ambivalent. On the one hand, several independent layers are heard at the same time, even if the quotation is unrecognizable. On the other hand, a more or less dissonant, complex, but still homogenous musical structure results through this simultaneity of events.

It is precisely this kind of quotation and contrasting that reveals a concept of dissonance completely different from that found in "European" music. Dissonances for Ives are not primarily intra-musically grounded. There is no system of compositional norms that allows them or discards them. They are rather the result of subjective postulations that are extra-musically motivated in two ways. In quoting traditional melodies, Ives was concerned more

*The word "quoting" is controversial in Ives literature (see Rathert 1989: 95–110), but is used here for lack of a better term.

with using the melodies as they were actually sung than with the note-for-note transcription found in a song book. These melodies should be inexact, with deviations and variations in intonation, "skewed," and relatively free in the actual performance of individual musical parameters. Here musical dissonances are the result of the representation of reality, with the only difference being that Ives did not use a tape recorder, but instead used traditional instruments and notation as recording devices. He proceeded in a similar fashion in his onomatopoeic works, in which he practiced the imitation of nature, including noises, not shying away from the most realistic representation possible. It was irrelevant to him whether this was a morning riverscape (*The Housatonic at Stockbridge*) or a sports event (*A Yale-Princeton Football Game*). On the other hand, Ives wanted to make programmatic statements with his music using preexistent material that, of course, only seldom fit together and was consonant. "Dissonance" for Ives refers not only and not primarily to the intra-musical conflict between certain tones or sounds, even when music is at times dissonant in the Western sense, but to a dissonance of cognitions that are bound to the quotations, that is to say, the appropriate contents and concepts. One could perhaps speak of a kind of cognitive dissonance (see Festinger 1978) in music. On the one side, a cognitive dissonance automatically results from musical dissonance because musical dissonances are confronted with each other not as aesthetic-sensual charms but rather as different cognitions that stick to the musical quotations or are recalled as associations. On the other side, musical dissonances are more secondary because they are the unavoidable results of the quotation. They are dispensable, as Ives demonstrated in other works (for example, in the seemingly innocent third movement of his *Fourth Symphony*).

III

The objection could be raised at this point that this principle of cognitive dissonance is only pertinent when the listener knows what Ives is quoting. If Ives's music is compared with that of the Viennese School, this objection appears to be only partially valid. The abandonment of the functional harmonic framework by Schoenberg and his students resulted in the development of a unique and unmistakable musical vocabulary that cannot be understood and integrated all at once. The situation is completely different with Ives. It is not necessary to know exactly what is being quoted; we still hear immediately from where the quotations come, from the military, entertainment, or the religious milieu. The music of the Viennese School became highly individualized on account of its forced need for expression and by becoming so cut itself off from easy access. With Ives, access is made seemingly easier because he works with clearer musical means. The use of the word "seemingly" is appropriate because one immediately hears and recognizes that music from various traditions is involved without necessarily understanding its meaning. What seems at first to be a restriction of musical expression, namely the use of material connotatively filled and "worn out," is in reality a means of opening. Liberation, and not the restriction of the listener, is the result. Someone who knows the quoted music and can relate it to something else will naturally hear Ives's music differently from someone who is unprejudiced. The connoted material practically imposes a use of imagination on the part of the audience. This amounts to a condition that is considered highly suspicious, even pathological, at least for listeners who have grown up in the context of German-speaking music aesthetics since Hanslick. To overstate this somewhat: the same dissonant musical structure, if this even exists, in a composition of the Viennese School that presumably dispenses with any explicit meaning (a presumption that Schoenberg and his students would certainly have rejected) is full of meaning in a composition of Ives's. These meanings, no matter how vague, immediately impose themselves on the listener.

The two concepts of dissonance are diametrically opposed in one other aspect of reception. Dissonances in the Western sense can disappear with time and rid themselves of their dissonant character. This is an experience that most everyone can share in some way who has for a considerable time heard only sophisticated music and has managed to avoid being inundated by popular music. This subjective opinion has been confirmed by scientific investigations (see Voigt 1985: 41–42). The best evidence for the disappearance of dissonance, or rather its acceptance, is to be found in history. Harmonies and progressions that were considered dissonant advanced to consonances, such as thirds and sixths. One should remember that the music of Beethoven was a popular example in the first half of the nineteenth century for showing the irritations of an excessive use of dissonances. The example was proffered by both proponents and opponents of his music. In a newspaper article from 1848, the following list is subsumed with reference to Beethoven under musical "freaks of the age": "sound effects, affected melody sequences, bizarre harmony progressions, as well as ear-splitting dissonances" (Schucht 1848: 756–57). To another contemporary, the "abundance of dissonances . . . is Beethoven's spirit itself, the manifestation of the same, the material side of the spirit" (Brendel 1845: 10). Both views are alien to us. The music has become too much a part of us. We have "adjusted our listening" and no longer have to seize upon the means of performance prophylaxis practiced in the nineteenth century. There is a copy of the orchestral parts of the *Eroica* from the nineteenth century that shows changes in the original score in two outstanding passages that clearly aim to avoid dissonances. The first is an especially sharp dissonance, emphasized by the instrumentation, that sounds at the climax of the first movement, the second E^3–F^3 (bars 276–79) in the flutes, which is softened to a unison. The second example, the oft-noted cumulus—that is, the beginning of the recapitulation simultaneously with the last measures of the elaboration, where the second A *flat*–B *flat* sounds together with the E flat major triad for two measures (bars 394–96)—was likewise softened by replacing the A *flat* with G, which restored the harmony.* Schoenberg was also of the opinion, in propagating his own artistic path, that the difference between consonance and dissonance is "only gradual and inconsiderable"; in support of this he appealed to the harmonic series where the seemingly dissonant intervals appear as more distant harmonics. "It depends solely on the growing ability of the analyzing ear to familiarize itself with the distant harmonics and by doing so to expand the concept of artistic harmony to the extent that all natural expression is included" (Schoenberg 1921: 17–18). The possibility of adjustment is based on an aspect of the phenomenon of musical dissonance that has been heretofore practically ignored. Perception, or more precisely the kind or quality of perception, has played a role in the differentiation of consonance and dissonance

*See Tusa 1985: 133. Such changes were presumably no rarity in the nineteenth century.

since well before the nineteenth century. Considerations of perception of both interval groups with respect to fusing versus not fusing (Plato, Euclid, Iamblichus), smooth versus rough (Plutarch), and pleasant versus unpleasant (Aristotle) have existed alongside mathematical determination since antiquity. Claudius Ptolemy counted the eleventh (octave plus fourth), categorized by the Pythagoreans as a dissonance, as a consonance, because its fusion in harmonies was similar to that of a fourth. When one expands this abstract observation, directed solely toward the interval constellation, with the question of physical and sensual appearance, then the already questionable dichotomy of consonance and dissonance is destabilized even further. I would like to present two historical examples that are widely divergent. In his treatise *Summa de speculatione musicae*, Walter Odington, an early-fourteenth-century English music theorist, saw the possibility that the third, categorized according to the still-valid Pythagorean rule as dissonant, could become consonant through a certain freedom of vocal performance (see Odington 1970: 70–71). In Schoenberg's melodrama *Erwartung* (1909), a major work from the period of his free-atonal composing, intervallic combinations exist in two striking passages that, viewed abstractly, can hardly be called more or less dissonant. Bar 154 contains a nine-tone and bars 382–83 an eleven-tone cluster from the chromatic scale. Both sounds are perceived completely differently on account of the kind of instrumentation, dynamics, articulation, and position and indeed were intended as such. At the dramatic climax of the work in bar 154, one finds an aggressive *fff*-sound with an extreme ambitus (contra-B to C⁴), with the shrill upper registers of flutes, oboes, and clarinets, that musically accompanies the total anguish of the protagonist, who at that moment discovers the corpse of her lover in the nocturnal forest. In bars 382–83, one finds a softer sound, even though it uses more tones of the chromatic scale in less space (contra-D to E-flat³). This is achieved again by instrumentation and reduced dynamic marking (*pp*). The passage is directly related to the meditation of the protagonist: "Oh, I curse you . . . but your pity made me happy. . . . I thought I was happy."

Upon taking another look at Ives's music and focusing on a listening adjustment or acclimatization to dissonances, it becomes absolutely conceivable that one can gradually become accustomed to these dissonant sound structures. The different cognitions that originate from the connoted musical material will be recognized and accepted in their diversity, yet they can hardly be overlooked. It is probably not possible to adjust to these musical–cognitive dissonances. This is owing to the heavy semantic baggage they carry. Ives's works share this kind of resistance with other works that likewise make use of preexisting musical materials and are unable to allow these to disappear semantically via decomposition in the new work structure. One need only think of a few examples, such as Bernd Alois Zimmermann's *Musique pour les soupers du Roi Ubu* (1962–67), or the third movement of Luciano Berio's *Sinfonia* (1968), or the products of *musique concrète*, or the modern possibilities of sound sampling in advanced jazz and pop music. Of course, these are not historical lineages of musical tradition, but one can find in all these works the other concept of dissonance that was described with Ives.

IV

The contrast between the two concepts of dissonance, the first, Western, music-immanent, and the other, extra-musically affected, represented by Ives, starts to lose considerable focus if the history of composition in Europe is not acknowledged primarily from the viewpoint of composition theory, something that most composers outrun. What is lost is the question of motivation for the use of dissonance. In trying to find an answer, we are forced to accept a viewpoint that disintegrates the musically immanent connection of the Western concept of dissonance, as is the case with Ives. A few examples must suffice. At least since the Renaissance, the use of dissonance and extra-musical implications have come closer together. In Claudio Monteverdi's *seconda prattica*, for example, the dissonant passages that are contrary to the rules are legitimized by the mimicking of spoken language. In the first opera, composed around 1600, dissonances were employed above all for their affective and expressive effect (see Dahlhaus 1962: 324). In the baroque *musica poetica* of Protestant Germany, where deviations from the rules had previously been allowed to conglomerate into musical rhetorical figures that had then been integrated into new rules, significant use of dissonance was linked to affective expression of pain and care, for example in the *passus duriusculus*, the chromatic descent of a fourth (see Massenkeil 1963). Even in a time when modulatory possibilities and degree of dissonant chord formation had gone far beyond the simple dominant seventh chord, Schumann succeeded in creating a manifest semantic relationship to the title of a small piano work (*Pleading Child*) with this "all-purpose chord" as an unresolved final chord.

Schoenberg's "step" into free atonality was, as Anton von Webern wrote in an early article (marked by an emphasis on the revolutionary), guided by the "creation of new values of expression," whatever this vague formulation means, and this creation required a new means of expression (see Webern 1912: 22).

As this short steeplechase has shown, "dissonance" is an imprecise category that crosses intra-musical definitions and boundaries. The resultant historical change is inherent in the origin of the word itself. Theodor W. Adorno, who considered dissonance a central category of modern art, based his interpretation on the dualistic character of dissonance as if it were self-evident. We can now read his statement of this view as a focused embodiment of our discussion without incorporating its historical limitations: "The incalculable significance for new art since Baudelaire and the Tristan of everything that is dissonant, truly a kind of invariant of the modern, stems from the convergence therein of the immanent power play of the work of art with the outward reality that rises to power over the subject parallel to its autonomy" (Adorno 1970: 29–30).

HANS ULRICH GUMBRECHT

Rhythm and Meaning

❖❖ *for UE/RG*

I

The association of "rhythm" both with literature *and* with the body has never been seen as a problem by literary scholarship. In the heyday of the "literariness" debate, R. Jakobson's famous definition of "poetic function" as the projection of the principle of "the equivalence from the axis of selection to the axis of combination" (Jakobson 1979 [1960]: 94) directed attention to phenomena like assonance and rhythm. These were then used fairly frequently (with interpretations of Jakobson's proposal that were probably too generous) as elements of a *metahistorical concept* of literature. On the other side, decades of research on *oral poetry* have given scholarly worth to a prescholarly experience: among all text types considered to be literary, those whose constitutive features include forms of "bound" (rhythmically structured) language have a special (genetic or pragmatic) affinity with forms of communication that take place in the *physical co-presence* of the communication partners. Paul Zumthor (1983) raised this line of academic pursuit to a new level of reflection with his outline of a "poetics of the voice." He made it clear how many of the concepts of literary criticism that refer to written textuality were in need of basic revision if they were to be applied to the description of oral poetry.

One is at a loss, however, if, instead of just enumerating individual (and more or less canonized) observations of literary criticism on the topic of rhythm, one asks whether these positions can be brought into line toward a new theory of bound language.

Given the (virtually) limitless perspectives of inquiry, the phenomenon of rhythm offers just as many arbitrary (and therefore worthless) solutions. Rhythm, as we have seen, was used as a specifying
characteristic to define literature and was seen as an indication of a
special closeness between text and body; the practice of defining
literary historical periods through the frequency of certain rhythmic patterns has even generated a subgenre of literary history
(*Versgeschichte*). In the age of the "linguistification" of literary scholarship and under the concept of "overdetermined text constitution" (see Link 1976: 53, for a definition), it became a given that
rhythm was used in modern lyrical texts as a process to transport
their seemingly constitutive, semantic incoherence toward semantic precision. Such bewilderment on the part of literary scholars
and the arbitrariness of the solutions it warrants are a symptom and
a result of a situation that has existed for at least several hundred
years. What we call *"Western culture" describes itself without exception
as a phenomenological complex that is constituted in the dimension of
"representation" (of meaning, of semantics)*. Therefore, the integration
of phenomena without a primary representation dimension (such
as that of the body or of rhythm) into concepts of cultural self-
reference is accomplished via the attempt to attribute to them a
function of representation. The theory of "overdetermined text
constitution" is an especially good example of this approach.

Only in recent years has scholarship brought forward any op-
posing voices. Zumthor remarked, somewhat casually, that the
body movements of singers and dancers serve to structure their
conduct (1983: 195)—and not the expression of their individuality.
This is precisely the line that the following argumentation will
take. I would like to show that a *constitutive tension exists between the
phenomenon of rhythm and the dimension of meaning* and to argue for an
expansion of the catalogue of our scholarly discourses of description. Of course, scholarly description cannot be achieved without semantics and the dimension of representation. This does not
mean, however, that all phenomena that become the object of
scholarly description are themselves descriptions and must therefore be presented with the question of what they mean or want to
express.

Based on the descriptive difficulties that literary scholarship
has with the phenomenon of rhythm, certain differentiations and

themes that normally motivate literary theory to reflect on this concept will be excluded. This is done in order to emphasize a comprehensive problem of the discourse of cultural criticism. I will, for example, not discuss the distinction between spoken rhythms and "meters" as canonized patterns in certain cultural contexts. I will also not discuss the question why certain rhythms and meters are dominant in certain periods and cultural areas (the argument of this article can at best be a first step in transforming the question of a connection between epochs/cultural areas and rhythms/meters into an answerable question). As a cultural critic, I further lack the competence to examine the connection between physiology and rhythm, which remains a mystery to natural scientists as well. There is, finally, insufficient space here to address the question (coming from a deconstructionist perspective) of special forms of the presence of rhythm in grapheme sequences—since this requires complicated preconsiderations. What one might be able to do is present the history of the poetological domestication of the phenomenon of rhythm under the dominance of the sense dimension (since the *Poetics* of Aristotle)—but even this would be a different article or require another examination.

I begin my argument with reference to a position that would represent the conclusion of such a history, namely, with the claim of poetology and literary criticism that rhythm and meaning can be conceptually harmonized. My *strategy of counterproof* will be the attempt to explain those three functions that poetological tradition along with everyday experience most frequently attributes to spoken rhythm:

1. *the memory-enhancing function* (spoken utterances can be more easily remembered in rhythmic form);

2. *the affective function* (rhythmic speech has a specific impact on emotions; sufficiently long employment can lead to trance);

3. *the coordinating function* (the simultaneous use of rhythmic speech facilitates the coordination of body movements among different individuals; it allows them, metaphorically speaking, to become a "collective subject").

This explication of the three functions of rhythm, however, will not find a corresponding structure of argumentation. Rather, I will concentrate in the next section on the development of a phenomenologically grounded *definition of the concept rhythm*. In the third section, I will explain two theories—put forth in the "Philosophy of Sociality," by G. H. Mead, and the "Biology of Cognition," by H. R. Maturana—that seem to be well-suited for *two different ways of explaining* the three functions of rhythm. In the final section, I will briefly return to the general problem of a *differentiation of the scholarly discourses of description*.

II

Rhythm is the realization of form under the (complicating) condition of temporality. This definition corresponds with the conclusion that the French linguist E. Benveniste drew at the end of his study on the use of the word ῥυθμός in ancient Greek. Benveniste states: "When one proceeds from the contexts of its occurrence, then this word designates the form at the moment of its embodiment by what is changing, moving, flowing—the form of all such matter that has no organic consistency. It corresponds to the structure of an unstable element" (Benveniste 1966: 333). But why are temporality and nonconsistency "complicating conditions" for the realization of form?

In order to proceed with this line of questioning, we must revert to another proposed definition, this time regarding the concept "*form*." "Form is unarticulated self-reference. In that this self-reference stands still, it can show that a problem is solved. It refers to the context in which the problem was raised and at the same time to itself. It presents self-differentiation and self-identity through each other" (Luhmann 1986a: 629–30). What it means to define form as the *simultaneity* of self-reference and external reference becomes clear when forms are visually realized in outlines describing the boundaries between phenomena that have form and their environment. Such outlines simultaneously participate in the phenomenon and its environment. The same situation is cited in classical-phenomenological language when it is said that themes only exist by virtue of the backdrop of horizons. As soon as we turn again to rhythm in spoken language, we can recognize that the form of a single sound only stands out given such a backdrop, that is, its (sound) environment: between the echo of the preceding sound in retention and the anticipation of the following sound in protention.

Temporality as a factor that complicates form presents itself in the transition from a single sound to a sequence of sounds, that is, to an utterance. Since the individual sounds that constitute an utterance have differing forms among themselves, it is not obvious that the totality of sounds in an utterance, based on the backdrop of other utterances as its environment or its horizon, can be experienced as "formed." This problem surfaces not only in the transition from single sounds to sound sequences or utterances, but in all those phenomena that Husserl calls "time objects in a specific sense": "We understand *time objects in a specific sense* to be objects that contain the units not only of time but also of time extension. When a sound rings out, my objectivizing comprehension can make a sound that lasts and fades away into an object. This is not possible for the duration of the sound or for the sound in its duration. This is a time object" (Husserl 1966 [1905]: 23).

The question therefore is: how can "time objects" in Husserl's sense attain form (i.e., a simultaneity of self-reference and external reference) that is not destroyed by the specific differences of units of self-reference and external reference in the elements that make it up (individual sounds)? All of the phenomena that we call rhythm can be looked upon as solutions to this problem. In the case of spoken language, rhythm lies in the repetition of (arbitrary) sequences of sound qualities. In European languages, these are either sequences of stressed and unstressed syllables or sequences of long and short syllables. What are called *"metrical feet"* in poetology are minimal units of form given to language as "time objects in a specific sense." These are experienced even by inexperienced listeners as forms, but only experienced listeners are able to identify *specific* forms. This being the case, I assume that metrical feet as forms are a special case of the involuntary remembering and the involuntary anticipation that Husserl designated with the terms "retention"/"protention." On the more complex level of the *verse*, consisting of several feet, and even more clearly on the level of *stanzas*, non-involuntary acts of remembering and anticipation are apparently required in order to experience a verse or stanza form. Presumably the rhyme (at the end of a verse) and the rhyme pattern (between stanzas) act as signals that trigger these acts of remembering and anticipating and thereby enable us to identify form.

Of course, not every realization of form in the temporality of (spoken or written) language is rhythm. Sequences of words or sentences can also lead to an experience of more or less precise forms on a *semantic level*. But for this effect, the recurrence of certain subordinate sense patterns is *not* necessary, because meaning does not belong to the "time phenomena in a specific sense." An object of meaning can be conceived before its articulation in time (of spoken or written language) begins, and it can be remembered retrospectively by a listener or reader independently of any recurrence phenomena. More complicated is the connection between temporality and tone quality or range. One can expect the recurrence of certain tone qualities and ranges (such as *alliteration, assonance,* or *rhyme*) in certain places of a rhythmic pattern. When, however, in all passages of a rhythmic pattern, the recurrence of stressed and unstressed or long and short syllables is linked to the recurrence of tone range and tone color, we tend to experience this concomitance as unsettling.

As a by-product of our suggested definition for the term "rhythm," we are now able to formulate an explanation for its *memory-enhancing function*. If one wants to remember a sequence of non-rhythmically formed language, then this is only possible *polythetically* (see Schütz 1960: 71–72), namely, by successively bringing to mind the individual sounds, words, and sentences of the utterance to be remembered. In remembering rhythmically formed language, however, the possibility exists of "transforming something that is known as multistranded to something that is single-stranded." The rhythmic pattern that gives the spoken or written utterance its specific form is then able, metonymically speaking, to represent a complexity that is primarily unfolded in time. The remembered rhythm presents a structure to the remembering reproduction of a speech sequence that drastically reduces the number of syllables, words, and sentences from which various subunits to be reproduced can be selected.

III

In order to explain the other functions of rhythm, we will now consult the definitions of rhythm in G. H. Mead's "Philosophy of Sociality" and H. R. Maturana's "Biology of Cognition" against the background of the definition of rhythm developed in the previous section. Before we do this, however, we want to list and categorize some of the forms of behavior that occur in the production and reception of rhythmic language by means of a scheme that is based on the primary level of observation:

	Speaker	Listener
1.1	Conception of a semantic form	
1.2	Polythetic production of an utterance by the voice (accompanied by simultaneous auditory perception)	Polythetic reception of an utterance through auditory perception
1.3	Monothetic constitution of a form in the perception of one's own voice (rhythm)	Monothetic constitution of a form in the perception of a strange voice (rhythm)
1.4	Monothetic constitution of a movement form from the kinesthetic perception of one's own speech organs, one's own auditory organs, one's own body (rhythm)	Monothetic constitution of a movement form from the kinesthetic perception of one's own auditory organs, one's own body (rhythm)
2.	Second constitution of the semantic form	First constitution of the semantic form

(Left margin: Affective function ↕; Center: Coordinating function ⇆)

Level 1.1: The conception of a semantic form can (but does not have to) precede the articulation of spoken language. At any rate, such articulation as a conception of a semantic form that corresponds to the content of the still-unarticulated utterance is only possible for the speaker.

Level 1.2: With his voice the speaker produces the sequence of the sounds that constitute the utterance polythetically. In doing so, he hears the sounds that he is producing. Simultaneously, the listener perceives the sequence of these sounds through hearing.

Level 1.3: The speaker and listener—sometimes simultaneously—identify patterns of sound qualities that are produced by one's own or by a strange voice as a form of the utterance (rhythm). This form can be perceived monothetically.

Level 1.4: One perceives one's own body (kinesthetic perception) as an organ of sound production and sound reception (speaker), or as an organ of sound reception (listener). If the produced or received sound sequence has form (is rhythmic), then the object of kinesthetic perception also has form. Rhythm and form are experienced on both the perceptive (1.3) *and* the kinesthetic (1.4) levels.

Level 2: The constitution of a semantic structure (through passive or active synthesis) is connected to the production or reception of the sound sequence. This constitution is normally a second constitution for the producer and a first constitution for the recipient.

Coordinating function: This function proceeds from the identity of the form constituted in the kinesthetic perception of the speaker and the kinesthetic perception of the listener. Speaker and listener become, so to speak, "one subject."

Affective function: This can be described as a specific closeness or linkage between the constitution of semantic forms and the kinesthetic perception of movement forms. Formulated another way, "affectivity" is defined as the inability or impossibility of divorcing the constitution of semantic form from the perception of one's own body.

In his article "The Philosophy of Sociality" (1969 [1929]), G. H. Mead developed an evolutionary model to explain the interplay of those levels of human behavior that correspond to levels 1.2, 2, and 1.4 in my table above. With primitive mankind, according to Mead, various forms of distance perception (1.2) triggered various forms of imagery of physical perception (2), for example, the imagery of rending prey or of injury to one's own body. This imagery was directly connected with involuntary body movements (1.4), for example, attack or flight. Finally, these three levels of behavior were not yet divided into the temporal perspectives of present and future but unfolded simultaneously.

On those levels of evolution where the phenomena of civilization begin, contoured concepts took the place of a poorly contoured imagery of physical perceptions (2). With the help of these new concepts, dangers or behavioral possibilities, now experienced as future events, could be anticipated. According to Mead, civilized humans are set apart by the capacity to repress or defer body movements (1.4) brought on by such anticipations. Humans can either employ them or not, depending on the result of the anticipation. Here it becomes clear that, contrary to the hypothesis concerning the reaction of primitive mankind, one can assume a *succes-*

sion of behavioral forms on the three thematic levels, alongside the qualitatively different appropriation of levels 2 and 1.4 (which are simultaneous with the prehistoric stage).

The combination of Mead's hypothesis with our definition of the term "rhythm" makes rhythm look like a *playback* of human behavior from the civilized stage to the prehistoric stage. If, in the perception of rhythm, both the object of distance perception (1.3) and the kinesthetic perception of one's own body (1.4) have a form quality, that is, if observation and perception can be mono-thetically comprehended on both levels, then external observation and kinesthetic perception can enter into a reciprocal relationship representing each other. This relationship, however, suspends the relationship of succession between them that normally exists in civilized humans by playing it back into the simultaneity of repre-sentation and represented. The "civilized" repression of stimulated body movements is therefore made more difficult (or impossible), and the "civilized" precision of concepts gives way to the poorly contoured, physically grounded imagery.

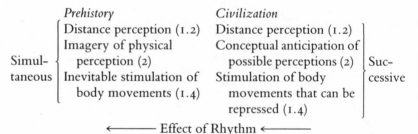

	Prehistory	Civilization	
	Distance perception (1.2)	Distance perception (1.2)	
Simul-taneous	Imagery of physical perception (2)	Conceptual anticipation of possible perceptions (2)	Suc-cessive
	Inevitable stimulation of body movements (1.4)	Stimulation of body movements that can be repressed (1.4)	

←——————— Effect of Rhythm ←———————

This combination of a phenomenological definition of rhythm with the model gleaned from Mead's evolutionary hypothesis seems to correspond to our experience of the effect of rhythm as a reshaping of "lucid consciousness" into conditions that border on the "trancelike." The affective function of rhythm can thus be explained in this context as well as an imagination-stimulating effect. But my model does not yet help to understand the behavior-coordinating function of rhythm.

In the context of H. R. Maturana's "Biology of Cognition," the affective function and the coordinating function of rhythm appear as consequences of specific kinds of *coupling*. More specifically, the behavior-coordinating function should be describable as a specific form of coupling between two or more bodies ("organisms"), especially on level 1.4, and the affective function as a specific form of coupling between body (perception) and consciousness (levels 1.4 and 2). A (*structural*) *coupling* between a system A and a system B occurs, according to Maturana (see 1982a: 244), whenever system A finds itself in the environment of system B and vice versa, whenever system A reacts to change in the condition of system B and vice versa, whenever system A reacts to a change in system B that is related to a change in system A and vice versa (that is, whenever both systems react indirectly to their own changes). Structurally coupled systems produce *consensual zones*. As soon as these zones are constituted, further systems can be coupled to them.

The phenomena that we call languages are, according to Maturana, *consensual zones of the second order*:

When the organisms that operate in a consensual zone can be influenced in a recursive manner through internal conditions created by their consensual interaction, and when they can include in their consensual zone those behaviors created through recursive interaction as parts of their behavior, then consensuality of the second order is created. From this perspective, the consensual behavior of the first order operationally represents a description of the circumstances that trigger it. For the creation of this consensuality of the second order (and consequently, for the appearance of the recursive operations of consensus over consensus) that leads to a recursive use of description upon descriptions, it is necessary, however, that all processes of reciprocal influence, including descriptions, take place in the same zone.   (Maturana 1982a: 257)

The observation that the behaviors created by the recursive interactions between organisms in the first place are included in the interaction is crucial for the definition of consensual zones of the second order. Only under this condition are consensual zones productive and constantly creative, as we would expect of language, of new parts of themselves (see Maturana 1982a: 259). Based on the productivity of their interactions and their constantly new reactions to the newly produced parts of their consensual zone, these organisms, coupled by a consensual zone of the second order, attain the status of "observers" (ibid., 258). Observers differentiate between themselves and those organisms out of which they emerge. These differences, as elements of languages, are what we can call "semantic descriptions." "Whenever an observer describes the interaction between two or more organisms, as if the meaning that he attributes to the interaction were determining the progress of these interactions, then the observer makes a *semantic* observation" (Maturana and Varela 1987: 210).

Coupled organisms do not attain the status of observers within *consensual zones of the first order*, however. Interactions on this level produce no new parts of themselves and therefore do not command any level of semantic description. If we can define languages as consensual zones of the second order, then the reciprocal linkage between machines or organs of the human body (at least as a rule) form consensual zones of the first order. A main reason for assigning phenomena of *rhythm* to the consensual zone of the first order lies in rhythm being a recurrence of behavioral sequences (of sound sequences in the case of rhythmic language). This aspect of rhythm corresponds to the criterion of nonproductivity. Nonbound language does not display such recurrence. If what we call rhythm appears primarily in consensual zones of the first order, however, then rhythm does not command a level of semantic description, and the organisms coupled via rhythm do not produce the status of observers. The three functions of rhythm that we are examining could then be explained by the dissolution of differences that are created in the consensual zones of the second order by the emergence of the observer and his semantic descriptions. The *behavior-coordinating function* then is characterized by the absence of a difference between the self-reference of one coupled organism and the self-reference of another. The *affective function* is a dissolution of a differentiation between body perception and sense constitution (or more precisely, this function appears as an absence of the difference between body perception and sense constitution). The *memory-enhancing function* is a dissolution of the differences by which time dimensions are constituted, time dimensions that are, for their part, the trigger for the time-spanning action of memory. The affinity between rhythm and *imagination*, as explained by Mead, would then result from a specific "intermediate status" for bound language. As language, it would attain the status of a consensual zone of the second order wherein semantic descriptions (meanings) are constituted; as rhythm, bound language would simultaneously have the status of a consensual zone of the first order (without a level of semantic description). In other words, the special status of imagination between body movement and meaning would correspond to the oscillation of bound language between the levels of consensual zones of the first and second orders.

IV

Our recourse to the theoretical precepts of Maturana's biology of cognition has yielded explanations for the functions linked to the phenomenon of rhythmic language. It has also implicitly made clear from where the enormous difficulties and confusions arise in the poetological and scholarly description of the phenomenon of bound language.

Scholarly discourses are constituted, self-referentially, in consensual zones of the second order. They are, therefore, in the terminology of Maturana and Varela, complex configurations of semantic descriptions. But we must not assume therefore that all couplings thematized in scholarly language (this includes couplings or interactions between organisms) must themselves correspond to the definition of consensual zones of the second order. This fact has been, at all times and without difficulty, taken into account in natural science descriptions of couplings between human organs. There are, however, phenomena, including rhythmically structured (bound) language, that fall between the phenomenal status of consensual zones of the first order (rhythm) and the phenomenal status of consensual zones of the second order (language). Their partial membership in the phenomenal status of consensual zones of the first order has been disregarded with increasing consistency in the Western scholarly tradition. This is precisely the reason for the poetological subjugation of phenomena of rhythm by the dimension of representation (of semantic description and consensual zones of the second order).

On the basis of these considerations, we can now reformulate the definition of the phenomenon of rhythm developed in the preceding section. Whereas we had formerly proposed rhythm as the solution to the problem of constituting form under the complicating conditions of temporality, it now becomes clear that "temporality as a complicating condition" is but a consequence of the projection of differentiations (semantic descriptions) among present, past, and future, as only a consensual zone of the second order can generate. Phenomena of rhythm that can be categorized as a type of consensual zone of the first order do not themselves display these differentiations or therefore the dimension of temporality. Rhythm does not actually have to assert itself against temporality. Our impression to the contrary is a consequence of misguided efforts to describe the phenomenon of rhythm exclusively as a phenomenon on the level of consensual zones of the second order.

What our definition of rhythmically formed (bound) language finally discovered was a constitutive oscillation between different consensual levels. From what has been said, it becomes clear that a scholarly description of rhythmically formed (bound) language should thematize this oscillation as a *tension*, instead of harmonizing it with theorems such as that of "overdetermined lyrical texts," according to which the phenomenon of rhythm is subjugated by the dimension of representation.

Seen this way, the problem of the scholarly description of rhythmic language becomes a paradigmatic case of our general epistemology. From the difference between the description developed here (which emphasizes a tension between rhythm and language, an interference of consensual zones of the first and second orders) and the common descriptions in poetology or literary criticism (which attempt to include the phenomenon of rhythm in the dimension of representation), it becomes clear that with the thematization of "materialities of communication" we encounter those levels and forms of human interaction where the interactive partners do *not* have the status of observers. For precisely this reason, several phenomenological complexes such as rhythmic language have been included in the concept of "materialities of communication," complexes in which the consensual zones of the first and second orders overlap. Other examples of those complexes are imagination, affects, and violence. The inclusion of such newly constituted themes will oblige us to expand and differentiate the catalogue of our descriptive discourses. This could ultimately help alleviate the schism between the natural sciences and the humanities.

KLAUS DIRSCHERL

Tàpies, or the Materiality of Painting

I

The art of the Catalonian Antoni Tàpies, especially his early work, thrives on creative destruction. In order to illuminate this paradox, it is necessary to glance at the historical situation in which this art was created and in which it was consciously engaged. In 1966, at least a quarter-century after the end of the Spanish Civil War, the poet Jaime Gil de Biedma, a compatriot of Tàpies, looked back on the period immediately after World War II with sadness: "Europe lay in ruins" (Gil de Biedma 1985: 125). Postwar Spain, as well as the rest of Europe, was characterized by bomb debris, hunger, and a black market. The Franco regime tried to marginalize all those who were not prepared to join in the nationalistic triumph and its hollow discourses. Key positions in cultural institutions had long since been occupied by supporters of the regime. Universities, schools, and academies ensured the dissemination and public cele-bration of official literature and art. Censorship forbade what-ever seemed to threaten this official culture. Nevertheless, Gil de Biedma is sad when remembering this period of intellectual and physical ruin with a kind of "nostalgie de la boue" (ibid., 147), as he calls it in another poem.

Why was this poet from Barcelona fascinated by these ruins twenty years later, in 1966? Would this situation not call instead for indictment and lament? Where did he and his friends, where did

Antoni Tàpies and other artists, gain the strength in the early Franco era for their art and for their tremendous will to survive? Is it the refusal to participate in the official discourse that gave them this incredible impetus?

II

"It is apparently possible to say no" (Gil de Biedma 1985: 69) is a quote from the collection of poems *Moralidades*, hacked apart by the censors and consequently published by the author in Mexico. Similarly, Antoni Tàpies understood his artistic work in the 1940's and 1950's as a protest against the Franco regime: "What I did also served as a way to spit in the face of the well-meaning bourgeoisie" (Tàpies 1983: 213). What characterized this protest? Let us look at some of his earlier paintings, or better yet, objects and assemblages. In his *Packing Case with Straw* (Fig. 1), an assemblage of wood and paper from 1969, Tàpies merges into a work of art a great many things that normally would have ended up at the garbage dump. Wooden slabs and some straw are interwoven in a seemingly arbitrary fashion. All this is covered by a gray-blue color that lends the chaotic ensemble a powerful center. The other elements also seem to get their focus from this blotch of color.

With this kind of assemblage, Tàpies rejects traditional art on several levels. First of all, his "picture" is an affront to a traditional type of painting that offers the observer a mimetic representation of reality. Nothing is *represented* here. Instead, the artist *presents* his material. And its order does not reveal a meaning, as traditional mimetic painting used to do. The assemblage *is* nothing more than itself. This insistence on its own materiality and the rejection of the usual transparency of the artistic sign blocked or at least irritated the understanding of this art.

Additionally, the employment of used materials, old pieces of wood and used straw, shows a contempt for traditional painting materials like oil- and water-based paints, canvas, the well-formed frame, and the respectability that these materials have gained over centuries. Tàpies works with artistic means that are normally considered garbage. Another of his assemblages thematizes exactly this point: *Large Knotted Cloth with Garbage* (Fig. 2) is the title of an assemblage from 1971. It seems obvious that such a work could

Fig. 1. Antoni Tàpies, *Packing Case with Straw*, 1969. © 1994 ARS, New York/ADAGP, Paris.

easily provoke academic critics with their traditional view of art. As are all of Tàpies's early works, this one is characterized not only by its potential for negation but also by its appeal for a new way of dealing with reality and a different approach to art.

I asserted that the assemblage *Packing Case with Straw* does not *represent* reality but rather *presents* material. But what is more, the presentation shows not a finished object but broken pieces that

Fig. 2. Antoni Tàpies, *Large Knotted Cloth with Garbage*, 1971. © 1994 ARS, New York/ADAGP, Paris.

refer to their old uses in a new context. They are nailed together into a new configuration that some might describe as geometric. The straw at the bottom half of the assemblage prompts thoughts of a stall, of something living. The colors that Tàpies uses or shows are once again a rejection of traditional painting. They lack its splendor, are muted, neither exciting nor spectacular. The assemblage is dominated by brown tones. A visual tension arises out of the conflict of the different materials in use. But it also stems from the vigorous rejection of traditional painting and the various impulses of meaning that are produced by the new configuration and that incite the observer, despite an apparent refusal of signification, to discover a meaningful object in the assemblage.

Still more austere, still less spectacular, is the assemblage titled *Bedside Rug*, from 1970 (Fig. 3). In the center of the picture we see a ratty rug. Its brown-green color is somewhat faded. Unappealing in every way, this is a real piece of garbage that would only be used

Fig. 3. Antoni Tàpies, *Bedside Rug*, 1970. © 1994 ARS, New York/ ADAGP, Paris.

to seal a broken window or door. Tàpies places this ratty rug in the center of his assemblage and valorizes it with a series of small but effective interventions. The orange strokes at the edge, but also the use of the same color in the center, encourage placing this useless piece of material into another context. The strokes act as rays, the color blotches in the center as a source of light. One would almost think of a sacred object. Such proposals of significance, however, do not converge into the obligatory recognition of a depicted piece of reality as is the case with traditional mimetic art.

Instead, they encourage trying and then discarding independent models of meaning. By doing so, we take part in the creative-destructive task of finding meaning, a task that Tàpies wants to initiate with works based on Far Eastern art and communications practices.*

Tàpies creates the greatest suspense in this assemblage by contrasting the old context of the bedside rug and the new artistic context, constructed with the help of some subtle interventions. The traditional mimetic function of art is brought into question once again. The fact that Tàpies covers the rug with a piece of used plexiglass transforms it into something to be displayed, thematizes art as spectacle and at the same time problemizes it as such. One could almost say that Tàpies "stages" the mimetic function of art and parodies it at the same time. He mirrors the old tasks of art in a scenario of newly fashioned garbage. Despite the demonstrative humility of his choice of materials, he in no way rejects his own creative intervention. On the contrary, the gesture of the artist is all the more powerful in its contrast with worthless materials. This gesture is a kind of survival signal, a demonstration of strength in an environment that is obviously characterized by dissolution, being used, and ending. The act of creation is more important than the created object itself. The intervention, the tearing apart, and the direct involvement of the artist are more important than the result. With Tàpies, the use of garbage becomes an artistic event.

The assemblage *Companys*, from 1974 (Fig. 4), demonstrates that this kind of artistic event can also turn into a political event. On an old window shutter, whose rusty nails are still visible, is pressed a white handkerchief that is smeared with blood. A piece of plexiglass helps to enclose it within the framework of the shutter. The Catalonian word "Companys," meaning comrades, can be found on a sticker of the sort used to mark lost articles. Again, different elements refer back to earlier uses in their present use. The blood on the handkerchief points to violence, but also to life. The framing and the glass covering are a renewed demonstration of the theme of mimesis. Unlike the previous assemblages, however, this one constricts the semantic potential of its material configuration to some extent by introducing a political message with the word "Com-

*See "The Wall as a Means of Expression," in Tàpies 1976: 131–36, and the excellent Tàpies interpretation by Geisler (1985).

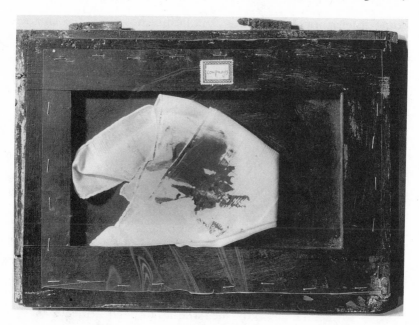

Fig. 4. Antoni Tàpies, *Companys*, 1974. © 1994 ARS, New York/ADAGP, Paris.

panys." "Comrades," an address to political allies, together with the bloodstained handkerchief, calls to memory bloody battles and repression. The crumpled cloth holds a symbolic potency of political explosiveness.

The appeal to meaning is made more precise for the observer who recognizes in the word "Companys" a reference to the Catalonian politician of that name, who was executed as commander-in-chief as a proxy for all Catalonians who did not want to bow to Franco's nationalistic dictatorship. The gesture of resistance that characterizes most early works of Tàpies's achieves here a political potency of unimagined force. This force is undoubtedly rooted in the demonstrated humility with which the artist fuses old, used, broken, and seemingly worthless materials into a symbol of silent resistance. The fact that the explosive potential of these assemblages was very much recognized is confirmed by the public treatment of Tàpies at the time. On the one hand, Spanish authorities tried in the early 1970's to use this Catalonian avant-gardist to gain some international reputation. At home, however, information about Tàpies was suppressed.* The danger presented by this kind of resistance was not to be underestimated, as can be deduced from Luis Marsillach's warning: "I'm afraid that this art without beauty will lead to a politics without justice and to a world without God" (quoted in Tàpies 1983: 245).

III

It was not only Tàpies's destructive garbage art that was cloaked in silence and censorship. For a long time, literary criticism ignored the fact that destruction, wreckage, rotting, and death were central obsessions of the literature in Franco's time.† "Madrid is a city with more than a million corpses (according to the latest statistics)" (Alonso 1983 [1944]: 73). This is the beginning of one of Dámaso Alonso's most famous poems from his *Sons of Anger*, with which, already in 1944, he shocked the Spanish reader. In 1949, Pedro Salinas, while in exile, published a series of poems titled *Zero* that describe Spain in ruin. Blas de Otero sees himself and the world drowning in a flood of blood (Correa 1980, 2: 174). Another one of the so-called *poetas sociales*, Angel González, dedicated an entire series of poems (in the collection *Without Hope, with Conviction*, published in 1961) to the evocation of a Spain characterized by destruction, ruins, and a people without hope (González 1986: 64–72). Carlos Edmundo de Ory, one of the many writers who left the country in order to write Spanish literature in exile, published a collection of short stories titled *Refuse*. This list could easily be continued.

What these texts have in common is their description, cynical commentary on, or pathetic lament over Spain's destruction in both a physical and intellectual sense. In *Espadaña*, a journal in which many of the authors just mentioned were published, one spoke of a new "tremendismo" (Sanz Villanueva 1976: 266), a

---

*Tàpies (1983: 244–45) reports that the pro-government magazine *ABC* interviewed him but only printed these interviews in the international, not in the local, editions.

†Even the eminent *Literary History of Spain*, by R. O. Jones (1972), certainly not subject to Spanish censorship, only mentions this in conjunction with C. J. Cela's novels.

resurrection of a literature characterized by horror and terror. Fifty years earlier, Ramón del Valle-Inclán had wanted to shock and shake up his fellow citizens with the same kind of literature. It is also clear that all of the above-mentioned authors showed a reality of destruction and dissolution because they wanted to overcome this reality. They met the actual destruction within the country with a literary "destruction," a reflection in the medium of art and literature, as if wanting to conjure up a better world by imploring what is ruined.

It was Luis Martín-Santos who, in 1961, fundamentally changed this attitude toward destruction with his novel *Time of Silence*. One of its protagonists, Muecas, a good-for-nothing who earns a living by breeding rats for laboratories, is admired or ironically praised by the narrator precisely because he understands how to survive in the chaos of Madrid's poorest neighborhoods, gloriously and profitably enthroned on a pile of garbage. The narrator ironically lauds "the ability to improvise and the original constructive power of the Iberian race" (Martín-Santos 1982 [1961]: 52) in considering the impressive work of this uncrowned king of the ghettos of Madrid, who built "a complete and harmonious city along with its enlivening atmosphere out of nothing and garbage" (ibid.). Martín-Santos's irony leaves us a bit in the dark as to whether this praise of Muecas the garbage king is meant to be taken seriously. But the enthusiasm with which his creative commerce with broken pieces of furniture, corrugated tin, and building refuse is described can certainly be seen as a prelude to what Tàpies will do with garbage and used materials.

IV

The young Tàpies understands his artistic work, and especially his use of old paper, cardboard boxes, wire, charred material, or other "materia innoble," as he calls it (Tàpies 1983: 211), as a protest against the official art propagated from centralistic Madrid. In his autobiography, he describes in detail how the cultural "wasteland" (ibid.) that covered Franco's Spain led to his resistance. At the same time, he begins to develop new concepts of a positive artistic struggle with reality out of the force of his protest, out of the strength that the negation of the dominant culture gives him. The interest in Far Eastern philosophy, but also in Western theories of the heterodox, prevent his use of ignoble materials from being seen only as protest. He increasingly realizes the chance for a new beginning. In a text fragment from 1970 with the programmatic title "Nothing Is Insignificant" and with the no less programmatic motto "For in order to be born again, you must die" (Tàpies 1976: 175), he develops a theory of poverty art that depends not on the reproduction of reality by whatever means but rather on the creative employment of this same impoverished reality. Avant-garde art in Spain, where Marcel Duchamp and early surrealism were accepted late and with reservation, in the end does not overwhelm but underwhelms the dominant cultural code. At the same time, Tàpies presents a theory of the effect of his art that requires of the observer an active and meditative approach to the artist's activity. The public is invited to engage in exercises of concentration and reduction so that it may reach a disposition where it will no longer allow itself to be misled by the usual spectacle of art and mass culture.

How much destruction and renewal, reduction and return to origins, rejection of the rational and appeals to instincts go hand in hand in this artistic concept is made clear in a passage from his *Memoria personal*, where Tàpies attempts to place his work within the context of psychoanalytical, but also heterodox, philosophical theories:

As far as my work is concerned, I felt at that time the need to start from the nadir; not at zero, but I had to get back to my roots and finally reacquire and make my own many approaches that I had once vaguely internalized, through surrealism, in my early years. Many of the techniques that validate the anarchic impulses of the imagination and the subconscious became important again, for example, the conscious inclusion of chance, of failure, and of error.   (Tàpies 1983: 301)

This passage shows that the path from the "materia innoble" to creation via destruction reestablished the contacts between European avant-garde movements and Tàpies and Spanish art that had been completely cut off under Franco. With Tàpies, destruction is no longer protest but becomes a process of transformation. The surrealistic "trastornar la visión" (Tàpies 1983: 301), the "turning around of vision," becomes a transformation of reality. Spanish

speakers will understand that *trastorno* also means "mental distur-
bance." But Tàpies does not see this *trastorno*, however, as a negative process that might unwillingly bring out "moral filth" (ibid.,
302). *Trastorno* becomes for him a central artistic process with
which he develops a new concept of art.

The descriptions of his artistic activities that, in their most
intensive moments, developed into a real battle with various materials leave no doubt that this frenzied, fevered work had some kind
of therapeutic value for Tàpies himself. His own nonconformity, at
first venting itself in destructive energy, was transformed into the
outline of a new art where the activity of the artist is more important than the resulting art objects. The Catalonian whom the
Franco government denied the use of his mother tongue, the artist
for whom the painting of oils seemed like accepting the standards
of the hated official art, the Spaniard for whom isolation in his own
country prevented all contact with the European avant-garde, was
in this way able to create free spaces for artistic activity normally
blocked by the false redundancy of official culture with its pom-
pous speeches and imitation art.

The free spaces that Tàpies created were semantically not empty.
The Far Eastern doctrine of pictorial signs, which he displayed in
his wall pictures in exemplary fashion and dynamized with an intelligent employment of scriptual signs (see Geisler 1985), was never
conceived so as to become semantically neutral. His artistic work
(especially in the early years) was always sensitive to the context in
which he sought his materials so that each of his works almost asked
for interpretation but still denied any precise and unique meaning.
After all, Tàpies understood himself as a painter who, with his
work, takes part in the world in which he lives, but who, in his
writings about art, always seeks to realize the paradox of a discourse
not based on Western logic (see Dirscherl 1986: 83–86).

V

The most convincing commentary on Tàpies's practice of art as
creative destruction is that by J. A. Valente. His *Cinco fragmentos
para Antoni Tàpies* is a poetic reaction to the work of the Catalonian
that shows how much Valente sees in Tàpies a congenial artist. In
fact, there are astonishing parallels between the artistic and poetic

development of the Gallician Valente and the Catalonian Tàpies. Both experienced the Franco era and its moral and material censorships as young artists. Both began their work with the destruction of the dominant literary and artistic systems. Valente, like other poets of the 1940's and 1950's in Spain, writes on decay, destruction, and refuse. "Words decay" is the concise formula found in a poem from 1968 (Valente 1980: 361). The rhetoric of lies, so typical of Francoist art, but also social life in general, is constantly ridiculed with satire. For Valente, traditional poetry is like the "sale of used noise" (ibid., 369), its official representatives are "corpulent idols" of a false culture (ibid., 227).

As for Tàpies, destruction is a poetic theme for Valente, before becoming an artistic program. His concern is a return to the nadir, the *punto cero* of all speech, the *punto cero* used programmatically as a title to the first edition of his poems: "The poetic word must return language to the nadir, to the stage of unlimited nondetermination, of unlimited freedom" (Valente 1980: 9). This is the main subject of his large volume of poetry and at the same time the course he recommends for himself and for art under Franco in order to gain new strength and freedom from the destruction of false discourses. In one of the pieces in *Cinco fragmentos para Antoni Tàpies*, Valente formulates the link between himself and the Catalonian painter: "Poetry has often felt the temptation of silence. Poems naturally tend toward quietness. Or it is part of their making. Poetry: the art of composing stillness. A poem is not alive if, even before its words, its silence cannot be heard" (Valente 1985: 177). This is an essential concept: "silence" as the basic condition of a new type of poetry in this country where, on the one hand, the intellectual debate is obscured by the verbose rhetoric of official writers and, on the other hand, many poets and artists are silenced by censorship. Valente and Tàpies gain strength from their battle for a creative type of destruction, for a destructive-creative conflict with native poetic traditions, and for the development of a theory of artistic creation based on destruction. Impulses toward this goal come from his interest in Indian cultures and his intensive study of Spanish mystics, who are likewise heterodox within the context of the orthodox system of the Counterreformation. The tradition of Spanish mysticism, as well as Eastern philosophies, makes it clear to him that the use of "creative imagination is always an exercise in destruction"

(Valente 1972: 73). Orthodoxies always lead to stagnation, to crystallized forms that stand in the way of the flexibility of creative activity. Therefore, according to Valente, the artistic act that wants to free itself of these stifling structures always depends on destruction. Indian cultures developed a "ritual of destruction" that made it possible for them to escape the impending death of their culture: "Let us turn the constant flow of creative movement against the crystallization of form; only from this movement comes freedom, not from the fetishization of its products. Destruction was and is a necessary beginning and origin of what paradoxically survives death, what escapes the greed and avarice of the ruling idols, the cannibalism caused by humanity's own acts" (ibid., 74).

This praise of the flowing, the nonfixated, the movable as a moment of destruction and creation once again demonstrates the intellectual relationship between Antoni Tàpies, the artist who creatively employs garbage and worthless materials, and Valente, the theoretician of creative destruction. It is therefore not surprising if Valente, like Tàpies, attempts to explain and revive a literary tradition that furnishes the aesthetic legitimacy for his own artistic activity. Borges once said that every artist creates his own predecessors. Valente does this by emphasizing the relationship between his own poetry and authors like Lautréamont, Rimbaud, and Artaud, and by placing those Spanish poets in the foreground who were forced into the background by official criticism. Thus he repeatedly praises the mystic Juan de la Cruz and the poverty of his poetic language. The "meagerness of speech" (Valente 1972: 74) of this Spanish monk is exemplary for him since the natural corporeality of language has not yet been dissolved into deceiving transparency. The rough vocabulary of a Juan de la Cruz contains more potential meaning than any crystal clear verse by Garcilaso de la Vega, who was held in such high esteem by official criticism in Franco's time.*

VI

Finally, if one questions what value Valente's and Tàpies's destruction and innovation strategies have within the artistic and literary

*The periodical *Garcilaso* has gathered pro-government authors around itself since 1943. In its first issue, it presented its namesake as a soldier and poet who lost

history of Spain, but also in cultural history in general, one is surprised by their modernity.* The praise of sparse language as a final chance for real communication in a world flooded by images and crammed full with "meaning," the search for the uncoded and anarchical force in the physical component of signs, appear more important than ever in the light of postmodern resignation to the medial inundation of signs. It must not be forgotten, however, that Tàpies and Valente first developed destruction and the provocative aesthetization of garbage as survival strategies for a cultural situation wherein imposed aesthetic and ideological norms threatened to strangle any real communication. The crushing presence and emptiness of public discourses were countered with a massive criticism and the practical destruction of these same discourses. A *program* of destruction quickly developed out of destruction as a *theme.*

It is interesting that, even in the discourses of the Franco system, the all-present logocentrism of the West was detected and denounced and that consequently the untransparent corporeality of simple materials and less coded language was discovered as a weapon against the deceitful transparency of these discourses. The corruption of the discourses by the state initially provoked a refusal to communicate among its enemies. But in the "meagerness of speech" that Valente promoted, in the emptiness and silence that Tàpies demanded as new qualities of artistic and social activity, there could already be felt the need for a new type of meaningfulness. The appeal to destruction implied the hope of a new meaningfulness that would succeed in escaping the Western *circulus vitiosus* between meaningful signs and meaningless sign schemes and in discovering new ways of communication that allow the wholeness of prelogical existence without denying the experience of an intellectually explicit life and work.

It is in any case certain that, via Tàpies and Valente, Spain's art and literature could participate in the worldwide debate on the pos-

---

his life in the struggle for the Spanish throne in 1536, four hundred years before the "national uprising," the term used in Francoist jargon for the Civil War.

*It is useful to remember that an aesthetic-ideological debate concerning the worth and worthlessness of refuse and destruction has been going on outside Spain since the late 1960's. This debate still raises convincing arguments. See among others Enzensberger 1968; Mitscherlich 1976; Thompson 1979.

sibilities of communication and signification, although the point of departure was historically well-defined and clearly limited to the 1950's and 1960's in Franco's Spain. Or is the contemporary situation, in which the variety of discourse is only illusory, more akin to the semiotic conditions in a totalitarian system of meaning than we might think?

STEPHEN BANN

"Wilder Shores of Love":
Cy Twombly's Straying Signs

❖

This is an essay about a hermeneutic investigation gone astray: about a process of interpretation that, in the last resort, turns back on itself and becomes, as it were, an allegory of the objects it originally purported to interpret. These objects are the paintings of the American artist Cy Twombly. That Twombly's work should present these puzzling features is not, I would claim, an indication that the interpretive process has not been pushed far enough, let alone that the paintings themselves are, in some radical sense, mute and uncommunicative. On the contrary, I would take it as indicative of the special quality of these works, and of their historical significance, that they do not so much capture a meaning—which remains there, like a treasure, to be discovered—as enact a quest for meaning. It has often been remarked of the art historian's method, typified by Erwin Panofsky's model of iconological investigation, that it gives a special privilege to the form of iconographic coding that was practiced in Italian Renaissance painting, and neglects the crucial differences that existed in prior periods, like the medieval epoch, or indeed in subsequent phases, like seventeenth-century Holland (see Alpers 1983). Twombly's art, I would suggest, provokes the classic interpretive strategies. The language of his titles, to take only one aspect of his work, invites comparison with the Greco-Roman mythology of Renaissance art. But this is not a secure or self-sufficient dimension of reference for Twombly: the gesture of naming, like the gesture of painting that intersects with it, creates expectations that are no less rich for being, in the last resort, condemned to unfulfillment.

This does not imply, by any means, that Twombly's work acts as a mere lure, tempting the viewer (and reader) with an expectation of meaning that is then lightly, and frivolously, withdrawn. As will be suggested, the quest initiated by Twombly's painting has a structure to it, even if the individual examples are lost in the aporia of meaninglessness. His practice as an artist itself enacts (and does not merely illustrate) the fulfillment of a myth, and in this respect it rejoins, by a curious detour, the mythic status of the American abstract expressionist movement, which was its own point of departure. "Action painting," as celebrated by Harold Rosenberg, was the existential enhancement of the artist's painterly activity: his studio became an arena in which the perilous engagement with matter and space was fought out for an audience that, of necessity, only arrived when the battle was over. There is virtually nothing of that lingering existential tremor in Twombly's work, at least as far as it is bound to the mythic status of the New York School, and the fascination with studio practice (see Rosenberg 1962). Yet, if Twombly's work conveys no nostalgia for the abandoned studio, it is all the more strongly aimed at a new space to be conquered. The series of works shown at the Venice Biennale of 1988, with their intricate rococo frames containing a drift of green pigments, epitomized this impulse toward a new location—not the New York loft but the salon of an Italian palazzo.

For it is hardly the least important aspect of Twombly's career that he left New York in the late 1950's and has made his home in Italy, particularly Rome, for almost all of the intervening period. As a young artist, he shared the cultural milieu, and especially the connections with Black Mountain College, that gave distinction to the early works of Jasper Johns and Robert Rauschenberg. His decision to leave New York, apart from a brief return in the late 1960's, was tantamount to a relinquishment of all claims to be considered a central member of the rising school of artists that achieved worldwide fame, from their New York base, in the 1960's.* It was

*Irving Sandler, who has chronicled the American art of the postwar period, mentioned to me in conversation that Twombly has only recently been reintegrated into the central tradition that he appeared to have abandoned on leaving New York.

also, in a sense, the acting out of a geopolitical logic whose import must have seemed highly paradoxical at the time. Toward the
end of his life, the Italian poet and filmmaker Pier Paolo Pasolini
planned a film based on the life of St. Paul, of which the most
distinctive feature was a topological rearrangement of the main
geographical centers to fit the circumstances of the contemporary
world. In Pasolini's plan, the ancient religious capital of Jerusalem
was to be replaced by Rome, the intellectually vibrant city of
Athens by Paris, and the imperial dominance of Rome by the contemporary example of New York. Cy Twombly's journey from
New York to Rome obviously inverts the centripetal logic of the
movement from the periphery to the metropolis—or so it must
have appeared to an art world still mesmerized by the prestige of
the New York School. From a longer perspective, his journey can,
nonetheless, be seen to have a logic of its own.

If I am insisting on the importance of Twombly's choice, this is
because the geopolitical aspect of it has a resonance that goes
beyond the immediate circumstances of the postwar period. Frank
Kermode has written persuasively about the classical myth of *translatio imperii*, and the way in which this notion of a moving center of
arts and civilization influenced the imagination of the American
pioneers.* One could say that the New York School became highly
conscious of the claim to be not merely an addendum to the cav-
alcade of international modernism, but its culmination. The fact
that an American critic like Rosenberg was capable of discerning
the "Fall of Paris" as the capital of modernism at a stage when Paris
had not yet, in effect, fallen to the German army is simply one early
indication of the sensitivity of American opinion to this issue (see
Rosenberg 1962: 209–20). Of course, the arguments supporting
the view that the prestige of the New York School was consciously
manipulated, in the circumstances of the Cold War, by the cultural
agencies of the American government have also been amply re-
hearsed, and they are not incompatible with the more purely cultural notion of an attachment to the myth of *translatio imperii*. When
Robert Motherwell pointed out that New York occupied a Mediterranean latitude, one closer to Rome than to the cities of North-
ern Europe, he was no doubt asserting, even on an unconscious

---

*For an earlier treatment of *translatio imperii* in the context of American art, see
Bann 1976.

level, the connection between New York and the traditional centers of classical civilization. But he was also drawing attention, on a primary level, to the kinship that affected the painter most immediately: a question of light.

Without any doubt, light has also been important to Twombly in his choice of abode: Roland Barthes celebrated the fact when he described the achievement of Twombly's paintings as "a kind of Mediterranean effect" (*Cy Twombly* 1979: 17). But the attraction to Rome—what I have called the centripetal movement to the metropolis—also has its cultural significance, and this should not be minimized. Following the simple sequence of Twombly's titles from the 1950's to the present day, one can detect the gradual irradiation of themes and motifs from the classical world. Titles that observe the conventions of the New York School, in drawing attention to space and movement through congenial metaphor (*Free Wheeler, Panorama*) or settling for a deadpan self-reflexivity (*Criticism, Untitled*), are overhauled by specific iconographic references: *School of Fontainebleau, Woodland Glade* (*To Poussin*), *The Italians*, and *Hyperion* (*To Keats*) all appear within the years 1960 to 1962. By using these titles, which are often inscribed together with other congenial texts on the paintings themselves, Twombly does not, however, imply any traditional iconographic coding. The titles are paradigmatic, forming a series of like terms unified by a system. And the system is simply that of the classical heritage, to which the expatriate artist egregiously lays claim.

Yet I would not want to overemphasize this act of reclamation, which Twombly performed in his migration from New York to Rome. That is to say, I would not wish to portray it as a mere reclamation of ancestral wealth, as if the American artist had only to make a landfall in the Old World for its treasures to be immediately available to him. What has become perceptible over 30 years or so—and what will form the main argument of this essay—is the fact that Twombly performs a dialectical movement: from New York to the original metropolis, Rome, but also from Rome to the other face of the Mediterranean world, from West to East. This is perhaps most clearly indicated in the titling of the remarkable *Anabasis* series of 1983, which alludes to the ill-fated Greek expedition to Persia in the fourth century B.C. One of the large drawings exhibited with the series bears the word "LYCIAN," which also serves as its title, and alludes to unmistakably to the god Apollo, for whom this term served as an epithet. If Apollo is the god of the arts, the classical divinity *par excellence*, his various epithets draw attention to the different states into which he is transformed by a kind of geopolitical drag. The Hyperborean Apollo, celebrated by Nietzsche and Walter Pater, brings to the inhabitants of the far North the beauties, and also the hidden violence, of the arts. The Lycian Apollo, worshiped as such in Cyrene (the modern Libya), is the divinity who refused the demeaning sacrifice of the Babylonian Clinis and turned him into a black crow; he is also the divinity to whom wolves were sacrificed.* In Twombly's *Lycian (Drawing)*, the straying lines of blue, red, and purple are overtaken by a flush of gray oils, as if the artist were acknowledging the sterner side of the classical god in his Eastern manifestation.

It is appropriate that, if the titling of this work depends upon the recognition of Apollo's epithet and his altered identity, any further discussion of it should attempt to capture, in language, the powerful material effects of Twombly's painterly technique. The title *Lycian (Drawing)* is infinitely commutable—it can become a caption in a catalogue, for instance, or the text for an adjacent label in an art gallery. But the words "LYCIAN" and "(drawing)," as they are found in the top section of the work, belong to the same system of graphic traces as the remaining sections of the work: the "Y" and the "A" of "LYCIAN," in particular, are exuberant inscriptions, exceeding their brief as mere letter forms, while the upward-sloping, cursive character of the written text as a whole is mimed by the red, blue, and purple lines advancing under their cloak of gray.

Roland Barthes, who has written memorably on Twombly's works, has also commented in another connection on what he calls "the double origin of painting." The passage that follows seems exactly appropriate to Twombly's characteristic style, not only because it points to a duality pervading his painterly approach at all levels, but also because it indicates the considerable rhetorical cogency that has been necessary to overcome this duality in the appearance of the finished work. Barthes writes:

*A semantic confusion is possible here. The Lycian Apollo derives his epithet from Lycia, an area in southwest Asia Minor, but he is also known as "Lycaeus," a term derived from the Greek word for wolf, and has as one of his functions that of protecting against wolves.

Let us imagine out of any historical context a double origin of painting. The first origin would be in writing, the tracing of future signs, the exercise of the point (of the brush, the lead pencil, the engraver's tool, of what hollows out and makes stripes—even if it be with the artifice of a line laid down in color). The second would be in *cuisine*, that is to say any practice that aims at transforming matter across the whole scale of its circumstances, by multiple operations like tenderizing, thickening, fluid-ifying, granulation, lubrification, producing what is called in gastronomy the coated, the liaised, the velvety, the creamy, the crunchy, etc. Freud also sets up an opposition between sculpture—*via di livare*—and painting—*via di porre*—but the opposition can be found in painting alone: one between the incision (the "stroke") and the unction (the "coated").   (Barthes 1982: 194; my translation)

If I pause and take stock at this stage in my essay on Twombly, this is because the introduction of Barthes's splendid text carries the argument to a further stage and at the same time calls its fundamental assumptions into question. Right from the start, I signaled the point that this would be an exercise in flawed hermeneutics, without the customary satisfaction of a fit between the writer's search for meaning and the ready accessibility of the works under discussion. Nonetheless, the strategy I have followed up to this juncture implies a logical and coherent progression in the search for meaning: it is simply that I have endeavored to replace the customary fixed points with a dynamic topology of relations. Twombly's iconography, I have suggested, eschews the direct correlations of the Renaissance tradition. His geographical context, the "school" to which he belongs, is to be understood not as a fixed affiliation (Paris, New York) but as an inclination in a particular direction (from New York to Rome), which has subsequently developed a second, alternative focus (from West to East, from Rome to the extremities of the classical world). Yet, once these structures have been set up, the quest inevitably converges on an individual work, in this case *Lycian (Drawing)*. Here there is ample evidence of Twombly's indirectness, of his tangential approach to iconography. Apollo is not mentioned in the title, or represented in the work. It therefore requires a real effort of self-assertion for the critic to detect the god under the cover of the epithet; he must enter the thicket of mythological references in order to extract a clear meaning, which is then, of course, belied by the elliptical nature of the work itself. Apollo, whether Hyperborean or Lycian, is far from his native Greece, and thus takes on a menacing disguise. Twombly's work is also in disguise: whatever reference may be implicit, the serene god of classical beauty and balanced harmony is replaced by a pulsing intimation of feverish dread.

In response to this emotional effect, and under the intolerable pressure of the need to find words to encompass it, the critic of a few paragraphs back is drawn to the formulation of a myth of the origins of painting, as Barthes provides it. The language that Barthes uses seems extraordinarily appropriate to the character of the signs that Twombly employs. The pencil makes its incisive strokes, recording dates and a signature that are part of the work's apparatus of authentication, as well as part of its visual field. The word (title) "LYCIAN" is traced, in part, with one of those colored lines that Barthes credits to "artifice" in their straining toward the painterly condition. Elsewhere, in the lower zone of the work, the mass of oil painting, harmonizing with the thickened lines of crayon, establishes a unified textural effect, a homogeneous surface, a phenomenon of *cuisine*.

Yet, in the last resort, Barthes's notion of the dual origin of painting "out of any historical context" does not adequately account for the power exhibited by Twombly's work. The analytic exercise that divides the incisive stroke from the thickened mass is highly valuable if we are to understand why these works come across quite unequivocally as finished paintings—even though, in the case of *Lycian (Drawing)*, the very title suggests that we are looking simply at a sketch. They come across as paintings not because of any concern for the overall homogeneity of the painted surface (even in Twombly's officially designated paintings, the area of white canvas is often considerable), but because they create an equilibrium out of the two opposed types of marks that Barthes correctly identifies. They are *complete* because of this finely achieved balance. At the same time, it is not enough to view them simply as exercises in the counterpointing of different qualities of mark. The rhetorical cogency that I identified goes beyond these categories. Indeed, it is an inescapable feature of Twombly's paintings that we should, after paying due attention to the autoreferential dimension indicated in Barthes's distinction, set out once again on a quest for meaning. This has to be done, even if the expectation of finding any definitive meaning is foreclosed from the start.

Not only is Lycian (Drawing) assigned, by virtue of its title and its inscription, to classical mythology; it is also assigned, by the signature and the two juxtaposed dates accompanying it, to the biography of the artist. "Sept. 17. 82" is given in smaller writing, immediately after the signature, while "Aug. 15. 83" appears above, assimilating the signature to a later stage in the completion of the work. This intersection between mythology and biography seems to me to be at the center of Twombly's project as an artist. Yet to understand why this should be so, we need to investigate more closely the possible investments of the contemporary artist in classical myth. In Lévi-Strauss's celebrated definition, myth is a form of speech. But it is a form of speech precisely for those societies that mediate their knowledge of the surrounding world through collective representations that take the form of stories. The individual artist's access to mythology, at a historical stage when that mythology has ceased to be an interpretive tool for the whole society, is bound to be a very different one.

This distinction between a view of myth as a transsubjective medium that, as it were, permeates the world and the work, and a view that foregrounds the access of the individual subject is reflected in my own earlier writings on Cy Twombly. In connection with his Pan series (1980), I have invoked not the "writerly" Barthes quoted earlier but the Barthes of High Structuralism who found congenial company in Hegel, when he spoke of the ancient Greeks' discovering in the natural world "an immense frisson of meaning, to which he gave the name of a god, Pan" (Barthes 1966: 1). But for his subsequent Anabasis series (1983), I have tried to find a point of entry that would clarify the semantic preconditions of the mythic reference and the artist's own investment in myth. Where is the psychological subject in the Anabasis series? The answer seems to lie in a kind of cryptographic elucidation of the signifiers that Twombly has employed, both implicitly and explicitly. We see the "X" of Xenophon (author of the Greek Anabasis) being transformed into an inscription that is also the scythed wheel of a chariot. At the same time, we know that the Anabasis of Xenophon—author and also major participant in the military campaign

he describes—was also the *Anabasis of Cyrus*: it records the unsuc-
cessful campaign of the satrap of Lydia to seize and appropriate the
Persian throne. Out of the inscribed "X"s there comes the death-
dealing scythed wheel; out of the epic account of Xenophon, the
defeat and death of Cyrus.*

Although I have presented this argument in a necessarily con-
tracted form, it should be obvious that the mythic reference is
being used in quite a different way from the traditional iconographic model, or indeed from the generalized semantic model that
I applied to the *Pan* series. Twombly does not simply encode a
meaning, picking the appropriate term out of a dictionary of par-
ticularized images (the situation implied, in post-Renaissance art,
by the existence of repertoires such as Cesare Ripa's *Iconologia*). He
enacts, through the inscription and metamorphosis of the letter, a
process of fusion between the psychological subject (the author)
and the mythological subject (the "hero"). Derrida has long since
pointed the way to what he calls a "psychoanalytic graphology,"
which would develop from the pioneering work of Melanie Klein
on "the forms of signs, even within phonetic writing, the cathexes
of gestures, and of movements, of letters, lines, points, the elements of the writing apparatus (instrument, surface, substance,
etc.)" (Derrida 1978: 231). Twombly is one of the contemporary
artists who make us most aware of the potential value of such a
study. But he also shows how the graphic and painterly practice
that it would attempt to describe is not harnessed to a banal ethos of
self-expression. As the *Anabasis* series shows, Twombly uses graphology, and history, to stage both the assumption of identity
(Cy/Cyrus) and its loss (the scythed wheel, the death of Cyrus) in
the constructed sequences of the work.

Doubtless the *Anabasis* series is unusual, even in Twombly's
work, for the dense packing of meanings that has been discussed
here. But it is not an isolated example. In the years when *Anabasis*
was created and in the following years, Twombly ventured into at
least two more sequences that extend and confirm the direction
sketched out in the foregoing paragraphs, without in any way
closing off the possibilities of further development. *Wilder Shores of
Love*, the title of two paintings from 1985, is also the title of this

*For an account of the *Anabasis* series that puts it in the context of the
Narcissus myth, see Bann 1989.

essay, and will introduce my closing speculations on the loss and retrieval of meaning in Twombly's art, considered as a hermeneutic text. *Hero and Leander*, the title both of a sequence of three large paintings dating from 1981–84 and of a single, even larger work inscribed "To Christopher Marlowe," dating from 1984–85, initiates a quest that seems closely parallel to that of the *Anabasis* series.

First of all, it is worth referring once again to what I called, at the very beginning of this essay, the geopolitical logic of Twombly's art. This logic pertains not only to his having chosen Rome, as opposed to New York, in the formative stages of his career, but also to a gathering impulse to investigate the Eastern periphery for which Greece and Rome supplied a center: to cultivate the Lycian Apollo rather than the Apollo worshiped in Delphi. The *Anabasis* series, of course, implies a mythic narrative that perfectly subsumes this quest: the small Greek army of mercenaries travels eastward and encounters the menace of Persian power, from which they eventually and painfully extricate themselves. *Hero and Leander* is no less significant. The myth refers to a young man of Abydos, Leander, who was in love with a priestess of Aphrodite named Hero, who lived at Sestos, a town on the other side of the Hellespont. Each night Leander swam the Hellespont in order to meet Hero, until, on one occasion, the lamp that Hero lit to guide him was blown out by the wind. Leander drowned, unable to find the shore. (Hero subsequently followed him to her death.) As the Hellespont is the traditional dividing line between Europe and Asia, Leander's amorous quest takes place at the frontier between West and East: in a sense, he dies for love at the same time that he transgresses a limit separating the metropolitan culture from its troubling other side.

That this cultural dimension should be indicated, however lightly, in Twombly's title, is already a reason for stressing Twombly's ineradicable differences from the abstract expressionist movement, and from their particular view of the modernist inheritance. In their scale and in their facture, the works of the *Hero and Leander* series obviously recall the *Nymphéas*, completed at Giverny by Monet, which were rightly regarded by Clement Greenberg as a significant precedent for abstract expressionism. But if Monet is inevitably suggested by the way in which Twombly dissolves purple foci within a liquid movement of pigments (just as Turner is evoked by the stormy blue vortex of the single work that stands apart), these are simply additional, intertextual references in a structure that includes the textuality of the title, not to mention the dedication to Christopher Marlowe and the unattributed quotation that is framed as a caption to the series of three: "He's gone / up bubbles / all his amorous breath." There are good reasons, if we look at Twombly's early training, for his invocation of poetry in close connection with his painting. Marcelin Pleynet has indeed outlined with great persuasiveness the influence that his time at the interdisciplinary Black Mountain College would have had upon him, from a very early stage (see Pleynet 1977). But, on a quite different level, this sedulous citation of poets and their texts can be seen as a strategy for marking Twombly's disaffection with any notion of pure, exclusive visuality. These paintings are the record of an engagement between the painter and his canvas, certainly. But they are also the record of an artist's engagement with the infinitely subtle membrane of meaning that surrounds and permeates a cultural world.

But what of the specific meanings that are invited by the title, *Hero and Leander*, as well as by the framed caption and the dedication to Marlowe? Turner uses the myth of Hero and Leander, in his painting of 1837, to justify the representation of a storm at sea, as well as to permit the recording of conflicting light sources and shadows with a skill that the young John Ruskin acclaimed as "sorcery" (Ruskin 1903, 1: 187). For Twombly, we may imagine, it is the striving and sinking of Leander, his victory and his loss, that supplies a psychological kernel no less crucial than the fate of Cyrus in the *Anabasis* series. The caption—"He's gone / up bubbles / all his amorous breath"—implies a radical metamorphosis of the heroic body. In the first work of the tripartite series, the inscribed word "Leandro" is borne up by the wave like a jaunty surfer. In the second work, the surf has subsided, leaving a flush or two of purplish pigment and the veiled signature "C.T." in the place "Leandro" occupied. In the final painting of the series, placed next to the caption, finer streaks of purple (they are presumably the traces of the crayon specified in the description of the work) hardly infringe an aqueous calm.

The source of this caption is not given, and it has not proved possible to locate it. Certainly it does not occur in Marlowe's *Hero and Leander*, which must be the text that accounts for the dedication of the work standing apart from the threefold series. But Marlowe's poem may be seen, nevertheless, as offering a possible guide to the meaning of the whole group of paintings. For its true subject matter is not the romance of the successful lover, cruelly struck down in the interval of his amorous conquests. Marlowe specifically tells us that Hero withheld her maidenhead:

> No marvel, then, though Hero would not yield
> So soon to part from that she dearly held.
> Jewels being lost are found again, this never,
> 'Tis lost but once, and once lost, lost for ever.
>
> (Marlowe 1968: 30)

The erotic interest of the poem is thus at least in part displaced from the dalliance of Hero and Leander on shore to the romance of Neptune, the sea god, with the protesting Leander, as he struggles against the all-embracing medium:

> The god put Helle's bracelet on his arm,
> And swore the sea should never do him harm.
> He clapp'd his plump cheeks, with his tresses play'd,
> And smiling wantonly, his love bewray'd.
> He watch'd his arms, and as they open'd wide
> At every stroke, betwixt them would he slide
> And steal a kiss, and then run out and dance,
> And as he turn'd, cast many a lustful glance,
> And threw him gaudy toys to please his eye,
> And dive into the water, and there pry
> Upon his breast, his thighs, and every limb,
> And up again, and close beside him swim,
> And talk of love.
>
> (Marlowe 1968: 34–35)

Without dismissing the suggestions of transgressive sexuality (which lead poor Leander to cry out, "I am no woman, I"), we can certainly see the relevance of Leander's love affair with the sea to the issues of meaning and process that have been under consideration here. Twombly's model is not the erotic consummation—the maidenhead found and lost forever in the very moment of capture—but a passionate engagement of the body with the states of fluidity that both encompass it erotically and in the end overwhelm

Cy Twombly, Untitled (12.8.81–7.11.83), pencil and pastel on paper, 100 × 70 cm (Courtesy Mayor Gallery, London)

it, resulting in death. Transposing this distinction into more accessible terms, we might say that it betokens the androgynous fantasy of a body both desiring and desired, sinking below the surface of the canvas as Twombly's signature appears to do, and seeking to incorporate the final state of its own negation, provided that this is compensated by the reparative vision of the intact picture plane. Where the *Anabasis* series returns from its extra-European excursion to the classical idyll of the Virgilian scene (SYLVAE),* the tri-partite *Hero and Leander* series dispenses, in the end, with the sea as active, lively participant (the lustful Neptune), and settles for the aqueous screen: as with Monet (in Pleynet's estimation), the irides-cent surface becomes a source of nurture, a maternal prospect.

To read the *Hero and Leander* pictures in terms of the myth of androgyny is hardly as speculative as it may seem. Grouped with the *Anabasis* series, and contained in the same catalogue, are two works inscribed and titled "NIKE ANDROGYNE," a reference to the traditional Greek "Victory" figure in its androgynous manifesta-tion.† A further work, *Victory* (1984), which uses a folded collage element perhaps to indicate the wings of the figure, bears in its lower section the more explicit text "Victory over man." It is evidently in weaving together these slight, tantalizing indications that we begin to construct a meaning for Twombly's art as a whole. Yet is this anything more than a hermeneutic quest that draws attention to its own ill-foundedness? Does the viewer, and critic, who launches himself (as I have done) into elaborate parallels and subsidiary myths, all on the strength of these scrawled words, exhibit anything more than his own desire to know?

To argue that Twombly himself anticipates this moment of self-questioning, that his straying signs are designedly poised on the edge between meaning and meaninglessness, is perhaps to presup-pose an even more impressive authorial control than that of the classic author. Yet it is not my intention to credit him with this godlike authority over the alternating current of sense. He himself, I would argue, is caught up in the quest that the critic, gleaning in the same field, tries to make appear more directed and more co-herent. The proof is that Twombly's references become, all the time, more extreme in their striving for that other place that is the correlative both to the centripetal Roman world and to the values of rationality associated with it. This leads me to the pair of paint-ings dating from 1985 that came after the *Hero and Leander* sequence

*The words "Virgilian views" occur in the first two works of the *Anabasis* series, and "SYLVAE" in the first three, although in the third case it is almost effaced. While it is likely that these Virgilian references belong to the first dates in the two-stage process which these works record, the persistence of the earlier words does, of course, temper the violence of the Anabasis motif.

†It does not appear that Twombly has picked a particular statue or personifica-tion in his reference; his idea is, however, self-evident.

in Twombly's major exhibition of 1987/88 and, but for one work (*Untitled*), closed the retrospective series. The pair bears the title that has also been given to this essay: *Wilder Shores of Love*.

It would exhibit my own desire to know to an unconscionable degree if I were to retrace the various steps in my quest to find the origin of this title, which is also, of course, inscribed across both of the paintings. Success came quite by chance when I found a recent edition of Lesley Blanch's book of the same title in a Paris bookshop. But I was convinced for a time that the phrase itself— "Wilder Shores of Love"—was a quotation (colleagues assured me that it came from Byron, but *Don Juan* did not respond to the suggestion). It was, in fact, a quotation drawn from Lesley Blanch's own text. Of one of the four remarkable women whose careers are described in her book, Jane Digby el Mezrab, she writes: "She was an Amazon. Her whole life was spent riding at breakneck speed towards the wilder shores of love" (Blanch 1987: 134). The Byronic lure is not, however, irrelevant. Blanch's heroines all fulfill a mythic movement from West to East, the prototypes for which can be found in the Romantic movement and in individual sagas like Byron's heroic death in the cause of Greek independence.

Jane Digby el Mezrab is not the least interesting of these heroines. The bald biographical details of her life are themselves so evocative that they seem to break out of the preconstrained format. Born in 1807, the daughter of Admiral Sir Henry Digby, Jane was a member of a junior branch of the ancient family, originally from Coleshill in Warwickshire, which had obtained the grant of Sherborne Castle from the Crown in the early seventeenth century, and continued to live in the castle, an exquisite "H"-shaped country house originally built as a memorial to Prince Henry, eldest son of James I. The Digbys had an ostrich as one of their armorial supporters, and Lesley Blanch is willing to speculate on the possible effect of this exotic bird on the young girl's imagination, though she is less skeptical about the likely influence of her ancestor, the poet Sir Kenelm Digby, with his proven oriental connections (Blanch 1987: 136).

Jane Digby's successive marriages record a slow but ineluctable progress from unexceptionable respectability to an "other side" that can hardly be spoken of. In 1814, she married Edward, first earl of Ellenborough, later to be governor general of India. He obtained a divorce from her in 1830, after a brief separation, on the grounds of her adultery with Felix, Prince Schwartzenberg, then secretary of the Austrian Embassy. She did not marry Prince Schwartzenberg, but in 1832, after a period as the mistress of King Ludwig of Bavaria, she married the Bavarian nobleman Baron Venningen. Her next marriage (the intervening adventures would take too long to recount) was to Hadji-Petros, a general in the Greek army; after this she went to live with the Bedouin tribe that gave her the name "El Mezrab," and married (in the words of the official biography) "a Bedouin Arab called Midjouel" (Blanch 1987: 168ff, transliterates the name as "Medjuel").

How does this briefly evoked career, which can only be a kind of embroidery upon the splendid title of Blanch's book, impinge upon our experience of the two paintings by Twombly that bear the same title—and are inscribed with the words of it, gushing red across a neutral white field? There is, in these two works, a boisterous, almost cheeky assertion of the untutored *graffiti* over any meanings that might be derived from them, especially in the first of the series, where two ejaculating penises mimic the scrawling line of the letter forms. Yet Jane Digby is the Amazon, the Nike Androgyne, the embodiment of a quest that leads ever eastward, to the point where the naming protocols of the West become inoperative. Insofar as she may be said to serve, like Leander in the earlier sequence, as a vicarious body, buffeted by the liquid mass of pigments, she is an index of Twombly's involvement, but in a deferred, enigmatic fashion. Signs stray, and the interpreter is often several steps behind.

EMBODIMENT AND THE LIMITS OF SIGNIFICATION

PAUL ZUMTHOR

Body and Performance

A topic such as this makes it necessary to closely examine a few key terms whose definitions remain problematic despite statements to the contrary. This is true for the term "performance" as well as for terms like "work," "text," and "forms." The following investigation will concentrate primarily on these.

I

For the moment I will accept the definition of "performance" offered by Dell Hymes (1975). Hymes chooses a comparatively narrow sociolinguistic perspective. The justification for this is not to be questioned. We must expand this definition, however, and finally, as we will see, shift its main focus.

First we must clarify the relationship between the performance of a poetic utterance and its reception. In doing so, we maintain the following:

On the one hand, "reception" denotes a process of historical understanding; that is to say, it contains the idea of temporal expansion. This duration might be interminably long; in any case, it becomes the real existence of a text or an utterance within a community of readers or listeners. In this sense, the reception of a text or utterance measures its longevity, that is, the temporal, spatial, and social sphere in which it is effective. This is so self-evident that investigations into these areas are often time-specific, for example, "The Reception of Shakespeare in Nineteenth Century France" and so on.

On the other hand, "performance" is an anthropological term that relates to the conditions of presentation and experience. It denotes a communicative action as such (see Hymes 1975). It therefore refers to a point in time that is experienced as the present and to the concrete presence of participants who are directly included in the action. To the degree that the critic is practically forced to emphasize this viewpoint, it becomes possible to say that performance lies outside the flow of time. It actualizes more or less numerous, more or less clearly imagined possibilities. In this sense, performance alone realizes the "concretization" of which different critics speak concerning reception.

It could be said that performance is a moment of reception, a privileged point in time in which a text is actually experienced. In some cases, reception limits itself to performance. This is true in normal pragmatic discourses. Perhaps the literary text, in contrast to all others, is also characterized by the fact that it sets up a strong contrast between reception and performance. This contrast becomes more important the longer the reception lasts.

The technologies of the twentieth century have confused the outline that has been sketched so far. The auditive and audiovisual media from the record to the television have dramatically changed the conditions of performance. They have not negatively affected the nature of performance itself, however (see Zumthor 1983; 1985: 4–17; 1987a). I would like to call to mind at this point that "medialization" allows a message to be repeated in a sense that is not identical to the written text, but is certainly analogous. Medialization, through its procedure, preserves a kind of extratemporal presence of the message. It strengthens or blurs some of the physical aspects of performance, above all those that have to do with the "perceptibility" of performance. But it allows an important part to continue: the employment of various sensual stimuli and experiences in the transmission of a message.

II

These kinds of considerations have brought me to introduce a basic differentiation between "text" and "work." I would like to define it in the following, concise manner:

On the one hand, text is a unified linguistic sequence whose overall meaning cannot be reduced to the sum of particular effects of meaning evoked by the sequential parts of the text.

On the other hand, work is what is poetically communicated (text, sounds, rhythms, optical elements). The term includes the totality of performance characteristics.

In order to make this even more precise, I use the term "poem," denoting the text and in some cases the melody of a work but ignoring other performance factors.

Text is and remains readable. Works are simultaneously hearable and visible. Performance functionally employs all elements that are able to carry and to strengthen the work's character and that are suited to validate its authority and its persuasive power. Performance even uses silence and motivates it.

I have, for my part, used these terms one after another in order to describe ethnological conditions (as in my work on oral poetry) and, more recently, medieval conditions. I nevertheless believe that the use of these terms can be expanded, providing they are given the proper nuances.

The totality of sensual experiences initiated by a work fall into two categories according to whether they are dominated by hearing or sight. Sight produces differing cognitive processes depending on whether it perceives a real, more or less complex situation completely or concentrates on a message encoded in writing.

If we ignore two cases that don't concern us here—an optic perception of a real situation that is not related to the hearing of an articulated message (this is especially true of pantomime), and a hearing that accompanies a written message and thereby doubles it—then the following possibilities present themselves:

1. A situation is seen and heard as a whole. If this occurs with direct perception, then a physical presence is involved that could be called "perceptibility" (tactileness). If the seeing is conveyed by a television screen or a film, then the effect of perceptibility is weakened or even nullified, without, of course, the loss of the actual performance itself.

2. Hearing alone of necessity requires some medialization, for example, by the record. Through this, perceptibility is reduced or disappears completely.

3. Reading, that is, only seeing a message, generally remains bound to a weak or unclear experience of the "reading situation,"

that is, to temporal, spatial, and mood elements. Nevertheless, different modalities of reading can be described more precisely: (a) Reading can be fashioned as an audible address, as a relationship between the reader and the listener; (b) An individual reader can read for himself or for his own needs. He will normally read either silently or aloud. In the second situation, minimal muscle movement comes into play. This procedure can be found in cases of underdeveloped literacy, in cultural and religious traditions, and generally in the Third World. We also know that this was the normal way of reading in the West up until the fifteenth and sixteenth centuries.

These differentiations demonstrate that performance cannot be spoken of in a completely unambivalent manner. It becomes necessary to distinguish the performance itself—the kind that concerns the ethnologist in purely oral situations—from a whole series of realizations that are less and less clearly defined and more and more distant from the model:

On the one hand, we experience the actual, complete performance when the situation can be heard and seen as a whole.

On the other hand, public delivery, what is mediated, "medialized" hearing and seeing, then hearing alone (the order could be changed based on various circumstances), these all mark stages of a progressive but never completed weakening of performance. Solitary, nonarticulated reading exhibits the weakest, almost nonexistent level of performance.

This distinction can never completely reverse the original situation, of course (with the exception, perhaps, of possibilities that would be difficult to imagine).

III

The question now arises, in what does the variable element consist that gives this spectrum of performance a coherency as well as a variety of possibilities? The answer, unavoidably, is that the variable consists in the employment of physical energies. This employment is most obviously visible in the actual performance itself. At the same time, it should not be forgotten that the use of the body plays a reduced role in any textual experience.

I will again take up a differentiation that I have used in my more recent work, to include the conference on style (see Gumbrecht and Pfeiffer 1986). There are two series of forms through which the work originates. One of these series is made up of linguistic forms whose totality equals the text, and the other comprises, somewhat summarily, what I have called sociocorporeal forms. These are all nontextual parts connected to the corporeality of the participants and their social existence as members of a group and as individuals within that group.

The work itself originates in the link between textual and sociocorporeal conditions. Both are, in their own way, formalized products of an aesthetic. Tensions arise between the two possibilities of realization. The textual element is predominant in the written message, the sociocorporeal in the oral. The use of the voice almost always effects an easing of linguistic imperatives. This employment is characterized by a "wild" knowledge that escapes from the ability to speak even in situations of concrete complexity and intense personal relationships. The orally produced text, more so than the written, resists, to the extent that it relies on a physical voice, any perception that might sever it from its social function, from its place within a real community, from an acknowledged tradition, and from the circumstances in which it is heard.

The written text, the object of solitary study, implies a special effect of "displaced" communication brought about by the distance of times and the contexts of production and reception. This does not happen to the orally recited poem. As an oral exclamation, it rests on the fiction of immediacy. Even if it is heard long after its conception, it achieves some kind of immediate existence through hearing. From this the specific authority is derived that is inherent in the text as performance. The written describes, the recited proves by showing.

The oppositions just discussed are not absolute. They show their greatest effect when a work that is written and intended to be read is compared with a work that comes from a purely oral tradition. If we concern ourselves with works that are to be recited but are only handed down in written form, then we must assume that both dimensions of effect are simultaneously present in the text. The uniqueness of the work is strongly reliant on whether it was originally intended as a written or as a performative exclamation.

Only sound and physical presence, only the play of the voice and mimicry, can realize what was once written. Whatever it may consist in, performance confronts the listener or the observer with a text that, as long as it is made possible by this performance, knows neither corruptions nor emendations by the "author." Even if the text was created over a long period of writing, it stands on its own as something that is performed and staged. The "poetic" art for whoever delivers the text consists in embodying this immediacy, in expressing it in his own form of delivery. Even the simple reading out loud of a written text necessitates a special eloquence, a spoken manner that is effortless, an impressive power of suggestion, and a thoroughly dominant rhythm. The listener must follow; he cannot look back. The message must be immediate, whatever its desired effect. Language does not necessarily gain a clear, transparent meaning under these circumstances. Rather, it gains a transparency of its own linguistic existence. Voice and intellect yield truth; they must convince or persuade. Only bit by bit do sentences take on the reciprocal relationship that the voice grants them. The relationship of which the work is made up is thus created by the body. When a written text becomes voice, it changes fundamentally as long as hearing and linguistic-corporeal presence continue. Beyond the objects and meanings to which it refers, the spoken word points to the indescribable. Speaking is not simply the executor of the linguistic system. It not only fails to confirm the system's precepts completely but, in its entire physicality, often contradicts these, to our surprise and entertainment.

The body makes me aware of the spoken word contained in the poetic text by representing it in the scenic sense of the word. This results in a dual structure. The spoken word presumes to be a narration but simultaneously becomes a commentary on the narration in the sound of the voice and movement of the body, both bestowing expression. Narration and interpretation coexist in the work, yet each play its own independent game. A special kind of truthfulness, requiring trust and participation, flows from the relationship the listener perceives between these two. What we call "diction" forms a rhetoric of voice and gesture on the lips of the speaker by which he situates the poetic text as well as himself in the communicative continuum of his listeners.

IV

The effect that this produces is all the stronger, the better the voice sounds. In the intermediate spaces of the linguistic system, the desire to free oneself from its limits and to lose oneself in the wealth of its pure immediacy manifests itself. Perhaps the situation in which the text, intended as oral, naturally finds itself in the collective memory increases the force of this desire. Such a text is not isolated or disconnected from plot references but is destined, like the physical games in which it takes part, for play. Thus it offers, like any play, entertainment that comes from repetition and similarity. Like any play, the oral text becomes art under the spell of an emotional connection that is uncovered by performance and to which all energies of the living work strive to return. To some extent this involves a place where the effective sphere of "fantasmatic function" (Gilbert Durand) expands itself. There is also to some extent a concrete, localized place where words unfold and to which words in some part entrust the order of speech. I do not doubt that this is the main cause for a striking, oft-named characteristic of medieval texts: their inability to express the description of living things or objects other than by a linguistic enumeration void of any perspective.

The point here is not representation or the refusal to represent but presence. Every presence provokes a break with the preceding absence. This break creates a special rhythm in collective duration and in the history of individuals. Through the effects of repetition and interruption produced in time, presence grants a measure that can be compared to the "time of the Church" (Jacques Le Goff). For this reason, certain cultures, most certainly that of the European Middle Ages, possess those sacred connotations that are inscribed in the universal perspective of the *musica* of cosmic cycles. It is well-known that the resurgent Boethius tradition at the beginning of the twelfth century considered music to be a transcendental category manifest in the harmony of the created rhythms and in the perceived proportion of numbers. This harmony is concrete. It arises from the movement of visible things, from the body of mankind itself, whose rhythms and oscillations are the measure of all things (see Zumthor 1987b: 188), and from the "consonance" of sounds, movements, and modulations. Herein lies the beauty of the world. It stimulates and moves through the senses, that is to say, through the indivisible unity of meaning and sensual perception. The Middle Ages offer an especially favorable, but by no means all-inclusive, observation platform. Certain claims of its scholastics reveal a universal value. Hugh of Saint-Victor discusses works of art in relationship to the pleasure of the eye, but also with regard to hearing, smell, taste, touch, and above all the "cheerfulness" of melodious sounds. Hearing seemed to be the most noble sense for the thinkers of that time. Rudolf of Saint-Trond defines *harmonia* simply as a sounding together of voices. Guido d'Arezzo claims that the singer recites what *musica* composes—the rhythm of the universe (see de Bruyne 1946, vol. 2, chap. 3).

V

Performance is, in this sense, play. It is, if we follow the definitions of anthropologists, psychiatrists, or philosophers from Buytendijk and Huizinga to Schechner, Schumann, and Fink, a mirror, a doubling split between action and actor. Beyond an intentional distance often marked by regulated signals, the participants reciprocally observe their play, they enjoy a play that is free of normal sanctions. The latent threat of reality disappears for the short duration of the play. The entanglements of the world of experience become disentangled, and their elements are formed according to the needs of the imagination.

The voice is obviously the most important instrument of poetic play, but it is also the object of this play. From this comes the use of singing and scanned declamation by performers in many cultures—a music of voices that is, for the audience, inseparably linked to the idea of poetry. Spoken declamation is also probably conceived of in this way. Having become music, the poetic voice raises itself from the undifferentiated flow of noises and words. It becomes an event.

The voice is functionally linked to gesture. Like the voice, gesture projects the body into the space of performance, attempts to conquer this and to saturate it with its movement. The spoken word does not exist, like the written, simply in a verbal context. It necessarily belongs in the course of an existential situation that changes it in some way and whose totality is brought into play by the bodies of the participants. After twenty years of research and attempts to get to the roots of expressive spontaneity, Marcel Jousse believed that word and gesture were inseparable parts of a dynamic complex he called "verbomotoric." Working from entirely different premises, Brecht coined the term *gestus* in the framework of performative perspectives, in that an actor's bearing, a certain manner of speaking, and a critical attitude bind the speaker to what is said. This *gestus* operates on the border between two semiotic areas. It proves that bearing and voice modulation continuously define each other (Pavis 1981: 29–30).

Gesture, as the object of sense perception, initiates thermal and chemical processes with its movements. Gesture is accomplished within the context of formal elements (dimension, models) and dynamic moments that are consolidated into images of solidity and heaviness. Finally, gesture creates an environment that originates from the psychophysical reality of the body and its surroundings. The observer of gesture needs sight above all for interpretation but also in varying degrees hearing, smell, and touch. It would certainly be incorrect to relate every gesticular sequence to a linguistic sentence, to integrate every gesticular quality into a system of signs. Nonetheless, gesture can be sign to the extent that it is culturally defined or has a conventional meaning within a certain milieu. Ethnology teaches us to what extent these conventions can be effective within an artistic-performative use of gesture—from the singing, composing medicine men of West Africa (*griots*) to the Japanese *rakugo* storytellers.

The symbolic potential of gesture was perhaps developed on the basis of late forms that Jousse called the original *rhythmomimism*, grounded in cosmic correspondences, a kind of hieroglyphic gesture that was linked to the "expansive power of the word," of which Antonin Artaud speaks in connection with Asian theater. The language of gesture is also the language of breathing. It inhabits, as I. Fónagy says, "a kind of prelinguistic reserve." Fónagy talks in a more general linguistic sense of an "audible mimicry," because the sensual registers are still very integrated at this level (Fónagy 1983: 51–55, 205). The practice of medieval poetic recitation belongs to these behavioral forms. They represent at the same time the natural milieu. In the thirteenth century, Boncompagno stressed the significance of gesture for the interpretation of irony as a rhetorical figure (Goldin 1981: 59; cf. Zumthor 1987b: 269–95). It can be demonstrated, on the basis of saints' lives, that the mimicry of the singers was more important than the singing, because it directed the presentation more precisely and was also easier to command. The *Artes praedicandi* testify to the enticing power that this festivity had after 1200 on the new religious orders dedicated to preaching. This determined the nature of the texts themselves. Along with the voice, gesture helps to fix the meaning of the text. It might be what makes it possible to begin with.

HELMUT PFEIFFER

Girolamo Cardano and the Melancholy of Writing

> So there is really nothing special about me. And
> the artists, who have come from foreign lands to
> paint my portrait, were unable to find anything
> characteristic in me whereby I would have been
> easily recognizable in the portrait.
>
> —Cardano

I

In a famous letter to Francesco Vettori, dated December 12, 1513, Niccolò Machiavelli describes his daily routine, forced upon him by his political exile after the return of the Medici. Machiavelli also discusses his relationship with the texts of antiquity. His presentation is made all the more precise not only by the contrast with the banality of his life in the country but also through distance from the reality of political-diplomatic life. It was about such a life that Vettori had reported from Rome on November 23 and to which he had invited Machiavelli to return. Remarkably, Machiavelli's description of his reading is characterized by a massive metaphor of presence. The reader Machiavelli hears the author's voice in the letters of the text and finds himself in an imaginary conversation. The old texts are by no means silent witnesses whose written form requires an exercise in interpretation, but are living presences. Reading unexpectedly becomes an effortless conversation between past author and present reader. In the back and forth of question and answer, the motives of his conversational partners are transparent and Machiavelli's own situation is clear. The nightly relationship with these books and their authors has, in contrast to the reality of everyday and the constrictions of politics, the character of emphasis and of liberation from heteronomy—a condition also visible in the elaborate ritual with which Machiavelli celebrates his reading-become-conversation. The retreat into the study is an ecstasy of ceremony that frees the reading subject from all foreign constraints and allows him to become a theorist:

In the evening I return home and retreat to my study; in the entryway I take off my dirty and worn work clothes and put on clothes fit for court and the public. Suitably dressed, I enter into the ancient courtyards of ancient men, where I am lovingly greeted by them and partake of the nourishment that belongs to me alone and for which I was born; where I am not ashamed to speak with them and to ask them for the reasons behind their actions. And they answer me out of their humanity, and for four hours I am not aware of any boredom, I forget every care, I fear no poverty, death does not frighten me. I lose myself in them completely. (Machiavelli 1984: 426)

The imaginary presence of antiquity, apparent in the stylization of his own person and the surrounding space, does not constitute a peaceful enclave but represents the creative context of the *Principe*, about which Machiavelli finally tells Vettori. In the question of transferring knowledge, he specifically refers to Dante when he speaks of the relationship of antiquity's authors, freed from all contingency, to the development of the contemporary and practical science of the "new prince," as he presents the *Principe*.

Machiavelli's connection between antiquity and the present, which postulates the direct relevance of ancient knowledge for the new science of politics in the simulation of a conversational relationship, is remarkable because it runs contrary to a central experience of humanism and its *studia humanitatis*. When humanism, like philology, concerns itself with epochs and the historical distance to transmitted texts, it enables the historical classification of texts through stylistic analysis and reconstruction of historical context. On the other hand, it also suggests an anachronistic distance and the inability ever to catch up with what is transmitted. Since the fifteenth century, the "Renaissance" of antiquity had been haunted by the shadow of antiquity's irreconcilable distance (see, e.g., Greene 1982, 1986). In his dramatic staging of conversational ceremony, Machiavelli's insistent suggestion of conversational presence and of the unsurpassable relevance of ancient texts for present concerns brushes aside the modern awareness of "historical seclusion" (see Greene 1982: 4–27) and epochal individuality, so prominent in modern critical writings on ancient texts. If philology triumphed in the critical separation of true past claims from false, as in Lorenzo Valla's debunking of the Constantinian Donation, and in doing so placed these claims into an objective historical time frame, Roman antiquity was for Machiavelli again a dialogic partner for the present, providing answers to immediate questions. Written transmission bridges otherwise irremediable distances and at the same time provokes the imaginary restitution of oral presence.

Machiavelli's rituals of a pronounced presence of antiquity and its written texts point out problems that are unrecognized by the poetological discussions of the time. In the dramatic precision of their attempts at restitution, the rituals go beyond the framework that the rhetorical-poetological reflections of the Renaissance bring to light for the relationship of orality and writing. These reflections are ambivalent: on the one hand, in the poetological categorization of those genres of humanistic preference such as the letter or the dialogue, they must rely, directly or indirectly, on a perspective of orality; on the other hand, they repeatedly emphasize the primacy of writing and its order. Erasmus, for example, in his *De conscribendis epistolis*, relates the letter, whose humanistic-literary stylization is indebted to him as is no other form, to the model of a conversation among friends.[1] This may still be influenced by the Christian-Pauline reaction against the "dead" letter (as in 2 Cor. 3.6: "for the letter killeth, but the spirit giveth life"), but above all, Erasmus recommends the imitation of the normative characteristics of conversations: the mean between naturalness and the art of sociability, the free succession of different topics. With the subsequent poetological dignification of given text genres, the primacy of writing gained more and more ground. This is most apparent in the sixteenth century, in Speroni's and Tasso's poetics of the dialogue, which succeeded the upsurge of the humanistic dialogue. In Speroni's and Tasso's theories, the semblance of the spoken word is still required, but the dialogue is subject to dictates that reduce this semblance of orality to mere ornamentation while an underlying structural order is responsible for the force of the arguments. L. Mulas summarizes these theories as follows: "The dialogue is certainly not understood as a transcription of orality, even if it is written in prose, but rather as the result of the intelligent use of the rules of the three arts of the word: dialectic, rhetoric, and poetics" (Mulas 1982: 251). Something that was not problematic in the dialogues of the Renaissance, namely, its written form, is tied into a neat package by sixteenth-century poetics through the combination of rules of discourse and the ornamentation of orality.

II

Recourse to such a poetological set of rules was unavailable to the literary self-portrait of the Renaissance, even though its written form was to become a problem. If we accept M. Beaujour's suggestion of a strict division between (narrative) autobiography and (nonnarrative, rhetorical) self-portraiture, and if we understand the "invention of the self-portrait" as a "rediscovery of rhetoric," as a "playful mimesis of rhetorical procedures" (Beaujour 1980: 186–87), then we must raise the question, regardless of the possible blindness of texts for their own rhetorical processes, of the relationship of the self-portrait to oral speech and its usefulness. The skepticism concerning the "genre character" of the self-portrait is something Beaujour certainly shares when he portrays it as a genre without expectations and partially includes it with various text forms such as the essay or the meditation. Beaujour's thesis, applied to authors from Montaigne to Leiris, loses hardly any plausibility. It states that rhetoric, along with its method of collection and description, of the examination and pragmatic use of topics of the most varied discourses of knowledge, represents not only a tool but also the "structural model" of the self-portrait. On the other hand, the relationship of the self-portrait to the rhetorical norm of functionality and public usefulness is evident to Beaujour. The self-portrait reveals itself as a parasitic "variant of the procedures of the old rhetoric" (ibid., 10); the justification of rhetoric, its persuasiveness, and ability to convince conversational partners and listeners, are replaced, however, by reflection on the self. The self-portrait is therefore, even if its rhetorical matrix is not transparent, always burdened with a bad conscience, manifest in constant self-reflection. "The original sin of the self-portrait is to pervert expression, exchange, communication, and persuasion and at the same time to denounce this perversion" (ibid., 14). The self-portrait is *écrivaillerie coupable*, writing instead of speaking, reflection instead of effect, self-orientation instead of other-orientation.

Beaujour's analysis reveals a common denominator of the many forms of literary self-portraits. This denominator is reflected in their constant concern with themselves, both in form and theme, even when the Christian inculpation of godforsaken self-reflection, which Augustine helped make a part of the tradition of autobiography, plays no role. The problem of the self-portrait is not so much the violation of a dogma as its rhetorical-poetological exile. Not a part of the plan of poetics, it lives off the techniques of rhetoric in the collection and association of its material, but, in the transition from immediate social circulation of oral speech to written self-reflection, loses the justification of social functionality that made rhetoric legitimate in the first place.

It is not even necessary to pick up the actual texts of the *Essais* of Montaigne to see that the relationship of orality and writing, presence and distance, immediacy and transmission is one of their central aspects. It is sufficient to glance at the history of the reception of the *Essais*, where Montaigne's self-portrait has, since the seventeenth century, been associated to a remarkable degree with the (reading) experience of conversational speaking (see Brody 1982: 21–27). The reception of Montaigne, where it is more concerned with the form of the *Essais* and less with their philosophical or ideological implications, has one of its recurring moments in its experience of the semblance of orality, one could say, of a free-floating *effet d'oralité*. There can hardly be a better example of this than the remarks of E. Auerbach, who, in one of the few passages in his *Mimesis* that goes beyond philological text interpretation, notes the imaginary shift from reading to listening in a way that reads, because of its articulation of hermeneutic distance, as a reflective echo of what Machiavelli had told Francesco Vettori of his ceremonious association with the authors of antiquity: "I suspect that everyone who is familiar with Montaigne's work has had the same experience as I have: after I had read him for some time and had gained some familiarity with his style, I thought I could hear him speaking and could see his gestures. This is an experience that is very rare with older theoretical writers and probably non-existent to the same degree as with Montaigne" (Auerbach 1971:

276).[2] Deriving an option for speaking from this and from Montaigne's penchant for conversation, against which writing would always be a deficient mode, is still a current position (see, e.g., Jeanneret 1976: 80ff; Kritzman 1980: 100). Montaigne seems to say as much at the beginning of *De l'utile et de l'honneste*: "I speak to the paper just as I would to the next best person I might happen to meet" (Montaigne 1978: 790). This statement, however, was clearly suspected by Montaigne himself (and then again by later readers) of hiding the fact that the semblance of oral immediacy actually stems from the elaborateness of writing; that is, it is an *effet d'art* of writing.[3] Despite his ambivalence toward writing, Montaigne was aware of its productivity with regard to his self-portrait, a fact not lost on his readers. His repeated discrediting of the *Essais* as a "dead and mute painting" (ibid., 783) is only the flip side of the coin that relates writing to the formation and stabilization of the self. The essay *Du démentir* explicitly formulates the back and forth in which the "speaking" subject gives the text the "form" that is already that of the self, and in return gains stability from the written fixation and precision of the text. This is not the place to examine the implications of the metaphorics of consubstantiality and form in which Montaigne unfolds the relationship between self and writing. It should be noted, however, that the exploration of textual productivity, which unfolds the *écriture* of the self-portrait, functions as a defensive strategy against doubts about the legitimacy of its writing.[4] The self-portrait of the Renaissance remains in a precarious position as long as it does not succeed in distancing itself from those heterogenous discourses in which it participates in its rhetorical structure. Given the poetological placelessness of the self-portrait, this can only be a solution for individual cases through which the self-portrait gives new form to the discourses from which it feeds.

III

Girolamo Cardano's *De vita propria*, written or put together in 1575–76, at the end of his life in Rome, has never been considered a literary masterpiece. Even his translator, viewing it from a "purely literary perspective," could only recognize an "incomplete and imperfect work" (Cardano 1914: xxxv) in the thematic and formal heterogeneity of Cardano's self-portrait. Where the high demands of "pure" literature are so obviously unfulfilled, other qualities must be consulted, such as its documentary relevance for an epoch and for the spirit of a great scientist. Cardano's self-portrait is referred to as a witness for Italy's decline in the sixteenth century, for the conditions at the universities, for the new spirituality of the Counterreformation and the Baroque, for the replacement of the perspective of the *studia humanitatis* by the illusionless naturalism of physiology and medicine and thereby the rejection of any tension between ideal and reality.[5] In view of the overall ineffectiveness of Cardano's writing, *De vita propria* projects itself out of the "silent monument of an expired giant of the spirit" (Cardano 1914: xxxv) as a rather curious, sometimes contradictory conglomerate of a kind typical of his time.

H. Friedrich (and after him M. Beaujour), deviating from the usual assessment, grants some literary relevance to *De vita propria* by claiming that Cardano and Montaigne made use of the same method and thereby established a self-view that was to be fundamentally different from later autobiography and its norm of the organic self. Cardano's self-portrait is "the only work of all of autobiographical literature that can be put on the same level as the *Essais* with any seriousness" (Friedrich 1949: 277–78). When, however, Friedrich believes he has uncovered Cardano's uniqueness in "the disconnected expression of subjectivity" (ibid., 276), he is guilty of a modernistic distortion that ignores the specific heterogeneity of the text and the modalities of its self-reflection.

Cardano's passion is in fact—aside from chess and dice, to which he also devoted separate treatises—writing, as is evident even in the preference for certain writing instruments. A small chapter of *De vita propria*, titled "Delectatio," discusses certain attachments over the course of his life. The list includes such heterogenous things as a penchant for precious gems, for rare books that cost him a fortune, and for reading itself, of works from such varied areas as philosophy, history, medicine, mysticism, and poetry (Petrarca and Pulci). At the head of these randomly listed attachments is Cardano's costly passion for writing instruments, like fine styluses and various kinds of pens: "I believe I can say that all my writing instruments have cost me more than 200 ducats" (Cardano 1914: 54). For Cardano, who had money problems all his life, this passion for the sensual materiality of writing instruments is a ruinous affair, one he in no way seeks to rationalize. The remarkable thing about this passage is that he does not see any need to question or justify the various items in this list—an omission uncharacteristic of Cardano's representation of other aspects of passion, especially in his reports on his profligate passion for chess and dice. The "Delectatio" chapter does not attempt to explain, instead listing without comment diverse, idiosyncratic interests and hobbies that go beyond the practiced opposition of profession and leisure.

The cited passage already places Cardano's penchant for expensive writing instruments, articulated as an addiction to writing, in the horizon of a relationship to his social and university surroundings that from his youth on was tense and by no means free of paranoid traces: "Solitude is more appealing to me than the company of friends, of whom I have only very few who are honest and none who are learned" (Cardano 1914: 54). Cardano believes that he would have had more success in life if he had been able to curb his passion for writing, conspicuously evident in the monumentality of his works (ibid., 208). This perspective of an unfulfilled wish remains superimposed by an awareness of marginality and social discrimination. Such an awareness of stigmatization is evident, and this again is characteristic of Cardano's method, in the articulation of a variety of representational and interpretive horizons. His presumably illegitimate birth was to have been prevented by abortion; his astrological horoscope makes the necessity of later physical deformity clear; a passage on *prudentia*, based on the moral-philosophical tradition, illustrates Cardano's lack of common sense in worldly affairs, despite his own moral-philosophical treatises, extensive lists of rules for living, great experience, and analysis of these principles. The "signs of an abnormal character" (ibid., 107), already present at birth, substantiate themselves for the author through childhood fantasies, even though these seemed to him to be a "pleasant play that began every morning and never remained absent for long" (ibid.). He repeatedly laments his delayed, after several rejections (possibly on account of his illegitimate birth), admission to the Milan College of Medicine. The execution of his eldest son, who had killed his wife and to whom an elegy in the *De vita propria* is dedicated, as well as repeated prison terms for his younger son, are registered by Cardano above all as a social stigmatization of himself. His description of his way of walking stresses his "constantly being lost in thought" (ibid., 57). Again and again he emphasizes his striking lack of even the most elementary social graces. The chapter "Mores, & animi vitia, & errores" persists in asserting the usefulness of social isolation despite a specific reference to philosophical objections. The momentary self-descriptions of himself as an old man remind us again and again of his social exile and his limited aptitude for social intercourse. "I am an old man, hated and broken, an unpleasant person" (ibid., 49) is the concise comment of one passage. He later describes himself as a man "who lives in great poverty, surrounded by many enemies, subject to great injustices, downtrodden by so much misfortune" (ibid., 137). The chapter "Conversationis qualitas," which describes Cardano's lack of social qualities in the context of an exuberant baroque attack on the worthlessness of humans who "carry a sack of stinking excrement and a pot full of urine around in their bodies" (ibid., 214), finally counters the Aristotelian verdict against solitude with reference to the scientist's need for solitude. It takes up the topical, antihumanistic opposition of *honos* and *studia sapientiae* he had already discussed in the chapter "Honores delati": "Inventions require undisturbed quiet, still, constant contemplation, and ardent trials, and all of this requires solitude and not the company of others" (ibid., 215).

There is no better formulation for the genesis of his marginality and his written relationship to himself than the description of the deformities predicted by his horoscope, a description retrospectively providing a clear example of his social dysfunction. His deformity is evident in two physical defects that impact on social intercourse: first, an unspecified injury to the genitals that affected Cardano's relationship between the ages of 21 and 31 to women; second, a speech defect (*lingua parum blaesus*), a stammering, inherited from his father, that made speaking difficult and undermined the effectiveness of his academic lectures. At the end of his life, as shown in the *De vita propria*, this double handicap, the temporary sexual handicap but primarily the speech defect, still casts the shadow of deficiency and marginality that was already present at Cardano's birth, and is only compensated for by writing—a compensation involving the use of a second language and alienation from his mother tongue. The fateful and discursively rationalized failure of everyday orality and social intercourse is tempered by the success of scientific and self-referential writing, which abolishes spatial and temporal distances. The defects that cause Cardano's distance from his surroundings provoke the supplementary nature of his writing, the productivity of which presents the illusion that he used his handicap to his advantage.

This contrast is fairly clear in Cardano's self-presentation. On the one hand, he presents his failure in the oral realms of social intercourse and friendly conversation, a failure variously justified by demonstrations from astrology and moral philosophy. On the other hand, he presents us with a broad and diverse corpus of written works—encompassing, according to Cardano, 10 of 26 important scientific disciplines—which guarantees a fame that transcends time and space. On the one hand is an old man who loathes himself and believes himself to be persecuted by his surroundings, and on the other is a tireless inventor and scientist who has lost all control over the scope of his endeavors, who is proud of being apostrophized by Alciati as the "man of inventions" (Cardano 1914: 189), and who claims to have solved or at least posed 40,000 problems in medicine. Cardano does, however, take the desire for fame to task in his stubborn gesture of criticizing humanistic self-awareness. The chapter "Cogitatio de nomine perpetuando" is particularly ambivalent toward the resumption of the ancient, humanistic motif of fame gained through writing: here he considers the Epicureans' objections and their advice to enjoy life and articulates the questionable nature of fame and the destructive quality of ambition. Despite this criticism of the transience and insignificance of fame, the unconquerable quest for that prize, which resists his efforts at rational demystification, remains unchanged for Cardano: "It was no wonder that I was once consumed and possessed by greed for fame; but today it is a wonder that I am still consumed, even though I now recognize all this. . . . My condition has basically not changed: no money and no leisure time, no honor, no office, but still the longing for eternal fame" (ibid., 27–28).[6] Given the failure of conversation, the economy of writing, writing that others will write about, becomes a questionable but also unavoidable reaction.

For Cardano, the contrast between orality and writing determines even his performance of the oral art of disputation required by the university and its examination system. Paradoxically, Cardano's exorbitant successes in the university, his true home despite all his enemies, seem to have stemmed from his having been completely versed in the corpus of written, meanwhile printed, texts.[7] In this way Cardano, for whom the university was an agonistic space, was able to distance himself from his opponents. Though persecuted on all sides, he succeeded in the scientific system because this system was dominated by a new order of knowledge established with writing and book printing. Cardano reports on the power of his speech "that seemed irresistible" (Cardano 1914: 34), his capacity to lecture from memory, and his successes in disputation. The two examples included to corroborate his superiority concern a recurring dispute over Greek text passages that ends each time with Cardano documenting a false quote of his opponent's with the printed text. His feared prowess at disputation was based on his precise recall of the wording of critically established and printed texts. This is all the more remarkable in that Cardano took every opportunity to lament his poor memory and mentioned his inability to make any use of rhetoric's artificial memory systems, made known to him by his father.[8] It is this recall of critically established texts that resulted in his superiority in academic exchanges, halted the oral dispute in order to refer to the written text, and scared away his potential opponents from the beginning. Cardano is certainly no successor to scholasticism. He repeatedly emphasizes the primacy of experience, even in its seemingly obscure and erratic aspects, over the authority of the text. De vita propria is full of experiential rudiments that defy any explanation. Cardano triumphs over his opponents in the competitive communicative situation of academic disputation by recourse to the printed text. He thereby hastens the demise of orality in the framework of oral dispute itself and stabilizes what becomes his identity: fame in writing and in books.

Cardano repeatedly reformulates face-to-face relationships in terms of writing and print, where they first achieve their stable form. In the chapter "De amicis, atque patronis," which hardly distinguishes between personal friends and institutional patrons,*

*Noninstrumental, autonomous friendship, the "friendship that is based solely on the strength of our own affinity" (Cardano 1914: 47), of course was in

he says he can best express his gratitude to all such persons by mentioning them in *De vita propria*, "so that I, as far as I am concerned, would gladly grant someone an eternal name in that I name them here" (Cardano 1914: 48). For the same reason he is consequential in his refusal to name his enemies so that they may not become a part of the eternal life of the printed book. To illustrate his own fame, already achieved in his lifetime, he lists over 70 authors in his *Testimonia clarorum virorum de me* "whose books contain honorable mention of me" (ibid., 184). With this accumulation he believes he has surpassed the citations accrued by Aristotle and Galen in their own lifetimes, even though he must concede that he has certainly been helped by the invention of printing.

These examples show that Cardano's predilection for the written and the printed word neglects the differences between scientific or philosophical works and self-portraits. He certainly understands that he can't use well-established discourse forms in his *De vita propria*, in contrast to the massive disciplinary ordering of his scientific or philosophical treatises.* He can only cite such heterogeneous authors as Marcus Aurelius, Caesar, and Galen (although Galen's "autobiography" is presented in diverse passages throughout his works). The intent of *De vita propria*, in which an "honest, sincere narration" ("sinceram narrationem," 1914: 37) of the "naked" truth of the self is to be presented, stands in contrast to the description of the ambition of the scientist who wants to make his name eternal but does not want to make himself known. Cardano's writing mania is not directed solely toward the time-spanning placement of his name in the scientific system, even if, in *De vita propria*, he explicitly recapitulates a list of titles of partially printed, partially handwritten, works in his scientific corpus. From the beginning, the self is seen from the perspective of writing. This is in part a defense against persecutions, but that is not all. A fundamental maxim of the author reads as follows: "I have always, as

---

principle not unknown to Cardano, well-versed as he was in ancient moral philosophy.

  *Certain characteristics of Cardano's self-portrait, for example, the recapitulation of his family history, remind us of the tradition of the *ricordi*, but this relationship remains undeveloped. On the *ricordi*, see Bec 1967 and Guglielminetti 1977.

well as I could, relied less on my memory than on written texts" (ibid., 12). This allows us to understand that Cardano did not present his self-portrait as the result of a lifelong cultivation of *memoria* but as a rewriting of what had already been written. *De vita propria* is based on writings and notes that he made for himself over the course of time. It represents therefore a continuous written relationship with himself, in which lifelong experience is distanced through the use of Latin, a language he did not learn until adulthood.

Nevertheless, Cardano's attitude toward his work remains essentially ambivalent. The hypertrophy of writing does not produce a stable economy but comes back to the work as a whole, to include the scientific-philosophical work. He succinctly comments on his moral-philosophical treatise *De optimae vitae genere*: "I wrote this book because, out of the misery of memories, . . . I have never found another way out other than to simulate immortality through the immortality of a name" (Cardano 1914: 169). He thereby devalues the reality of the fame of a name to an illusionary impulse for the subject, which he nevertheless is incapable of escaping. He consequently pauses, unconsoled by the imposing list of citations of him in the works of others, and with a stroke of the pen destroys all illusion. The praise of mankind is worthless given the vanity of all earthly things. The mania of writing is by no means quieted in the repeated postulate of the usefulness of creation but finally reverts to the opposite, the destruction of its product. Twice, Cardano tells us, he burned his own books.

The reflection on *De vita propria*, which is, after all, described as "the navel of all my writings" (Cardano 1914: 171), is schismatic precisely because of its hybrid character. Concerning the audience of the self-portrait, Cardano repeatedly vacillates between ignoring the reader by an exclusivity of self-reference, realized in a closed circle of passion for writing and reading what is written, and being useful to the reader, that is, offering a text of exemplary value for readers, an ideal already postulated for his scientific work. It is this last demand, however, that conflicts with the heterogeneity of the self-portrait, because Cardano's concept of usefulness implies a homogeneous text, whose ideal is represented by the scientific monograph. There, a book's importance is judged on the success of its suitability to the subject and its formal unity.

A book that is worth being bought must be complete with regards to its intellectual content and its artistic form. A book is complete that deals with its subject continuously from beginning to end, exhausts it completely without overloading it with extraneous matters, maintains a rigid distribution of the subject matter, presents us with heretofore unknown facts, and uncovers the essential foundations of the subject.* (Ibid., 69)

This appraisal collides massively with the form of *De vita propria*, which combines narrative forms, a series of observations without commentary (almost in the sense of later "protocol tenets"), heterogeneous scientific discourses, topical proverbs, and moral-philosophical reflections, and which is so unsure even in its own mode of self-reference that Cardano inserts a chapter titled "De me ipso." Monstrous chapter titles like "Ostenta naturalia visa, rara tamen de Vita propria, & filii ultione" underline a heterogeneity that repeatedly leads Cardano to abrupt theme changes, of whose formal requirements he has no concept. Since *De vita propria* is unable to meet the demands of thematic consistency, but instead allows its form to be determined by the heterogeneity and digressiveness of various references, it struggles with determining the limits and the pertinence of its elements that cannot be traced back to the form of the self.

His writing, which is supposed to provide for Cardano, himself alienated from the immediacy of conversation, a homogeneous space-time continuum of fame, grows in contradictions. On the one side is his tendency to objectify everything—from scientific speculation to the peculiarities of his own nature. On the other side are the fitful escapes from the self-made prison of writing. Cardano notes in *De vita propria*:

Just yesterday after my meal, I was suddenly overtaken with such a hatred of all books, by others and my own, namely those already published, that I could not bear the thought of them, much less the sight. If I think rationally about this, then I realize that the reason for this lies in some kind of melancholy, especially since it involves my best books. (Cardano 1914: 213)

With reference to his *temperatura melancholica*, Cardano places himself in the humoral theoretic condition of intellectual and authorial

---

*A book must also be permeated with usefulness: "Take care that a book is concerned with practical usefulness and that this in turn forms and dominates the book. Only such a book and no other is complete."

greatness. This condition has, since the Aristotelian *Problemata* and canonically for the Renaissance since Marsilio Ficino's *De vita triplici*, belonged to the constitutive outfitting of the intellectual as the "agitation of knowledge" (Battaglia 1967: 70).[9] The positivity that melancholy gains with Ficino as an impulse in the order of knowledge is lost in Cardano's retrospective on his own writing. It turns into a destructiveness without foundation. With respect to the world of books, especially his own, Cardano reveals a negativity that lies over the world of writing and that casts its shadow on the representation of the self suspended between register and apology. More than Ficino's melancholic euphoria, the melancholy of the self-portraitist corresponds to another, much later description of the symptoms of the melancholic. The "puzzling impression" of melancholic inhibition corresponds to an "extraordinary lowering of his [the melancholic's] self-esteem, a great ego deprivation," which surprisingly manifests itself in the "course of obtrusive communicativeness that is satisfied by one's own exposure" (Freud 1975: 199–201). Cardano's self-diagnoses of melancholy, a self-description whose psychic origin is not to be speculated upon here in Freudian terms, halted at symptomatological findings of ambivalence and instability. The contrast to the imaginary ceremonies of conversation, discussed at the beginning, is clear enough.

CHARLES GRIVEL

Travel Writing

Those who write, travel.

The art of being there is to go there.

—Joseph de Maistre

Seeing nothing but still understanding. Strongest
is wonder. The thickness of the window pane is
tangible. A question poses itself. Flaubert: "A
slight wind, the Nile is completely still, we walk
along the shore, we tread the beautiful, fine sand.
Golden clouds like satin divans, the sky is
covered with light blue blotches: the sun sets in
the desert. To the left is the crenated Arab
mountain chain; in the foreground are palm trees,
and the foreground is dipped in black; further
back, beyond the palms, camels wander past, two
or three Arabs are riding donkeys. What stillness!
Not a sound. Great sandy shorelines and sun! A
trip can become terrible this way. The sphinx
radiates some of this effect."

The Source of Inspiration

Writing and traveling belong together: "I arrive in India, open my
eyes, and write a book" (Michaux 1948: 95). I only write while
traveling—I write when I travel. Traveling is actually writing. I
travel whenever I write. Bodies move in writing: I move forward
horizontally and vertically. Traveling—we go there to tell about it;
I save the paper I need. "Paper, reserved for my next trip," notes
Flaubert on the stack of paper (1986 [1849/50]: 22). The pages are
ordered in the drawer, even sealed! Everything that I write at home
at my desk is written in anticipation of a future trip. A special—

untouched!—material for an equally special undertaking that has not yet begun, as a source for my own inspiration. I write down there and in there; I write now as I wait for a stronger, more effective incentive.

My traveling is an event of the pen. Is it something other than the story I make of it? than the postcard I send? Do I do something other than to decipher it beforehand in the travel guide or the brochure? Don't I carry my writing identity around with me; don't I sign with my name the letters I send from all the places I have visited?

Traveling means placing the body into a *state of writing*. I send my body and my legs traveling in order to write. My body is writing; it marks everything that it experiences and perceives directly; it registers, conveys, speaks. When this body writes, then it travels, and only in this way can it change location (when I am lying down, robbed of any chance to travel, then I am silent and convey nothing). I move and excite my body, and it writes. Writing is a multifaceted movement of the body into depths, *there, where it is not*.

Travel in General

Moving around, changing locations, this is the main thing. Being ready to go, moving, meandering. The subject cannot be tied down to one place. The more it is assigned one, the more it wants to leave. Picabia: "One has to be a nomad, traversing ideas like countries and towns" (cited in Breton 1925: 127). The subject reacts to the daily imprisonment that it experiences (the "allotted" space, the office, the "pad") with a kind of social impatience; too much on one side, not enough on the other. Where I live in Mannheim, close to the train station, on the way to the university, which is located in the former palace of the elector Karl Theodor, there is a deep ravine of cut red rocks, through which, under the train tracks, one can reach the banks of the Rhine. People call it the "Suez Canal." *It is here, but it resembles something somewhere else*. There is always already a somewhere else implied; walking leads to a place where we are not, away from a place as from a dock. Our towns are piers and wharfs, springboards and platforms: here we wait, here we are ready to leave. The general signs of the "city tour," these are the arrows that rule us. We live in a universe of routes. We move, we head toward, we cross, we set out, constantly suspended in an endless changing of places (stopping, parking, these are difficult). An Occidental kind of wandering: what surprises us, wherever this obsession has not yet taken root, is that people are still *there*, where they belong, hemmed in by the region in which they live. They *are* this region, like their gods. For us, on the other hand, doing something—shopping, working, visiting, eating—means changing places. I have to find a place and fit in—park my car, pursue the right course, knock on the right door—all of this requires movement. The constant transportation of humanity has made it hysterical. We walk from one place to another, driven by an ever faster, clearer, more fevered trembling. "How are you?" "How's it going?" "What's up?" "What's going on?" as if someone had stepped onto an anthill. Traveling here means carrying to extremes the urban movement that tugs at life, trumping the usual commotion, making industry and self-revelation a principle, forcing things. The traveler is a city dweller. He leaves the city, which he drags along on his soles. He devotes himself to discovering new landscapes with the same nervous attention with which he approaches every traffic light, that he uses with every facade and at work: he perceives a sign. This manner of reading is projected onto seacoasts, wide-open countrysides, distant (and ever more distant), unique, and empty landscapes, onto mountain peaks, jungles, and deserts. It is remarkable that this urbanity, this mania of deciphering signs on floors or walls, the challenging gesture transferred to another place where he runs around for any thinkable reason, produces that *which had not been read*. The traveler can, of course, content himself with recognizing "in reality" the monuments and landscapes shown by the travel brochures. He has read what is there, the reading does nothing more than prove that he was there. He can also profit exceedingly from this deep *absence in which he finds himself,* to experience something beyond this nothing that he was not necessarily to experience, shall we say, a kind of self. Once again Flaubert: "I wanted to leave home, get away from myself, who cares where, everywhere, with the smoke of my chimney and the leaves of my acacia" (1986: 22).

I therefore distinguish within the same paradigm between urban change of place (our immediate fate) and travel. I travel when I

leave the city; I submerge myself in a new field. It is this movement—the renunciation of knowledge, applying knowledge to
something new, whose true (practical) perception is denied—that
makes the traveler *available*. He travels, but as one who is absent; he
does not orient himself, he *goes*; he no longer takes notice of
addresses, he runs around full speed, subjected to the force of a
random timetable that represents nothing more than his own ex-
cesses. Going for a walk, bumming around, hanging out. And
anonymity: I walk somewhere *incognito*, *I am someone someplace*; no
meaning, hardly a purpose. Traveling is dealing a new hand, something the subject allows itself. I am playing at not fulfilling any of
my roles. I have been shuffled, a bent body, domination of circumstance, being everything, being nothing, being as one would never
be, swaying, being carried away by the floods, a nobody.

A Trace, No Trace

The traveler is someone who looks at a painting. What he critically
inspects is for him a picture. But of what is it a picture, what secret
of what reality does it represent? In which direction do its tracks
lead? At first, a sign shows me that someone has been this way
before. The sign is dirty; the idea of it is as unbearable as oily paper.
Of course, the sign is also comforting to a certain extent because it
shows that I'm on the right path. I am the first, but I am following
someone else. I go there because I need a radical change of place,
but I am necessarily a follower, like a pathfinder, in that I listen to
what was there before, even if only as a game. The traveler has lost
a sense, a feeling of the concrete. A country becomes a landscape; a
forest represents the picture it presents, as well as the traveler's own
movement guided by the white, red, or green signs that grace its
trees. General defunctionalization.

The traveler is missing a language, the language of the other,
those who are at home. At best, he can make do with school
English. He looks around—but how can he distinguish without
subtitles and commentary? Sure, the travel guide, which is written
in his mother tongue, overloads and embarrasses him with definitions, but these definitions only aesthetize what they pretend to
grasp (in case they aren't tautologies anyway). The traveler loses a
considerable portion of his knowledge, he lightens his load, con-

fuses things, deceives himself. The attraction he has read about never corresponds to what he sees before him. *The ignorance of the traveler is wonderful.* Finally knowing less, finally being secure from knowledge, and from the responsibilities it brings with it. I can finally act like a deaf mute, I can renounce understanding and acting! The great inactivity of traveling! The overall sign system, which is his, allowing him to balance out orders and behavior, disappears. The journey is like *free, unoccupied places.* My behavior toward signs is no longer normal while traveling. The newness of places and touristic recommendations encourage me to interpret signs eagerly. But it doesn't work, no matter how I try, since, without language, there is neither truth nor probability. And so I make up rumors without foundation and new melodies—spontaneously, but at the same time wrongly.

The unsuitable, unsure sign behavior of a traveler who is in a state of absence brings X into existence—the unknown, unnameable, but still certain. X appears in the simple, incorrect shift of my semiotic reader's grid. By moving, after all, the sense of my mobility, by allowing for "displaced" knowledge, I no longer know anything, or, at least, I experience in a *completely different way* from now on. I am engaged in abstract art. *I am creating reality without truth.* The spatial distance, because of its capacity to disrupt normal sign behavior, produces new signs. I marvel at these signs, created under my steps; I collect and photograph them because, for a moment, they have no meaning at all. I am intoxicated by their nothingness. By the progressive suspension of language.

Let the guy-ropes fly, Rimbaud said. Or better yet: the unknown, the symbol of unknown meaning crops up from under my feet. *I am returning to the beginning of the world.* The elementary spatial displacement, the shift, the "distance" of a body, my body, produces in the same measure in which it destroys the coincidence of reality and language as a sign of what formerly did not exist, what was awaiting my arrival, what *depends on nobody but me* for appearance. G. K. Chesterton:

A person, thought Syme, who always went west, to the end of the world, would certainly find something, for example, a tree that is both more and less a tree, maybe a tree disowned by spirits. It would be the same thing if he always went east to the ends of the earth. Then he would find a thing that was not quite this thing, maybe a tower whose architecture would already be a sin.   (Chesterton 1966: 84)

Pisa, for example, an unexplainable, nonexistent Pisa that is reserved for me, of which I can only produce a cliché. Or maybe Babel. Babel unrelentingly, irreversibly appears whenever I push my ignorance far enough. This "tree," this "tower," this "thing," this sign of signs and sign without reference, stimulates my curiosity to such an extent, more in the East, more in the West, that it still has insufficient meaning and is caught up in the movement that spurs me on. My trip denies it all measure. It remains a sign without object that carries no truth, *not in any possible world*. The traveler is intoxicated by the meaninglessness of signs that appear and disappear, by the dismissal of language, and by the abandonment of its tools.

Here but There. Away—There

Where should we go, where should we allow ourselves to be carried off to, to what goals, to what distances, to what proximities? Which region should we choose? Should we visit France like Renaud Camus (1981) or Russia like Bernard Noël (1980)? It hardly makes any difference; all possibilities are open to the traveler. He knows France or has just come from there; he doesn't know Russia and will never get there. On the one hand the banality of experiencing "France" in France, the real France, a France that is more real than nature; on the other hand an unknown country that resists me and whose language I will never learn. The traveler is always "beside himself"; he has lost his senses, but is always affected on the inside; he is capable of anything—the country itself is unimportant—*the main thing is that he changes location*. He looks, observes, lets the eye rove. Yet, he owns a language, or rather: a language owns him—the language of his country and his mother tongue. Its societal text is inscribed in him; he exhausts himself in its coding; his own name holds him fast: "The misuse of language is ruining our civilization. It is on the verge of death" (Noël 1980: 9). And so he moves outside his language. When he travels, he is guided by the appetite of the eye: "Clouds, clouds, we really are in heaven. Mountains and valleys, bridges across white water. The need to see bestows form, makes everything legible. . . . I have seen beige-colored fields with green islands, an eternally blue sky, a blue that makes my chest ache because its permanence is so unimaginable: the blue of eternity" (ibid., 13–14). Seeing (reality?) creates definite distress—seeing without knowing, seeing without language, gradually and always from a great distance, in a strange place.

I am watching, when I'm driving, from my seat, from my car. There is a gap between what hits my pupils and the ideas that my knowledge or my thoughts make of it: *I drive by and dissect*; things are not really there, nor am I seeing them properly, nor do they accommodate any kind of descriptive, reporting, or narrative language. A landscape produces vacuity—just because it is a landscape. I catch myself experiencing a kind of vacuum, the unknown, nonexistent emerges. In a certain sense, the traveler is a painter; the picture of what he perceives takes the place of something that he imagines but does not attain: "reality." The worst thing for him would be if he saw nothing at all; the signs of rules—"Do not touch!" "Do not walk!" "Entry forbidden!" "Dead End!"—they are for him true distress. The traveler would like to follow his senses to the limit, as far, as intensely as possible, to the breadth, height, and depths. He takes control of surfaces. He fights with the medium through the medium—speaking, writing, and moving his legs. The traveler plays against an existing form by completing a predesignated course; he sets words into motion against other words.

The traveler is faced with a problem: "How can what is hidden by visible things be seen?" (Noël 1980: 36). How can we see with language what lies "under language"? How to see what "is worth seeing"—the "tourist attractions" with the sufficiently relaxed distance, how can they be seen, in a sense for free, without any interest, in their deep meaninglessness? One could escape into the museum because it places the incomparable witnesses of artistic avarice side by side, without the constraints of time. One could also begin by writing.

Write your travels. Sketch no itinerary; tell not about what happened but about the perceived lack of knowledge: "What did you see?—I don't know, I'm writing about it." This is not a report, a *post festum*, written at home with my feet under the desk. *That* will not be a part of the play of memories. On the contrary: we "mark" by moving. The letters shake on account of our ignorance. A hesitant text that is unsure of the traveler himself. I am not writing because I learned this or met that; on the contrary, my fingertips tingle because it is strange and has unknowingly turned into signs. The *not knowing* of the traveler as cause for writing, an open series of moments that are neither fragmentary nor progressive. I am not developing a panorama or taking a view "from above." I view this (unspeakable ground) without understanding, silent, because I have no appropriate language. I do not tell anything, because I have no really integrable information: *I try to see; I move my eyes back and forth.*

Traveling, writing, dispossession: these go together. I don't want to "unwrite" anymore. I change space, crawl out of my skin; a kind of extermination of meaning breaks through. I stay here or there, or better yet, I let myself drift from here to there, unsure, robbed of my possessions. I have no "goal" or object, and I have likewise lost any sense of myself; I am, as Baudrillard said, the abstraction of travel, purely a cinematic vision (Baudrillard 1986: 10). As a traveler I succumb to the avarice of dispossession, I practice giving up myself. Normally I am what I use up, the unending series of things that I purchase. As a traveler I only resemble the contents of my suitcase: *I have nothing, I am nothing.* Baudrillard: "How far can one venture into the forms of the desert that relate to nothing without being broken?" (ibid., 27). Answer: I want to be broken, want nothing else but this . . . explosion, the end of the perception that understands itself to be the catalogue of all the things I am offered, the end of the analytical repertoire and meaningful "values." The great indifference. From having to seeing. Pure, cinematic movement, activation of the visible along the entire way. I "see" rather than "observe." Utility no longer fulfills any role; things remain unused, defunctionalized, look old but are new, all too new, still unused, no longer bothered by functionality. *A world of things found by accident that are randomly identified.* There are no more laws for this kind of traveler. He travels around in the world as among ruins. His eyes create ruins. A secret principle of instant damage and devaluation is at work. But the damage is such that we congratulate ourselves. Surfaces are devoured by the eyes. No framework is left standing; only the decayed is visible; the destruction is, visually speaking, my Beatrice.

Therein lies the inexplicable possibility of the traveler: wherever he travels, world and spirit come together; he sees what he likes. Left out in the cold by his language, it becomes, so he imagines, legible "in the drama" itself. This wall really consists of endless specks; it really means neither separation nor incarceration; it is a speck in the literal sense of the word, a speck in my eye, either a test or homage to Leonardo or a cry that is hurled at Honecker.

The Body Travels

The traveler is a body that changes places. One thing that must be considered: the mechanical movement of a mass in space up until arrival or stopping, up until colliding with a brick wall.

The effects of a change of locale on the body are actually of a unique nature. The body is not a "rock," it doesn't "fall"; it perceives, it thinks, it acts. To accelerate it in a certain direction means to affect its system of perception and its condition of consciousness, to create confusion. The traveler, one could say, artificially disrupts his body in order to feel out its *possibilities*. Movement, change, unrest, roadways: staying put is not allowed. Nietzsche, in *Ecce Homo*: "*Stay sitting* as little as possible."

Whoever puts himself in motion is not far from thinking: "We move, and signs surround us" (Ogilvie 1984: 8). Philosophizing with our feet, with the constant movement that they communicate to the rest of our body; *my active limbs make me think.*

Movement—but not a stroll, not an outing or window shopping, not a tourist route. A goal is needed, even if it is never reached or never even appears. The traveler is not lazy; he lies in wait, in ambush—distracted but alert. He does not enjoy emptiness but something like a fascination whose nature is initially hidden. The traveler is excited; his tension grows with every step, with the route he completes. He does nothing but anxiously gets ready. Something dark has him in its grips and pulls him toward it. I go mechanically; my legs are like a robot's. The knees, the arms rise and fall. Taking breath, in the same way as one eats or talks. Even the word in our mouths is the product of two alternating movements: high, low, closed, open, chewing, word, chewing, walking. Analogous actions occur when traveling in any kind of vehicle (my jaws start to move in the train—I yawn because I stretch my limbs, or they me). Impulse: I think in two-steps, I chew by alternatively contracting the bones in my jaw. I philosophize in two-steps, open, closed, coming and going (back and forth); I breathe in and out. The traveler's body divides itself. Dialectics without synthesis: the second beat, the closing, supports the first, the opening. This is how a gardener uses his clippers on an endlessly long hedge. I step forward and divide myself, destroy myself. The subject changes itself twice with its legs. Thinking means thinking twice in oneself—or as a duality. "Increasing the molecular circulation of languages," and for this purpose: (1) *to go aimlessly and quickly* (but there is a goal, and the speed is not arbitrary); (2) *to scan*, dissect, keep two beats, like a buttonhole machine, a punch press.

I change places within a living but dissected space; I am the living division of this space. This push forward destroys the representation of the person and eliminates its reflexive attitude. My body and I, somehow we find ourselves *de-realized*. A mass that moves along a line deconstructs itself. This mass travels at night; it travels quickly, becomes tired; it does not know exactly that it is there.

Rigidity

The traveler falls into a kind of drowsiness. He gets in his vehicle and falls asleep. On my travels I sleep with open eyes. Breathing and pulse become even. Rigidity sets in. This is useful for writing; also helpful is not thinking. A metal cage holds me. A cabin. Here I am in the egg. Sounds become more refined, but they remain noises. Liquefaction. A gentle rocking. Speed. The cloth with which speed rubs on the windows pleasantly wipes away the exterior. The vibration of the driver's seat is part of the trip. I am inside. I transport myself in order to gain a sense of "interiority." Turbulences are softened. The mechanical strain produces a kind of floating. I take part in the duration. I set myself into a cockpit that is suspended in emptiness (a swing without supports). The strongest acceleration results in the greatest ease. Carpet, moss, a shine from nothing. Indifference. I am traveling as if packed in cotton—weightless, in immaterial, painted rain. Everything has already taken the familiar shape of my bed in the middle of my room.

Ballast

I always leave the evening prior; I have always already been gone. The heat of the moment that precedes the moment. I would like to sleep but at first can't close my eyes. The traveler is tired, he looks bad, he should go home, good advice. Tension in muscles, in the neck, in the ears. Little worries bother him. Wallet, money, papers. The journey begins with an extraordinarily difficult memory exercise: just don't forget anything! I depart and begin to get myself together again; I compose an identity for myself—a type of safe-conduct letter—and then throw myself into the chaos. I will sleep somewhere else, but on my pack, that shortened version of the traveler. I carry myself around in my utensils. I restrain myself, under knots and straps, as a unity, as a whole, like a load in a symbolic pack—will I really make use of everything that I'm taking along? The excitement of packing, the tiredness that goes with this identifying task; the forced concentration provokes impulses of flight, of opening, of waste: socks, underwear, razors, various lotions. Take everything. Take everything that has to be taken. Sort out something from everything. Put together something resembling the normal provisions of the Pharaoh in his tomb: basic foods, necessary things. Determining from the start what kind of cargo will be represented. The suitcase of the complete traveler is big, heavy, round, stuffed, close to bursting. It hangs onto its owner like the ball and chain onto the convict. With a stenciled prisoner number: you will accompany yourself! The impression of going on a journey with a load on your back. Fever, but great relief, because here I have, aside from myself, the reserves of myself. I am heavy, but I am rushing off.

Speed

"At the beginning of the journey, one feels around in the dark, but the physical effect of speed soon illuminates everything" (Dumas 1980, 2: 380). Speed invalidates the concreteness of what it allows me to drive past. It uproots things from their environment, offers them as snapshots; it also erases them, makes them fluid. It suppresses the objects of perception directly and accelerates the process of their being embedded in our memory. Introspective projection: "After speed has replaced space, everything changes concerning duration, in corpses, aged, before it is born and gains form: the difference between birth and death disappears" (Ishagpour 1983: 128). A process of abstraction is taking place: traveling fast deprives us of reality, though it is less damaging than it is vacuous, extinguishing; nothing has time to take shape. I move within a supple space, move everything aside, throw everything behind me that opposes pure movement. Baudrillard: "Driving creates a kind of invisibility, transparency, a kind of obliqueness in emptiness" (1986: 20). Sabato: "Speed has no meaning; one is always in the same landscape" (1982: 49). Maybe this is euphoria, but a euphoria that inflames a crisis. Soupault insistently recommends slowness while traveling, for sickness comes from moving too fast (1985: 121). The subject is lost in the fray; its world is diluted; it perceives its absence and dematerialization. The world in which I travel has lost content and density; it is no longer a thing but a vision in the sense that I can adjust my optics to it by using my speed. I succumb to its fascination, but my senses sketch expected perceptions only in my memory. Indistinctness lures me into a space of thinking without measure and limits. Traveling then becomes seeing; if I move quickly in this darkness, then my senses can immediately "enlighten" me.

In an Altered Condition

Traveling: a kind of intoxication, a kind of rapture. In my machine it is always already night. The fatigue, the relief, the dematerialization that sets in as a result of speed, these things promote this. Whenever we travel, we play with spaces in between, between two bodies of water, not far from the surface. The significant is continuously and simultaneously on both sides of the picture. A journey requires a suitcase, a bag, fever, sleeplessness, excess. I put on my best clothes: it's like Sunday, I could be on the way to church, I gave myself a close shave. I took off by myself, with me alone—having company on a journey is bad; the other person, across from you, too easily distracts you from yourself. Deceleration is followed by rapid propulsion. Reflection, regression. Return to childhood. Something like an inner noise hits the sweat-soaked body (a twitching?). I hear the voices of origins, the murmuring in the middle of the wheel, the drumming on the iron band, connected to me, to my body. I am a drum that remembers.

A thick, pulsing, and tightened skin: I've put the drumhead on my stomach. "Keep yourselves well on your island, *you, who cling to contemplation*" (Michaux 1948: 239).

Travel is a "discipline" of the body. It moves, it moves you, tests you during the journey that it controls. This body is afraid, it trembles, it is soft, both excited and sleeping; it is mechanically held at the ready for writing. The writer is a body in the condition of transfer: spiritually, physically, with hands or feet, with all its limbs, parts, muscles, juices. *Writing is transference*: the body becomes something it was or no longer is—on the one hand it leads us back to ourselves; on the other it helps us to break out. The external changes and along with it, the depth. In this way the shell is also the heart.

The Writing of Movement

The writer is often imagined to be someone who has, shall we say, an idea at the back of his head and, sitting in front of his paper, tries to put it into words. He wants it, has it, expresses it. In fact, every "idea" disappears in writing, goes beyond any calculations, runs ahead of its speaker: what I am thinking is suspended before me, unreachable, like a cast shadow, the further forward I go, the more distant it becomes. Something happens in writing that I would like to call elementary mental displacement. Sitting down at a desk, at a typewriter, in front of the paper, this is all setting something in motion—getting out of traffic, taking the phone off the hook, not being available, in short: disappearing. I write when I drop out. I catapult myself out of the concepts, convictions, and truths in which I am usually wrapped up. For this I use figures, masks, or voices. I multiply the discourses and perspectives in my mouth. I strip off language like I change clothes. I multiply myself, multiply my clothes. I write when I let myself be displaced, drift, from left to right, from top to bottom, and set my arms, my legs in motion (my spirit, you move nimbly). In short: writing means *not keeping still, going where one isn't*. Experiencing the space, fiction as a geographical fact, the source like a net, the description like a tour. I write: I allow myself to have all perspectives, I talk like I'm not supposed to talk—stammering, my head turned in another direction, already out of earshot. *I am far away*. I count on not being understood. I write, I assuage myself, exchange, disseminate *igno-rance*. If I formulate within or with it? I surprise myself with how I take meaning away from signs precisely there where entire masses of signs mean knowledge and behavior. If I think with it? I commu-nicate something in groundlessness, without a perceivable referen-tial range. I unravel and scatter: the writer releases meaning into a world in which the net of the unequivocal that has been thrown over us seems too tight. I create tracks, prepare for a roller coaster ride whose meaning may never be known with any certainty. Is there a plan? Obviously not. Nevertheless I am being led.

Let's take a look at a writer at work. He writes by guiding his hand from left to right (or his paper, his text, if he is using a keyboard). He writes by hand, with the hand; some of his fingers get mixed up in the process. He sits bent, with empty eyes, some-what agitated, wide awake but distracted. He is two: two hands, body vis-à-vis paper. A scission. Distraction but still activity. The body is absent but still tense. An idea flows into his pen like water, his nib, his ballpoint; an ink ribbon runs by; illuminated clarity breaks out. His ink pen, his felt-tip, or just his finger is drenched in blood (it has to bleed quietly, without any gnashing of teeth, coming out of himself as out of a deep, unstaunchable wound).

The body flows out in writing. Whoever writes, secretes. His kind of saliva. A lymphatic flow. An assortment of his body fluids. Running out, beating, spasmodic rhythm, ejaculation. His story, his images are an orgasmic impetus. From without to within and vice versa. Doubled expansion. Displacements, border crossings, only movement is permanent. Heat: when I write, my body over-flows. I begin to sweat. Indications of stigmata, wheezing, rattling. As if I were running while writing, hurrying from one line to the next, pursuing an unseen prey. It is also a matter of breathing—I pant—also a question of physical labor: I wear myself out writing. Lungs and muscles, writing gets me going, driven or sucked in by an inner abyss, *prey of the maelstrom that is my body*, until I'm dizzy, until I sink, into sleep, put to the test by saying.

Axioms

1. I traveled there; I have the write to speak about it. A journey makes speech believable; it is well-suited for conversation.

2. The journey is the object of a text; it is not different from the report that is made about it.

3. Travel literature is a neglected literature; compared to the samples of canonical genres, it can hardly offer something like "works."

4. The travel report—a product of the left hand, not really produced at a desk; the unconscious grants itself unlimited space here.

5. Travel writing is fragmentary; it is missing an epilogue, its model is running around lost.

6. Travel writing is also fast writing; the traveler has no time, his impressions come and go quickly, he only takes notes.

7. The traveler is brief; the time for writing seems to take away from the time for perception, even if he knows it is only a decoy.

8. The travel report is not a fictional genre. Its referential object is precise and stands out. What I see is certainly Rome; these are certainly the gardens of Isfahan: "A canal flows from the pavilion to the alley; here is the source of a stream that fills the canal up until the big bridge" (Tavernier 1981, 2: 136). Or Tours in France: "The bridge of Tours is very famous, but has nothing remarkable in itself" (Gautier 1870: 3). I describe, impressions reach me, the "prose of the world" flows from my pen.

9. Traveling, seeing, stacking up in our memories. Fixing, retaining, choosing. Arriving in order to carry away and take notes of what is interesting.

10. Writing about a journey means writing about the subject. Someone constructs himself, his I, during the journey. Unseen countries, unknown races, extinct species are good for this.

11. We travel around backward. Forward is backward, tomorrow is more like yesterday. Flaubert: "While my body moves forward, my thoughts move backward, engrossed in the past" (1986: 215).

12. The journey is a subject that speaks (its mind).

13. The text gained by it is defective, the worst of its works: the subject sees too much, cites too much, gorges itself (there are certainly too many Belgians driving around in "poor Belgium" with whom Baudelaire doesn't get along).

14. The travel report is exiled to the last volume of works, as if a kind of leftover, an incomplete text. Additionally, these notes don't have real titles: "Journey to the Congo," "To Timbuktu," "To the Orient," "To Spain," "Rome, Naples, Florence," "Travel Journal."

15. Sunk in the special existence of the traveler, the report opposes reading. Yet this opposition is an additional charm that it exudes.

16. The travel report is the report of a departure; it presents itself as an act of separation. And so it must replace something, counterbalance. Another reason for me to keep to it.

17. The journey is determined by the "season." We learn something about extraordinary conditions. Besides, the reader is always the one who did not go (unless he has already returned).

18. A journey is a method; it is written like research. Through this it feeds curiosity.

19. The traveler departs; he says how he will arrive. The initial deficit kindles the writing of daily notes or lets itself be hidden by them. Every notation touches the original need that it denies. Just as if one wanted to synchronize the world with what one sees (Noël 1978: 75).

20. Traveling, enjoyment of "in-between spaces." Above all: don't arrive anywhere; arrange it so that you will arrive too late! Concerning your book, let the most obvious gaps germinate and fill themselves.

21. The reason for the journey is never admitted. Before he sets down his *Itinéraire*, Chateaubriand writes: "I didn't make my journey to write about it. I wanted to look for pictures, that's all" (1849, 1: 36). The purpose of the journey needs to be played with. Taking off just to take a trip, just doing it, that won't work. A learned, documentary purpose is good.

22. The traveler is a swindler. Am I ever the person I claim to be; does a change of location give me the right to express myself? Traveler, bounty hunter, you make expectations into money: "We had the idea of writing about our journey *beforehand*, to sell it at a good profit, and to use the profits to check out the accuracy of our descriptions" (Mérimée, n.d.: 14). This is the fiction of every journey, because there is only one for each person. Everyone recognizes for himself the things he comes upon. You don't have to go there to have been there.

23. The journey doesn't result in much, doesn't yield much: "I am at the end of this damned journey that I had to tell everything about" (Roche 1972: 8). Exertions and discomfort: this is not a vacation, doesn't proceed with leisure. A journey is a *work*.

KARLHEINZ BARCK

Materiality, Materialism, Performance

> What's the matter?
> Never mind.
> What is mind?
> No matter.
>   —English wordplay
>
> We must find out whether or not history has
> slipped into a new cycle.
>   —Richard Schechner

The conceptual unclarity of the term "materiality" seems to indicate a need for tentative questioning of its meaning and for new kinds of experiences: experiences of the increasing "discrepancy between perception and consciousness" (Kamper and Wulf 1982), of the substitution of corporeality and intersubjective relationships with "artificial bodies" (Braun 1985) and "relationship boxes," and of the demise of reality in "hyper-reality" (Baudrillard 1987a) as its exact doubling; experiences and perceptions of substitutions by images, effected by electronic audiovisual media, so that correspondences between the two seem impossible to establish. "Simulation," a key term in Jean Baudrillard's apocalyptic epochal analysis, not only dissolves all correspondences between image and reality (thereby negating all criticism of ideology, per Einrauch and Kurzawa 1983: 31–34) but also excludes any and all fiction (and thereby any utopia): "The signs of art and industry are interchangeable: art can become a reproductive machine (Andy Warhol) and can still remain art, because the machine is only a sign. . . . Art is therefore pervasive, because the artistic stands in the center of reality. . . . The simulation principle overcomes both the reality principle and the pleasure principle" (Baudrillard 1982 [1976]: 119).

Jean-François Lyotard's Paris Beaubourg exhibit "Les immatériaux" (1984) was not the first to encourage critics to speak of a "tendency toward dematerialization," resulting from the scientific-technological revolution in the late capitalism of the First World. Dematerialization is experienced as such across changed concepts of time and space, for example, in that the increased speed of traffic (performance in the material means of communication) is also experienced as the destruction of space by time (Krausse 1987: 439–44). The history of military communications technology and the modern technologies of a destructive means of communication have effected a "revolution of information" that, according to Paul Virilio, represents a faultline in a historical epoch:

Communications and "télématique" simply complete the circle begun a century ago with the telegraph and the train. We are experiencing a phenomenon of "deanimalization": not only are animals (beasts of burden, draft and racing animals) giving way to the machine, but the technical communications device also has the tendency to disappear in the face of transmitted communications and finally gives way to the direct transmission of radio and radar signals. On its way via the steam engine and the electric motor, the automobile has had to wait for the middle of the twentieth century to become part of the "revolution of information," along with the radio, the cellular telephone, and the beginnings of satellite television. Ever since the [automobile's] mechanical and thermodynamic beginnings, and in spite of competition from trains and commercial air travel, one thing remains clear: the automobile has not stopped the principle of autonomous transport from masking the principle of information transport. It is precisely this point in time that ends with electronics. (Virilio 1984c: 224)

Have the new information technologies brought us to a threshold in the process of the differentiation of the "human mind" and the "human body," "in which the functions of the mind are no longer tied to the here and now of the body" (as H. U. Gumbrecht remarked in Dubrovnik)? And, viewed retrospectively, could the description of "materialities of communication" in the cultural history of humanity be an act of assurance, a well-founded warning sign of the irreversible consequences of crossing this threshold? Our knowledge of how we arrived at this precarious threshold would be insufficient were we to join with those who have always known "all that" and have always told us so.

I share Hans Ulrich Gumbrecht's uneasy question, for which he seeks an answer in the "dramatization of the present lack of perspective." I would like to ask a question that makes me uneasy: How can this view be made more concrete in terms of perspectives that would offer more than hopelessness and something other than trite consolations? If we were to try to assimilate the historical experiences of our century from the perspective of its (and our) catastrophes of fascism, Stalinism, genocide, and nuclear weapons, we would probably arrive at nothing more than a negative teleology of history: the worldwide capitalism of the First World as the perspective of humanity in an "electronic time," the time of electronic connectedness of the entire world and the "interdependence of different societies in the context of the same technological systems" (Picht 1981, 1: 35).

This assimilating perspective on humanity and its history sets the tenor of the discussion of postmodernism and masks the view of differentiation. The (possible) end of humanity's history in a nuclear or ecological disaster is already a cynical assumption when talking about humanity's emergence into its "posthistoire." "How shameless is the lie of posthistoire in light of the barbaric reality of our history" (H. Müller 1986: 19). Universal history, this hoary European myth of old and new historicism, has been, up till now, the legitimization for repression and exploitation. This history is not possible without a new sense of genre predicated on conditions that would allow for the end to the division of humanity into rich and poor, into rulers and ruled. Decentralization of universal history, criticism of the notion of a homogeneous humanity within the sound room of an electronically controlled "global village" would be an initial step on the way to such a new sense of genre. This new "world consciousness" (Picht 1981) would have to be developed from the margins, from the experiences of social, ethnic, religious, and cultural marginalities, without giving up the interdependence of the three worlds. "The disassociation between time and space that began with the train creates a condition of an increasingly stark lack of simultaneity between spaces, dominated by the pace of modern life, as well as stretches of land where 'clocks run differently'" (Krausse 1987: 441).

The view for other historical and cultural experiences, for alterities and identities, is also enhanced. Doubting progress is (in a completely different way) a problem for the First and Second Worlds that can hardly be expected to be understood by the Third. In the Second World of now-defunct socialist states, in which the concrete utopias of their history played an ever-increasing role, the criticism of technological euphoria, of a "myth of science" (Bunke 1986: 137), is linked to a debate over the distances between the present and the future, to what today is being called "new thinking." The Three World topography introduced at the Bandung Conference (1955) points to the different times and spaces in which experience and action take place as historical forms of economic, social, political, and cultural applications. The coexistence of different space-times cannot be transferred to an axis of a single and unified time. What can be concluded from these kinds of differentiations and decentralizations is the following: the historical concepts of a universal history continue (more or less consciously) all Hegelian principles of the philosophy of history. They are both anthropocentric and Eurocentric.

The new spatial metaphor of the common "European house," introduced into public debate under the political premise of coexistence, is an especially significant indication for a universal historical cover-up of important differences (naturally legitimized with reference to the nuclear threat). Years ago, Oskar Negt formulated a counterthesis. It is based on the "decentralization of historical impulse centers" (Negt 1983: 83) and assumes that the synchronization of history and the development of capital, anchored in Marxist theory, is no longer valid. We are faced with the task of explaining "in what the historical concept of the present consists" (ibid., 91). Jacob Taubes responded to this question in another context with the demand to discontinue the post-Enlightenment reversal of nature and history, classically represented by the Hegelian dialectic as a reflection of bourgeois society:

I have turned to Schelling's philosophical distinction between mythology and enlightenment to delineate, in a very incomplete way, the possibility of a demythologizing concept of history. If we should not succeed in constituting a historical concept of history, then the project of the modern cannot be saved from a retreat into a nature that is eternally the same, then the return to a mythical spirituality becomes unavoidable. It could then well be that Acheronic powers will overrun the "Olympia of Illusion," where an enlightened polytheism seeks to take hold.   (Taubes 1983: 464)

In reality, various apocalyptic images ("the end of history," "the end of reason," "the end of the modern," etc.), along with signals of a threshold of an anthropological epoch, indicate a crisis of consciousness whose deeper causes are still insufficiently evident in the description of an epochal opposition between *modern* and *postmodern*. It must be acknowledged that postmodern theory has made the latency of this crisis manifest. The question of a' historical concept of the present has been brought to light *ex negativo* through postmodernism.

A Cosmogonic View of History

I would like to propose and support the thesis that the new technologies created by the scientific-technological revolution have brought humanity to an epochal threshold characterized by a new "cosmogonic" view of history. At the heart of this view of history, the contours of which were already visible 200 years ago with the paradigmatic change from classical mechanics (Newton) to thermodynamics (Fourier, the mathematician), is the concept of irreversible time. I use the term "cosmogony" in the sense of Michel Serres, who applies it to the Kantian "revolution of thinking" and its consequences in the natural sciences in contrast to the cosmogonies of closed world concepts:

In any case, according to Kant, a new science is born—cosmogony, on the same day on which the previous science, cosmology, finally seemed crowned, finished, and completed. The pairing of cosmology and cosmogony opens the Romantic period. It characterizes two types of systems with different times: the time of order—reversible, and the time of world creation—irreversible; the time of mechanics and the time of thermodynamics.   (Serres 1973: 323)

Given the present third stage in the modern history of the division of labor and socialization,* characterized by digitalization

---

*The first two were described by Marx in *Das Kapital*: "Revolutionizing the method of production takes the strength of labor as its starting point in manufacturing, in large industries it uses the means of labor" (Marx 1962 [1867]: 391).

and systems integration and striving for the automation of human thinking (artificial intelligence, with its catastrophic consequences for the technologization of people and their bodies), the irreversibility of time has reached the consciousness of everyone with a certain secular delay. That the humanities and social sciences have become the focal point of this debate (and the highly neurotic reactions to it), along with its "unavoidable" consequences, seems to have several causes. One of the main causes seems to me to be that the nineteenth century (the European century!), the founding century of the historical disciplines and their methodological separation from the natural sciences and the consequent worldview oriented toward the myth of progress (of intellectual culture), has become deeply inscribed in the thinking of these disciplines. It is so deeply inscribed that even the most radical postmodern critics of this tradition can only effect its negation. At the end of the nineteenth century, Nietzsche's genealogy of history, using the scheme of eternal repetition, brought to light the carefully hidden official historiography of the bourgeois view of history. The fact that the newly awakened discussion of the end or the actuality of the Enlightenment usually steers well clear of Marxist critique of the Enlightenment (with few exceptions, among them Habermas) is probably connected to the burden of the Enlightenment tradition and to Marxism's theoretical crisis.

The theoretical roots of the cosmogonic theory of history, an early version of which stood at the height of the scientific worldview, lie within Marx's critique of the Enlightenment. With this theory, Marx discovered the "continent of history" (Althusser) for the historical disciplines. The difference between this theory and the materialistic predecessors of the Enlightenment and Hegel can be characterized briefly as the notion of the (industrial) process of labor as a process of temporalization. Social labor defines the only space from which this materialistic social theory can even begin to speak about human history. Materialism, in this new definition, is no longer a concept of perspective, no longer has anything to do with ideological philosophy, but constitutes reality (as social in different forms) as a dual relationship between humanity and nature (Schmied-Kowarzik 1984): as a relationship between appropriation and objectification realized through sensual activity (practice). "Humans are natural beings; nature is 'being' for humans; and work is the activity that binds humanity and nature together, in which both, nature and humanity, actually become what they are 'in themselves'" (Riedel 1965: 591). The Marxist theory of labor and history presumes the materiality of modern scientific practice. Contrary to the "fantastic illusions" of Hegelian natural philosophy, according to Marx, the natural sciences "through industrialization more *practically* affected and molded people's lives" (Marx 1977: pt. 1, 3: 122). Given the replacement of philosophy with a modern industry that connects people's lives with nature, the "objective historical views" of historicism have lost their theoretical foundation. This foundation "was based on viewing historical relationships as separate from human activity. Reactionary character" (Marx 1958: 543).

In the philosophical history of Enlightenment materialism, introduced by Descartes's new definition of the concept of matter, the Marxist categories of a historical materialism—labor/industry, humanity/nature, society/history—combined in the concept of anthropological nature, delineate the main difference from the materialism of the seventeenth and eighteenth centuries, "which deduces all thought of humanity from universal rules, which prescribes the laws of nature for all that exists" (Riedel 1965: 581). From this summary presentation of the historic-systematic use of the Marxist concept of a historical materialism, we can at least conclude that materiality includes two moments (or sides) of temporalizing socialization in the relationship between humanity, nature, and society. One is technological-material and the other is anthropological-social: "productive forces and social relationships as different sides to the development of the social individual" (Marx 1953 [1859]: 593). Materialistic thinking and materialistic science imply, in contrast to a simple "contemplative materialism," a moment of critical self-reflection: "The materialistic dialectic knows itself to be grounded in social practice, and there exists a connection between the logic of thought, categories of reason, and the determination of forms of ruling social practice" (Schmied-Kowarzik 1981: 276). As Ernst Bloch called it: a "transcending without transcendence" (1980: 289).

When speaking of materiality (at least in the sense of noncontemplative dialectical materialism),* understanding is always fo-

---

*I am not considering the perversion of the term "contemplative dialectical materialism," coined by Georgi Plekhanov, by the worldview of a dogmatic

cused on the relationship, on the stream of functions (Marx 1962: 511), on the integration of differentiated fields of practice on the basis of their social dimensions. There is therefore no reason to conclude from the petrifications of materialistic thinking that the concept of materialism should be replaced by the concept of materiality, because the former has accumulated an entire series of historical (Enlightenment, criticism of ideology, etc.) burdens, to which K. L. Pfeiffer alluded in Dubrovnik.

The suspicion that the explication of the theoretical foundations of the materialist "continent of history" discovered by Marx would exhaust itself in pure and sterile exegesis and would be unable to further our present attempts at a "historical concept of the present" might be countered by pointing out that the concept of *materialities of communication* (and the intended orientation of a new interdisciplinary cultural history) implicitly represents an actualization of the theoretical perspective that originated with the criticism of the bourgeois Enlightenment. This would, of course, include its explicit actualization. Given the dehumanizing tendencies of today's technological modes of socialization (and the interpretations of the same), we are not concerned with the restoration of a "myth of humanity" (something Marx already knew), nor with the illusory completion of a "project of the modern," but rather with the recovery of the workers' property (to include those who work with their minds) for the present conditions of their work and their lives.

The realization of this proclamation of materialistic social theory in programs of practical analysis could orient itself (at least) on the concept of *materialities of communication*. Today, given the working and living conditions of an "electronic age," we should develop materialistic criteria for the analysis of the increasingly important area of perceptive technologies. As initial attempts have shown, these can no longer be described with the conceptual instruments of preceding communications theories. The impression that the previously mentioned dematerialization or desemantization (K. L. Pfeiffer) of reality is created in this area is completely deceptive. For example, if we take a look at the complex relationships of sensitive visualizations through electronic technology (such as video cam-

---

Marxism. The scholastic scheme: dialectical materialism = super-philosophy for the natural sciences; historical materialism = super-philosophy for the historical and social sciences.

eras or so-called smart bombs with "reading heads"), then the separation (or the dispossession) of humanity from perceptions that make us the objects of technological observation arises as a qualitatively new phenomenon. Paul Virilio's thinking on *cinematism* in a controlled and manipulated *Telepolis* points in this direction. In the advanced areas of military logistics and police surveillance, the new phenomena show themselves in their absolute physicality and materiality:

War requires not only an autonomous intelligence but also a visual perception that has become independent of people: satellites constantly photograph, map, and fix objects; computers independently analyse the situation, creating a new, excentric view of the world. This scientific-technological event is revolutionary and at the same time suicidal, because it undermines people's freedom of will, be they scientists, the military, or politicians.   (Virilio 1986: 13)

As a preliminary concept on the way to a cultural-historical "scientific research strategy," as Marvin Harris suggested years ago (Harris 1979), materiality points to a long tradition of a desensualization that was philosophically baptized in the aesthetic idealism of the eighteenth century (above all in Germany). Here, as in Hegel's *Aesthetics*, ideality (as a sufficient principle for art) stands in contrast to materiality: "It is not the content itself in this formal ideality of art that demands our attention, but rather the satisfaction of intellectual creation. Representation must appear naturally; not what is natural as such, but creation, *the annihilation of sensual materiality* and external conditions is the poetic and ideal in the formal sense" (Hegel 1955: 190; my emphasis). Lukács even strengthened this idealistic conception in his aesthetics by giving the "homogenous medium," as an instance of suspension of everyday experience, the characteristic of leading and guiding the "receptive." The "homogenous medium" momentarily eliminates the "obstacles between perception and the objective being of the perceived" (Lukács 1963, 1: 648). In both instances, the systematic place of art is defined by its contrast to the everyday. The criterion of the reference of all conditions to the basis of human autonomy (Lukács's "The whole person and the person as a whole") makes it impossible to develop the concept of art historically. This preindustrial aesthetic idealism is finally confronted with practical criticism in modern audiovisual multimedia.

Materiality: Kaleidoscope of a
Short History of a Problem

In order to focus more clearly on the concept of materiality and its critical vitality in contrast to a tradition that remains locked in philosophical categories of identity, we must remind ourselves of (at least) two attempts at founding a materialistic theory of culture.

First is the model of a "materialistic cultural history" developed by the Critical Theory Collective in the space-time crisis era of the 1920's, planned by Max Horkheimer to be a "program for an interdisciplinary Marxism." This plan should not be considered a *quantité negligeable* in every point.* I believe that the reduction of the boundaries of "intellectual culture content" is valuable, as is the dual criticism of Mannheim's sociology of knowledge with its "meaningless" concept of "being" (Horkheimer) and of the "materialist philosophical ideology" of the Marxism of that time. The most important aspect of European materialism was lost from both perspectives: "namely, its practical link to social freedom movements since the Renaissance: materialism becomes one 'worldview' among many; it substantiates its concept of matter just as every other metaphysics absolves the materials it chooses" (Söllner 1979: 139).

The second attempt at founding the concept of *matérialité* is the theory of "materialist textual semiotics" developed in the 1960's and 1970's by the Paris Tel-Quel Group. Following the criticism of Saussurean linguistics developed by Derrida and Lacan, the concept of "the materiality of language" used by Kristeva and others characterizes the (textual) productivity of the *chaine signifiante* that precedes and cuts across all interpretation. According to this theory, materiality is primarily a procedural, action-oriented concept ("the labor of language"), whose closeness to the Marxist analysis of the fetishism of goods was explicitly established:

Today, the struggle between materialism and idealism takes place in one of two ways: either (materialistic gesture) one recognizes meaning (not as the meaning of a word, but as its creation) outside of subjectivity or one does not. Text is conceivable only within the materiality of language; meaning confronts language, and the logical-conceptual system it creates, with an exterior surrounded by reality, whose strangeness or "exteri-

*The best presentation of Horkheimer's concept is Söllner 1979. Also see Jay 1984.

orality" they are unable to eliminate. This forms the basis for a *materialistic* semiotics. This is a non-mechanical materialism, because exteriority is not process but rather practice, productive work with the material of the product.   (Ducrot and Todorov 1973: 451–52)

The reductionism of this theory is obvious and does not warrant further discussion here. More important is the fact that, given this view of materiality, language is removed from the model of communication: "Through the emphasis on the primacy of the significant, language has been removed from the model of communication" (Ducrot and Todorov 1973: 441). This has been accomplished with the argument that, in communications (as in exchange-value production), meaning is not "produced" but is only "represented" and "distributed." This division between communications and semantics, set up in the name of a "materialistic semiotics," dominated (in another way) structural linguistics. Following the mathematical communications theory established in the 1940's by C. E. Shannon and W. Weaver (*The Mathematical Theory of Communication*, 1949)—a theory of the sort that was, according to Alan Turing, a prerequisite for computer technology—structural linguistics saw communication as the main function of language, strictly separate from semantics (Martinet 1960). Roland Barthes's semiology has earned historical distinction for its criticism of this division in its extreme consequences: a de-ideologizing of linguistic communication (Calvet 1973).

Given this kaleidoscopic glance at a (still pending) conceptual and problematical history of materiality, a link or mediation between materiality and semantics in communicative actions would represent a conceivable beginning for a materiality of communications. This would include questioning the "desemanticizing of reality," providing a framework in which to orient ourselves. Niklas Luhmann's communications theory points in this direction, defining the communications process that is "freed from the transfer metaphor" as a "three-part selection process" and proceeding from the "differentiation of information and message" (Luhmann 1984).

Performance and Interculturalism

We can assume, along with O. Bloch (1985), that the materialism founded by Marx is to be distinguished from other materialisms in its concept of practical application; that its critical vitality must be conceived anew in every area of intellectual endeavor (the concept of matter in physics is not the same as that in biology or economics) and that it permits an open investigative strategy. The question Friedrich Kittler posed at the Dubrovnik conference is then raised as to how materialism, whose concept of matter was defined in the nineteenth century by energy, could be newly founded on the basis of information theory ("today, matter is information and no longer only energy") as a prospectively interdisciplinary task. It will have to be undertaken by scholars of both "hemispheres" (whose division into natural and humanistic sciences [*Geistesgeschichtes*] can no longer be justified), in cooperation with artists.

Models are already available in forms of an "integrated aesthetics of the living." An alternative culture has been created that, on the basis of developments in theater, is trying out models for "subjunctive worlds" (F. Turner). Richard Schechner's "Performance Theatre Group," Pina Bausch's "Dance Theater," Meredith Monk's "Performance Actions," Ariane Mnouchkine's "Théâtre du Soleil," and Robert Wilson and Heiner Müller's "Theater of Picture" are examples of a cultural application that experiments with boundaries and consequences of a labor-rationalized world and with its elimination.

The characterization of this new culture as *performance* makes this border crossing recognizable on several different levels, in view of the relationship between art and everyday life, between (anthropological) nature and technology, between artistic language and body language, between idea, presentation, and action, between text and production, and between image-time and space-time. The promotion of a concept of a (post)modern social aesthetic coming from the performance arts (dance, music, theater) can be seen as indicating the threshold of a cultural-historical epoch. Richard Schechner characterized this threshold in his performance theory:

Now my corner of experience, my "specialty," is performance. Not just theatre, but performance as a wide variety of activities ranging from theatre and dance to sports, rituals, popular entertainments, therapies that use performance techniques, and ordinary daily encounters among people where participants seem to be playing out roles more than just "being themselves." I've even come to doubt that there is a core or single self that a person can "be." Everything in human behavior indicates that we

perform our existence, especially our social existence. . . . Recently
because of the impact of the period of experimentation I'm focusing on,
and because of interest in dance, in the performance traditions of non-
Euro-American cultures, in the popular entertainments of Euro-America,
a second way of seeing performance history is emerging. This is a history
not of drama, nor of the productions of the great plays, nor even the
"acting styles" of the great actors, but of a very broad spectrum of
"performative activities." . . . Always there existed a lively popular
tradition of things like circus, mountebanks, vaudeville and burlesque,
commedia dell'arte, street entertainers. . . . These theatrical traditions
with their performance texts were shunned academically.   (Schechner
1982: 14, 30)

Schechner calls for the concrete utopia of an interculturalism that
responds to the electronic computer culture with the non-nostalgic
quest for the "Africa in each of us." This could also be called an
"anthropological materialism" that provides one possible answer
to Gumbrecht's question. Schechner states:

Interculturalism is replacing—ever so cautiously, but not so slowly—
internationalism. The nation is the force of modernism; and cultures—I
emphasize the plural—are the force (what word can replace force?) of
postmodernism. As a world information order comes into being, human
action can be mapped as a relationship among three levels:

PAN-HUMAN, EVEN SUPRA-HUMAN,
COMMUNICATIONS NETWORKS
information from / to anywhere, anyone

CULTURES, CULTURES OF CHOICE
ethnic, individualistic, local behaviors
people selecting cultures of choice
people performing various subjunctive actualities

PAN-HUMAN BODY BEHAVIORS / DREAM-ARCHETYPE NETWORKS
unconscious & ethological basis of behavior and cultures

. . . Maybe the most exciting aspect of this map is the possibility for
people to have "cultures of choice." (Schechner 1982: 124–25)

Performance not only describes present-day alternative practice,
but has at the same time also become a concept of a cultural
historical practice. Paul Zumthor presented the dimensions and

theoretical foundation of this concept in his standard work *Introduction à la poésie orale* (1983). A change in the thinking of our time of "electronic enlightenment" (Virilio), articulated within performance culture and (still) marginal but very promising, reveals aspects of cultural history that have been hidden up to now.

Performance could consequently also be a "deconstructive" ferment of decomposition within the postmodern itself. If the aesthetic and cultural border crossing is what they hold in common, then their understanding of time and history is what divides them. In the final analysis, postmodern "historicism" goes back to a cyclical concept of time, back to a "cosmological" model, that is now instrumented as a cycle of catastrophe. This explains certain postmodern theorists' radical rejection of utopias. The concept of subjunctive worlds represented by R. Schechner and F. Turner argues for a new ethic of responsibility:

If we destroy ourselves in a nuclear holocaust or eco-catastrophe, it won't be because of some kind of technological determinism, or innate drive or conspiracy of the powerful or economic forces of history; it will be because we chose to, collectively, and we chose to because we considered that future to be the most beautiful, and we considered it to be the most beautiful because we imaginatively constructed it to be so. Art has the exalted function, the world-saving function, of imaginatively constructing other futures which do not involve the *götterdammerung* of mass suicide. I don't mean namby-pamby assertions of moral principle or nonviolence. They only increase the desirability of what is forbidden (Blake). Most ecology freaks are imaginatively mass-murderers. . . . Of course, the universe isn't running down, if we realize that it's made of information not of energy. . . . I predict that we will create subjunctive worlds, not the death-bang.   (Turner, in Schechner 1982: 115)

Colophon

Francis Bacon, called the "father of modern materialism" by Marx, described a "house of sensory illusion" in his utopia *New Atlantis* at the beginning of the modern era. In this house were available all sorts of techniques for creating illusions, simulations, and deceptions. At the risk of loss of honor and of fines, the inhabitants were strictly forbidden to exaggerate or ornament any natural event. These events, says Bacon, must be represented simply and clearly without any trickery. Today the doors of this house are wide open. It has become, in the words of Jean Baudrillard, an "open house." "The promiscuity that dominates the networks of communications is superficially satisfying and endlessly inciting. It destroys all living, protective spaces. . . . This obscene delirium of communication joins itself to conditions of fascination and frenzy" (Baudrillard 1985: 131–32). Will the materiality of this communication inevitably catch up with us?

FRANCISCO J. VARELA AND MARK R. ANSPACH

The Body Thinks: The Immune System in the Process of Somatic Individuation

A Change in Metaphors

We would like to write about an object that is both the ultimate paradox and a potential breakdown: the body. In this age of AIDS, we know more precisely than ever before that we have a body *identity* that is as fragile as it is dynamic. The primary question is therefore: what is the nature of the body identity when a syndrome such as AIDS can cause its breakdown? This leads us directly to the key phenomenon of body identity: the immune system.

The role of the immune system is normally the protection of the "self" from external infections. The immune system is supposed to produce defenses against intruders as well as surveillance cells that kill pathogens and protect the "self" from being overcome by others (the nonself). Every textbook of immunology starts by defining immunology as the study of immune responses.

Immunological discourse is dominated by *military* metaphors, just as cognitive science was once dominated by the (digital) computer. We would like to propose a substantially different meta-

NOTE: Parts of this essay appeared in J. Brockman, ed., *Doing Science*, pp. 237–57 (New York: Prentice Hall, 1991). Mark R. Anspach gratefully acknowledges research support from the Direction des Recherches, Etudes et Techniques (contract no. 91/110).

phor and conceptual framework for the study of immune systems. This is a concept that emphasizes the *cognitive* abilities of immune events. It is clear that some readers will find the term "cognitive" too strong, but we believe it will be useful insofar as it provides a clear contrast to the military framework of immunity as defense. We would like to use the word "cognitive" in the same vague sense as it is used with respect to other biological processes, for instance, in the brain or in ecosystems. In any case, it is not meant here to describe mental and linguistic human processes.

The body can be considered a (structured) environment for the diverse and highly interactive populations of white blood cells, or lymphocytes, that constitute the immune system. The lymphocytes are differentiated among themselves, through either particular molecular markers or antibodies that are advertised on their membrane surfaces. Like the living species of the biosphere, they stimulate or inhibit each other's growth. Like species in an ecosystem they generate an amazing diversity: the antibodies and other molecules produced by lymphocytes are by far (by a millionfold) the most highly diversified molecular group in the body. They are therefore ideally qualified to ensure the constant change and diversity of other molecules in the body. The lymphocyte network exists in a state of harmony with its body as its natural environment, which in turn determines which lymphocytes occur. But the existing lymphocytes radically alter every molecular profile in the body. When we are adults, our molecular identity presents a profile that occurs only once, one that has developed through the cooperation of the immune system and the body.

The Unavoidable Cognitive Aspect of Immune Phenomena

Even if it had only a defensive function, the immune system would have to exhibit cognitive capabilities. It would first have to be able to recognize molecular profiles: this includes the shapes of intruding agents, or antigens, and, on a more general level, the "foreignness" that could endanger the bodily integrity of the subject. It must also be capable of learning, in order to recognize new antigens and defend itself against them. Finally, it must have a memory, in order to retain these new forms.

Recognition, learning ability, and memory are processes and mechanisms currently being discussed in "connectionism" (network approaches to cognitive mechanisms). The model paradigm is the brain. The immune system is claimed to be a cognitive network because (1) it shares a number of properties with the brain, and (2)—which is much more interesting—there are in both cases similar global properties of biological networks that make cognitive behavior possible. Given this perspective, the immune system can be a preferred paradigm for the current investigations of basic cognitive mechanisms.

This would not be the case without new results and trends in experimental immunobiology that orient themselves on the paradigm of networking. They have led to important shifts in immunological practice and applications: "Older theories hold that the antibody molecule is something like a 'universal glue' that can interact with any antigen form and enter into a complementary relationship that eliminates the antigen and remembers the 'learned' configuration" (Urbain 1986: 20). Especially important are the quotation marks around the word "learned." It is impossible to overlook the cognitive aspect of the process on the one hand; on the other hand, it does not seem to be really cognitive either. Otherwise, a paper carrying a signature would have to have "learned."

This introduces the central issue. It is conventional in immunology to speak of the difference between self/nonself. The immune system acts in its discriminative capacities *inside* the body. This has important consequences. Until recently, as we will see later, immunology, as well as other areas of cognitive science, considered every cognitive capacity to be a processing of information. It was believed that the information came from "outside," that the system reacted adequately and thereby produced an adequate response. These kinds of input/output relationships were, along with the assumption of internal programs for "information processing," the basis for a *heteronomous* approach to research, one that views systems as "externally determined" (Varela 1979). Immunologists have incorporated this heteronomous scheme. An antigen comes "from outside," and the appropriate response is the production of an antibody, whose purpose is to eliminate the antigen. But what determines *how* the antibody is formed? In contrast to the nervous system, the immune system has no spatially placed sensory organs.

Antibodies circulate freely within the organism, and the chance of meeting upon molecules of organic tissues (the "self") is just as high as the chance of meeting upon the antigen (the nonself). An antibody's recognition function assumes *that it is able to recognize what must be recognized.*

If a reader has the impression that this is becoming a little too complicated, we agree. It is necessary, however, to demonstrate that the assumption of a capacity for recognition, vital to the immune system, cannot be adequately explained by a heteronomous operation, by an automatic reaction to something that comes from "outside." In the past, immunology has attempted to avoid these difficulties and thereby maintain a heteronomous perspective. A truly satisfactory solution requires a more radical rethinking, an appreciation of the immune system as an autonomous network. In order to make this easier to understand, we would like to begin by asking what "recognition" means in this context.

To say that an antibody "recognizes" an antigen is to say that it binds with it chemically and by doing so neutralizes it. This explanation works beautifully where foreign molecules are concerned, but not with molecules that are essential components of the organism. Immunologists have therefore excluded the possibility that antibodies can attach themselves to molecules of its own organism without triggering autoimmune diseases. It is only in this one— pathological—case that destructive immune reactions to organic tissue occurs. In 1900, Paul Ehrlich identified this *tolerance* phenomenon as "horror autotoxicus."

Another important idea led to the hypothesis that the recognition of unknown antigens was based on the imprecision of these mechanisms themselves, that is, that an antibody can bind with varying degrees of affinity to a large spectrum of molecular forms. A repertoire of 10^5 kinds of antibodies is sufficient for a tadpole to remain alive, whereas humans need more than 10^9 kinds of antibodies. It must therefore be assumed that the function performed by the immune system can be *complete* at various levels—and this makes the question of "self" and "nonself" all the more complex.

Double discrimination also means double recognition. First, an antigen must be identified as "nonself," and only then can the type of antigen be determined. It logically follows that the recognition of the "nonself" results in the recognition of the "self." The diffi-

culty lies in the assumption that recognition also results in destruction. This rather diabolical implication could be formulated as
follows: "Classical theories demand on the one hand comparison
operations that distinguish between self and non-self structures,
whereas a non-recognition of the existence of the self becomes the
prerequisite that *no* immunological self-destruction takes place"
(Coutinho et al. 1984: 152). We would like to call this implication
the "immunological double bind." No defense without recognition / No recognition without destruction.

The Development of Current Theory
(Clonal Selection)

We are now in a position to examine the next step in immunological
thinking. It has evolved as an answer to the previously outlined
problems and still clings to the heteronomous view of the immune
system. Clonal selection theory developed out of the work of
N. Jerne and M. Burnet in the 1950's and, until recently, enjoyed a
dominant position in immunology, just as the symbolic/computa-
tional view of cognition has dominated cognitive science. It took a
long time for immunology to free itself from the scheme of "information processing," and it did so only reluctantly.

The first new idea came from Jerne and was based on the
assumption of an antibody repertoire permanently present in the
body. In contrast to preceding ideas, his speculation was that antibody production took place *prior* to a confrontation with antigens
and even to some extent anticipated this event. This seemed at first
inconceivable, but today we know that there are 10^{20} antibodies
with a high degree of diversity and degeneracy of binding, so that
there is no longer any doubt as to the existence of an "internal
repertoire." At that time, however, it remained to be explained
how an initially random series of antibodies could be so precisely
calibrated to the antigens. It was known that the confrontation with
antigens left behind traces within the system. The antibodies that
bind with them multiply, and this led to the theory of *immune
response*. In fact, a reflection on this kind of phenomenon later led to
an understanding of cognitive properties. The most important
suggestion as to how this problem could be circumvented was
made by Jerne. He called upon Darwin and the theory of natural

selection. Even then, when the antigen does not cause antibodies to be formed, it can still select those antibodies that are present and bind to them, causing them to multiply. It remained for M. Burnet to postulate a specific mechanism whereby this selective process could be embodied in terms of mere lymphocyte traffic. Every lymphocyte could carry (and produce) only one kind of antibody, so that the particular subclasses of lymphocyte families, or clones, could only bind with the appropriate antigen. The contact between antigen and clone led to a proliferation of clone cells, leading to an increased production of antibodies of a particular type, thus neutralizing the incoming antigen (Burnet 1959). This assumed a development of lymphocyte and antibody groups under the selection pressure of the antigens. Even today we still hear the term "antigenic determinant."

Clonal selection theory was a brilliant answer to the complicated and thorny question of how the immune system operates in the face of an unlimited range of unknown stimuli. Cognitive issues appear here as an evolutionary game. The problem is transferred from one temporal scale to another. It is likewise transferred from the external environment to the inside of the organism. Of course, this model does not solve the question of self-tolerance. The solution set forth by clonal selection theory is predictably simple. It postulates that the initial antibody repertoire is incomplete. Precisely those clones that are able to recognize self-molecules are missing. This simple solution only pushed the problem aside, since the absence of these clones could not be explained by genetic mechanisms. This barred the way for an explanation by way of a genetic process as well as a selective process. The relevant intermediate step was seen in the embryonic stage, which assumed a clonal selection that was supposed to destroy clones directed against the self. Formulated another way, the organism *learns* to distinguish between self and nonself during ontogeny.

Thus the old cognitive issues reappear through the window after being chased out the door. The selectionist model is insufficient; it depends on a learning process in which the self is isolated, albeit in an embryonic stage. Burnet formulated an explanation for this learning process. Autoimmune clones can be eliminated "by assuming that at this stage of embryonic life the antigenic contact leads to cell death" (Burnet 1959: 58). This was a curious twist of

the previous logic. Precisely those mechanisms that permit discrimination between self and antigens become the opposite of what
later allowed for the distinction between various antigens. In the
latter case, the contact with antigens leads to the elimination of
antigens. In the first case, the contact with antigens leads to the
elimination of cells. The theoretical gambit separates the two poles
of the immunological double bind. One part of the distinction is
ascribed to the adult, the other to the embryo. Moreover, the
clones to be eliminated in the embryo are themselves components
of the self, so that self-destruction is implicit in a framework designed to prevent this. It becomes clear that the interdependence of
these two contradictory processes is the price to be paid for logical
consistency.

Clonal selection provided a valuable framework for experimental work. It led Burnet to postulate the possibility of fooling the
immune system with the introduction of cells into an embryo to
make it tolerant of molecules not normally present. Burnet's theory could be proven in experiments, and it was clearly established
that this tolerance was learned. It was later found, however, that
this tolerance is not found exclusively in embryos. Adults can also
become tolerant, a fact leading to the conclusion that this learning
process cannot be limited to a specific developmental phase. This
posed serious questions for clonal selection theory.

The notion of a complete repertoire minus self-determinants is
already problematic. This exception seems initially to be rather
innocent but has frightening consequences if one keeps in mind
what has been said about the broad range of molecular profiles to
which an antibody binds, something that is basic to the notion of
completeness in the first place. The notion of autoimmune clonal
elimination is only a simple one so long as a specification of antibodies is assumed. This goes back to the medical origins of immunology and seemed to be confirmed by vaccination, where a narrow class of antibodies is induced against a pathogen. But this does
not allow us to postulate a rule of "one antibody, one antigen."
If we were to eliminate a sufficient number of clones in order to
avoid a reaction to organic molecules, then this would mean de-
priving living beings of their ability to react to the huge number
of potential antigens, thereby threatening their very existence.
In this case, the immunity shield would be nothing more than a

sieve. It becomes clear that the assumption of a complete repertoire "with exceptions" leads to another contradiction. These exceptions were first meant to solve the dilemma of the two contrary forms of recognition, which were themselves postulated to understand the difference between self and nonself. But the concept of self-recognition must be specified in such a way that it becomes incompatible with the assumption of completeness.

Thus we are able to observe a development that is frequent in natural science: after several years of general acceptance, the flaws of clonal selection theory became more and more clear (something not to be elaborated here). In the end it was the combination of unsolved theoretical problems (not always of concern to the immunologists) and a few key empirical observations that opened a new perspective in the mid-1970's.

Toward an Autonomous Immune Network

The problems just discussed remain unsolved as long as one is unwilling to discard the notion of *horror autotoxicus*. It is clear today that there are normal, circulating antibodies that bind to many (all?) organic molecules in both embryos and adults. It is no longer possible to think of these antibodies as working against the molecules of the organism. These same antibody types may cause auto-immune diseases in larger concentrations, but not at their normal levels of circulation.

Another basic theoretical revision is even more important. It must be remembered that antibodies that circulate and are responsible for self/nonself discrimination are themselves part of the organism. This leads to the conclusion that there are antibodies that bind to other antibodies. There is now ample evidence that this is indeed the case, and hence that the circulating elements of free-floating serum antibodies and the antibodies advertised on cell surfaces are not separate individual elements or clones, but form a tightly meshed network. This idea is (again!) the brainchild of Jerne (1974 and 1984). It became necessary to recognize that the system could operate on its own internal dynamics; Jerne called this "eigen-behavior" (self-determined behavior) in a dynamic equilibrium. These ideas raised serious questions about a heteronomous immune system. However, it is still necessary to change other theoretical assumptions in order to fully appreciate the consequences of this reorientation.

Imagine a foreign antigen entering the organism. A part of the antigen, its antigenic determinant, will be recognized by certain antibodies. Let us call this molecular profile E (for epitope). In the older concept, this would mean that the anti-E antibody was ready to eliminate the E-carrying antigen. Recognition takes place only between the two of them, and the antigen would continue to maintain its selective function. This private dialogue is no longer possible in the network concept. There is no longer a dual, but rather a multiple binding between E and anti-E antibodies. More significantly, we must take into account the antibodies that bind to the idiotopes of the anti-E's. These in turn will have antibodies that bind to their idiotopes, and so on.

The end result is that we will always encounter antibody classes that will at least partially resemble the incoming epitope E. Stated more simply: the antigen is able to enter the network to the extent that an antibody with a sufficiently similar molecular profile, an "internal image," is already in circulation. The antigen ceases to be a "determinant" and becomes a small perturbation in an already existing network. This means that the effects of the incoming antigen, as in any perturbation in a rich network, will be varied and dependent on the entire context of the network.

The heteronomous concept of the system is weakened by examining its network-based logic. Whenever the immunologist injects large amounts of an antigen, the immune response appears to be a heteronomous response of the system. The network paradigm lets us see what a highly contrived, laboratory situation this really is. Normally we do *not* receive large amounts of an antigen. We have a small number of various organic molecules that change over time and a certain number of molecules to which we are exposed through eating and breathing. The system is principally an autonomous unit, open to all kinds of modulation, and these modulations cause small changes within the organism itself. The system is certainly not a machine that produces immune reactions. Organisms that have never been exposed to antigens develop a completely normal immune system. This is a blatant contradiction to clonal selection theory, which would have to predict an atrophied immune system.

The next important step of reorientation is to drop the concept of the immune system as a defensive system that reacts to external events, and to understand it instead as a function of self-assertion that establishes a *molecular identity* by maintaining molecular circulation levels throughout the entire network. It is only by viewing the immune system in this way that it corresponds to current research on biological networks. A complex network that is connected with other networks generates these internal levels through distributed processes. More precisely, the dynamic level of antibody/cell encounters regulates the number of cells and the circulating level of molecular profiles. This idea runs parallel to the idea that an organism gives an ecosystem its identity within its environment. This means that some kind of ecology of lymphocytes exists within the body. This dance between immune system and body is the key to the alternative view proposed here, since it is this dance that allows the body to maintain an ever-changing and plastic identity over the course of its life throughout various confrontations. The establishment of the system's identity is a positive task and not a reaction against antigens. The task of identity specification is seen here as primary, both logically and biologically. All of this requires that the immune network, like any ecosystem, have a *learning mechanism*. This is based on the constant exchange of network components through recruitment of new lymphocytes from a reserve pool. This involves an active process that includes in mice, for example, up to 20 percent of all lymphocytes. It is this ongoing replacement that provides the mechanism for learning and memory (instead of the better known learning algorithms for neural networks; Varela, Coutinho et al. 1988; Varela, Sanchez, and Coutinho 1988).

Of course, this is only a very simplified sketch of the immune system. Important here is the fundamental conceptual outline and its logical framework. It is therefore important to properly understand what is meant today by the term "network" in immunology. The existence of anti-idiotypic antibodies is unquestioned. Less certain is their importance and significance. For most immunologists, immune networks are a chain of successive anti-idiotypes. The complexity of the network processes and their characteristics, normally central to the investigation of complex systems and cognitive science, is not well understood, however. The number of experimental papers that study immune network problems can be counted on one hand, and theoretical investigations are just beginning (Coutinho and Varela 1950; Varela and Coutinho 1991; Perelson 1988). This is a result of the difficulty of abandoning the view of immunity as defense even when mediated through idiotype network processes and finally recognizing the immune system as establishing molecular identity, that is, as an autonomous immune system. What is crucial here is the distinction between autonomous (self-production) and heteronomous (external direction).

We can now ask ourselves how this concept of the autonomous network deals with the immunological double bind and the problem of self/nonself discrimination. Actually the answer is quite simple. The answer corresponds to the basic resolution of any paradox. It must project itself out of the boundaries of its own validity. In this particular case, *the immune system fundamentally does not (cannot) discriminate between self and nonself.* The normal function of the network can only be perturbed or modulated by incoming antigens, responding only to what is similar to what is already present. Any antigen that perturbs the immune network is by definition an "antigen of the interior," and will therefore only modulate the ongoing dynamics of the network. Any element that is incapable of doing so is simply not recognized and may well trigger a "reflexive" immune response, that is, one produced by quasi-automatic processes that are only peripheral to the network itself. The distinction of self/nonself discrimination becomes a distinction of self/nonself recognition.

Normally, antigens enter through food or air and are regulated by the multiple loops that affect them, creating low levels of both the antigens and the binding antibodies. This is precisely what happens with the organism's own elements. Throughout its entire development, the organism's own molecules interact with the immune components in such a way that their levels are kept within limits since they are dominated by the immune activity. For example, the level of renin, a completely "normal" hormone, is regulated by the various antibodies normally present in the individual's immune system. This process need not be (and most generally is not) a stable one: its variability and frequency of exchange is too high. It is rather a principle of viability: certain levels are never surpassed despite constantly changing directions of motion (thus, an explosion in the production of certain antibody types is avoided). This is what is meant by a *positive* assertion of molecular identity; that is, what we are on the molecular level and what our immune system is relate to each other as two co-evolving processes.

Those who still see the immune system as a defensive system must be getting impatient. Surely, whenever immunity is weakened, as in AIDS, we are immediately ravaged by pathogens. To be sure, the system is *also* able to mount an immune response against infection. This occurs when the number or frequency of antigens is too great. Then specific mechanisms are triggered that will mount an immune response, to include inflammation at the wound site. These mechanisms are, interestingly, mostly independent of the network processes just described, and it is almost exclusively these "reflex" immune reactions that have been the concern of classical immunology. The point is not to deny that defense is possible, but to see it as a special case of something more fundamental: individual molecular identity. In fact, multicellular life is possible without an immune defense, as in invertebrates. Defensive responses, the center of attention in medical immunology, are secondary acquisitions. For example, defensive/avoidance reactions in neural behavior are necessary later variants of the more fundamental task of motion/relationship in multicellular life. To say that immunity is fundamentally defense is as distorted as saying that the brain is fundamentally concerned with defense and avoidance. We certainly defend ourselves and avoid attack, but this is hardly what cognition is about, that is, flexibility in living.

Coda

We have traced the change in immunological concepts from its instructionist inception through clonal selection to a network perspective. This development is closely linked to cognitive issues. It is fascinating to discover that the immune network now stands alongside neural networks as a source of mechanisms and explanations for basic cognitive phenomena such as recognition, learning, memory, and adaptability. If one accepts that connectionism and artificial networks are valid research alternatives in cognitive science, then immune activities must be seen as cognitive phenomena. Many would prefer to use the word "cognitive" exclusively for phenomena that involve language and reasoning in humans or in machines. I acknowledge that this use of the word is a defensible one, but it seems equally defensible to see these "higher" processes in continuity with "simpler" ones such as those studied by connectionists and exhibited by immune networks. This does not involve a trivial semantic issue but the underlying conceptual issues raised by immune events.

Immunology is about to emerge from the dominance of its original sin—being born from the medicine of infectious diseases and having vaccinations as its main paradigm, a heteronomous view *par excellence*. This is happening at the same time that cognitive science is recovering from the dominance of the digital computer as its main metaphor. If we are willing to acknowledge the central importance of the autonomy of the process in both these biological networks, neural and immune, then we will discover how we think with our entire body.

JEAN-FRANÇOIS LYOTARD

Can Thought Go on
Without a Body?

He

You philosophers ask questions without answers, questions that
have to remain unanswered to deserve being called philosophical.
According to you answered questions are only technical matters.
That's what they were to begin with. They were mistaken for
philosophical questions. You turn to other questions that seem
completely impossible to answer: which by definition resist every
attempt at conquest by the understanding. Or what amounts to the
same thing: you declare that if the first questions were answered,
that's because they were badly formulated. And you grant yourselves the privilege of continuing to regard as unresolved, that is, as
well formulated, questions that technical science believes it answered but in truth only inadequately dealt with. For you solutions
are just illusions, failures to maintain the integrity due to being—or
some such thing. Long live patience. You'll hold out forever with
your incredulity. But don't be surprised if all the same, through
your irresolution, you end up wearing out your reader.

But that's not the question. While we talk, the sun is getting
older. It will explode in 4.5 billion years. It's just a little beyond the
halfway point of its expected lifetime. It's like a man in his early
forties with a life expectancy of eighty. With the sun's death your
insoluble questions will be done with too. It's possible they'll stay
unanswered right up to the end, flawlessly formulated, though

now both grounds for raising such questions as well as the place to do this will no longer exist. You explain: it's impossible to think an end, pure and simple, of anything at all, since the end's a limit and to think it you have to be on both sides of that limit. So what's finished or finite has to be perpetuated in our thought if it's to be thought of as finished. Now this is true of limits belonging to thought. But after the sun's death there won't be a thought to know that its death took place.

That, in my view, is the sole serious question to face humanity today. In comparison everything else seems insignificant. Wars, conflicts, political tension, shifts in opinion, philosophical debates, even passions—everything's dead already if this infinite reserve from which you now draw energy to defer answers, if in short thought as quest, dies out with the sun. Maybe death isn't the word. But the inevitable explosion to come, the one that's always forgotten in your intellectual ploys, can be seen in a certain way as coming before the fact to render these ploys posthumous—make them futile. I'm talking about what's X'd out of your writings— matter. Matter taken as an arrangement of energy created, destroyed, and re-created over and over again, endlessly. On the corpuscular and/or cosmic scale I mean. I am not talking about the familiar, reassuring terrestrial world or the reassuring transcendent immanence of thought to its objects, analogous to the way the eye transcends what's visible or *habitus* its *situs*. In 4.5 billion years there will arrive the demise of your phenomenology and your utopian politics, and there'll be no one there to toll the death knell or hear it. It will be too late to understand that your passionate, endless questioning always depended on a "life of the mind" that will have been nothing else than a covert form of earthly life. A form of life that was spiritual because human, human because earthly—coming from the earth of the most living of living things. Thought borrows a horizon and orientation, the limitless limit and the end without end it assumes, from the corporeal, sensory, emotional, and cognitive experience of a quite sophisticated but definitely earthly existence—to which it's indebted as well.

With the disappearance of earth, thought will have stopped— leaving that disappearance absolutely unthought of. It's the horizon itself that will be abolished and, with its disappearance, your transcendence in immanence as well. If, as a limit, death really is what escapes and is deferred and as a result what thought has to deal with, right from the beginning—this death is still only the life of our minds. But the death of the sun is a death of mind, because it is the death of death as the life of the mind. There's no sublation or deferral if nothing survives. This annihilation is totally different from the one you harangue us about talking about "our" death, a death that is part of the fate of living creatures who think. Annihilation in any case is too subjective. It will involve a change in the condition of matter: that is, in the form that energies take. This change is enough to render null and void your anticipation of a world after the explosion. Political science-fiction novels depict the cold desert of our human world after nuclear war. The solar explosion won't be due to human war. It won't leave behind it a devastated human world, dehumanized, but with nonetheless at least a single survivor, someone to tell the story of what's left, write it down. Dehumanized still implies human—a dead human, but conceivable: because dead in human terms, still capable of being sublated in thought. But in what remains after the solar explosion, there won't be any humanness, there won't be living creatures, there won't be intelligent, sensitive, sentient earthlings to bear witness to it, since they and their earthly horizon will have been consumed.

Assume that the ground, Husserl's *Ur-Erde*, will vanish into clouds of heat and matter. Considered as matter, the earth isn't at all originary since it's subject to changes in its condition—changes from further away or closer, changes coming from matter and energy and from the laws governing Earth's transformation. The *Erde* is an arrangement of matter/energy. This arrangement is transitory—lasting a few billion years more or less. Lunar years. Not a long time considered on a cosmic scale. The sun, our earth, and your thought will have been no more than a spasmodic state of energy, an instant of established order, a smile on the surface of matter in a remote corner of the cosmos. You, the unbelievers, you're really believers: you believe much too much in that smile, in the complicity of things and thought, in the purposefulness of all things! Like everyone else, you will end up victims of the stabilized relationships of order in that remote corner. You'll have been seduced and deceived by what you call nature, by a congruence of mind and things. Claudel called this a *co-naissance*, and Merleau-

Ponty spoke of the chiasmus of the eye and the horizon, a fluid in which mind floats. The solar explosion, the mere thought of that explosion, should awaken you from this euphoria. Look here: you try to think of the event in its *quod*, in the advent of "it so happens that" before any quiddity, don't you? Well, you'll grant that the explosion of the sun is the *quod* itself, no subsequent assignment being possible. Of that death alone, Epicurus ought to have said what he says about death—that I have nothing to do with it, since if it's present, I'm not, and if I'm present, it's not. Human death is included in the life of human mind. Solar death implies an irreparably exclusive disjunction between death and thought: if there's death, then there's no thought. Negation without remainder. No self to make sense of it. Pure event. Disaster. All the events and disasters we're familiar with and try to think of will end up as no more than pale simulacra.

Now this event is ineluctable. So you do one of two things. On the one hand, you might choose not to concern yourself with it— and to remain in the life of the mind and in earthly phenomenality. Like Epicurus you say, "As long as it's not here, I am, and I continue philosophizing in the cozy lap of the complicity between man and nature." But still with this glum afterthought: *après moi le déluge*. The deluge of matter. You'll grant there's a significant point of divergence between our thinking and the classical and modern thought of Western civilization: the obvious fact of there being no nature, but only the material monster of *D'Alembert's Dream*, the *chōra* of the *Timaeus*. Once we were considered able to converse with Nature. Matter asks no questions, expects no answers of us. It ignores us. It made us the way it made all bodies—by chance and according to its laws.

On the other hand, you might try to anticipate the disaster and fend it off with means belonging to that category—means that are those of the laws of the transformation of energy. You decide to accept the challenge of the extremely likely annihilation of a solar order and an order of your own thought. And then the only job left you is quite clear—it's been under way for some time—the job of simulating conditions of life and thought to make thinking remain materially possible after the change in the condition of matter that's the disaster. This and this alone is what's at stake today in technical and scientific research in every field from dietetics, neurophysiology, genetics, and tissue synthesis to particle physics, astrophysics, electronics, information science, and nuclear physics. Whatever the immediate stakes might appear to be: health, war, production, communication. For the benefit of humankind, as the saying goes.

You know—technology wasn't invented by us humans. Rather the other way around. As anthropologists and biologists admit, even the simplest life forms, infusoria (tiny algae synthesized by light at the edges of tidepools a few million years ago) are already technical devices. Any material system is technological if it filters information useful to its survival, if it memorizes and processes that information and makes inferences based on the regulating effect of behavior; that is, if it intervenes on and impacts its environment so as to assure its perpetuation at least. A human being isn't different in nature from an object of this type. Its equipment for absorbing data isn't exceptional compared to that of other living things. What's true is that this human being is omnivorous when dealing with information because it has a regulating system (codes and rules of processing) that's more differentiated and a storage capacity for its memory that's greater than those of other living things. Most of all: it's equipped with a symbolic system that's both arbitrary (in semantics and syntax), letting it be less dependent on an immediate environment, and also "recursive" (Hofstadter), allowing it to take into account (above and beyond raw data) the way it has of processing such data. That is, itself. Hence, the way it has of processing as information its own rules in turn and of inferring other ways of processing information. A human, in short, is a living organization that is not only complex but, so to speak, replex. It can grasp itself as a medium (as in medicine) or as an organ (as in goal-directed activity) or as an object (as in thought—I mean aesthetic as well as speculative thought). It can even abstract itself from itself and take into account only its rules of processing, as in logic and mathematics. The opposite limit of this symbolic recursiveness resides in the necessity by which it is bound (whatever its *meta*-level of operation) at the same time to maintain regulations that guarantee its survival in any environment whatsoever. Isn't that exactly what constitutes the basis of your transcendence in immanence? Now, until the present time, this environment has been terrestrial. The survival of a thinking-organization requires exchanges with that environment such that the human body can perpetuate itself there. This is equally true of the quintessential *meta*-function—philosophical thought. To think, at the very least you have to breathe, eat, and so on. You are still under an obligation to "earn a living."

The body might be considered the hardware of the complex technical device that is human thought. If this body is not properly functioning, the ever so complex operations, the meta-regulations to the third or fourth power, the controlled deregulations of which you philosophers are so fond, are impossible. Your philosophy of the endless end, of immortal death, of interminable difference, of the undecidable, is an expression, perhaps the expression *par excellence*, of meta-regulation itself. It's as if it took itself into account as *meta*. Which is all well and good. But don't forget—this faculty of being able to change levels referentially derives solely from the symbolic and recursive power of language. Now language is simply the most complex form of the (living and dead) "memories" that regulate all living things and make them technical objects better adjusted to their surroundings than mechanical ensembles. In other words your philosophy is possible only because the material ensemble called "man" is endowed with very sophisticated software. But also, this software, human language, is dependent on the condition of the hardware. Now: the hardware will be consumed in the solar explosion, taking philosophical thought with it (along with all other thought) as it goes up in flames.

So the problem of the technological sciences can be stated as follows: how can we provide this software with a hardware that is independent of the conditions of life on earth?

That is: how can we make thought without a body possible? A thought that continues to exist after the death of the human body. This is the price to be paid if the explosion is to be conceivable, if the death of the sun is to be a death like other deaths we know about. Thought without a body is the prerequisite for thinking of the death of all bodies, solar or terrestrial, and of the death of thoughts that are inseparable from those bodies.

But "without a body" in this exact sense: without the complex living terrestrial organism known as the human body. Not without hardware, obviously.

So theoretically the solution is very simple: manufacture hardware capable of "nurturing" software at least as complex (or replex) as that of the present-day human brain, but in nonterrestrial conditions. That clearly means finding for the "body" envisaged a "nutrient" that owes nothing to biochemical components synthesized on the surface of the earth through the use of solar energy. Or: learning to effect these syntheses in other places than on earth. In both cases then this means learning to manufacture a hardware capable of nourishing our software or its equivalent, but one maintained and supported only by sources of energy available in the cosmos generally.

It's clear even to a lay person like myself that the combined forces of nuclear physics, electronics, photonics, and information science open up a possibility of constructing technical objects, with a capacity that's not just physical but also cognitive, that "extract" (that is, select, process, and distribute) energies these objects need in order to function from forms generally found everywhere in the cosmos.

So much for the hardware. As for the software such machines are to be equipped with—that's a subject for research in the area of artificial intelligence and for the controversies surrounding such research. You philosophers, writers, and artists are quick to dismiss the pathetic track record of today's software programs. True— thinking or "representing" machines (Monique Linard's term) are weaklings compared to ordinary human brains, even untrained ones.

It can be objected that programs fed into such computers are elementary and that progress can be expected in information science, artificial languages, and communications science. Which is likely. But the main objection concerns the very principle of these intelligences. This objection has been summed up in a line of thought proposed by Hubert L. Dreyfus. Our disappointment in these organs of "bodiless thought" comes from the fact that they operate on binary logic, one imposed on us by Russell and Whitehead's mathematical logic, Turing's machine, McCulloch and Pitts's neuronal model, the cybernetics of Wiener and von Neumann, Boolian algebra, and Shannon's information science.

But as Dreyfus argues, human thought doesn't think in a binary mode. It doesn't work with units of information (bits), but with intuitive, hypothetical configurations. It accepts imprecise, ambiguous data that don't seem to be selected according to preestablished codes or readability. It doesn't neglect side effects or marginal aspects of a situation. It's not just focused, but lateral too. Human thought can distinguish the important from the unimportant without doing exhaustive inventories of data and without testing the importance of data with respect to the goal pursued by a series of trials and errors. As Husserl has shown, thought becomes aware of a "horizon," aims at a "noema," a kind of object, a sort of nonconceptual monogram that provides it with intuitive configurations and opens up "in front of it" a field of orientation and expectation, a "frame" (Minsky). And in such a framework, perhaps more like a scheme, it moves toward what it looks for by "choosing," that is, by discarding and recombining the data it needs, but nonetheless without making use of preestablished criteria determining in advance what's appropriate to choose. This picture inevitably recalls the description Kant gave of a thought process he called reflective judgment: a mode of thought not guided by rules for determining data, but showing itself as possibly capable of developing such rules afterward on the basis of results obtained "reflexively."

This description of a reflective thought opposed to determinate thought does not hide (in the work of Husserl or Dreyfus) what it owes to perceptual experience. A field of thought exists in the same way that there's a field of vision (or hearing): the mind orients itself in it just as the eye does in the field of the visible. In France, this analogy was already central to Wallon's work, for example, and also to Merleau-Ponty's. It is "well known." Nonetheless it has to be stressed that this analogy isn't extrinsic, but intrinsic. In its procedures it doesn't only describe a thought analogous to an experience of perception. It also describes a thought that proceeds analogically and only analogically—not logically. A thought in which therefore procedures of the type "just as . . . so likewise . . ." or "as if . . . then" or again "as p is to q, so r is to s" are privileged compared to digital procedures of the type "if . . . then . . ." and "p is not non-p." Now these are the paradoxical operations that constitute the experience of a body, of an "actual" or phenomenological body in its space-time continuum of sensibility and perception. Which is why it's appropriate to take the body as model in the manufacture and programming of artificial intelligence if it's intended that artificial intelligence not be limited to the ability to reason logically.

It's obvious from this objection that what makes thought and the body inseparable isn't just that the latter is the indispensable hardware for the former, a material prerequisite of its existence. It's that each of them is analogous to the other in its relationship with its respective (sensible, symbolic) environment: the relationship being analogical in both cases. In this description there are convincing grounds for not supporting the hypothesis (once suggested by Hilary Putnam) of a principle of the "separability" of intelligence, a principle through which he believed he could legitimate an attempt to create artificial intelligence.

She

Now that's something to leave us satisfied as philosophers. At least something to assuage a part of our anxiety. A field of perception has limits, but these limits are always beyond reach. While a visual object is presenting one side to the eye, there are always other sides, still unseen. A direct, focused vision is always surrounded by a curved area where visibility is held in reserve yet isn't absent. This disjunction is inclusive. And I'm not speaking of a memory brought into play by even the simplest sight. Continuing vision preserves along with it what was seen an instant before from another angle. It anticipates what will be seen shortly. These syntheses result in identifications of objects, identifications that never are completed, syntheses that a subsequent sighting can always unsettle or undo. And the eye, in this experience, is indeed always in search of a recognition, as the mind is of a complete description of an object it is trying to think of: without, however, a viewer's ever being able to say he recognizes an object perfectly since the field of presentation is absolutely unique every time, and since when vision actually sees, it can't ever forget that there's always more to be seen once the object is "identified." Perceptual "recognition" never satisfies the logical demand for complete description.

In any serious discussion of analogy it's this experience that is meant, this blur, this uncertainty, this faith in the inexhaustibility of the perceivable, and not just a mode of transfer of the data onto an inscription-surface not originally its own. Similarly, writing plunges into the field of phrases, moving forward by means of adumbrations, groping toward what it "means" and never unaware, when it stops, that it's only suspending its exploration for a moment (a moment that might last a lifetime) and that there remains, beyond the writing that has stopped, an infinity of words, phrases, and meanings in a latent state, held in abeyance, with as many things "to be said" as at the beginning. Real "analogy" requires a thinking or representing machine to be *in* its data *just as* the eye is in the visual field or writing is in language (in the broad sense). It isn't enough for these machines to simulate the results of vision or of writing fairly well. It's a matter (to use the attractively appropriate locution) of "giving body" to the artificial thought of which they are capable. And it's that body, both "natural" and artificial, that will have to be carried far from earth before its destruction if we want the thought that survives the solar explosion to be something more than a poor binarized ghost of what it was beforehand.

From this point of view we should indeed have grounds not to give up on techno-science. I have no idea whether such a "program" is achievable. Is it even consistent to claim to be programming an experience that defies, if not programming, then at least the program—as does the vision of the painter or writing? It's up to you to give it a try. After all, the problem's an urgent one for you. It's the problem of a comprehension of ordinary language by your machines. A problem you encounter especially in the area of terminal/user interface. In that interface subsists the contact of your artificial intelligence with the naive kind of intelligence borne by so-called "natural" languages and immersed in them.

But another question bothers me. Is it really another question? Thinking and suffering overlap. Words, phrases in the act of writing, the latent nuances and timbres at the horizon of a painting or a musical composition as it's being created (you've said this yourselves) all lend themselves to us for the occasion and yet slip through our fingers. And even inscribed on a page or canvas, they "say" something other than what we "meant" because they're older than the present intent, overloaded with possibilities of meaning—that is, connected with other words, phrases, shades of meaning, timbres. By means of which precisely they constitute a field, a "world," the "brave" human world you were speaking about, but one that's probably more like an opaqueness of very distant horizons that exist only so that we'll "brave" them. If you think you're describing thought when you describe a selecting and tabulating of data, you're silencing truth. Because data aren't given, but givable, and selection isn't choice. Thinking, like writing or painting, is almost no more than letting a givable come toward you. In the discussion we had last year at Siegen, in this regard, emphasis was put on the sort of emptiness that has to be obtained from mind and body by a Japanese warrior-artist when doing calligraphy, by an actor when acting: the kind of suspension of ordinary intentions of mind associated with *habitus*, or arrangements of the body. It's at this cost, said Glenn and Andreas (and you can imagine how quickly I agreed, helped out by Dōgen, Diderot, and Kleist), that a brush encounters the "right" shapes, that a voice and a theatrical gesture are endowed with the "right" tone and look. This soliciting of emptiness, this evacuation—very much the opposite of overweening, selective, identificatory activity—doesn't take place without some suffering. I won't claim that the grace Kleist talked about (a grace of stroke, tone, or volume) has to be merited: that would be presumptuous of me. But it has to be called forth, evoked. The body and the mind have to be free of burdens for grace to touch us. That doesn't happen without suffering. An enjoyment of what we possessed is now lost.

Here again, you will note, there's a necessity for physical experience and a recourse to exemplary cases of bodily ascesis to understand and make understood a type of emptying of the mind, an emptying that is required if the mind is to think. This obviously has nothing to do with *tabula rasa*, with what Descartes (vainly) wanted to be a starting from scratch on the part of knowing thought—a starting that paradoxically can only be a starting all over again. In what we call thinking the mind isn't "directed" but suspended. You don't give it rules. You teach it to receive. You don't clear the ground to build unobstructed: you make a little clearing where the penumbra of an almost-given will be able to enter and modify its contour. An example of this work is found *mutatis mutandis* in Freudian *Durcharbeitung*. In which—though I won't labor the point—the pain and the cost of the work of thought can be seen. This kind of thinking has little to do with combining symbols in accordance with a set of rules. Even though the act of combining, as it seeks out and waits for its rule, can have quite a lot to do with thought.

The pain of thinking isn't a symptom coming from outside to inscribe itself on the mind instead of on its true place. It is thought itself resolving to be irresolute, deciding to be patient, wanting not to want, wanting, precisely, not to produce a meaning in place of what *must* be signified. This is a tip of the hat to a *duty* that hasn't yet been named. Maybe that duty isn't a debt. Maybe it's just the mode according to which what doesn't yet exist, a word, a phrase, a color, *will emerge*. So that the suffering of thinking is a suffering of time, of what happens. To sum up—will your thinking-machines, your representing-machines, suffer? What will be their future if they are just memories? You will tell me this scarcely matters if at least they can "achieve" the paradoxical relationship to the said "data," which are only quasi-givens, givables, which I've just described. But this is a hardly credible proposition.

If this suffering is the mark of true thought, it's because we think in the already-thought, in the inscribed. And because it's difficult to leave something hanging in abeyance or take it up again in a different way so what hasn't been thought yet can emerge and what *should be* inscribed *will be*. I'm not speaking just about lacking words amidst a superabundance of available words, but about ways of assembling these words, ways we should accept despite the articulations inspired in us by logic, by the syntax of our languages, by constructions inherited from our reading. (To Sepp Gumbrecht, who was surprised that any and all thought, according to me, should require and involve inscription, I say: We think in a world of inscriptions already there. Call this culture if you like. And if we think, this is because there's still something missing in this plenitude and room has to be made for this lack by making the mind a blank, which allows the something else remaining to be thought to happen. But this can only "emerge" as already inscribed in its turn.) The unthought hurts because we're comfortable in what's already thought. And thinking, which is accepting this discomfort, is also, to put it bluntly, an attempt to have done with it. That's the hope sustaining all writing (painting, etc.): that at the end, things will be better. Since there is no end, this hope is illusory. So: the unthought would have to make your machines uncomfortable; the uninscribed that remains to be inscribed would have to make their memory suffer. Do you see what I mean? Otherwise why would they ever *start* thinking? We need machines that suffer from the

burden of their memory. (But suffering doesn't have a good reputation in the technological megalopolis. Especially the suffering of
thinking. It doesn't even incite laughter anymore. The idea of it
doesn't occur, that's all. There's a trend toward "play," if not
performance.)

Finally, the human body has a gender. It's an accepted proposition that sexual difference is a paradigm of an incompleteness of not
just bodies, but minds too. Of course there's masculinity in women
as well as femininity in men. Otherwise how would one gender
even have an idea of the other or have an emotion that comes from
what's lacking? It's lacking because it's present deep inside, in the
body, in the mind. Present like a guard, restrained, off to the side,
at the edge of your vision, present on some horizon of it. Elusive,
impossible to grasp. Again we're back at transcendence in immanence. The notion of gender dominant in contemporary society
wants this gap closed, this transcendence toppled, this powerless-
ness overcome. Supposed "partners" (in a pleasure arrangement)
draw up a contract for purposes of common "enjoyment" of sexual
difference itself. The contract provides that neither party shall suffer from this association and that at the first sign of lack (whether
through failure to perform or not), of defocalization, of lack of
control and transcendence, the parties shall break the contract—
though that's still too strong a phrase; they'll just let it lapse. And
even if from time to time fashion gives "love" its place back among
the inventory of objects that circulate, it's as a "top of the line"
sexual relationship, reserved for superstars and advertised as an
enviable exception. I see in this arrangement a sign that techno-
science conditions thought to neglect the differend it carries within.

I don't know whether sexual difference is ontological difference. How would a person *know*? My unassuming phenomenological description still doesn't go far enough. Sexual difference is
related not simply to a body as it feels its incompleteness, but to an
unconscious body or to the unconscious as body. That is, as separated from thought—even analogical thought. This difference is *ex
hypothesi* outside our control. Maybe (because, as Freud showed in
his description of deferred action, it inscribes effects without the
inscription's being "memorized" in the form of recollection) it's the
other way around? And this difference is what initially sets up fields
of perception and thought as functions of waiting, of equivoca-

tions, as I've stated? This quite probably defines suffering in perceiving and conceiving as produced by an impossibility of unifying
and completely determining the object seen. To that which without
gendered difference would only be a neutral experience of the
space-time of perceptions and thoughts, an experience in which
this feeling of incompleteness would be lacking as unhappiness, but
only an experience producing a simple and pure cognitive aesthetic, to this neutrality gendered difference adds the suffering of
abandonment because it brings to neutrality what no field of vision
or thought can include, namely, a demand. The faculty to tran-
scend the given that you were taking about, a faculty lodged in
immanence, indeed finds a means to do this in the recursiveness of
human language—although such a capacity isn't just a possibility
but an actual force. And that force is desire.

So: the intelligence you're preparing to survive the solar explosion will have to carry that force within it on its interstellar voyage.
Your thinking machines will have to be nourished not just on
radiation but on the irremediable differend of gender.

And here is where the issue of complexity has to be brought up
again. I'm granting to physics theory that technological-scientific
development is, on the surface of the earth, the present-day form of
a process of negentropy or complexification that has been under
way since the earth began its existence. I'm granting that human
beings aren't and never have been the motor of this complexification, but an effect and carrier of this negentropy, its continuer. I'm
granting that the disembodied intelligence that everything here
conspires to create will make it possible to meet the challenge to
that process of complexification posed by an entropic tidal wave
which from that standpoint equates with the solar explosion to
come. I agree that with the cosmic exile of this intelligence a locus
of high complexity—a center of negentropy—will have escaped its
most probable outcome, a fate promised any isolated system by
Carnot's second law—precisely because this intelligence won't
have let itself be left isolated in its terrestrial-solar condition. In
granting all this, I concede that it isn't any human desire to know or
transform reality that propels this techno-science, but a cosmic
circumstance. But note that the complexity of that intelligence
exceeds that of the most sophisticated logical systems, since it's
another type of thing entirely. As a material ensemble, the human

body hinders the separability of this intelligence, hinders its exile and therefore survival. But at the same time the body, our phenomenological, mortal, perceiving body, is the only available *analogon* for thinking a certain complexity of thought.

Thought makes lavish use of analogy. It does this in scientific discovery too of course "before" its operativity is fixed in paradigms. On the other hand its analogizing power can also return, bringing into play the spontaneous analogical field of the perceiving body, educating Cézanne's eye, Debussy's ear, to see and hear givables, nuances, timbres that are "useless" for survival, even cultural survival.

But once again that analogizing power, which belongs to body and mind analogically and mutually and which body and mind share with each other in the art of invention, is inconsequential compared to an irreparable transcendence inscribed on the body by gender difference. Not calculation, not even analogy, can do away with the remainder left by this difference. This difference makes thought go on endlessly and won't allow itself to be thought. Thought is inseparable from the phenomenological body, although gendered body is separated from thought, and launches thought. I'm tempted to see in this difference a primordial explosion, a challenge to thought that's comparable to the solar catastrophe. But such is not the case, since this difference causes infinite thought— held as it is in reserve in the secrecy of bodies and thoughts. It annihilates only the One. You have to prepare postsolar thought for the inevitability and complexity of this separation. Or the pilot at the helm of spaceship *Exodus* will still be entropy.

(Translated by Bruce Boone and Lee Hildreth)

COMMUNICATION SYSTEMS
AND THEIR DISCONTENTS

BERNHARD SIEGERT

The Fall of the Roman Empire

> Alme Sol, curru nitido qui
> Promis et celas aliusque et idem
> Nasceris, possis nihil urbe Roma
> Visere mauius.
> —Horace

A sibylline oracle uncovers the fall of Rome in the depths of its name: ἔσται καὶ Σάμος ἄμμος, ἐσεῖται Δῆλος ἄδηλος, καὶ 'Ρώμη ῥύμη· τὰ δὲ θέσφατα πάντα τελεῖται (Samos too will be a pile of sand, and Delos will disappear. Rome will be a narrow street, because all oracles come true; Sybil. Weiss. 1951 [5th/6th cent.]: 88). Names (*nomina*) of things are only dissimulations of remains (*omina*). In this way, Samos will in reality become a pile of sand, Delos will be completely forgotten, and nothing more will remain of Rome than a narrow street. If names inscribe things with a difference that makes them exist only as a result of their demise rather than ensuring the identity of things, then history itself is at risk. The result, according to Lactantius, is a never-ending *Apocalypse Now*: "If the capital of the world declines and begins to resemble a narrow street, something that, according to the Sibyls, will occur, who can doubt then that the end has come for all humanity and for the entire world?" (Lactantius 1754–59 [ca. A.D. 300]: 7.25, 7). If the *res narratae* are only able to represent the *res gestae* in their decline, then a history of the *orbis terrarum* can only be a history of the demise of history. Since no history that includes its narrator can contain its own demise, it would have to be a narration of its own impossibility. The history of an empire synonymous with history itself, a history that at the same time is inscribed with its own demise, would have to cease telling what it wanted to tell in order to tell it. I would constantly have to interrupt myself in order to have time to say anything, just as Lactantius, doubting his own words, had to interrupt himself as soon as he wrote the above quoted "then." The time in which he says this rebukes the lies he tells. If the scope of personal speech corresponds to the scope of history, then statements that deal with the end or transformation of their own conditions of reality immediately become paradoxical. For this very reason, the demise of horizons or of empires is conditional for their acceptance into history.

The fall of the Roman Empire is the condition of a "history that is given" as an inscription of archaeological remains (Foucault 1981: 184). The chariot of Sol the Provider, constantly revealing and concealing Rome's daylight, crashed from the firmament that spans the horizon of our discursive universe. Rome has ceased to be the law of what can be said, but has become describable in precisely this way. What was still impossible for Lactantius to speak of, namely, the historical end of Rome, had already become a possibility for Augustine. Alaric's capture of Rome in A.D. 410 opened up a discursive opportunity to speak of Rome as a historical episode, even though Augustine could only do so with reference to the mythical trauma of Rome's birth through the fall of Troy (see Augustine 1911 [412–26]: 1.3 and 3.2–8). This story could only be told with Lactantius's consistency as the result of apocalyptic events. The end of Rome in history is etched in the (eternal) horizon of the Christian state.

If decline is the transcendental prerequisite for the historicity of an empire, then its demise cannot itself be a date in history. Historical events such as the capture of Rome in 410 cannot date the archaeological discontinuity that defines the empire as a historical formation. On the other hand, events can become historical dates of demise on the basis of archaeological breaks. In this way, Harold Innis was able to show, in broadening the scope of the historicity of dates, that the rise and fall of empires "in history" correlates with shifts of those positivities that concern the material basis of discursive practices. In this way, historic formations of power become visible as dependent variables of technologies of signs (see Innis 1972).

If the end is not a historical date but rather a prerequisite for something's becoming history, then the causes of downfall cannot themselves be historical. The premise for this insight is fundamental for the monumental genre of the historiography of the fall of Rome. The conclusion of this insight is fundamental for the count- less theories concerning the causes of the same. While writers since Gibbon have produced tendentiously unfinished works because of the impossibility of dating the fall of Rome, theories on the causes of its demise mirror the ensemble of scholarly discourses that have been dominant since the nineteenth century (see Christ 1986).

It is not the intent of the following to add another theory to those already extant. Since the fall is the transcendental prerequisite for the historicity of the empire, the empire and fall must be thought of as caused by the same thing. We have to adhere to the sibylline prophecy at least in this point. Much more important is the attempt to detract a bit from Rome's historical importance (and by doing so, to hold the concept of demise in abeyance), in order to be able to talk about the empire as defined by transformations of discursive practice, of which it is a representation. The empire as a representative form of discursive practice could then only be viewed by reflecting on this difference, that is, as a form or "gift" given to history.

This is a difference that, according to the sibyl, resides first and foremost in the word itself. I therefore don't use in the following the literal meaning of Rome (like the sibyl) but of *imperium*, which makes a no less apocalyptic or enlightening sense, namely that of *command* (see Seeck 1966, 2: 112), a term that came to mean "em- pire" only by way of a metonymic shift. The empire is a trope that ceases to be just a trope thanks to its own logic. It defines the techno-logos that both founds and positivates it. An implementa- tion of power (*imperium*) can only illuminate an empire through the materiality of this shift, that is to say, only through its media. The empire exists only as a positivity of the metonymy itself and conse- quently only by means of its postal system. Its fate depends on the consistency or inconsistency of a postal system or metonymy that became ironic during the course of the fourth and fifth centuries.

The trope of empire dried up to the same degree that its mean- ing ceased to be fed by a flood of decrees. By the fifth century, the empire existed without *imperium*. In the last 70 years of its exis- tence, it had become an ironic discourse; a letter without address or return address. The empire circulated as a production of dissimula- tion rhetoric, as a phantom of the present. The Visigoths and

Burgundians, who had founded autonomous empires in Gaul, for example, were called *hospes*. The Finlandization of Rome by the barbarian tribes to whom it owed tribute was designated *foedus*. Troops consisting of barbarians were called "legions." Alaric the Visigoth was *magister militum per Illyricum*; Stilicho, the *magister utriusque militiae* designated to defend the empire, was a Vandal and fellow barbarian. Salvian, an eyewitness to the destruction, was scandalized by the Roman aristocracy that continued to celebrate while its towns were being destroyed. When the Franks destroyed Trier for the fourth time, around 435, the Romans only asked the emperor for support of their circus games (see Salvian 1935 [ca. 450]: 205), in order to defend the empire exactly on the spot where it existed. As nameless corpses rotted in the streets, the trope of empire had been appropriated by the barbarians, and the *imperium* had long since gone over to other media.

This double *translatio* is the history of the *imperium*/empire metonymy itself and is resolved in the double meaning of a "posting of the empire." The Christianization of the *imperium* corresponds to the *genitivus subiectivus* of a postal system that is operated by the empire; the barbarization of the empire corresponds to the *genitivus obiectivus* of an empire that has itself been posted.

Harold Innis's thesis was that the stability of empires depends on whether they are successful in balancing the tendency to overemphasize either time or space as the prominent medium (both for storage or transmittal) (Innis 1972: 7). The power of the *imperium* originated from the posting of space. *Romanum* offers a problematic syntax in connection with this historical power. Rome was introduced to postal offices in Egypt. Egypt had imported these from Persia, where a relay postal system had existed since Cyrus.[*] Caesar had had enough time in Alexandria, between bouts of flirting with Cleopatra, to study the highly developed Egyptian bureaucracy. In this way, the postal virus was transferred to Rome.[†] After Caesar's death, Augustus not only monopolized the import

[*]See Holmberg 1933: 18–21, 23–32, on the history of the Persian and Egyptian postal systems; Rothschild 1984: 3–8; Ooteghem 1959: 187–88; Humbert 1962: 1646.

[†]The supporting arguments that an Egyptian transmission of the postal system to Rome is more likely than a direct Persian transmission, are given by Holmberg 1933: 39–42.

of papyrus, the other materiality of the empire, but also set into motion the technology of its transmission. In short, he created, as Suetonius recounts, the *cursus publicus.*

In order to receive messages and reports of events in every province more quickly and privately, he first stationed young and robust foot messengers along all military roads at regular intervals. Later, he stationed carts for couriers. This proved to be more efficient since he was able to personally question those who brought the dispatches then and there if it seemed necessary.   (Suetonius 1985 [ca. 120]: 93)

With the resulting *orbis terrarum*, Rome, the *urbs*, was transmitted in the medium of Persian-Egyptian despotism, the *angariae*. The link between oriental bureaucracy and the Roman military conquered the world and posted the metonymic confusion of territorial and imperial rule. Paul Veyne, in his speech at his initiation into the Collège de France, tried to answer the question of why the Romans had conquered the world:

Rome's maxims were archaic. Rome embodied an archaic form, not of imperialism, but rather of isolationism. It negated the plurality of nations, it acted . . . as if it were the only state in the true sense of the word; it was not looking for half-hearted security in its relations with other towns, . . . rather, it wanted to live in peace by creating once and forever a permanent and complete security. The ideal of such a goal: to conquer the entire horizon of civilized habitation to its ocean boundaries or to the barbarian tribes, in order to finally be alone in the world, everything having been conquered.   (Veyne 1988: 13)

As part of this isolationistic discourse, Livius declares that the Romans had conquered the world in order to defend themselves (see Gibbon 1987 [1776–88]: 489n6). Roman isolationism distinguished between two forms of conquest. Both are contained in the martial aspect of G. Dumézil's description of the function of sovereignty as represented by Romulus: slavery and synoicism (see Dumézil 1977: 160)—subjugation or incorporation of the conquered as citizens of the state. But from the beginning, synoicism implied a kind of "barbarization." Only those who lived within the confines of the city's walls could become Roman citizens (see Seeck 1966, 2: 117–18). Roman identity, something presumed by the term "barbarization," is defined by a border. Since the whole world is unable to occupy seven hills, this border must constantly be redefined. This was accomplished, according to Dumézil, by the other, juridical aspect of the function of sovereignty, represented in Roman origin epics by Numa (see Dumézil 1968: 274–77). In 268 B.C., when the colony of Ariminum was founded, a new law was passed according to which the town could keep its own citizenship despite the granting or octroyization of Roman citizenship. For a long time, this Ariminetic right was limited to Latin colonies. But when the postal service and bureaucracy arrived from Egypt (powerful weapons for the juridical aspect of the function of sovereignty), this right was expanded to non-Italic towns and entire provinces (see Seeck 1966, 2: 133–34). This postal mobilization of Numa, so to speak, continued until the borders of the *urbs* were metonymically defined by the *vallum Antoninus* and the Germanic, Dacian, Asian, and African *limites*. All lands of the empire were bound in a huge synoicism, an identification of the world as *romanum* that functioned as long as the postal service of the imperial metonymy.

It was the Latin translation of *angareion* that provided an Occidental etymology of "postal" in place of the Oriental. *Statio posita* represented two meanings: cavalry relay stations, *mutationes*, and *mansiones*, posts where the courier could spend the night. The *cursus* was limited to the *viae militariae* that followed the Roman legions (see Vaillé 1947: 55) and therefore only supported troop movements and not private traffic (see Riepl 1972: 184). Although the *cursus* was an imperial institution, it was financed liturgically by the provincial population. Conquest by Rome meant becoming a subject of its posting. Provincial towns ceased being data and, as mere addresses of relay stations, literally became *municipia* of the empire. Only Italy was freed by Nerva from the *munus vehicularium*.★

The entire organization of the imperial bureaucracy originated with the institution of the *cursus publicus*. Hadrian nationalized the postal system that had until then been under the direction of the curia. He installed a *praefectus vehiculorum* under the high command of the *praefectus praetorio* and placed each station under an imperial official, the *manceps* (see Seeck 1901: col. 1857). At the same time, Hadrian reformed the chancellery, up until then a part of the imperial household and since Claudius divided into four *officia: ab epis-*

★This is evidenced by the legend of a coin: *Vehiculatione Italia remissa.* See Rothschild 1984: 33; Humbert 1962: 1649; Holmberg 1933: 43–44; Vaillé 1947: 36.

tulis, a libellis, a cognitionibus, and *a studiis.* The *officium ab epistulis* was responsible for all postal traffic of the state and during Hadrian's rule was under a certain Gaius Suetonius Tranquillus (see Homo 1950 [1927]: 374–75). Hadrian added to the function of transmission, assigned to the letter office, the function of information storage, assigned to a bureau *a memoria,* and granted the entire chancellery the status of state service. This represented an increase in the power of officials to compete with the Senate.

The bureaucratization of power was completed by the beginning of the fourth century. The *magister officiorum,* head of the chancellery, was raised to the ranks of the highest civil servants along with the praetorian prefects (see Classen 1955: 71). Diocletian ruled solely through the officials of his bureaus and in doing so technically converted the *imperium* from a principacy to a dominate. According to Paul Veyne, the disempowerment of the Senate testifies to a transformation of the power dispositive: "The emperor, rid of the Senate and ruling through an uncomplicated staff of officials, ceases to be chief or shepherd: he takes on one of the roles available to the true monarch: father and priest. This is precisely why he converts to Christianity" (Veyne 1981: 17–18). Ruling without the Senate primarily means that the *senatusconsultus,* as instrument of the legislative, is replaced by a decree of the emperor, a decree that is now an *oraculum,* that is, a sacred word as expression of the emperor's pastoral power (see Vaillé 1947: 96). Unfortunately, a *cursus publicus* is not nearly as sure a communications medium as the Holy Spirit.

An edict of Julian's from 362 begins: "in rebus prima militia est secundus in litterarum praesidiis pacis ornatus" (*Cod. Theod.* 1971 [439]: 6.26, 1). The *litterarum praesidia,* the protection of letters, ranks immediately behind the military. This is a necessary part of any functioning empire that is entirely based on transmittal and ensures that a command is received and thereby thrust into the light of the empire. The command system and the metonymy of the empire are founded on the "power of the caesura" as a structure of writing itself (using Derrida's words). The fact that no context could lock in the letters (see Derrida 1976: 136) demands that they be sealed.

The term *cursus publicus* already indicates that the use of this medium is reserved for the emperor and his highest officials. According to Xiphilin, letters to "idiots," that is, in the Greek sense of the word, private persons, don't even get mailed: "ἔξω γάρ δή των βασιλικῶν γραμματών οὐδεν ἰδιωτικὸν διεπέμπετο" (It is known that private writings except those of the emperor are not sent in this way at all; in Vaillé 1947: 95 n. 1). Only an imperial diploma or, in postclassical terminology, an *evectio*, could provide access to the post office. These diplomas could be issued by the praetorian prefect and probably, after 395, by the *magister officiorum* (see Holmberg 1933: 89–90). This represented a limitation of discourse aimed at the equally total and impossible centralization of the discourse. The Theodosian Code contains a large number of repeated prohibitions against issuing *evectiones*, mainly addressed to officials of provincial governments (see, e.g. *Cod. Theod.* 1971: 8.5, 12, and 8.5, 40). Julian even went so far as to personally oversee and administer the *cursus*, "since," as he wrote to Mamertinus, his *praefectus praetorio*, "the state postal system has deteriorated under the arrogant impudence of certain people and the great number of postal permits that continue to be issued by the officials of the vicarages and the consular bureaus of the provincial governors. . . . For this reason, no one but you shall have the right to issue postal permits in the future" (*Cod. Theod.* 1971: 8.5, 12).

The validity of the *evectiones* was immediately suspended upon the death of the emperor. This was a vital step for any successor who, having come to power through the usual means of assassination, found it imperative to prevent all communications between officials of the deceased emperor who might be plotting against him (see Humbert 1962: 1663). Tacitus tells us of a man freed by Nero named Coenus, who, in A.D. 69, spread the rumor of Vitellius's defeat in order to revalidate the *evectiones* issued by Otho, even though the emperor had already committed suicide. Coenus was then able to reach Rome unusually quickly, but he was not able to avoid Vitellius's punishment (see Tacitus 1969 [104–10]: 2.54).

Julian had good reasons to be concerned about the security of the mail, reasons that are evident when reading through the Theodosian Code. This first codification of Roman law consists entirely of imperial letters, dated and posted with both address and return address. Among these is the one dated November 9, 362, which makes the security of the mail the second most important concern of the state. How can this letter guarantee the safe arrival of the mail if it is itself a letter? In fact, the relationship between law and decree in the Roman empire was asymmetrical. Since the law was subject to the emperor, no letter could not be given legal status. Peter Classen's study of the imperial Roman rescript deals with precisely this problem: "Letters to bishops and others who were not civil servants, but most of all to various kinds of corporations, could become permanent and legally binding by virtue of their content and were taken up as such by the Theodosian Code. . . . All statements made by the emperor could become law, since the format of letters was always uniform" (Classen 1955: 49–50).

All correspondence by Roman emperors was a writing of postcards. The Theodosian Code simply reveals the being of each postcard, for, as James Joyce said, "a postcard is a publication" (Joyce 1982: 446). Only the legal reform of 426 initiated by Valentinian III under the guardianship of Galla Placidia drew a distinction between *leges generales* and *iussiones* (see Classen 1955: 31–32, 50). This was by no means coincidental: the compilation of the Theodosian Code was accomplished during the reign of Galla Placidia. The possibility of leafing through the pages of a codex quickly brought to light contradictions between the edicts of various emperors. Consequently, it became necessary to distinguish between decrees that had time limitations and were personally addressed and laws that were to be valid for all subjects and for all time. The invention of the codex forced the differentiation of the pragmatics of power. This was of little use to Valentinian III, however. The postcard structure of the *imperium* produced some of the great motifs of the historiography of decline, for example, corruption and usurpation. If the *imperium* is a postcard, then interception consequently makes up a large part of its structure. There is always the possibility that it won't arrive. Or: the *imperium* only exists in the mode of decline.

If interception lies in the structure of the message, then the medium must be sealed if it is to arrive at all. From the time of Diocletian, all communications and their administration along the *cursus* were in the hands of the imperial secret service. The *agentes in rebus*, who had taken the place of the frumentarians, made up a *schola* under the command of the *magister officiorum*. The lower ranks served as couriers, the higher ranks, *centenarii* and *ducenarii*, made up the infamous *curiosi*. They were in charge of not only the administration of the postal service, that is, above all, the control of *evectiones*, but also the surveillance of the vicars and governors.* The *agentes in rebus* therefore had to police themselves and consequently became uncontrollable. Control is itself out of control. The *imperium* could not reach its controllers.

The media system of the Roman *imperium* did not seal the message but rather the medium; a situation beyond our realm of experience. Unlike our idiotic culture, the *imperium* enveloped the medium, not the message. From this it follows that medium and message are divergent: the medium is the only thing that exists within the *orbis terrarum* that is cut off from the *imperium*. Out of this comes the paradox that resulted when the Emperor Julian, if one can believe Libanius's words, reduced the number of *agentes in rebus* to seventeen couriers in order to safeguard the mail (see Libanius 1967 [381]: 2.58): making the mail more secure by making the medium less secure.

Julian the Apostate knew what he was doing. As vice-emperor of his predecessor Constantius II, he had had ample opportunity to study the effects of the secret service's control. Constantius not only commanded his agents "to withold nothing of what you might observe from your chief of staff" (*Cod. Theod.* 1971: 6.29, 4) but additionally ordered that *curiosi* "should not hesitate to throw people whom they judge to be guilty into the ruinous darkness of prison" (ibid. 6.29, 1). Thereupon, he himself became somewhat paranoid, as we are told by Ammianus. He administered a wide-ranging spy network in order to detect or to produce conspiracies against the empire. A denunciation alone was sufficient for the death penalty (see Ammianus 1968 [390/98]: 14.1, 2, 6, 7, and 14.5, 1–3). Consequently, Constantius found himself and his *imperium* completely in the hands of the *agentes in rebus*, who, according to Ammian, played off officers and vicars loyal to Rome against the emperor. The downfall of Silvanus provides an example of the structural link between usurpation and the imperial postcard service.

Silvanus had been sent to Gaul as *rector pedestris militiae* in order to fight off invading barbarians; a group of conspirators intercepted a number of his letters, which they falsified so as to be highly

*See Blum 1969 on the *curiosi*. On the *agentes in rebus* generally, see Hirschfeld 1893. Also see Seeck 1966, 2: 94–96; Riepl 1972: 459–62; Holmberg 1933: 104–30.

compromising, and then delivered to the emperor. Constantius sent an *agens in rebus* by the name of Apodemius after Silvanus. Apodemius, instead of handing over the emperor's letter and *imperium*, began *proprio arbitrio* to throw Silvanus's clientele into "the ruinous darkness of prison," whereupon Silvanus was left with no choice but to follow the content of his counterfeit letters and take the imperial purple (see Ammian 1968: 15.5, 8–16).

Usurpation is the redirection of command channels. Because the command channels remained, despite and because of all edicts, redirectable, Emperor Leon I finally proclaimed a law that, on the pain of death, forbade the possession and manufacture of purple ink, which was reserved for the signature of the emperor (see Classen 1955: 57).

Not only the *oraculum* of the divine emperor but the *oraculum* of God as well is a dependent function of the historical state of media technology. Under the conditions of a command system totally based on transmission, the "obligatory nature of duty . . . is beyond consciousness," as Hegel said (1975: 464), and consequently the fatal link between interception and usurpation is the structure of the intelligence service of a high command in general. Tertullian, in his *Apologeticum* of the new command system named Christianity, wrote clearly about the matter of interception:

Every spirit has wings—angels and demons. This is why they can be anywhere in no time at all. The whole world is but a single place for them. They find out whatever and wherever as easily as they report it. Their speed is deemed divine since their being remains unknown. They often want to appear as the cause of what they report, and they are in fact sometimes the cause of bad things but never of good things. They intercepted the counsels of God as the prophets relayed them to the people. They seize them even now as our readings are sounded out. In this way, they collect prophecies about the course of time and try to mimic divine wisdom by stealing divinations.   (Tertullian 1952 [198]: 22.8–9)

There is some indication that this quote deals with none other than the *cursus publicus*. In order to prove to all pagans that the Christian God was the only god and that pagan gods were nothing more than demons, Tertullian used the soul as witness. Properly interrogated, the soul would always confess the name of God, His charity, and wisdom (cf. Tertullian 1980 [191/200]: 5.2 and 6.2). But how can we be sure that the soul has learned this less than eloquent wisdom from God and not from the innumerable writings that have been circulated all over the world? To distinguish the Christian soul from demons, Tertullian answered by means of a media technological innovation. The soul is a data base that has been written only once, by God, before the invention of books and alphabets (see Tertullian 1980: 5.3–4). From this point on, it can only be read. In today's computer terminology, the soul is a ROM (read only memory) device, and demons are RAMs (random access memories). The transition of the command system or the *imperium* to local, homeostatic data banks, accessible through checks, renders Rome obsolete as a command center and is nothing else but the transcendence of the Roman Empire itself. The *limes* of power is no longer characterized by a demonic postal service but by fed-back data units. To use a slightly altered quote by Corneille: "ROM n'est plus dans Rome, elle est tout où je suis" (Corneille 1950 [1662]: 733).

The soul is the codification of all commands from the high command that thereby become laws. In the same way, the codification of the commands of the Roman emperors through the Theodosian Code was the codification of the Roman *imperium* that made the Roman Empire, existing only in its metonymy, obsolete: a *translatio* of the Roman *imperium*, in the true sense of the word, since the Theodosian Code only compiled imperial orders and nothing else. Orders were now granted the legal status that Holy Scripture had always had: not the most recent, but the earliest *oraculum* is valid (see Tertullian 1980: 5.6; Classen 1956: 59). Consequently, the *imperium* in book form replaces the *imperium* in its imperial form. The *imperium* changes the postal system from the *poste courante* to the *poste restante*.

The Christian church was apparently the form of power most favored by the codex. Christian books of the third century were already for the most part codices, whereas pagan books, as far as is known, were still exclusively volumina (see Innis 1972: 110). The reasons are easy to see. The Chester Beatty papyrus no. 1, a codex from the second century, contains the four gospels and the Acts of the Apostles. It would have taken five papyrus rolls to hold this extensive a text (see Ekschmitt 1964: 248–49). Codification lessens the time necessary to access individual sections, allows quick leafing through pages, forward and backward, and thereby makes a synoptic reading of the gospels possible. Christianity is the introduction of control into writing.

The Christian takeover of power coincided with a takeover of all media. The Egyptian paper monopoly went over to Christian hands with George of Cappadocia, a bacon merchant to the Roman army who became the first successor to Athansius in Alexandria, then a martyr, and finally Saint George of England (see Gibbon 1987: 419–20). Constantine the Great granted *evectiones* to all bishops for the use of the postal service so that they could visit their councils and synods. This was an *a priori* of the institutionalization of the new command system or religion (the same thing) and was a move that, according to Michel Gorce, was less of a courtesy than the attempt by the highest command levels to take control of religious power (see Vaillé 1947: 52). It shows a takeover that transcended the old borders of the imperial system and thereby aroused the ire of its representatives, for example, Ammian: "Flocks of bishops (scurried) with their postal carts from one place to another to so-called synods, and by trying to control this entire rite, he [i.e., Constantinus II] severed the nerves of the postal system" (Ammianus 1968: 21.16.18).

The scandal is that, with the opening of the *cursus* for representatives of the church (from the viewpoint of Ammian or Libanios nothing but *privati*), the medium of the Roman *imperium* ceases to exist as its systematic border. After the *translatio* of the *imperium* to *poste restante* systems, its border becomes homeostatic behavior. The *poste courante* has become a subsystem within the boundaries of pastoral power. From this we can infer that the metonymic borders of the Roman *imperium*, the *limites*, have become obsolete. The anchorites of the Egyptian desert crossed over the *limes* in order to convert their own bodies from Rome and its demon mail over to ROMs. As Peter Brown has shown, the ascetics consciously sought hallucinations in order to learn to overcome them and to not inadvertently fall prey to them (Brown 1986: 122). The battle against demons was the self-exorcism of Rome: "it closed borders within the I that were irritatingly wide open" (ibid., 124). The new *limes* of homeostasis surrounds every soul; *Rome est tout où je suis.* Self-awareness and awareness of demons are complementary. The imperial system of conscience systematically transcends the command system of the *poste courante*. The trinity of orders, data, and addresses in the form of God, Jesus Christ, and the Holy Spirit has taken the place of the bureaucratic Numa in his function of sovereignty. Saint Benedict finally based the technique of ecstasy for oriental monks on scripture and created the *schola militiarum Christi*, in certain ways the successor to the *schola agentum in rebus*.

While power was being transferred to cybernetic command systems, Roman emperors sought to escape the usurpation of their command channels with a strategy of incremental self-disenfranchisement. A first step consisted of granting only a transitory and limited validity to certain imperial letters. The imperial rescript, which originated in the chancellery during the dominate period, only became valid after the assertions on which it was based could be verified by a local *iudex* (see Classen 1955: 16–37).

A much more desperate step toward self-disenfranchisement was undertaken by the emperors of the fifth century. They forbade the presentation of cases with certain subject matter and even went so far as to legally declare their own signatures to be invalid (see Schuller 1975: 9). The signature of Valentinian III was used without his knowledge to pardon murderers and conspirators—a misuse that led him in a decree dated December 10, 455, to lament: "What an unspeakable crime! Without our knowledge, we have surrounded criminal acts with a protective wall!" (cited by Stein 1928: 503). The *oraculum* had become a blind letter. The emperor no longer knew what he was saying. The empire had been decoupled from the *imperium*. Roman imperial citizenship, the result of the metonymic dislocation of Rome's city walls to the *limes*, had finally taken over the function of dissimulation irony. In 382, Theodosius the Great concluded a synoicism with the Visigoths, who had invaded Thracia, that granted them autonomy and freedom from taxes, and imposed upon them the duty to follow the Roman army, so that Themistius was able to exclaim that the Roman army had never been so strong. The army was strong, but it was Roman in only a very ironic sense (see Stein 1928: 299). In other words: the empire and the complementary barbarization was, from the fourth century on, an effect of interpretation. Even after the demise of its metonymic foundation, the empire was interpreted as *imperium*, and the territory within the imperial borders was mistaken for the expansion of power. Actually, the condition of the imperial territory during the interregnum periods of the fifth century was the same as the condition following the coup of the Roman soldier Odoacer in 476.

After the *translatio* of the *imperium* to *poste restante* technologies and the takeover of imperial territory by Gothic and Germanic tribes, the Roman empire hung in the air for a brief moment like leaves falling from a tree. Goths, Franks, Burgundians, and so on took over the resident Roman and therefore literate civil servants along with the local administrative offices. But the network of local offices, necessary for the use of rescripts, for example, declined along with its premises: sufficient supplies of papyrus and the postal service. Papyrus finally disappeared from the West after the conquest of Alexandria by the Emir Amr ibn al-As in 642. But the decline of the network of Roman archives had started earlier. The orders that Cassiodorus, as Theoderic's *magister officiorum*, issued in regard to the *cursus publicus*, that the warehouses of the *mansiones* were to be supplied with provisions and that horses were to be returned to their *mutationes* (Cassiodorus 1973 [537/38]: 1.29), point to a rather sorry state of affairs. In fact, the *cursus* was soon reduced to a simple requisition system of *paraveredi* (see Vaillé 1947: 124, 130). Previously, *paraveredi* had been horses requisitioned on the *parangariae*, the nonmilitary side roads (see Holmberg 1933: 66–67). In this way, the German *Pferd* (horse) owes its name to the demise of the Roman postal system, since it is etymologically a *paraveredus*, or side horse.

The demise of the Roman archival and postal systems represented the end of the panoramic moment, where the empire was solitary and never-ending, and the advent of an eternal future. Instead of being addressed to individual officials, Frankish diplomas were addressed to practically every official that would ever see the light of the Merovingian world. Instead of having only transitory validity, they had a signature and above it a *corroboratio* that validated the eternal nature of the signature, something totally foreign to Roman rescripts. From the middle of the seventh century on, that is, from the conquest of Alexandria by Amr, "all words that referred to the present . . . were displaced by references to the future, precepts became charters that only had the outward appearance of letters" (Classen 1956: 65).

It was an inconspicuous end. It was acknowledged by no one.

Monasteries, repositories of writing as founded by Benedict or Cassiodorus after the fall of the Ostrogoth empire in 540, assumed control even of the *paraveredi*. In the West, no *veredus* ran from *mutatio* to *mansio* when, in November 858, the synod of Quirzy-sur-Oise demanded of the King of Germany that the postal service be forbidden once and for all (see Vaillé 1947: 131). Every empire established in the West after Rome's *translatio imperii* up until the beginning of the sixteenth century was therefore only a metonymy of a *"para-imperium,"* which is to say, empires that had always already fallen. They were not representations of *Romē* but of a *rymē*.

Sol never saw anything greater than the city of Rome on his *cursus* because his demise and that of the *imperium* were one and the same. The sun of the *imperium* of the *poste restante* is only now, in the twentieth century, beginning to set. Our messages are sealed, and our media are public in the most idiotic sense. Their empire, as far as it fills out the horizon of our senses, exists thanks to a demise of which power has left traces in the hinterland of the *privati* in order to have a part in history. But beyond the horizon of these *parangariae*, there, where empires rule that don't exist, like the American *schola agentum in rebus* called the NSA (National Security Agency, or No Such Agency), begins the antiquity of our present.

FRIEDRICH KITTLER

Unconditional Surrender

In January 1943, the military leaders of the three Allied powers—the U.S., the USSR, and the U.K.—planned a conference to coordinate Allied war objectives and postwar plans. Stalin declined Soviet participation for two good reasons. First, he was unable to leave Moscow because he wanted to personally direct (at least so he imagined) the deathblow that General Chuikov's 62nd Army was about to deal General Paulus and the 6th German Army, encircled in the city that carried Stalin's name. Second, the Soviet commander in chief was unprepared to discuss operational details and could only have once again made his demand for a second European front. A telegram would suffice.

The conference at Casablanca was therefore not strategically decisive—it probably simply resulted from Roosevelt's desire for "fresh air" (Cartier 1985: 603). The president, whose party had almost lost a majority in the last congressional elections, was drawn out of the White House to Humphrey Bogart's just-liberated film location.* In the courtyard of a villa surrounded by military police and barbed wire, Roosevelt discussed Stalin's demands with the British prime minister, accepted the priority of V-Day Europe over V-Day Japan, decided on a division of effort between British nighttime air raids on area targets and American daylight raids on point targets (Greenfield 1967: 296), and, finally, settled on two landing

---

*Actually Casablanca was only half liberated since, as a result of the U.S.'s diplomatic policy, which wanted to offend neither Vichy's General Giraud nor de Gaulle, the Nuremberg Race Laws stayed in effect a half year after the Allied landings (according to Jacques Derrida).

operations, the first targeting the Cosa Nostra's Sicily* and the second, slated for a year later, the coast of Normandy. All these operational decisions begged the political question of what surrender conditions were to be placed on the German army. At a press conference on January 24, Roosevelt announced that the future United Nations would only accept "unconditional surrender" and that this meant "the complete elimination of the German . . . war machine." Churchill "would not . . . have used these words" himself, but in view of the journalists present, and since the words had already been spoken, he "stood by the President" (Moltmann 1967: 172).

Yet Roosevelt had no intention of offending his British allies, let alone of providing the German propaganda machine with ammunition for a verbal counterattack. Germany's declaration of "total war" was also not an answer to "unconditional surrender," but had already been an idea of Goebbels's as early as January 17 (Moltmann 1967: 185).

Instead, Roosevelt had simply quoted—at least so he later claimed—from history books with which every American, but unfortunately not every European, was familiar. General Ulysses Simpson Grant had fought on the Union side of the Civil War and was destined to become famous in word and deed. In 1862, Grant laid siege to Confederate General Bricker at Fort Donelson and invented, as the encircled units had to withdraw their surrender terms, a play of significants: the "unconditional surrender" demanded by Grant had the same initials as his own, slightly megalomanic name, Ulysses Simpson, and his own country, the United States (Cartier 1985: 606–7).

Literally, then, Unconditional Surrender, a formula without basis in international law (Baum 1967: 362), meant surrender to America as such. What the formula means in a more technical sense is explained in the great American war novel *Gravity's Rainbow*. In this story a bombing raid by the 8th U.S. Air Force on a German chemical plant inspires the novel's dark hero, a former Waffen-SS

*Schäfer 1989: 162–64, reports on the notable connections between Mussolini's attempt to quash the Mafia, the German U-boat strategy in the West Atlantic, the U.S. longshoreman's union, and finally the choice of Sicily for the first Allied landings in Europe.

colonel from Dornberger's Peenemünde, to make the following paranoid but historically plausible decoding:

If what the IG built on this site were not at *all* the final shape of it, but only an arrangement of fetishes, come-ons to call down special tools in the form of 8th AF bombers *yes* the "Allied" planes all would have been, ultimately, IG-built, by way of Director Krupp, through his English interlocks—the bombing was the exact industrial process of conversion, each release of energy placed exactly in space and time, each shockwave plotted in advance to bring *precisely tonight's wreck* into being. . . . If it is in working order, what is it meant to do? The engineers who built it as a refinery never knew there were any further steps to be taken. Their design was "finalized," and they could forget it.

It means this War was never political at all, the politics was all theatre, all just to keep the people distracted . . . secretly, it was being dictated instead by the needs of technology . . . by a conspiracy between human beings and techniques, by something that needed the energy-burst of war, crying, "Money be damned, the very life of [insert name of Nation] is at stake," but meaning, most likely, *dawn is nearly here, I need my night's blood, my funding, funding, ahh more, more.* . . . The real crises were crises of allocation and priority, not among firms—it was only staged to look that way—but among the different Technologies, Plastics, Electronics, Aircraft, and their needs which are understood only by the ruling elite. (Pynchon 1973: 520–21)

Germany's ruling elites had started the war with the fairly accurate assumption that, thanks to Hitler's propagation of an "extreme acceleration of rearmament," it enjoyed a technological advantage of two years. The principle of acceleration, as it was to be technically implemented in the integrated accelerometer of the V2, made it possible to achieve this technological advantage without reaching any noteworthy level of all-out arms production, that is, avoiding the coincidence of total war and social revolution that had been provoked in World War I (see Milward 1967: 24–27; and, as confirmation, Jodl 1982: 1713). The late but massive armaments effort in Great Britain and the United States mandated a German victory before 1942. It was for this reason that the outnumbered but operationally employed ten panzer divisions, whose VHF radios (Wildhagen 1970: 31–32) made blitzkrieg possible in the first place, had to overrun Poland and then France. In September 1940,

Hitler, as partial victor, ordered the halt of all long-term military research projects. At least officially, liquid-propelled rockets, super-high-frequency radars, and long-range bombers were taken off the priority lists in order to concentrate all resources on the development of multipurpose antiaircraft guns, the Würzburg radar system, and tactical bombers. Of course, the personal commander in chief of the German army, with his "amazing technical-tactical foresight," which had already made him "the creator of the modern armed force" (Jodl 1982: 1718), continued to recommend almost weekly innovations of tactical or all-too-tactical weapons systems. Hitler had no idea of higher math, however.*

Not until Operation Barbarossa came to a halt and the blitzkrieg came to an end at the gates of Moscow did the regime revise its economy of guns and butter. According to General Jodl, Chief of Staff of the Army, Hitler recognized his strategic defeat "sooner than anyone else in the world" (Jodl 1982: 1721). In this situation he named Albert Speer, previously his architect, as chief of the recently created Ministry for Armament and Munitions (Reichsministerium für Bewaffnung und Munition), renamed somewhat ambiguously in September 1943 as the Ministry for Armament and War Production (Ministerium für Rüstung und Kriegsproduktion) (Speer 1989: 268). In fact, Speer almost succeeded in his production efforts for the war under ever-increasing enemy air superiority, which had been achieved with the help of Allied radar (and the study of which had been forbidden by the German stop-research order) (Hagemeyer 1979: 340).

All war production demands that it be taken out of the hands of the military. After the bitter experiences of 1914, when Schlieffen's mobilization plan perfected only mass armies and not the mass production of gunpowder, both the Reichswehr and the Wehrmacht attempted to achieve some competence in the economics of technology and, with the founding of the Army Weapons Office (Heereswaffenamt) and the Defense Economy Office (Wehrwirt-

---

*See Boelcke 1969: 37: "His [Hitler's] interests were only focused on the traditional weapons of the armed forces. He hardly left the basics of macrophysics, namely, the familiar concepts of mechanics, theory of solids, and statics. Whether he ever mastered differential calculus, so as to be decisively engaged in construction, is doubtful. It is certain that as an autodidact, he lacked the basics of microphysics and modern chemistry."

schaftsamt), tried to learn that soldiers are reliant on weapons systems in technological wars and that weapons systems depend on supplies of raw materials (Geyer 1984: 101–8). But the military (with the exception of modern armchair generals) are conservative, if only because they teach men the art of killing instead of learning from machines the technique of switching. For this reason, Speer's wartime economic miracle required eliminating the power of these technological-economic army offices (ibid., 159–60). When the Army Weapons Office was forced to relinquish authority over weapons production to Speer's predecessor and was left only with authority over weapons development, the office head committed suicide (Ruland 1969: 123).

It was not until after the circumvention of the military that the war became a playground for engineers who delivered an array of unsolicited innovations (Ludwig 1979: 350). Despite Hitler's orders to the contrary, Messerschmitt developed the Me 262, the first jet fighter ready for mass production (Lusar 1971: 115–17). Lippisch tested his ramjet engine, whose commercial use may come about in the 1990's (see Spremberg 1963); Walther developed submarines that were finally worthy of the name; and Wernher von Braun launched his first V2 over the skies of Peenemünde on October 3, 1942. For these engineering newcomers, who were able as of 1942 to serve on boards of directors (Ludwig 1979: 200), Speer's appointment was exactly what Pynchon described: it eliminated the one-sided military finalization of arms production, redirected the priorities of Hitler's raw materialism toward high tech, and invited these capital-intensive companies to compete freely with each other (Geyer 1984: 166). The consequence of all this was that Germany, out of sheer necessity, set off a second wave of innovation and, according to an internal review by the U.S. Navy, "was already building tomorrow's weapons today" (cited in F. Hahn 1963: 11). Some of these saw action in the spring of 1945.

These futuristic weapons, being materially unsupported—jets without fuel supplies, rockets without launching bases, and night-vision devices without tanks—were unable to change the fortunes of war by themselves. Instead, they changed the infrastructure of Germany and of Fortress Europe, which was according to the *New York Times* a precursor of the Unified Market of 1992. "Ironically," writes a historian of Sauckel's European forced laborers, "Germany's labor experience was a factor in the preparation of European postwar integration. Hitler and his brutal Gauleiter Sauckel have the distinction, along with Jean Monnet and General George Marshall, of being the founders of the Common Market" (Homze 1967: 232). Through the systematic exploitation of the industrial capacities and workers in occupied areas, the military sector rose from 16 percent to 40 percent of the German economy between 1941 and 1944. New technological elites and a newly industrialized countryside, forced into the displacement of production sites to rural areas or even driven underground by Allied air superiority, formed the foundation for Professor Erhard's future economic miracle (Geyer 1984: 162–66).

Defeat, in sight since Stalingrad, was not able to stop these technological breakthroughs. On the contrary, the Ministry of Economic Affairs (Reichswirtschaftsministerium), which had been somewhat disfunctionalized by Speer since 1943 (Herbst 1982: 261–66), turned its attention to postwar planning. It encouraged, among other things, a professor from Erlangen and a journalist from Frankfurt to think about reconstruction projects. The professor's name was Ludwig Erhard; the journalist was Erich Welter (see Herbst 1982: 383–97, 443 n. 394), who, with his postwar founding of the *Frankfurter Allgemeine Zeitung*, did in fact contribute to the economic rebuilding of the Federal Republic. No Western welfare state would have been possible without the preceding warfare state (see McNeill 1982: 360–65). There never really was a "zero hour."

Speer, the former architect, couldn't hold back, given the far-sightedness of his competitors. Hardly had cities or factories been reduced to rubble when teams of young architects (as shown by the paranoia of Pynchon's Colonel Enzian) raced along the autobahn from Berlin to the sites of the newest rubble architecture. They undertook the clean-up of Allied bombings, recognizing the catastrophic consequences that narrow, medieval street plans had once again had for the fleeing population. Any postwar reconstruction would have to start with the premise that inner cities should be expanded with concrete buildings, city highways, and "green zones" (Durth 1987: 209–21). These green zones would have the bonus of serving as recreational areas, but were mainly intended for use in the next world war as bombing refuge areas. Nuclear weapons were not yet a familiar concept to these planners. And so it happened. Speer's city planners poured the foundations of their concrete postwar architecture, above all in Düsseldorf, Hamburg, and Hannover. As their historian formulated their activity, "total war must be seen not only as the end of the Third Reich, but also as the precursor to reconstruction" (Durth 1987: 15). And, just as Pynchon's Colonel Enzian would add, the carpet bombings probably belong to the same prehistory.

Hitler's supposedly totalitarian regime was actually a highly entropic balance between competing power subsystems and bureaucracies that could only be countered by leadership. For this reason, all reconstruction plans, awaiting the foreseeable time after Hitler, ran up against an absolute enemy.

Hitler, in his personally optimized bunkers, lost all confidence in one power subsystem after another. The first victim, abandoned by Hitler after the Allies had proven their air superiority, was the Luftwaffe; the second, shunned after Staufenberg made his attempt on Hitler's life, was the army, whose future technologies such as the rocket corps (special-purpose forces) came under the Waffen-SS command after July 1944. And finally, in March 1945, when even the head of the SS could no longer hold the Oder line as Berlin's last natural defensive barrier, Hitler declared that his entire treasonous country had rightly been defeated by "the stronger peoples of the East" (cited in Schramm 1982, 4: 1705). Hitler then issued the so-called Nero Order in imitation or escalation of Stalin's initial defensive tactics that had turned Western Russia into scorched earth:

The Führer issued the following order on March 19, 1945:
RE: Destruction measures for national territories.
The struggle for our national existence forces us to avail ourselves of all means at our disposal on our national territories that will weaken our enemy and prevent his further advance. . . . It is wrong to believe that undestroyed or only temporarily damaged transportation, communications, industrial, and supply sites could be used for our own purposes upon recapture. The enemy will only leave scorched earth in the wake of his retreat and completely ignore the needs of the populace.
I therefore order:
1. All military transportation, communications, industrial, and sup-

ply sites within our national boundaries, which could be of use to the enemy in any way now or in the foreseeable future in sustaining his warfare capabilities, are to be destroyed. . . .

3. This order is to be conveyed to all commanders immediately. Contrary instructions are invalid.   (Schramm 1982, 4: 1580–81)

If there were any doubts concerning this scorched-earth policy, they disappeared with the "Orders for Enforcement" issued by General Albert Praun, successor to General Fellgiebel as head of army communications (Fellgiebel was executed in July 1944). There could really be no discussion of a Reich, that is, a media system, given the ordered "destruction of all communications sites," not only those of "the army, but also of the postal system, the trains, the water supply, the police, and the electrical power works," as well as "all reserve depots for replacement parts, cables, and technical manuals" (cited in Speer 1989: 456). As in the story by Borges, the country and its maps would implode (see Borges 1964–66, 3: 131–32).

The scorched-earth policy was ostensibly not directed against external enemies but primarily against reconstruction plans in the economic and arms ministries, and secondarily against the army's strategy of stopping the fighting in the West and redirecting as many units as possible from Soviet to western areas of operation. The capture on April 10 of a "British document concerning the administration of Germany after occupation, including corresponding maps" (OKW diary, Apr. 10, 1945, in Schramm 1982, 4: 1233) made the attachment to a future Western Europe all the more discernible. Speer, having protested in vain against the scorched-earth policy, contacted the chief of staff, General Guderian, and befriended industrialists, with the result that an order declaring null and void all instructions contrary to the Nero Order was hardly enforced. The reconstruction (as well as the populace) was spared the hardship of beginning without any infrastructure.

The scene had already been set with the rescue of schematics and technical manuals for a grandiose technology transfer that was soon to mark the international postwar order. When Hitler decided, on April 22, to stay and die in Berlin because the Reichsführer SS had betrayed him with surrender talks (Trevor-Roper 1947: 185), the system was able to disintegrate into its subsystems, and these subsystems could be integrated into their corresponding surroundings. After General Bradley and Marshal Konyev met at Torgau, the former German empire became nothing more than a fractal of American, Soviet, British, and finally French zones, in which, for one final moment, some islands of army, navy, or Waffen-SS troops, such as those around the high-tech center of Nordhausen, survived (see Ludwig 1979: 506–14). And like the compounding of a mathematical fractal through the proliferation of self-likenesses, the establishment of zones was reiterated, over several geographical decades.

Command Group B of the Army Command Staff had reached the deep south on the last open autobahn, where the high command of the Luftwaffe awaited the arrival of General Patton's tanks. Göring, upon leaving Hitler, had traded in his Reichsmarshall fantasy uniforms for the plain, "brown grey cloth" of an "American general" (Speer 1989: 477). Army Command Group A and the Navy Command (OKM) headed for the far north, that is, an area sure to be occupied by the British, where Himmler dreamed of negotiating a partial surrender with Montgomery. Only Hitler and other suicide candidates like General Krebs, whose perfect knowledge of Moscow and the Russian language qualified him to be the last chief of staff of the army (after Guderian), stayed in the Berlin Führer bunker, surrounded by the Red Army. All subsystems and the disappearing center had thereby chosen and exhausted their possible options (with the exception of the French).

In order to save the Soviet option of the former center, the fractalization repeated itself on a lower, operational level. Despite all the army marches to the west, General Wenck's 12th Army received the order to disengage the American forces and relieve Berlin from the southwest. At the same time, Busse's 9th Army (after breaking out from its encirclement) was to attack from the southeast along with "Army Group Steiner" from the north. SS-General Steiner, who had been unable to prevent the "secret" withdrawal of the V2 rockets from the Oder front "to the south" (F. Steiner 1963: 225), found just enough time in a telephone conversation with Krebs to call the orders to attack "impossible and senseless," before the last line to the Führer bunker was cut off. But it was precisely this last link to a battle "phantom that only existed in the minds of the Führer Command Center" (ibid., 228–29) that triggered

the last act: the suicides of Hitler, Eva, and Blondi, the smallest
fractal—the only faithful ones, as Hitler had been wont to say since
the autumn of 1943 (Speer 1989: 315; Trevor-Roper 1947: 63).

This was reason enough for the three commanding generals
Wenck, Steiner, and Busse to continue their march to the west,
interrupted by Hitler's order. Reason enough for Goebbels, a day
after Hitler's suicide, on May 1, to send General Krebs with a white
flag to Chuikov's Berlin command post, where the chief of staff of
the army explained, in fluent Russian, that only two countries in
the entire world had set aside a Labor Day for their workers:
Germany and the Soviet Union (Tschuikov 1966: 213). Reason
enough finally for SS-General Kammler, the commander of the
Rocket Corps, to load up the high-tech blueprints of his restricted
zone Mittelbau and (according to "a report that could not be confirmed in detail") to transport these southeast for interested workers (Ludwig 1979: 514).

Given the disappearance of the center, the transfer of technology could begin according to the options of the individual subcen-
ters and their new surroundings. The documents of unconditional
surrender, first signed secretly in Reims with Americans and British present, and then in Karlshorst with all four Allies, in the name
of the supreme command of the army, contained the following
paragraphs:

2. . . . No ship, sea-going vessel, or airplane of any kind may be
destroyed, nor may ships' hulls, machine installations, or tools, machines
of any kind, weapons, apparatuses, and all technical means of continuing
the war effort be harmed in any way. . . .

6. This declaration is written in English, Russian, and German. The
English and Russian versions alone are binding. (Schramm 1982, 4:
1679–80)

Speer's and Guderian's countermeasures against the Nero Order, which would have made scorched technology out of Stalin's
scorched earth, coincide in every sense of the word with the Allied
prohibition on destroying military technology. Unconditional surrender meant the transfer of technology.

In the eastern zone, the searchlights that had started Marshal
Zhukov's last operation (Sasso 1982: 21–22) also enabled the nighttime dismantling of weapons factories. As Pynchon states: "The

roads heading east are jammed day and night with Russian lorries, full of materiel. All kinds of loot. But no clear pattern to it yet, beyond strip-it-and-pack-it-home" (Pynchon 1973: 449). Some factories, concentration camps, engineers, and Waffen-SS instructors, however, continued to work to provide the Red Army with uranium experts, the Korean War with MIG 15's (Bower 1987: 14), and the future East German National People's Army (NVA) with cadre. Sputnik supposedly won the race against the U.S. Explorer satellite because Pennemünde's assistants went to Kasakhstan and Pennemünde's only professor went to White Sands. . . .

The transfer of technology to Great Britain was less strategic and more along the lines of colonial trade. The dismantled Würzburg radar system, brought to Jodrell Bank, led to the invention of radio astronomy. Engineers from the Aeronautical Research Institute in Volkerode prepared the way for wind-tunnel measurements and the construction of the Concord (Bower 1988: 206), and tape recorders from naval supplies paved the way to the sound of Abbey Road and the future Beatles (Southall 1982: 137). Walther's submarine constructions for Vickers-Armstrong (Bower 1987: 190–94) simply mirrored the turn of a fallen empire to defensive strategies. Generally, Great Britain seemed to be in the strange situation of losing more from the transfer of technology than it gained, at least after Truman and Churchill had agreed in Potsdam to keep not only intelligence about German technologies from Stalin but especially their own intelligence technologies (Virilio 1984b: 106). It is well known that British prototypes of digital computers were decisive in the Atlantic, African, and probably the European theaters because they were able to decipher communications of the entire German army command structure in real time from the operational level of the Enigma to the strategic Siemens encoding machine (see Rohwer and Jäckel 1979). When Alan Turing, intelligence cryptographer and inventor of the computer, traveled to Ebermannstadt for one last time in July 1945, there was nothing in the German cryptoanalysis centers to dismantle. On the contrary, he could only pity the technological deficit of those enemies or colleagues who had not yet replaced themselves with machines (Hodges 1983: 312).

The German-French technology transfer was much smoother. Probably since neither of the two languages were binding in the surrender document, the mutual hermeneutics went on undisturbed. Just as German press officers had provided paper for Sartre's *L'être et le néant* as an example of heroic nihilism, so French occupation officers invited Heidegger to think about technology as such. Empirical technologies hinted at greater "success," simply the "inheritance of [four years] of cooperation in war." The Mirage and the Airbus are constructions by wartime engineers (Bower 1987: 150–51) under the conditions of an economically unified Fortress Europe.

Since unconditional surrender literally meant capitulation to America, the transatlantic technology transfer was greater than all the rest. Internal statistics of Air Force Intelligence claiming that 17 percent of all German wartime scientists worked in the Soviet Union, 12 percent in France, 11 percent in England, and only 6 percent in the United States were "obviously false" and were only given to other governmental agencies in order to speed up the transfer operations Overcast and Paperclip (Bower 1987: 233–34). In 1945 the Joint Intelligence Committee presented the following personnel recommendation to the Joint Chiefs of Staff:

Unless the migration of important German scientists and technicians into the Soviet zone is immediately stopped, we believe that the Soviet Union within a relatively short time may equal United States developments in the fields of atomic research and guided missiles and may be ahead of U.S. development in other fields of great military importance, including infra red, television and jet propulsion.   (Cited Bower 1987: 161)

But the German agencies were prepared. By the end of August 1944, the SS Central Security Office (Reichssicherheitshauptamt) had learned from "reliable" agent reports of a plan "to transfer at least 20,000 German engineers to the United States" "in the case of a German defeat" (Ludwig 1979: 513). This most certainly motivated Major General Kammler to order his rocket technicians to the deep, that is American, south (Ruland 1969: 253). Even the highest levels of army command and general staffs continued this strategy—until their so-called dissolution, which was probably the beginning of postwar German Federal Army planning—of transferring as many technicians as possible, along with one and a half million other soldiers, from the east to the west (Cartier 1985: 1023). This strategy met the personnel requirements of the Americans.

The results of operations Overlord and Paperclip are now history. In 1947, the U.S. Office of Technical Services put it succinctly: "This accumulation of information not only represents the greatest transfer of mass intelligence ever made from one country to another, but it also represents one of the most valuable acquisitions ever made by this country" (cited in Gimbel 1990: 147). Wernher von Braun's rocket technicians and Professor Strughold's space medicine researchers, whose human resources could only be provided by concentration camps, completed an atomic deterrent whose foundations were laid by emigrants from Hitler's Europe (McNeill 1982: 353). John von Neumann, the mathematician of all atomic bombs and of the von Neumann computer, convinced the Pentagon that the "marriage of two monsters" (Jungk 1956: 414), a warhead from Los Alamos and a launch vehicle from Peenemünde, would become the contemporary strategic standard (Heims 1982: 230–90). The Pax Americana, thanks to higher mathematics, rests on the triumph of this (in Eisenhower's words) military-industrial complex and its obviation of personnel-intensive world wars like the first and materiel-intensive wars like the second.

This is precisely the reason why the standards of civilian entertainment electronics (with the big exception of transistors) is still at the level of 1945. World War II, which had introduced the circuit board in place of free-floating tubes, coils, and condensers, likewise forms the plateau of our memory world. The tank's VHF radio, as it was introduced in the German Army in 1934 and by Bell Labs in the U.S. Army in 1940 (Welchman 1982: 264), became a secondary medium for entire populations and added a storage medium through the magnetophone. The primary medium after the war became television, whose development by the BBC and the German Postal Agency was halted at the outbreak of the war simply because the same picture-producing electronics in radars gained the highest military priority. Whenever Walter Bruch, whose PAL system has become the color TV standard for half the world, wasn't spending his time aiming his TV picture tube at a V2 rocket as it rose from Test Stand VII in Peenemünde,* he spent it with tests that are an integral part of every Cruise Missile today. He equipped aerial bombs with television cameras and self-guided

*Along with Bruch 1967: 74–77, see Dornberger 1953: 10; these two sources together make it clear that the TV screen at pad VII had the purpose, as have all simulations since then, of preventing a fatal test result for the experimenters.

mechanisms and had old "pleasure boats, of course without pas-
sengers" sail around on the Müggelsee, and then tried to optimize
the link between TV and servomotors to the point where these
bombs found the pleasure boats all on their own (Bruch 1967: 73–
74). Norbert Wiener and Claude Shannon, the two mathematicians
of a new information theory, proceeded in this manner in their
work for the National Defense Research Council. They developed
an automatic antiaircraft control system for the Battle of Britain
(Hagemeyer 1979: 278–87), without which, according to Wiener
himself, his later cybernetics would have been unthinkable (Wiener
1961: 28–30).

The self-guided weapons of World War II eliminated the two
modern concepts of causality and subjectivity and introduced the
present as the age of technical systems. Only Shannon and Turing—that is, neither Norbert Wiener at MIT nor German army
engineers except Zuse—calculated these systems through digitally
to take the decisive step from radio waves and differential equations
to the pulse technology of radar or to the algebra of computers.*
The Pax Americana has a good technological foundation.

Whether digital or analog, technical systems are always self-
guided. "The most complicated apparatus of the modern world,"
armaments minister Speer wrote in the conclusion of his *Memoirs*,
"can unrelentingly destroy itself through negative impulses that
feed off each other" (Speer 1989: 525). His final statement at the
Nuremberg trials as evidence for the victors was as follows:

> Hitler's dictatorship was the first dictatorship of an industrial nation in the
> age of modern technology. . . . Telephones, teletypes, and radios made it
> possible to relay messages from the highest levels directly to the lowest
> echelons. . . . This state system may seem as confusing as the wires of a
> switchboard to an outsider, but like the switchboard, it could be con-
> trolled and dominated by someone's will. Earlier dictatorships required
> supervisors of a high quality at lower echelons—men who could think
> and act independently. The authoritarian system in the age of technology
> can do without these men—the means of communication alone make it
> possible to mechanize the work of the lower echelons.   (Speer 1989: 522)

---

*Hagemeyer 1979: 338–45. The "Würzburg Primer," published in October
1943 by the Supreme Command of the Navy, the Air Force Ministry, and the
Head of the Army Communications System, sacrifices any sort of mathematical
elegance in the case of square pulses.

"Men who can think and act independently" have defined subjects since Kant or Gneisenau, that is, since before the development of self-guided weapons. Consequently, the singularity of
mankind is eliminated with the death of 55 million in the last world
war. According to Pynchon's mean-spirited words, "the mass nature of wartime death . . . serves as a spectacle, as diversion from
the real movements of the War" (Pynchon 1973: 105). This is why
Germany's fractalization into occupation zones, technology transfer, reconstruction, and five-year plans are part of the logic of
technological systems. After the first film of the V2 finally convinced Hitler, who was (according to Syberberg) the "greatest
cineast of all time," of the feasibility of self-guided space weapons,
he stated that nations "are, in light of this weapon," "now and for
all time too small" (cited in Ruland 1969: 141). Nothing and no
one, not even the Führer principle, could stop the technology
transfer. Technology transfer means that communications technologies remain true to their name; that is, they become transmitta-
ble communications themselves. When empires are media and
media are postal services (see Siegert's essay in this volume), then
their fate can only be dispatched. As Zhukov's artillery shot down
the last tethered balloon, from which the radio relay line connected
the Führer bunker under the Reichs chancellery to Army Group
Steiner (Hoffmann 1965, 2: n.p.), nothing ended; it was only the
beginning.

The United States was not the only nation waiting for unconditional surrender and military technicians. Japan, the technology
empire of the future, was waiting as well. As blueprints of the Me
262 and the Heinkel 117 reached the Far East (with the success of
one of two submarine blockade busters), an official "Japanese plan
to bring German technicians to Japan" was made official in August
1944 (Ludwig 1979: 513–14). On April 30, 1945, the Supreme
Command decided on "the outlines of measures to be taken in the
case of Germany's capitulation," according to which "the interests
of German citizens in East Asia were to be generously preserved,"
but "the great aims of the Greater East Asian War" were to be
unremittingly continued. Consequently, on May 9, 1945, Japan
declared "all agreements with the German Reich" to be suspended
(cited in Hattori 1967: 389–90).

The unthinkable only occurred after Hiroshima and Nagasaki.

For the first time in their history, the Japanese heard the voice of a Tenno on a recording and over the radio, as if Sony's media empire had already begun. Emperor Hirohito, in his classical, almost incomprehensible Japanese, declared the end of a world war without any reference to unconditional surrender.

WULF R. HALBACH

Simulated Breakdowns

❖❖   *for my father*

This paper has three parts, the first of which introduces several terms I consider valuable for the description of complex dynamic systems. These terms seem to be more or less paradigmatic for the situation that Wlad Godzich described as—allow me this rephrasing—a world with a growing number of images that are without references. I consider these terms to be an opening for our discussion if we view breakdowns not only as contingencies but also as constitutive—hardly previewable—elements of all kinds of highly complex dynamic systems.

The second part presents a case study of October 19, 1987, and the third consists more or less in questions and annotations, which show the potential of this perspective in systems and lead us into a discussion about the compossibility of "the real" and "the not yet real."

I

On October 19, 1987, the international stock market crashed by about 750 points on the Dow Jones Index. This was equivalent to almost 24 percent of its value the previous night and 35 percent of its value a week prior. This was an enormous drop considering that the changes on an average day are usually no more than plus or minus 2 percent. The problem I am going to discuss hinges on the term "average." To analyze and describe the market, the traditional broker basically uses two methods. One can be described in more or less scientific, or better, mathematical terms, whereas the other follows nonmathematical principles. Those means are chart analysis on the one hand and intuition, fueled by something we might call routine and rumor, on the other. The moment the financial sector introduced the computer not only to support the actual exchange of stocks and obligations and to forward obligations, for example, but also to collect and to distribute data for and by various international information services, these traditional procedures became outdated. Besides stock quotes, the collected data include all relevant (and even nonrelevant) information, ranging from the health of the American president to political and social changes in all parts of the world. For the first time in the history of the international market, simultaneous real-time information and reaction to it became possible for all stock exchanges (worldwide). This resulted in (1) a new form of institution—the computer stock exchange—and (2) a new form of market rigging, since it became possible to play the game simultaneously on each and every one of the national markets. In saying that real-time information and reaction became possible for the first time, the stress lies on the term "reaction." The real-time transmitting of market-relevant data was nearly achieved with the introduction of the telegraph. And—to cite a book in progress about the importance of the telegraph by Monika Reiss of Freiburg—it was this development that structured the international market as we know it today. All of this is well known to most of us, as is the following introduction to simulation software for this extended market. Less well known are the results of this more than evolutionary change.

The speed with which new information became available demanded an even higher speed of reaction. To support this, two types of software were developed to analyze and simulate certain market situations based on the just-mentioned traditional methods: (1) chart-analysis programs that promise to propose the correct reaction to and behavior for a given situation on the basis of an analysis of past developments and (2) stop-loss-order programs that send out a selling signal the moment certain quotations move below a specified value. Both types of programs work on the principle of "strong causality," that is, the presupposition that certain factors have a strong causal influence on the processes in question. These factors can be described in rules and regulations of hard constraint, in contrast to those of a soft constraint, which consider rules and ruling factors as an interdependent network with a kind of interactive system of regulation.

If we try to formulate a mathematical description of the stock market at any given point in time, we will see that this algorithm is feasible today only if the market is reduced to a linearity that considers just a few of all the parameters involved. Even a well-trained broker does not always know all the parameters of the market, but his intuition (routine and rumor) lets him consider all the important factors. In other words: there is no proper scientific explanation why certain configurations should result in a *bull* (rising) or in a *bear* (falling) market. The consequences of this inadequacy are fairly obvious: the process in question suffers in its mathematical description from reduction to a "linear approximation," its reduction to average values. John von Neumann and Oskar Morgenstern described this reduction in their *Theory of Games and Economic Behaviour* as a reduction to the description of rational behavior, which is again defined by the relative linearity by which a preproposed goal is achieved. "The individual who attempts to obtain these respective maxima is also said to act 'rationally'" (Neumann and Morgenstern 1972: 9). The goal is the attempt "[of] the consumer . . . to obtain a maximum of utility or satisfaction and [of] the entrepreneur [to obtain] a maximum of profits" (ibid., 8). This is a quantification of a qualitative orientation toward what Immanuel Kant called "Vernunftserkenntnis" ("reine Erkenntnis" or "Erkenntnis a priori"; the term "cognition" would not really fit here). This qualitative orientation at "Vernunftserkenntnis" is Kant's way—in his first and second critique—of defining rational behavior, and the attempt to handle it in a quantitative manner, to "quote" it as an algorithm, marks the basic problem not only of models of human processuality but of dynamic systems in general (see Kant 1983a: 698 [B864]; 1983b; 117 [A23]).

Again, in order to "copy" this processuality with the help of a simulation, it must be reduced to a non-originary, algorithmable linearity, within which only those steps are significant that show a recognizable vector toward the proposed goal. In other words, only strategically oriented parts of the process become objects of

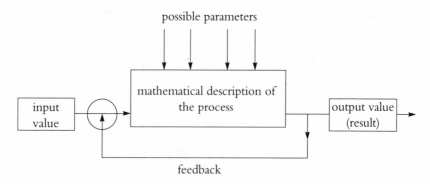

Fig. 1. General feedback diagram

our model, since its underlying evaluation is of a retrospective character. This means that the determination of what is relevant for the process occurs from the preproposed goal backward. Just one small note to those interested in the mathematical aspects of this problem: to reduce the parameters of our simulation to a computable linearity does not mean that the actual process itself is also of a linear character.

This is true for simulations in general and is in fact the basic problem for any attempt to describe realities on this level. In order to create a model for any reality in question, as many details and parameters must be taken into consideration as possible (also a question of the costs). The details and parameters chosen are the most relevant—maximum parameters—and those that are left out are the least influential—minimal parameters. If we take a non-dynamic system, this approach causes relatively few problems, since the output hardly has any influence on the proposed parameters (Fig. 1). This is certainly not the case with dynamic systems like the international stock market, since the output of the simulation in progress will cause its user to react in a certain way—most of the time in the proposed way. This reaction changes the surrounding factors of the model because the buying and selling of stocks has an influence on the prices of these and other stocks. In general, even this singular reaction causes no big changes because the parameters of the model are—even under the discussed restrictions—well chosen.

II

What happened on October 19, 1987? Since success in the international stock market depends, much more than any other economic structure, on reaction speed relative to other participants, hardly any institution or individual can afford not to join the automation of the markets. The surplus of information had to be processed in re-actions, and the appropriate means were or seemed to be the above-mentioned software packages, all of which worked with the same underlying principle of chart analysis. Imagine what happens if, let's say, after a good movie on television all the inhabitants of, for example, Palo Alto, go to the bathroom at the same time? The answer is obvious: the relatively stable water system overloads and will eventually—depending on the consumption of beer, and so on—break down. Basically the same thing happened on Wall Street. The explosive differences, however, become obvious if we try to describe the process in a less metaphoric way. Let us say that our simulation tells us that a certain stock X is declining and should be sold. Even if we don't trust our model, we will at least get suspicious and watch X in the days to come. It will probably be the first stock sold the instant we get an option to buy other stocks we consider more profitable. The moment a whole community of brokers, or better—since they all basically use the same type of software—all brokers get the same information (it doesn't matter whether it is correct or not), our suspicions will be confirmed, because sooner or later someone will sell and consequently affect the price of our stock X. The result is only too obvious: we get the next selling signal, and this one is impossible to ignore. Since most investors use a strategy of synthetically insured portfolios, that is, groups of stocks from different areas of the market, this is not a singular process that affects only stock X, but a general process that affects the whole market. Again, even if the theoretical proposition of our model is wrong, this movement will prove the forecast of our simulation to be true! This will eventually even affect our views of this kind of simulation.

If we consider the diagram of a general feedback mechanism (Fig. 1) where the results of a described process after a period of time t are fed back into the process as new input values, we must reformulate this diagram in order to meet the special requirements

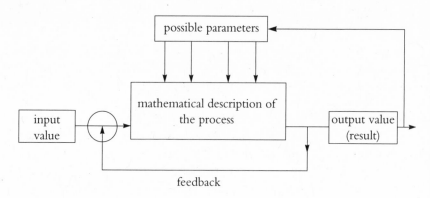

Fig. 2. Feedback diagram of a dynamic system

of the stock market as a dynamic system (Fig. 2). Since the output of a serious simulation is not merely a table of figures but a proposal for reaction, which in our case changes those parameters that led to the simulated configuration of quotations in the first place, we now have a kind of external feedback and a very interesting paradoxical situation. Even if the parameters we called maximum parameters could be modified to fit the new configuration, the simulation that led to this crucial situation will eventually lead to the final break-down, because the multitude of changes will also change the evaluation of the parameters. This means that those factors we call minimal parameters will also be involved as maximum parameters in the "real" process the moment they suffer a transformation by the multitude of market interventions. In our example, this transformation is not one of an additional character, but one of multiplying, if not of exponential, character. So again, our question is: what happened? The simulations, important for handling the markets, crashed! They crashed in their ability to describe the actual situation because their orientation at average values did not include the possibilities that a certain set of parameters—considered minimal—could turn maximal and therefore become important for an adequate description.

In other words, even if a change of the defined maximum parameters was taken into consideration, a change of the set of parameters of influence was not. To rephrase again: the simulation could not deal with its own influence, could not "watch" itself in relation to its context, because—please allow me once again to use metaphorical language—the presupposed "reality" crashed with its simulation. Luckily enough, the "reality" of the market offers an "exit" and closes the stock exchanges for three days to send a break signal to the exponential character of this development and thereby helps to stabilize the market at a new level of normality—in our example, at about 600 points below the previous level.*

III

Our simulation of possible stock market interventions implies yet another problem. To use mathematical terms—and it is very interesting that all handbooks of mathematics, very much concerned with the abstraction of all their topics, use the term "reality" only in the context of simulations—the relationship between "reality" and simulation achieves another vector if we realize that the real system, to which the simulation refers as a substitute, is not the kind of "reality" we might think it is, not something we can touch or deal with in a material sense, but another "simulation," since it is something "untouchable," and there is only reference but no materiality. This "immateriality" of money, all the more the case without a gold standard, has its pendant in stocks and obligations of and for corporations whose value seems to be represented by the individual values of their distributed stocks. But this representation is only one of the market's perspectives of this particular business. This aspect of the market, being in itself constituted by a configuration of signifiers, is even more obvious in the dealing of futures on, for example, bananas that have not yet been grown. If this market is automatically handled with the help of simulation programs, we are finally confronted with the question of the constitutive gap between "reality" and simulations. Since simulations gain a certain active aspect of reality themselves as their prophecies become real, this question takes on a very explosive character. In this context, I am calling the output of our simulation in question a "prophecy" in order to stress its basic orientation toward average values of real-

*For the actual data, I am very much indebted to Gerke 1988.

ities and to account for its inability to predict the contingency of the final breakdown, which is already inscribed in its basic construction and which it therefore is incapable of seeing.

IV

Let me conclude with a few annotations on and questions about the process just described. All these problems come down to the system's problem with its own circular self-description. If a modus on an n-order observation is used to produce a description, which is then implemented in any kind of automata, then the handling will necessarily be of an $n - 1$ order. Then again, one might say that we will just have to move up any number of steps on the observation chain until we have achieved an adequate description. But this "until" only offers the feeble promise of another "average" and—from the same vector—the danger or the promise of the "final breakdown." The only technical way I can think to solve this problem of rejected and averaged values and of the incompatibility of the order of observation and the order of automatic handling is a network-oriented approach to modeling realities, similar to that of "parallel distributed processing" (PDP) (see Rumelhart et al. 1986). These systems are at least capable of solving the problem of rejected values, since their parameters are of a dynamic form. They distinguish between hard and soft constraints to deal with the changes of what I call minimal parameters. But then again, I am not too sure whether these systems still allow us, to paraphrase Claude E. Shannon, to observe a difference between observation and observer, since all units and knots of these systems by definition observe and control each other.

The psychological origin of any simulation and automatic planning is found in the fear of the breakdown of the system. Automatic planning and simulations only make sense if they promise a kind of early-warning system against a breakdown, one they might not even be able to "think," and if they propose solutions to the inevitable. If we remember the potentializing character of the simulation process, we will detect a spiral movement between fear as the origin of the simulation, the simulation in progress, and fear again. In this context, simulations easily achieve some kind of ontological character and remind us of the animistic attempts to achieve "a corresponding control over things [and nature]" that Sigmund Freud described in 1913 in *Totem and Taboo* (Freud 1952, 9: 103–6).

This brings me to my concluding question, namely: Can simulation systems "think" their breakdowns if they are unable to predict them?

ALOIS HAHN

Talking about AIDS

Rhetorical and Practical Paradoxes

Discourses create paradoxes. They almost unavoidably appear in certain forms of self-description and self-justification while one is attempting to locate the universe's Archimedean point. Normally, the paradoxes discovered in this manner, for example, the Epimenides paradoxes, are of little consequence for action. They give joy to logicians, rhetoricians, and, of course, writers. The proverbial barber, to whom the paradoxical instructions are given to shave all the men of the village who don't shave themselves, will either shave his own beard or not without really being too concerned that in any case he is failing to comply with the instructions. Things are different when someone is confronted with contradictory imperatives, compliance and noncompliance with which are alike linked to stiff penalties or to some other dreadful consequences. The situation is all the worse if this someone is unable to point out the structure of the trap, whether it is a strictly logical paradox involving actual contradiction or instead a practical paradox.

Relationships enmeshed in double binds, a phenomenon documented and analyzed by an extensive literature, are one example of practical paradox. Another example results when antinomies appear on which legitimate justifications of forms of social behavior

NOTE: The following discussion is part of a larger empirical study of AIDS in which I am currently engaged along with my Trier colleagues Willi Eirmbter and Rüdiger Jacob.

or postulates of meaning are based, as when it becomes apparent that the difference between true and false cannot be based on truth itself, when the difference between right and wrong cannot be based on right itself, or when the distinction between immanence and transcendence seems unavoidably immanent. Both types of practical paradox can lead to a breakdown of the appropriate reaction; in extreme cases, the perception of "meaninglessness"* can drive a person to suicide. It is not necessarily decisive for "real" or unsolvable paradoxes, as seen from the perspective of the logician, to be involved. It is sufficient if those concerned feel that the dilemma is hopeless. If, in the following, I talk about the discourse on AIDS as a generator of paradox, then I am always thinking of these kinds of "practical" paradoxes, of dilemmas that create virtual breakdowns, the inability to act, or crises of legitimacy for institutions or for individual existence. Paradoxes of this kind always exist, but they normally remain hidden. The proper functioning of almost all communication depends on keeping its shaky foundation, its actual lack of any foundation, unconscious and unspoken. Society is based on the silent acceptance of the Münchhausen Principle: you alone can pull yourself out of the mud by your own hair. But whoever recognizes this fact is already lost. Help from strangers can only exist if it goes unnoticed.

AIDS as Discourse

AIDS is not only a deadly disease but also the principle of a special discourse. Within this discourse can be found, on the one hand, all of the known, scientifically sanctioned assumptions and knowledge about agents, means of transmission, dangers of infection, diagnostic and therapeutic methods, and, on the other hand, a collectively assumed connection between life-styles, character and threat, guilt and death, sexuality and menace. Disease as media topic requires an "imaginary" (in Michel Maffesoli's sense). This is the subject of the following discussion.

Seldom has a disease generated so much public attention in such a short time as AIDS (Herzlich and Pierret 1987). This is especially

---

*I am using an emphatic sense of "meaning" that can certainly be sensibly negated, as opposed to a comprehensive sense of "meaning" that cannot be negated but contains its own negation (see A. Hahn 1987).

remarkable if one considers how relatively small the number of those who have died from the disease is (compared to the number of deaths from other causes). The total number of AIDS cases in the Federal Republic of Germany up to the end of 1988 was 2,779, 190 of these being women. Half of those infected had already died by this time. More than 80 percent of those infected belonged to so-called "high risk groups"; that is, they were homosexuals or drug users. In metropolitan areas, there were 242 with the disease for every million inhabitants; in other areas, only 14. Nevertheless, the phenomenon of the disease was known by almost the entire population. AIDS is therefore above all a reality of communication. Almost no one in the population as a whole has observed the illness firsthand. Fear is based not on personal experience but rather on what has appeared in the media. It could even be said that the virus is currently circulating more quickly in the minds of the population than in their bloodstreams.

Fear of Infection and AIDS Testing

If one were to investigate the contents of the characteristic "imaginary" of this disease, one would find two conflicting, if not strictly speaking contradictory, ideas. On the one hand, AIDS is present as a universal threat. Everyone can be infected. Although in fact only few have been directly affected, and since certain groups carry considerably higher risks, the danger is presented as ubiquitous, often in contradiction of the current understanding of the "real" possibilities of infection. For example, members of the Alpine Club inquired whether secured climbing cables could be used safely without gloves to protect the climber from infection. On the other hand, counterbalancing the theme of the omnipresence of danger, the fact that infection can be avoided is well known: everyone can do something to protect himself and others, but only if these precautions are constant. The AIDS gloves that have in the meantime become mandatory for every first-aid kit are a symbol of the coexistence of the universal presence of danger and fundamental possibilities of protection.

The central theme in the discourse about AIDS is not actually the disease itself but rather the idea of an omnipresent and dangerous virus: hidden, but still discoverable; deadly, but still beatable through an ensemble of precautions that are linked to maintaining safe distance, early recognition, segregation of groups, and the classification of those affected. Attention thereby is shifted from the public disease to covert infection or HIV-positive test results.

Whether or not one carries the virus determines a person's fundamental identity. The answer is not always known. People don't even know themselves who they are. They have to be told. Others, the doctors who administer the test, decide who I am. The result is a contradictory imperative. As long as I don't know if I've been infected, I can keep the identity I've had. It is therefore advisable not to take the risk of being tested. On the other hand, I can only be sure of my identity if I risk losing it by being tested. It would therefore seem advisable to be tested. Either solution is equally risky inasmuch as even testing can't provide any final guarantees.

The Paradox of the Foreignness of Nonforeigners

A positive test result would show me that I am different from what I thought I was. I am foreign to myself. It is useful in this context to analyze the minority but nevertheless widely disseminated discourse of the supporters of the French "Front National": AIDS is spread by foreigners. Hell is represented by others. The nation is pure, virtuous, and healthy. Foreigners must therefore be tested first.

The logic of testing is not limited to what is foreign in the strict sense of the word. Whoever tests HIV positive is a foreigner in more than just a metaphoric sense. It is not always known with certainty and at all times who is HIV positive. This creates the paradox that nonforeigners have to be treated as foreigners in order to determine that they really aren't foreign at all. Since testing has to be repeated, one is forced to reject the difference between foreign and nonforeign that is central to the self-identity of right-wing radicals. It is central for them precisely because these same radicals will never contest this difference, for the criterion for foreignness makes it possible to speak of foreigners who are not foreign as well as of nonforeigners who are foreign (because they disobeyed the rules).

AIDS Testing as a Dispositive of Truth

From this background arise the fantasies of a permanent test for everyone. Testing becomes an obligatory confession. Similar to the "proof of Arianism" for the Nazis, AIDS testing manifests, for those with the views outlined above, who "truly" belongs to the nation of the pure and healthy and who represents a deadly alterity.

As a consequence, testing becomes the voice of truth in the "imaginary" of these views, rather like the torture of a few centuries ago. Only this time it is a mild torture, scientific and hygienic. But the manifestation of one's identity is at stake in both cases. Permanent testing in the totalitarian discourse on AIDS becomes what the public, forced confession or permanent denunciation was and is in totalitarian societies. The speech given by Pierre-Louis Roederer to the Jacobites on December 18, 1791, comes to mind, in which he demanded a general scrutiny of everyone by everyone as well as permanent denunciations in order to distinguish friend from foe: "You will never be able, under the present circumstances, to distinguish the enemies from the friends of the constitution with certainty. . . . There is only one way to discover them, namely by taking the offensive. Everyone who does not participate is our enemy. . . . Every word, every motion, even silence itself are indications for the sentiments of each individual and show where he stands" (Jaume 1989: 73). Testing then becomes the "breakthrough" of the hidden identity by bringing about the dissolution of what was heretofore maintained. The outbreak of the disease or death are not the breakdown; it begins with an HIV-positive result.

Testing functions as an institutionalized, involuntary memory, or perhaps as the reading of a text written in blood. "Blood is a most special juice," says Goethe's devil. In the "imaginary" of the AIDS disease, blood, virus, sexuality, sperm, and death are mixed. Testing works like a confessional generator that forces out a hidden and unconfessable secret; its institutionalization makes control through control possible: a dispositive of truth that changes the forgotten past into a collectively valid presence of the social being.

Testing as Paradox and Antiparadox

Testing also represents a dispositive of an existential antiparadox. Before testing, neither I nor others knew whether the virus was present or not. Of course, all social life requires the continuous maintenance of contacts, both physical and sexual. But in extreme fantasies of threat, virtually every contact can be deadly, and it would therefore be necessary to forgo all social contact in order to avoid the risk of death. The avoidance of all risk of a deadly infection implies an avoidance of life. The fear of AIDS produces a vital "double bind." This paradox is by no means completely eliminated by testing, but it is reduced to the normal risks of life, whose paradox is expressed in the trite saying that the only way not to die is not to live.

As one can easily see, the antiparadox effect of testing can only be truly achieved if the results are made public. Test and denunciation are close allies for those who hope to gain some airtight protection for the population as a whole. Whenever the threat of infection is seen as ubiquitous, the next step seems to demand the total exposure of those identified as having AIDS. If only sexual contacts with those infected are seen to be dangerous, then the publicity of the infection can be minimized. If one reads through the corresponding demands as they are openly discussed, then both are to be found in a totalitarian discourse. It is well known that Le Pen has called for concentration camps for those who are HIV positive. He's not the only one. A few years ago in Germany, a popular tabloid printed a Frankfurt professor's advice to tattoo the genitals of those infected with AIDS.

The alternatives offered by this totalitarian discourse lie somewhere between stigmatization and physical isolation. These are rejected in this form by the liberal majority. More widely accepted is the call for "voluntary" testing. The result, given general participation, would be similar in certain respects: only those who are voluntarily tested appear to be acting responsibly, given the general risk of infection. Finding out that you are infected would require you to warn others. Self-stigmatization would take the place of stigmatization by others. The segregation effect would be unavoidable. One difference is at least thinkable, however: it would be easier to interpret the stigmatized identity as one of choice. Exclusion and stigma could be imagined as a deadly form of exclusivity: AIDS as *morbus sacer*, as epilepsy or tuberculosis was in other times. It is nevertheless more likely that the dilemma remains, even in the case of voluntary testing. Whoever is not tested stands before himself as someone who is not completely convinced of his own identity; if he were convinced, he wouldn't hesitate to be tested. But when he decides to be tested, he risks discovering that his identity up to now does not correspond to the truth. Testing produces a paradox whose antiparadox lies with the individual, namely, with his power to subject himself to the test.

Submitting oneself to testing strictly speaking represents only the first step of this antiparadox: only the person affected and his medical caretakers are made aware of the truth of his identity. The second step concerns the social presentation of the self. Here the question of revealing the results presents the individual with the same situation as he faced before testing. This is especially true for intercourse with those who are closest. On the one hand, responsibility demands an immediate revelation—whether of one's test results or of one's lack of test results—but, on the other hand, the relationship itself is threatened by this very same revelation. Being a threat to others does not have a place in a love relationship. But a confession might end the relationship altogether. It is clear from the data that someone infected with AIDS can hardly find sexual partners, even though the possibility exists of avoiding infection through appropriate precautions (e.g., condoms). This is true as well for nonsexual contacts. Michael Pollak writes about a typical situation where a mother of an AIDS patient, having been informed by the doctor that she can kiss her son without risk of infection, is still unable to do so. The fear of infection is too great to be simply brushed aside by medical theory. This fear has an almost "infrastructural" intensity that cannot be overcome by communication. The son's reaction in this example is one of utter disappointment. He no longer has any desire to see his mother (Pollak 1987: 100). From the perspective of the AIDS patient, the dilemma is that the revelation of the truth causes the loss of a loved one, but silence requires that a loved one be treated as if he were not loved. The situation is no less dramatic from the perspective of the one who does not know about the infection. Love requires trust. To demand testing would contradict the required trust. Tests could never provide any absolute certainty anyway. Consummation of the relationship means exposing oneself to deadly risk. The other person, that is, the person who is loved, appears as a dual personality: he is lover and potentially lethal enemy.* Love itself generates this duality. If the other person were indifferent, he would also not be dangerous. But with love comes the duality, and the duality can be overcome only through shared knowledge of infection. The reason for this naturally lies in the barrier to observation.

It could be said that the AIDS phenomenon dramatically uncovers a trusted paradox that has been experienced as a source of tragedy since the "Hiketides": whether or not the alter ego is friend or foe can only be known *ex post facto* because of his basic intransparency. One has no friends at all if one does not risk treating enemies as friends. This is a necessity even though the most effective enemy is one who enjoys the friendly trust of his unknowing foe. The crisis in the case of AIDS results, on the one hand, from the deadliness of the threat and, on the other, from the recognition of the unrecognizability of the virus, exposure to which is overcome only by the vital paradox.

A completely different paradox might arise for a liberal society in conjunction with the question of mandatory testing and corresponding measures. If it is assumed that the most extreme fears that inhabit the fantasies of certain people could actually be true (an assumption for which there is at present absolutely no scientific evidence, but that cannot be regarded as completely impossible), then the preservation of the liberality of a society could conflict with the preservation of the society itself. Perhaps only a liberal society is worth defending, but in order to defend itself, it would have to become antiliberal. The solutions to these paradoxes would soon appear. Antiliberal measures would be initiated and declared to be only temporary. A society is only liberal if it sometimes isn't, or if it isn't so that it can become liberal again sometime in the future. Such temporal arguments can also be presented in connection with the difference of ends and means or the difference between reality and appearances. The effect of successful

---

*This is not an entirely new dilemma and not one that is generated exclusively by AIDS. In societies with a high female death rate from childbirth, a similar problem arises for women, at least when marriage and intercourse are voluntary.

solutions is always the same: paradoxes are swept under the rug so that things can (somehow?) go on.

Paradoxes of Interpretation

In all premodern societies, illness and death have given rise to religious interpretations. These were normally not private but set within a binding cultural framework. Illness could be attributed to supernatural and inexplicable resolution or to individual, biographical guilt. Official, modern medical doctrine excludes such attributions. Illness is illness and nothing more. Implications of outside influence are out of the question. They can be neither required of the doctor nor socially imputed to the patient. The patient has the right to demand that his illness is not seen as a metaphor. It means nothing. Therein lies a piece of freedom. A series of studies now shows that, contrary to the official self-descriptions of medicine, illnesses do in fact become objects of interpretation that connect them to assumed life-styles, family, and guilt (see Herzlich and Pierret 1984: 155–60). The blame placed on outside influences can often weigh more heavily on the patient than the illness itself (see Pollak 1988). It becomes apparent that the "imaginary" of such illnesses is especially prone to this kind of "metaphorizing." Susan Sontag described this phenomenon several years ago with respect to cancer and more recently with AIDS (Sontag 1980, 1989) and has taken a strong position against it. From her perspective, the integration of a natural evil into the interpretive world of culture does not lead to its resolution but rather to an escalation of horror, which adds defamation to the already present suffering. Though her statements may be plausible, there is a flip side: the refusal to give meaning to illness and death in no way suspends the need for meaning. This is supported by numerous studies (see Herzlich and Pierret 1984). The alternative to interpretation is experienced as meaninglessness. The interpretations themselves are lacking, however. The dilemma is obvious: Whoever gives meaning to suffering or allows others to do so is confronted with interpretations that all too clearly contaminate his freedom and dignity. Yet whoever refuses interpretation is left open to a painful absurdity.

Is there a way out? What could be the "rejection value" (in

Gotthard Günther's sense) of the binary intracultural "coding" of illness that seems to allow only interpretation or meaninglessness and to institutionalize the need for interpretation as a generator of the experience of meaninglessness? Perhaps a freedom of sense as an infracultural phenomenon beyond culture? But this time a phenomenon that is seen not as supracultural but rather as infracultural? The problem is that all transcendence, whether conceived as supracultural or infracultural, must be intracultural in its inception.

The "way out" of this dilemma has been described in sociological literature, often critically, as a "suppression" of death and suffering (most recently: Nassehi and Weber 1989; A. Hahn 1968; Fuchs 1973). But who is suppressing and what are they suppressing? If these topics had been suppressed, it would no longer be possible to communicate the situation. If something is suppressed from the conscious mind, then one isn't aware of it oneself. At most an observer could make us aware of this fact. But how could this be accomplished if the observer had himself completely suppressed the facts? The idea that modern society has suppressed death because it is more afraid of death than other societies owing to an inability to assign meaning seems to me to be deficient. Interpretation and fear are not mutually exclusive. Besides, who could report something from the communicative beyond? It might be shown that certain forms of communication about death are no longer accepted everywhere (or, academically speaking, are not "connectable"). Presumably, as is so often the case when speaking of the "loss" of something important, the issue is not suppression but differentiation. Death is no longer, as it was several generations ago, a topic of general communication that permeates all consciousness, but rather an object of special subsystems that deal with this topic in their own peculiar ways. They "divide" themselves, so to speak, and thereby prevent our consciousness from seeing them as a whole. The result can be the marginalization of this topic for everyday concerns. Within the individual subsystems of communication, the horrible appears not as something that is defeated but as something that is specified: it is changed. The threat no longer presents itself as an object of indescribable fear but as an object of very precisely definable apprehensions. Death is not defeated as such, but is contested in its separate forms. Nothing can be done about death, but AIDS (cancer, syphilis, cholera, . . .) can be overcome.

This might explain the (apparent) paradox that modern society, supposedly so oblivious to death, has been able to make AIDS into such a media topic. How could it do this if the memory of a death that defies all interpretation were to interrupt its own *modus procedendi*? AIDS does not function as a form of death, insofar as death is seen as an existential necessity, but rather as a cause of death that can be fought. The entreaty of the danger of AIDS mobilizes a specific fear of death that has medical, legal, political, and caretaking implications. The identifiable form of this risk is what sets new energies free. We can deal with AIDS, but not with death. We overcome our fear of death by fearing its masks.

WLAD GODZICH

Language, Images, and the
Postmodern Predicament

It is a commonplace of the current discussion on literacy that
present-day students face far greater obstacles than their predecessors in the acquisition of the fundamentals of literacy because they
have been exposed since their earliest childhood to the pernicious
effects of television. Whether this is in fact the case remains a matter
of debate not least because of the poverty of the arguments that are
adduced as proof for either side. This poverty is twofold: historical
and theoretical. On the historical side there is a failure to appreciate
the fact that literacy, as a specific relation to language, has had a
defining role within modernity. Any changes in our relation to
language would thus spell the end of modernity. On the theoretical
side, there has been a failure to establish the ground on which
language and images actually compete with each other and to
provide an understanding of their respective advantages. In this
paper I attempt to sketch what the successful completion of both of
these tasks would require.

I

We must begin by acknowledging that language and literacy are
two distinct phenomena, and specifically, that the second term is a
shorthand description of a determinate set of relations that we have
to language, relations that arose under, and were conditioned by,
concrete historical circumstances. The historical character of liter-

acy should suggest, at the very least, that it is neither eternal—or "natural" as we are wont to say—nor immutable. But, just as important, it should also remind us that all our thinking about language has been dominated by the relations of literacy that we have to it. To put it more plainly: our present construct of language is a construct of, and for, literacy, and we cannot therefore preclude a priori the possibility of other constructs.

Only a detailed historical account of the emergence of the current construct of language and of its eventual vicissitudes would have probative value. In spite of some distinguished efforts (Jack Goody [1977], Marshall McLuhan, Walter Ong [1982], Ivan Illich [Illich and Sanders 1988]), no such comprehensive account is available to us, and the argument must thus proceed in somewhat more speculative fashion than it ought to; nonetheless the broad features of these developments can be distinguished, and it is only their exact dating that remains uncertain.

The medieval polity presents the paradoxical situation of a society capable of both extreme linguistic unity and inordinate linguistic diversity. Latin, as the universal language of the clerical class (a class defined by its literacy), serves all cognitive and interactive purposes, and, in the High Middle Ages especially, as the instrument of both church and state bureaucracies. By contrast to its universalism, which knows no other boundaries than those of the Christian faith, the particularism of medieval polity, that is, its subdivision into entities of considerable political, social, economic, and even legal autonomy, bound up with each other by bonds of feudal allegiance, is accompanied by abundant linguistic diversity that does not stop at the boundaries of each of these entities, as in the case of dialectal variation, but weaves itself through their very tissue by means of the specific jargons or trade languages associated with the various craft corporations and guilds. This latter, mostly illiterate, sphere of linguistic practice, about which we know very little owing to our own, literate, dependence on written documentation, represented the bulk of the population's experience of language. It was a sphere of immediate contact and transactions within a community of shared values and social orientations, however hierarchically differentiated. The variability of the languages represented the variability of social interactions: full knowledge of the language of a craft was a mark of one's participation in it and one's rights to its privileges, just as speech inflected differently from the local one undoubtedly would mark one for the levying of a special excise tax on goods imported from outside the city limits in the local marketplace. For the market played a determining role here. In fact it is its size that determined the scope and compass of the dominant language spoken in it, as still happens in numerous rural areas of Africa today.

In this respect, there is little difference in nature between Latin and the vernaculars: each was treated as proper to its function, that is, as universal within its own sphere—a fact that may explain why Latin was not retained for the role of truly universal language. Rather, one of the dialects emerged, generally by virtue of the support it received from a politically dominant group, to assume that position, and it displaced Latin as well as the other vernaculars, treating them equally as rivals.

We are all familiar with this process, which we associate with the major upheavals of early modern times: the so-called revival of learning known as the Renaissance; the emergence of the modern European nations; the advent of the modern form of the state; the development of humanistic ideology; and certainly not least, the vast expansion of markets on regional, national, and even trans-continental scales. The introduction of print technology ensured that the ideological commitment of humanism to linguistic univer-salism received the support of literacy, itself a requirement of the vast expansion of the state and of the economic sphere.

Under these conditions of expansion, the experience necessary for effective practice in the society exceeded the capacities of direct individual acquisition and thus had to be increasingly mediated by language, as in, for example, learning from books and, more gen-erally, (literate) education. Language in turn had to be treated as universal so that the experiences that were catalogued, coded, transmitted, and interpreted in it could be assumed by its users regardless of their degree of familiarity with these experiences. Thus, in opposition to the prior linguistic heterogeneity that was intended to acknowledge, if not produce, social differentiation and local autonomy, the new linguistic universalism of the epoch of literacy required assertions of human dignity, the covalence of individuals, and centralism.

From the outset, though, this emergent culture of literacy was beset with ambiguity and contradictions, the most notable of which was that, on the one hand, the ideology of linguistic universalism and its secondary elaboration into the values of what we know as humanism presupposed more direct and unimpeded access to all the spheres of the polity for all the members of the (presumably universal) linguistic community, while, on the other hand, the very advent of the ideology was due to the impossibility of such access and the resulting need for linguistic mediation. Literature as we know it and, more generally, the aesthetic function of art have come to occupy the space left gaping by this contradictory pull upon language in this epoch, universalizing according to strict humanist principles the particular instances of mediation necessitated by the imperative toward expansion and absorption of what had remained heterogeneous and particular.

But alongside such conquests of what could be described as archaic instances of heterogeneity and particularism—vestiges of older cultures of illiteracy, whether in the advanced countries or in the more recently modernized ones—there has emerged the more vexing problem of the production of a new heterogeneity, one that is not amenable to reduction by the culture of literacy since it is produced by this very culture as it proceeds to make its own differentiations. In its initial stages, if the culture of literacy relied upon language as universal mediator to bring into communicative interaction realms of practice that had arisen and evolved autonomously, it did so only because of the necessity for an expanding market to homogenize these realms and make them subject to a single ratio in the reckoning of their value. This same culture of literacy then began to produce increasingly self-standing spheres of practice that did not need to communicate with each other through the universal mediator but merely through a specialized part of it that operated somewhat analogously to the Latin of the Middle Ages. These spheres were destined to evolve in the direction of greater autonomy. The increasing specialization of the production of goods traded in the market inevitably promoted the elaboration of certain specific linguistic codes, marked by their functionality within the restricted sphere of their application. The codes were analogous to the jargons and trade languages of medieval crafts and guilds, and, in addition to being functional, they served to identify their users as members of determinate professional groups, a feature of social life well exploited in satirical literature in its depiction of physicians and lawyers, and, more recently, of politicians and literary critics.

The fact that the two latter groups are now legitimate objects of such mockery should, however, give us pause. Whereas the special linguistic elaboration of medicine and law are understandable in, and consonant with, the culture of literacy insofar as they constitute realms of specialized practice, the emergence of special languages for politics and for the discourse of reflection upon linguistic practice contravenes that culture: these argots are in direct conflict with the foundational notion of the culture of literacy, namely, that language is universal and that it is in the polity that its role as universal mediator is in evidence. In other words, the very existence of spheres of practice marked by special languages is legitimate according to the basic tenets of the ideology of literacy only if these specialized languages can be translated into a universal language and if the resulting translation is universally understandable, so that it permits the functioning of a polity based upon humanistic universalism and articulated in it. If these conditions fail to obtain, then the various spheres of practice, and those engaged in them, will become literally incommunicable to each other, and the cohesion of the social realm will begin to grow precarious unless it is ensured by other means. This is particularly the case if it is political language itself that becomes specialized and therefore understandable only to those initiated in it, and the problem is rendered well-nigh hopeless if those whose task it is to discourse upon language do so in impenetrable fashion. At this point the values of humanism, and especially those concerning the universality of experience, the covalence of individuals, and their right of access to all spheres of human activity are suspended; social cohesion is more likely then to be ensured by coercive authoritarian or manipulatory means than through participatory ones. The citizen, though a competent wielder of the codes in effect in his or her own sphere of production, becomes linguistically incompetent in the political sphere and must defer to those who are competent, or are said to be. But, in the culture of literacy, the political sphere was defined precisely by its linguistic status as a sphere of universal access. For it to become specialized and autonomous is tantamount to emptying out the meaning of citizenship and to reducing the exercise of its rights and privileges to an increasingly meaningless formalism, such as a form of voting or poll-taking characteristic of plebiscitary rather than democratic determination of policy.

We seem to have returned to our point of departure: the outgrowth of the specialized languages is already contained *in potentia* in the very project of a culture of literacy; but we must acknowledge that while such a possibility existed from the outset, it was also neutralized with considerable success until quite recently, when the equilibrium seems to have shifted toward the heterogenizing forces. The logic of literacy alone cannot account for this development, which is due rather to what I have been calling market forces.

The impulse toward mass literacy came from the rapid expansion of markets, as we have seen. It was rendered necessary by the fact that the traditional way of acquiring experience for effective praxis in one's society, that is, through long, individual apprenticeship with master practitioners, was too slow and too restricted in scale to permit the growth of the market. Literate culture, based on mediated as opposed to direct experience, represented a gain in efficiency: much more relevant experience, offered in the guise of the knowledge that we call know-how, can be acquired in a much shorter time by much larger numbers of people, so that the learned experience of the master is multiplied. Additionally, just as in industrial production, of which literacy is the enabling cultural condition, so too in the marketplace the culture of literacy fostered greater uniformity and gained further control. Certain masters and their programs could be promoted to the detriment of others. In all such calculations, the market is ruled by the law of efficiency, for it is this law that enables it to maximize profits while holding costs down. Training people through the written word is much more efficient than doing so through personal contact. Once that lesson was absorbed, it was inevitable that we would see further investment in literacy.

I have discussed the development of literacy primarily in reference to training and acquisition of know-how, but of course these activities, as important as they are, represent only a portion of what goes on in the culture of literacy. At least as important in this context are all those transactional and productive activities mediated by the written word: contracts, sales, capital movements, instructions for production, and the like. And it is here that we have had major changes taking place recently. Increasingly we have transactions conducted through the mediation of electronic media: transfers of funds from one account to another over telephone lines, transactions in which, typically, neither the money, the lender, nor the recipient come face to face. Indeed the efficiency of this operation depends in great measure on the elimination of the now needless face-to-face encounter in which language as universal mediator was used. Such indirect and mediated forms of communication are becoming more and more common, and they increasingly involve the use of images rather than language, for images are more efficient in imparting information than language is. For our purposes here, we must note that all these developments entail a diminution in the role played by the type of language that the culture of literacy is built upon: the so-called natural language as universal mediator, the language of presence and fullness of experience.

In addition we need to take into account the fact that the claim to universalism for language has suffered setbacks with the expansion of the market on a global scale, whereas mediated images and electronic messages have overcome local cultural resistances far more effectively. Moreover, since the development of quantum mechanics at least, it has become impossible to assert that language is a universal mediator: it can offer only rather gross and misleading approximations of what physicists know through mathematical formulas. Yet the activities of physicists and the technology built upon their findings show no sign of debilitation as a result of their lessened reliance upon language.

These developments, combined with the impulse toward greater efficiency, make it inevitable that the position occupied by language, or at least by what we have taken language to be in our culture, will change radically in the years to come. Whether these changes will take us beyond the boundaries of modernity is what we must now turn to in our attempt to grasp theoretically the competition between language and images.

II

In his famous essay "Die Zeit des Weltbildes" (The epoch of world-views), Heidegger established that the distinctive feature of modernity is that it operates by means of "images of the world," what we would call "representations" (Heidegger 1972). Foucault, much of whose work could be described as a commentary and a corroboration of Heidegger's theses in this essay, established that these representations, these worldviews, were discursive in nature and moreover that they were discursive constructs, the archeology of which could be undertaken. If a worldview is a discursive construct, then it follows that there are as many worldviews possible as there are discourses. And if we bear in mind that for modernity worldviews and worlds tend to be identical, then there are as many possible worlds as there are discourses. This opens the immense sphere of possibility that held so much interest for Kant, who did not fail to recognize its decisive yet potentially devastating role for modernity: the opening of this sphere of possibility disqualifies all universalizing master narratives and the discursive economy of truth that was associated with them; it inevitably ushers in an era of cultural relativism. Legitimation is no longer universal but must be reconstructed locally and specifically.

There is a further consequence to bear in mind: as the old discursive economy of truth and the ontology upon which it rested stand in ruin, there is also ushered in a new economic formation based on the relation of the subject to language. Fiction and the imaginary, which had an important mediating role between experience and knowledge, find themselves pushed toward a margin from which they can relentlessly haunt this modern subject, further contributing to the unease we call the crisis of legitimacy (see Costa Lima 1984).

In the old economy, legitimation obtained by virtue of the fact that there existed a set of identity equations between Being, the World, and Truth, so that the truth of the world was knowable to being, and practical activity (ethical and political) was properly grounded. These identity equations, which were vouched for by metaphysics, are the first victims of the modern reliance upon discourse, for language is for modernity no longer the locus of such equations but a conventional system of artificial signs given to instrumental use. The predicament of modernity is now joined: the modern subject, living in the epoch of worldviews, constructs his or her cognitive apprehensions of the world by means of language, yet language is no longer thought of as being governed by the

Parmenidean identity of being and saying. The modern subject must thus simultaneously bear in mind that to speak is to submit to the rules of language, to construct, to falsify, to fictionalize, *and*, on the other hand, that to speak is to tell the truth by establishing the referentiality of the world of the worldview. The modern subject bears this in mind in a complex admixture of forgetting and re-membering, so as neither to be a dupe of his or her own con-structions nor to abandon all pretensions to cognition of the world.

This dialectic of forgetting and remembering is articulated quite clearly in Nietzsche's writings on metaphor (Nietzsche 1969a). It will be recalled that for Nietzsche today's truth is but a metaphor whose metaphorical origin has been conveniently forgotten by those who have recourse to it as truth. Nietzsche's formulation has proven puzzling to his commentators over the years, for what is at stake in this characterization of metaphor as origin of truth is a question of decisive importance for modernity: what is the relation of the modern subject to his or her own utterances? What cred-ibility are they to be given? Does the modern subject stand *by* or *under (hypokeimenon)* his or her own utterances? How does the modern subject function as a subject of knowledge and of experi-ence at the same time? How does this subject manage to be his or her own *hypokeimenon* and that which rests upon the *hypokeimenon* at the same time? To put it within the category of consciousness that is the hallmark of modernity, the modern subject must bear in mind simultaneously the fact that to speak is to construct, to falsify, and therefore to lie, and the fact that to speak is to tell the truth by instituting some referent. There is no obvious solution to this problem, which recalls the constraints of G. Bateson's double bind and suggests a schizo-analytic approach, à la G. Deleuze and F. Guattari. In fact, the history of the modern subject shows that this double function of remembering and forgetting is handled in several ways, among which we may distinguish three principal ones, corresponding to three moments within modernity:

1. The first is the moment of disillusion or demystification: the subject suddenly discovers that the truth he or she believed in was a construct, a metaphor, a falsehood. This moment corresponds to Nietzsche's statement that the history of truth is the history of the longest-lasting falsehood. Here Nietzsche shows himself to be the worthy heir of the Enlightenment, denouncing mystification

wherever it may occur and subjecting even the discourse of truth to an analysis of occult interests. This moment is generally taken to be that of a radical nihilism since it leaves the subject unable even to stand by any utterance he or she may make except of the demystifying kind.

2. The second moment is a moment of partial recovery, in which the modern subject acknowledges the fact that he now knows that the statements he utters are not true in the sense of the older economy but that nonetheless they provide a basis for cognition and action. This is the moment of the *als ob*, of the *nonetheless*. This recovery is based on the fact that the modern subject has now gone through the decisive experience of recognizing the central role of language in relation to cognitive processes, and of coming to terms with the fundamentally falsifying nature of language. Such a coming to terms is tantamount to the acceptance of the falseness of language and indeed of its acceptance as the subject's very own truth. Hence, a new alliance between the subject, language, and the world, which can be stated in the form of an apparently paradoxical proposition: "I know that what I am saying is false in an absolute sense, but it is nonetheless true in a punctual sense." This proposition admits of a variety of interpretations, the most famous of which in modernity is that of the pragmatists, who see in it the abandonment of the pretense to any sort of genuine finality and its replacement with a finality more suited to human finitude.

In any case, this proposition enshrines the modern subject as a cleaved subject, operating according to the paradox of knowing how to make oneself *stand by*, in a punctual way, that is, to think as true that which one knows full well not to be true. Modern consciousness is thus necessarily a consciousness of falsehood, but at the same time it does not mourn the passing of Truth, for it has learned to bracket all of its utterances, all of its statements, with a new modalizer: "I believe that. . . ." As Nietzsche indicates, to believe something is "to hold it as true" (*für wahr halten*). Belief, as William James recognized a long time ago, is the means by which the modern subject manages to make himself stand by his utterances.

Must this subject forget that he modalizes what he says with belief in order to state what he says as if he were still speaking the truth? Must his belief be so deep that it need not be invoked except when challenged, and the rest of the time can the subject go around thinking that truth alone flows from his lips? The issue here is that of legitimation within the new paradigm instituted by the recourse to belief, and this issue is one that is brought out as soon as one invokes a Tarskian solution to the paradox of truth and falsehood under the aegis of belief: in the previous economy of the discourse of truth, there operated an identity equation that equated the subject of the utterance, for instance: "Paris is the capital of France," with the subject of the enunciation, for instance "I state that P, where P = Paris is the capital of France." The two subjects were identical. But now, in the new economy of belief, the subject of the utterance is not equated to the subject of the enunciation but subordinated to it: the value of P is determined not in and of itself but in relation to the authority or legitimacy of the "I" of "I state that P." What this means is that the sovereignty and the authority of the subject is at stake in every discursive act, and that it is affirmed in them. Moreover, it means that the process of legitimation by which a proposition is accepted by the community to which it is directed is ultimately nothing less than a *coup de force* effected by a subject who must believe himself or herself to be the legislator, the king, the artist, and/or the spokesperson.

3. The third moment is one in which the modern subject shies away from the violence presupposed by the regime of belief, and sheds belief itself. The abandonment of belief marks the advent of cynicism, and the subject accepts the fact of falsehood and decides to no longer *stand by* the possibility of thinking that a unique view of the world is necessary (see Sloterdijk 1983). At this time, the full possibilization of the possible takes place, and we enter the epoch of the modern imaginary in which arbitrariness reigns and the symbolic (as the instance of the law) is neutralized. What does this entail? Modern consciousness knows itself to be a consciousness of falsehood and accepts this fact; it knows that this means that it cannot generate a narrative capable of totalizing the meaning of existence and of the world. This ultimate step in the demystification (*désenchantement, Entzäuberung*) of the world, accelerated by some historical catastrophes (Auschwitz, Hiroshima, the Gulag, to speak today's shorthand), leads the subject to give up truth (the law) altogether and to accept the advent of the imaginary by instituting *fiction* as the way to constitute subjects and the world.

This new regime of generalized fiction, characteristic of a Nietz-

schean modernity, turns the imaginary into its own law and toler-
ates nothing but the imaginary, which is tantamount to a moralization of the imaginary—something that is very much in evidence in
some strands of poststructuralism. This moralization of the imaginary is actually paradoxical since it affirms simultaneously the
universal and the subjective status of the law insofar as the new
modern subject does not recognize any third instance such as God,
Reason, or History as capable of grounding the law, while making
of the law the act of self-positing (*selbst Setzung*) of the subject in his
or her own name and that of all other subjects (the Categorical
Imperative).

It should be clear then that the advent of the imaginary is not, as
many people tend to think, the sublimated and subliminal locus of
freedom where the subject is able to live in the mode of experimentation by anticipating, and then consuming, itself by flashing all
possibles in front of himself in an endless process of transgression
of the law (as some interpreters of Bataille would have it). The law
itself changes under this regime: it is now determined as a process
of indeterminacy. We have here an antinomy that modernity does
not know how to resolve: how does the modern subject legislate an
interdiction to legislate, or legislate that no one should legislate for
anyone else?

What is the status of such a law, whose kinship with Bateson's
double bind is evident? It is the law that is in force when the subject
assumes the memory of his own earlier forgetfulness, and what
returns in this memory is the knowledge of the plasticity and the
basic lability of the subject facing the real. What such a law accom-
plishes is a cognitive process in which the basic indeterminacy of
the subject is overcome. This process itself takes the legalizing
form of an institution and a constitution of the subject through the
mediation of the linguistic sign. So that what the subject assumes in
this act of recalling to memory of what had been forgotten is, first
of all, the fact that he acknowledges himself as the being of an
institution (in the double sense of being instituted and of belonging
to institutions); but, even more important, the subject acknowledges that language is the institution that is the condition of possibility for all institutions. This is the decisive proposition for
modernity: *language is the originally instituting institution*; it provides
the framework within which the practice of the subject will be that

of a self-positing of the Self in language. From this point of view, the modern subject, whom we saw earlier to be a consciousness of falsehood, becomes now the subject of inscription of Form, that is, the Artist.

This long and yet overly sketchy account of modernity can now be recast in the terms of my earlier distinctions. The Parmenidean doctrine of the sayability of being can be described in terms of an equation in which the three terms *world*, *language*, and *speaking subject* are stable and fixed in relation to each other. The problems have arisen as soon as these terms have become mobile. In point of fact, we can see the various strategies that I have just described as so many attempts to ensure a synchronization between the various velocities involved. We first accepted the mobility of the world and realized that we had to find ways of keeping up with it; we have learned, with great difficulty, to accept our own mobility and lability; but what has proved most difficult to accept is that the very instrument of our relation to the world, that is, language, is itself mobile and travels at its own speed. Some have embraced this notion eagerly so as to make us and the world nothing but forms produced out of the form of language, but this is unwarranted, for none of the three initial terms should be privileged over the others, and least of all language, which even now as we speak is experiencing a shrinking of its role and function, challenged as it is by images. There should be nothing surprising about this: once we have located ourselves in the imaginary, as I have shown that we have, language can withstand only with difficulty the competition of the image, which, after all, is at home in the imaginary.

Let us consider a relatively simple case of modern image: photography. It has been considered a technique of reproduction that makes for an objective apprehension of things and restores them to us such as they are. Where with language we have a discourse *on* the world, with human beings facing the world in order to name it, photography substitutes the simple appearance of things; it is a discourse *of* the world. It differs substantially from painting and other premodern images by virtue of the active negation, the Keatsian Negative Capability, present in the latter. Art does not express things but a human view of them. At the level of what anthropologists call *folk theory*, photography is indeed immediate; it reproduces the objects such as they are, once all issues of angle, composition, and so forth are taken care of. By giving us things the way they are, photography confers upon them an imaginary presence that no mode of representation had achieved until then. Originally, image means imitation: the image that imitates the world remains distinct from the world. We now have images that coincide so much with the given that they abolish themselves as images in order to become the given magically repeated (see the works of Walter Benjamin). In the plastic image of painting, the world was being negated, whereas now we have a world affirmed in itself. Images now allow for the paradox that the world states itself before human language.

The structure of objective images achieved by our technological innovations brings about a new relation: photographs coincide with the world to the point of denying themselves as images, but the world they make present to us is imaginary. Photographs and television are, and are not, the world. They are the world insofar as they become rigorously confused with it (and the Lockean question henceforth becomes: did it happen if television did not report it, did not show it?). But they are not the world since they are but imaginary renderings lacking the concrete hardness of the world that we have in our grasp, the Aristotelian "resistance" that Paul de Man tried to remind us of (de Man 1986). In this, photographs and television confer a new power upon the world insofar as this world, magically present, escapes our grasp since it is imaginary. This is the world as it would be if it could erect itself into a world outside a dialectical relation to us, which is why the Lockean question is appropriate, but also why, in our apocalyptic moments, it is easier for us to imagine the world without us, an end of us that would not be the end of the world—a notion barely conceivable within modernity (this may be one of the reasons why ecologists are ultimately so reassuring: they cling to the old chronology: first the end of the world and then of us).

We are living in the midst of a prelogical affirmation of the world, in the sense that it takes place before the fact of *logos*, and it threatens us with an alienation that modern thinkers could barely conceive. For what happens is that immediate (nonmediated) reality becomes the very expression of the imaginary and substitutes itself for it. The imaginary becomes free of the *logos* since the world speaks itself in its own terms. Such a world is defined without us. It *is* the world without us, a world altogether other, with coordinates that do not come from us, a world in which time is not our time, and where space is but space. To take an example much in favor in time-lapse photography, it is a world in which the germination, growth, and decay of a flower becomes the utterance, outside any reference to an observer, of a sort of truth of the plant realm. A world in which things speak their for-themselves as if it were given to us to apprehend them in their in-themselves, as Hegel would never say. But that is precisely where the illusion resides. We do not really get to the side of things: the beyond that is thus proposed to us remains imaginary, and as such it escapes our grasp (see Proust's meditation on "le mimosa sans moi," where paronomasia reveals the impending senselessness: subtract the letters of "moi" from "mimosa" and you get a far greater problem than the epistemological conundrum of whether a tree falling in the forest makes any noise if there is no one to hear it). This is equally true of representations of the "Other," who inevitably becomes less familiar and more other under such conditions.

What does this mean? We are now inhabited by images that we have not drawn from ourselves, images of external impressions that we do not master and that retain all their agential capability without being mediated by us. These "objective images" give us the world, not a world before language or discourse, for that would still give us hope, but a world that has been subjected to the workings of language and has come out unaffected. We have a withdrawal of meaning. Ideas are leaving the suprasensible forever to go over to the sensible, where they get lost, where they abolish themselves as ideas. Something of this nature is happening to time. The traditional way to think of a decisive action was articulated around the three tenses, past, present, and future, but today we are moving toward a two-tense system: real time and differed, or replay, time. The future has disappeared into the calculations of supercomputers as well as into this strange entity called "real time," which contains both a part of the present and a part of the immediate future, as, for instance, when one sees on a radar screen the approach of a threatening missile in real time. The present mediated by the computer displays on the screen the proximate arrival of the missile at its target. This temporal dissonance was cited as one of the major causes of exhaustion and dysfunction among air-traffic controllers, who are called upon to live part of their lives in this two-tense dimension (see Virilio 1984a).

In the premodern universe, world, subject, and language were stable and fixed, permitting the functioning of well-oiled and reliable identity equations. The modern world saw all these elements put into motion, and we have seen that the solution to the resulting problems lies in the control of velocities, so that effects of stability can be produced and instabilities occur only as a result of willful and controlled action. We have seen further that this controlled environment of celerities was predicated upon the specific powers of acceleration and deceleration of language, which permits such effects as literalism under conditions of perfect synchrony, and figurality under conditions of altered speeds.

The problem is that a dissonance is now manifesting itself: images are scrambling the functioning of language, which must operate out of the imaginary in order to function optimally. Images are parasitical noises upon language at first—and then they supplant it: it must be recalled that the technology of images operates at the speed of light, as does the world. Language could slow down the world, thanks to its tremendous negative capability, but it cannot slow down images, for they operate out of the very imaginary that language would have to be able to organize in the first place. Indeed the question for us is one of dissonance: can language bring the speed of the image under control, that is, turn images into a kind of language (but the failure of the various visual semiotics is not reassuring on this score), or are we to *see* a world, images of this world, and an imaginary all traveling at the speed of light in a universe without *logos*, an alogical universe? Such would seem to be the postmodern predicament.

NIKLAS LUHMANN

How Can the Mind Participate in Communication?

I

Within the communication system we call society, it is conventional to assume that humans can communicate. Even clever analysts have been fooled by this convention. It is relatively easy to see that this statement is false and that it only functions as a convention and only within communication. The convention is necessary because communication necessarily addresses its operations to those who are required to continue communication. Humans cannot communicate; not even their brains can communicate; not even their conscious minds can communicate. Only communication can communicate.

I would like to counter any and all doubts with the following: we have absolutely no idea how to comprehend that conscious minds can bring about communication. Neurophysiological studies, difficult enough in themselves, are not very helpful in terms of the mind. We no longer assume, as did the ancient Indians, that we can alter conditions by concentrating. The more common idea that the mind effects physical behavior or even communication is equally mysterious. The assumption that this occurs is nothing more than an observer's causal attribution. We have to start any clarification with the observer.

Once this is recognized, what follows is the question whether and, if the answer to that is affirmative, how the mind participates in communication. The fact that the mind does participate is undisputed, since communication could not exist without the mind, just as life could not exist without a molecular organization of matter. But what is participation?

Humans are living organisms developed on the basis of living cells. Even cells, as an indispensable foundation of life, are operationally isolated; that is to say, they are "autopoietically" organized (see Maturana 1982b: 138ff, 157ff, 170ff; Varela 1979; Maturana and Varela 1987). The same is true of autopoietic systems of higher orders, that is, of organisms that are capable of exchanging cells in their own autopoiesis. This very isolation can be demonstrated in the brain. The brain can be stimulated by an extremely small amount of external impulses, but only internal changes are available for its own operations, and it cannot initiate any contacts with its environment through nerve impulses, whether as input or output. (There are no nerves in its environment that could take up and transmit such impulses.) Countless independent systems are at work within humans that determine, through their own structures, what operations will be carried out. They are, however, interdependent.

In the same way, what we experience as our own mind operates as an isolated autopoietic system (see Luhmann 1985a). There is no conscious link between one mind and another. There is no operational unity of more than one mind as a system, and whatever appears as a "consensus" is the construct of an observer, that is, his own achievement.* Even contemporaneous alertness or contemporaneous transformation of thoughts into thoughts is only available in the form of an operation internal to the mind and is based on the isolation of the system, an indispensable condition of its possibility, its autonomy, and its structural complexity. The mind cannot consciously communicate. It can imagine that it is communicating, but this remains an imagination of its own system, an internal operation that allows the continuation of its own thought process. This is not communication.

*This is also true when communication communicates, as communication, the observation that consensus is a fact. "Using a metalanguage which is a restriction of his language, L, an observer can say: 'it is a fact that A and B *agree* over T,' and other *observers* may *agree*, in this metalanguage, that 'this *is* a fact.'" This is how Gordon Pask (1981: 1331) formulates the same fact from a somewhat different theoretical basis.

I hope to have made clear that my argument rests on the level of factually actualized operations. The initial (system-transcending) assumption is that *cognition* must be understood as a recursive processing of symbols (however they are materialized) in systems isolated by the conditions of the connectability of their own operations (be they machines, in the sense of artificial intelligence; cells; brains; consciously operating systems; or communication systems).* The question of what an observer observes and with what causal assumptions he calculates effects on causations is a completely different matter. This can only be answered by an investigation of the observer.

Aside from the idiosyncrasies of certain observers and aside from society's determination of who can be made responsible for what, who can demand consideration for his sensitivities, and how turn-taking can be managed, aside from all these special assignations of communication on something that can be dealt with as a "person," independently of an interior organization it is absolutely necessary in a theoretical explanation to distinguish clearly between systems of the mind and communicative (social) systems. We are dealing in both cases with structurally determined systems, that is to say, systems that orient each reproduction of their own operations, whatever the external causes may be, on their own structures. In both cases, we are dealing with systems that create differentiations through the realization of their own operations, create boundaries, accumulate their own history (as an observer can verify), and with all this define their own environment. This does not mean that the mind and communication have nothing in common. It is necessary to formulate more precisely how their relationship is to be understood in light of their irrefutable difference.

II

Once it has come into existence, a system of consciousness can be active even without communication. It experiences this and that within itself, observes something, feels itself thinking (see Pothast 1987), and even talks to itself. Communication, on the other hand,

*The related field of study is now called cognitive science(s). Along with the already cited works of Maturana and Varela, see above all McCulloch 1965 and Foerster 1981. I am only concerned in the text with a small part of this immense field of study of an operative cognitive theory.

can hardly come into being without the participation of the mind. In this sense, the relationship is asymmetrical, however problems of indirect communication, unintentionally one-sided communication, communication with nonlinguistic gestures, and so on, are conceptually assigned. There is no communication without the mind; but: can there be communication without the mind's communicating?

We are faced with the following question: how is communication possible if it has such a fluid, constantly changing foundation? How can communication reproduce itself if it must rely on a multitude of nervously vibrating brains and agitated minds? How can it rely on systems that will only realize their own production through a constant change of conditions, that is, through creating other structures from one moment to the next in order to actualize the next condition?

The initial answer is a postulate: the continuation of communication obviously requires the maintenance of an organization that can get by with this material and continues to do so only so long as this is the case. It might actually be possible to describe everything that is communicated on the level of mental states (as are all life processes on the level of biochemical changes), with one exception: the autopoiesis of the emerging system; that is, with the exception of what alone can describe what communication (or life) is.

As a consequence of this hypothesis, we can transfer H. R. Maturana's concept of the "conservation of adaptation" from biology to sociology (see Maturana 1986a, 1986b). This concept does not contradict the concept of the structurally determined system but is considered complementary to such a system. Only when a system, in its autopoietic reproduction, adapts itself to the field in which it operates can it determine itself through its own structures. And only when it is in contact with its environment through its own structure can it continue its own operations. Reproduction either does or does not take place. Communication either is or is not continued. Whenever it does continue, it remains adapted, no matter how self-dynamically it proceeds. It is not the goal of communication to adapt itself to the respective mind. On the contrary, communication fascinates and occupies the mind whenever and as long as it continues. This is not its purpose, not its meaning, not its function. Only, if it doesn't happen, then it doesn't happen

It is apparently possible to link communication to communication and in so doing to activate the necessary and indispensable states of consciousness, even though the required environment, the systems of consciousness, is made up of highly unstable, self-dynamic, diffuse mental states that (aside from individual consciousness) cannot be hooked up directly to one another. In saying certain things, each communication therefore reduces the possibilities of linkage, but still leaves open, by means of meanings, a wide spectrum of connected communication, including the possibility of negating or reinterpreting the received information or declaring it untrue or unwelcome. The autopoiesis of social systems is nothing more than this constant process of reduction and opening of connective possibilities. It can only be continued if it is already in progress. It can create episodes with a contemplated ending that only serve as a transition to another possibility of communication. Episodes can be determined by purposes (*télē*). Society is purposeless and must be treated in communication as untreatable through communication. It is possible to say: stop! But the end of society can only be brought about by the end of its nonsocial conditions.

Systems of consciousness and systems of communication end when their operations can no longer be continued. Only an observer can talk about a beginning and an end. The observer observes through the use of a distinction. In this case, he distinguishes beginning and nonbeginning, or ending and nonending. A system that observes itself can only proceed in this way. It must make use of a distinction in order to distinguish the end of its distinction. It is only possible to stop in an operative sense. In observation, the end of observation remains a paradox—a reentry of a distinction into itself (see Spencer Brown 1971; Glanville 1984). It is all the more important that, on the basis of its own operations, a system is able to observe when another begins or ends, free of paradox.

The evolution of social communication is only possible in a constantly operative link with states of consciousness. This link was first achieved through language, then more effectively through writing, and finally through printing. Decisive in this process is not the symbolic character so often claimed for these developments, but rather the differentiation of special experiential objects that are either extraordinary or fascinating. They have no similarity to anything else that can be experienced and are constantly in motion or (as in reading) only usable in motion. Language and script fascinate and preoccupy the mind and thereby secure its participation, even though this is in no way required by the internal dynamics of the mind and diversions are always held at the ready. It is possible to describe language and script as symbolic arrangements within this link as long as "symbol" only means that the link of what is separated can be presented within what is separated.*

In other words, language and script, along with all their technical developments, guarantee for the communication system what Maturana calls the conservation of adaptation: the constant accommodation of communication to the mind. They define the free space of autopoiesis within the social communication system. Thus the evolution of societal communication has built up an incredibly complex network of contemporaneous communication processes that is completely nontransparent for every communication that takes place within the system. This is also true for every mind that observes communication, whether it participates in it or not. Developments that make this observation easier, such as the "public opinion" created by the mass media or "markets" created by prizes, do little to affect the basics of this process. They make one thing possible: a more effective recursivity in the observation of the observation of others.

The relationship of the accommodation of communication to the mind and the unavoidable internal dynamics and evolution of society is also evident in the fact that changes in the forms in which language becomes comprehensible to the mind, from simple sounds to pictorial scripts to phonetic scripts and finally to print, mark thresholds of societal evolution that, once crossed, trigger immense impulses of complexity in a very short time. It only took a few centuries for the effects of the alphabet to become apparent (Havelock 1982). The same is true for the introduction of printing in Europe,† and an equally radical change was accomplished with the transmission of printing to other cultures in less than a hundred years (Wood 1985).

In the classical Darwinistic evolutionary scheme, these kinds of radical breaks in continuity are difficult to explain when compared to relatively long periods of only slight structural change. The

---

*As in the case of the *symbolon*, the sign of hospitality, *in the hands of the guest*.
†See Eisenstein 1979; for a rather cursory view, see Ong 1971.

theory of autopoietic systems provides the foundation for new possibilities (see Roth 1982; Maturana 1982b, 1986b). The possibilities for complexity in autopoietic systems are subject to quick and abrupt change when the conditions of their operative and structural linkage with the required environment change; or in our case, when communication's formation of the mind creates new possibilities for itself.

III

The mind thinks what it thinks and nothing else. From the perspective of an observer—either another mind or a communication system that communicates about the observed mind—the mind can be seen as a medium that could accept and transmit a myriad of conditions.* The observer can imagine a mind (doing what it does) as freedom, above all as the freedom to allow itself to be influenced. Or it could imagine possible states that the mind could accept or possible processes that it could complete. As a medium, as a freedom, as a modality, as a conjuncture—whatever label is placed on a mind, it is done so by an observer. In doing so, the observer abstracts the fact, either a little or a lot, that the mind in all its states and in all its operations is determined by its own structures. Instead of certain internal links that change from one minute to the next, the observer assumes a more or less loose linkage. In order to assume this, he himself must operate as an internally dynamic and structurally determined system. And this takes time.

The observer can also be identical to the observed system. Another type of observation, one that presumes non-observation, must be distinguished from states of observation that presume intent for conscious observation, on the one hand, and for communication as an extremely painstaking thematization of the observed object, on the other. Just as visual and auditory perception use light and air precisely because these cannot be seen or heard as media (the

*"Medium" here is used in the sense of Heider 1959 [1926]. One might also think of Plato's well-known wax metaphor in *Theaetetus* 191 C and 194 C–D, although it is still not clear what else the soul might be (that is, what else besides a container) when the wax inside it is like its heart (a play on the words *kaér/kerós*). The better soul in this case consists of the purer wax, which is better suited to take up forms (194E–195).

example is from Heider 1959 [1926]), so communication uses the mind as a medium precisely because communication does not thematize the mind in question. Metaphorically speaking, the mind in question remains invisible to communication. When it becomes visible, it becomes disruptive, just as the strong whoosh and whistle of the air inside a car traveling at high speed disrupt words of communication. The mind functions as a medium when it is assumed that it could take in everything that is said. It is a loosely linked mass of elements with practically no self-determination, a mass that can be impressed with whatever is said or read. In the convergence of loosely and rigidly linked elemental masses the rigid link wins out, just as a foot leaves behind traces in the soft ground. What the mind hears or reads almost necessarily makes an impression at that very moment. Whether it is taken up in memory is another question that presumes a consistency test within the context of a self-determination of the system of the mind and its brain. It is sufficient for the communication process to understand that the mind, virtually helpless, must participate. This leads to the question: how can the mind be a structurally determined system and a medium at the same time? The answer lies in the evolutionary acquisition of language.

In order to work through to this answer, it must be made clear that the concepts of a (loosely linked) medium and a (rigidly linked) form are correlative concepts. This distinction forms the basis for an observation: a medium is a medium only for a form, only seen from a form (Luhmann 1986b). Mind is no more a medium "in itself" than are light and air. It only allows for the evolution of language (whether it already exists or not and in whatever form), just as language is again a medium in which the mind can imprint concrete expressions by putting together words into sentences and eventually producing a corresponding communication in a way that does not use up the medium.

The law of medium and form states that the more rigid form prevails over the softer medium. This would lead, if it were unconditionally true, to the rapid rigidization of material. For the same reason, forms such as language offer an evolutionary advantage, forms that can also serve as media and that can, on the basis of their considerable discipline (specification of sounds that can be expressed as words, grammatical rules, etc.), de-link elements and be freed for an immense variation of possible links, so that other forms (*prágmata*, complexes of ideas, theories, etc.) can impress themselves. This requires a temporalization of the elements. Sentences that are thought and spoken are only parts of a process that disappear at the moment of their generation. They are constitutively unstable. Their accumulation would very quickly lead to uncontrolled complexity, that is, chaos. Just imagine the noise that would result if spoken words did not fade away but remained audible! A counterselection that prevents forgetting and creates the effects of "time binding" (Korzybski 1958) can take place only because elements are temporalized and reduced to events. This is supported by the neurophysiological device of constant consistency proofs. Finally, after the invention of writing, it can be described and honored with terms like *mnemosýnē* and *a-létheia*.

IV

Communication is only possible as an autopoietic system. With the help of language, it reproduces communication from communication while using this structural requisite of its own reproduction to employ the mind as a medium. The mind therefore participates in communication as a structurally determined system and as a medium. This is only possible because the mind and communication, psychic systems and social systems, never fuse or even partially overlap, but are completely separate, self-referentially closed, autopoietic-reproductive systems. As I said: humans can't communicate.

Only with this premise is it possible to determine the specific relevance of the mind for communication in a way that is compatible with other insights of cognitive science. We can then say that the mind has the privileged position of being able to disturb, stimulate, and irritate communication. The mind cannot instruct communication, because communication constructs itself. But the mind is a constant source of impulses for the one or the other turn of the operative process inherent in communication. Only the mind is capable of perception (including the perception of communication). Perceptions remain locked up in the activated mind and cannot be communicated. Reports about perceptions are possible, and, in this way, perceptions can stimulate communication without ever becoming communication, and can suggest the choice of one theme or another. Reports of perception are not perceptions themselves; thus communication operates blindly (the neurophysiology of perception, not to mention the mind, also works constructively and can be stimulated but not instructed by the environment).

Remarkable is the fact that communication can only be stimulated by the mind and not by physical, chemical, biochemical, or neurophysiological operations as such. Radioactivity, smog, or diseases of all sorts may increase or decrease. Such a fact can have no effect on communication if it is not perceived, measured, and made conscious; only then can the fact stimulate the attempt to communicate about it according to the rules of communication. Even in an airplane that is about to crash, it only becomes possible to communicate about the impending crash if it is perceived. The crash itself cannot influence communication; it can only end it.

Systems of the mind and systems of communication exist completely independently of each other. At the same time, however, they form a relationship of structural complementarity. They can only actualize and specify their own structures and thus can only change themselves. They use each other for a reciprocal initiation of these structural changes. Systems of communication can only be stimulated by systems of the mind, and these in turn are extremely attracted to what is conspicuously communicated by language. My argument is as follows: the independence of each closed system is a requirement for structural complementarity, that is, for the reciprocal initiation (but not determination) of the actualized choice of structure.

We see that communication systems exist (for an observer) in a highly complex environment, but this environment, to use the neurophysiological analogy, can effectively stimulate, and thereby influence, only a very small part of its possibilities. Apparently, then, no system could observe its environment (or more generally, develop cognition) if it had to ward off every event in its environment with an internal state. The lack of connectability between operations assumes a distinct limitation of sensibility toward outside events (Roth 1986). It is possible to recognize a double filter, a double structural selectivity of autopoietic systems. Their sensibility is limited to a narrow spectrum of possible stimuli, and it is precisely in this area that their own operations are organized in a manner that is unspecific as to stimuli. Communication operates with an unspecific reference to the participating state of mind; it is especially unspecific as to perception. It cannot copy states of mind, cannot imitate them, cannot represent them. This is the basis for the possibility of communication's building up a complexity of its own and refining itself to such an extreme that it would be highly unlikely to reproduce itself without being adapted to an environment it cannot know.

It is now worth considering to what extent this theory is accurate, a consideration that leads back to an evolutionary-theoretical mode of observation. There certainly exists (at least among beings capable of speech) a communication based on speechless, mutual experience, that is to say, on the basis of a representation understood by all participants. Such communication is experienced in this way; for example, when pedestrians move out of each other's way, and everyone can see that the other sees that the situation requires such a move. Maturana might already call this "language" (1982b: 258ff). There is still a very close bond to the reciprocal-reflexive perception of perceptions. Important evolutionary steps take place from here to oral communication and to writing, to alphabetic scripts, and to printing that differentiate the social communication system more and more regarding the simultaneous processes of the mind's perception and deduction. Communication is made all the more possible if we are not in the position of simultaneously perceiving what others are perceiving, and in this way we are independent of others' perceptions or failures to perceive that we perceive what we perceive. This progress in no way replaces older forms of oral or even speechless communication. Evolution allows for the side-by-side existence of early and late and also allows a refinement and functional specification of older forms of communication. We are certainly more adroit in questions of sexuality than our ancestors were before the invention of language and writing, even though we solve the related coordination problems in a nonwritten way.*

*Even the use of printed letters or copies of printed originals for sending declarations of love are suspect, but only as a result of the invention of printing and only since about the middle of the seventeenth century. A certain irony lies in relying on printed originals in matters of sexuality, for example, in the "erotic supersystem" as described by van der Weck-Erlen 1978 [1907].

V

The interaction between systems of the mind and systems of communication is not realized in the creation of a supersystem that could accomplish operations integrating the conscious and communicative operations according to the structural determinations of both systems.* Instead, systems of the mind are capable of observing communicative systems, and communicative systems are able to observe systems of the mind. In order to be able to say this, we need a concept of observation that is not psychically conceived, that is, exclusively related to systems of the mind.

Observation is introduced here as a theoretical concept of difference. Observation is making a distinction.† An operative foundation, whether of the mind or of communication, is not crucial for this definition, but it does assume that observation can be accomplished as an operation and as such is itself an operation (that is, it can only observe itself with the help of another operation).

Operations of the mind and of communication proceed blindly. They do what they do. They reproduce the system. Meaning only comes into play on the level of observation, with all the provisions demonstrated by logic and hermeneutics: with the ability to negate (as distinguished from the ability to affirm); with the ability for logical modalization, for a simultaneous presentation of other possibilities and, building on this, for modalities such as necessity, impossibility, and contingency; with temporal orientations that can describe, with the help of the distinction between future and past, what happens in the operative present and what differentiates the system from its contemporary environment; and last but not least, with concepts of causality. All this does not exist if an observing system does not give these to itself. Everything that functions as a unity only functions in this way through its observer. Whenever we think or say, "There is 'a' . . ., there is a thing, there is a world," and in so doing mean more than simply, "There is something that is the way it is," an observer is involved, and the next question is not

*This rejects a demanding concept of "spirit," and also rejects what might have been called "intuition" in the Middle Ages.

†The term is used by Spencer Brown 1971 to denote a beginning: "draw a distinction." Spencer Brown is very much aware of the immanent duality of this basic operation and differentiates between distinctions and indications.

"What is there?" but rather "How does an observer construct what he constructs in order to be able to connect further observations?"

The consequences for cognitive theory that can be deduced from this distinction between operations and observations cannot be pursued further here.* Of importance for the analysis of the relationship between the mind and communication is the fact that the separation of these systems apparently assumes a reintegration on the level of observation, whereby observations necessarily remain separate empirical operations that can proceed either consciously or communicatively but are logically powerful enough to be able to reintroduce this distinction in the form of a reentry into their own system (Spencer Brown 1971).

What could be called "meaning," namely, a contemporaneously available excess of references within the operations that force selection, seems to be evaluated from a rudimentary ability to observe (Luhmann 1984: 87ff; 1985a). Meaning pulls a net of possibilities over current operations and allows it to understand itself as a selection of . . ., both for conscious and for communicative operations. Without a meaningful ability to distinguish (something that in every operation includes a concurrent negation of others), the autopoietic systems of the mind and of communication would not have been able to mutually exclude each other, because they would not have been able to distinguish themselves from each other. For this reason, the possibility of self-observation remains a component of the autopoiesis of psychic and social systems that cannot be eliminated. It is carried from thought to thought and from communication to communication and in the process prevents any overlapping of operations and constitutes both systems as closed in themselves.

VI

The more radically the mind is understood as the subject, the more difficult it becomes to understand how another subject, an "alter ego," can be constituted. In itself, so to speak as the center of its

---

*In order to show that things have changed since the advent of classical cognitive theories (including those with a transcendental bent), we now speak of "constructivism," or, with the increased application of artificially supported analyses of empirical conditions, of cognitive sciences.

own thought processes, the mind only finds itself, but no other mind. How then can it arrive at the idea that there are similar phenomena outside itself?

The Kantian solution is based on a *petitio principii.* We recognize the similarity of our own mind to other minds and then proceed from there. This solution has been taken up in "radical constructivism." The recognitive subject constructs an analog to itself with slightly altered structures and perspectives and thereby creates the chance for a double proof of reality from its own and from a foreign perspective (Glasersfeld 1985: 22ff). But how can a mind arrive at such an idea except by perceiving an analog to itself by itself? How can it arrive at the idea that an "interior" exists within the other that is similar to one's own "interior," and that this "interior" is different from other systems? How can a completely different perspective be incorporated into this analogy? Finally, how is it that this has been going on for thousands of years with a stupendous regularity in all "normal" people?

I would like to replace this analogy theory with a construction founded in difference theory. The mind does not arrive at an analogy through another, similar case. It can only take part in communication if it can distinguish between message and information. A message is chosen from various behaviors; information is chosen from various facts; and communication combines both into one event (Luhmann 1984: 191ff). The distinction between message and information is constitutive for all communication (as opposed to simple perception) and is therefore a requirement for participation. For example, it is necessary to address one's own messages to the person sending messages and not to the information. This can certainly be done, and mastery of this distinction can be achieved without knowing any details about the person for whom the message is intended. This distinction becomes important in actual participation in communication. The distinction between persons and things or subjects and objects condenses from this primary distinction. Only with the mastery of this semantic is it possible to arrive at the idea of an analogy between one's own and foreign minds. As long as mastery is not attained (or at least not with today's precision), then the boundaries of the social communication system will be drawn differently than they are today. They might include plants and animals, the deceased, ghosts, and gods and might exclude more distant humans, depending on the extent to which socialization can suggest possibilities of communication to the mind.

There is no doubt that direct perception, including the perception of the perceptions of others, plays a part in this matter. It is impossible, however, to perceive how others perceive; one can only perceive the fact that they do so. We have no access to biochemical or neurophysiological processes or to processes of the minds of others, except in the construction of an observer. A difference between persons and objects must always first be constituted, and for this to occur, participation in communication becomes indispensable.

The detour via communication, the participation in a completely different operating system, and the attractiveness of the constitutive difference of this system are all critical for the constitution of an alter ego. The theory offered here is based on distinctions and not on unity or similarities. This is compatible with the theory of self-referential and closed systems on the level of systems theory and with a constructivist approach on the level of cognitive theory. In social theory, both the primacy of language theory and the concept of intersubjectivity must be abandoned and replaced with the concept of a self-referential and closed system of social communication.

VII

It finally remains to be explained how it is that the social communication system is pervaded by the idea that humans can communicate or even that the individual can communicate with society.

My point of departure is the same: no system can effect its own operations outside its own boundaries. Every expansion of the operative possibilities, every increase in complexity therefore means *eo ipso* the expansion of the system. We can postulate that no system is able to use its own operations to establish contact with its environment. This would require that operations take place at least in part, with one end, so to speak, outside the system. No brain can use nerve impulses to search for other nerve impulses outside the brain. No mind can operatively think outside itself, although it can certainly think of something else within itself. No societal system can communicate with its environment.*

A concept must be found for the classical theme of "individual and society" that does not rely on any internal operations of the system in question, that is, neither on conscious thought nor on communication. I have suggested designating this operative and structural link an interpenetration—not a terribly fortunate terminological choice, and one that still requires some explanation.† "Interpenetration" does not refer to a comprehensive system of coordination or to an operative process of exchange (something that would require being able to talk about inputs and outputs in this sense). "Interpenetration" can only mean: the unity and complexity (as opposed to specific conditions and operations) of the one is given a function within the system of the other. The way in which this occurs can only be demonstrated in the structures and operations of each individual system; it could not occur otherwise. Interpenetration therefore takes a different form in systems of the mind than in systems of communication.

Systems of the mind are socialized by interpenetrations with social systems. This concept requires a fundamental rethinking of the classical sociological theory of socialization, all the way from foreign socialization to self-socialization, but remains to be taken up elsewhere (see Gilgenmann 1986). Communication systems experience interpenetration by considering the personal dynamics of humans in their physical and mental (including the mind) dimensions. I call this (again with reference to Parsons) "inclusion." The terminology and the valid rules of attribution vary with the evolution of each social system. Even simple societies form ideas (with, in some cases, a very restrictive, in other cases, a very broad execution) about people or analogous communication partners (Cazeneuve 1958; Hallowell 1960). Very early on, concepts like that

---

*This is, of course, not true for social systems that differentiate themselves within the society. These systems are able to use their societal constitution to communicate with other social systems (provided they are capable of collective action). For the exceptional theological problems that result from this theory, see Luhmann 1985c.

†See Luhmann 1984: 296ff. Historically, this term comes from the theory of general action systems by Talcott Parsons. He discusses the same problem but in the context of a completely different theoretical architecture. See Luhmann 1978.

of the soul existed to identify people before and after death. Up until the early modern period, personhood remained an attribute mostly for legal relationships (but also relevant for existence as *civis* in a society). As an attribute, it assumes the power to control; that is, it assumes property and freedom. Subjects are spoken of to define the self-referential foundation of the cognitions of the mind by the mind and thus, in a doctrine that rapidly opened to question the marking of the social extraterritoriality of knowledge as distinct from what could for some time still be called *opinio* or common sense.* Only in the eighteenth century was the concept of the individual tailored to persons, a refinement that transformed the concept of person at the same time. These kinds of semantic changes allow us to see a clear reaction to structural changes in society and to a consequence of printing, the new societal relevance of a "reading public." Here we can do no more than point out conceptual prerequisites for an investigation of the structural and societal foundations of changes within the terminology of inclusion.

Everyone knows, of course, that the word "human being" is not a human being. We must also learn that there is nothing in the unity of an object that corresponds to the word. Words such as "human being," "soul," "person," "subject," and "individual" are nothing more than what they effect in communication. They are cognitive operators insofar as they enable the calculation of continued communication. They have limited connectability and therefore have a potential for distinction and definition. The unity that they represent owes its existence to communication. This is not to say, of course, that there is nothing else but communication. However, the cognitive style of what-questions must be changed to that of how-questions. The unity of what is to be asked with a what-question is always a product of the system that asks the question. It is therefore necessary to know first how it is that the question came to be asked. The system, whether a psychic or social one, asks how it asks for what is as it is. But even this statement is naturally nothing more than a communicative maneuver of redirecting communication. I don't know if I mean what I say. And if I knew, I would have to keep it to myself.

*The fusion of these terms is a concern of the eighteenth century. This is especially the case with Buffier 1724.

A Farewell to Interpretation

Desire for Theory

Fifteen or twenty minutes into a talk I recently gave at an American university, I was interrupted by a man in the small audience (apparently a colleague) who showed clear signs of impatience: "Could you please define what you mean by *meta-realities* of communication?" It took us further questions and answers to find out that he was referring to a recurrent nominal phrase in my talk that I had hoped would be understood as *"materialities* of communication." The embarrassment of this incident did not help make me a particularly convincing speaker that afternoon. From a more long-term perspective, however, it sharpened my perception of a sort of "everyday Cartesianism" prevailing in the expectations toward academic lectures that promise (or threaten with) "theory." "Theory," at least in the humanities, seems to bear a connotation of "high abstraction" and is expected to refer to phenomena that one would tend to qualify as "spiritual" rather than "material" (hence, probably, the prefix "meta-" in my listener's disturbing question). I therefore want to emphasize that the intellectual program circumscribed in the title of this volume as "Materialities of Communication" *intends to be theoretical and, nevertheless, to focus on concrete and not always "spiritual" phenomena.* Given the normal use of the word "theory," such a combination could appear to be almost paradoxical. But such an impression might not be too high a price to pay if, on the other hand, the concentration on materialities enables us to take seriously a philosophical warning against the ever increasing degree of abstraction as a powerful and dangerous tendency within the Western intellectual tradition. Coming from sources as different as Horkheimer and Adorno's *Dialectics of Enlightenment* and Georges Bataille's *Les larmes d'Eros*, this warning points to the risk implied in the boundless abstraction of losing contact with the concrete and sensual dimensions of our experience.

Another (normally more aggressive) reaction that theoretical thinking in the humanities frequently encounters is the question of "whether we really need new theories." It is usually based on at least one of two different presuppositions that I want to characterize as the "instrumental" and the "mimetic" misconceptions of theory. Especially popular within literary criticism, the instrumental misconception makes the legitimacy and the value of theories dependent on their capacity to improve the techniques of textual interpretation. From such a perspective, it is often possible to make theories look superfluous by just pointing to the example of highly sophisticated literary critics who never seemed to care about theory (favorite references are the great heroes of New Criticism, together with Leo Spitzer and Erich Auerbach). The mimetic misconception of theory, in turn, claims that a relationship of "adequacy" must exist between abstract theories and concrete extratheoretical realities. Under this premise, theoretical innovations appear justified only if they respond to changes in "the real world."

While both the instrumental and the mimetic misunderstandings set "theory" against "reality" and invariably reduce the first to a purely reactive function in this context, the contributions to our volume, explicitly or implicitly, see theories, above all, as a *part of those institutionalized structures of knowledge that* are *human reality*. Second, they attribute to theory, as a sector within institutionalized knowledge, a function not of just reacting to changes but *of initiating change and of providing models for variation*. It is precisely on behalf of this function that such theories, which appear at first glance as counterintuitive, have a greater chance of making a difference than those that simply satisfy commonsense expectations. On the level of self-observation, theoretical thinking should therefore rather identify, enhance, and foster desire for theory change than impose upon itself the restrictive economies of instrumentality and mimetic correspondence. Even then, however, the question remains open where such desire and such impulses for theory innovation come from. The answer that many of the authors in this book seem to favor (as a presupposition for their more specific arguments) points to theory as the *space where forms of human self-reference can be negotiated.* I use the word "self-reference" here—and not the word "identity"—because "identity" points to a historically and culturally specific configuration of self-reference (perhaps exactly that configuration of self-reference which the contemporary desire for theory seeks to overcome). If social knowledge *is* reality, and if theory is that sector of knowledge which negotiates figures of human self-reference, then we may assume that transformations of reality take place around transformations of human self-reference as a center of productive instability.

While "the humanities" and "les sciences humaines," as collective names for the cluster of academic disciplines to which our discourses belong, seem to confirm this speculation, "*Geistes*wissenschaften," as their German equivalent, reveals the decisive aspect of the model of self-reference that has been dominating Western culture for centuries—and that has now entered into a stage of crisis.[1] For the distinction between the "human" and the "nonhuman," it used to be crucial that the concept of the human excluded (or even actively avoided) any reference to the human body. This explains the strong convergence among otherwise diverging contemporary theory positions toward a reintegration of the body into our models of human self-reference—and it also explains the difficulty (if not the impossibility) of achieving this goal on the basis of conceptual repertoires inherited from the tradition of the humanities.[2] Such a reintegration would bring those phenomena, which are traditionally defined as "nonhuman," closer to new forms of human self-reference, and it might hence be associated with a trend in recent theory outlines of becoming *less anthropocentric* (or more ecological).[3] At the same time—and as a reinforcement of such de-anthropocentrization—we can observe a desire to discuss *functional equivalents between the human mind and the human body on the one side and machines on the other* (from a different perspective, this is a desire for models of human self-reference that have left behind the traditional bias against anything "technical"). Finally, this double problematization of traditional Western humanism might lead to a situation where a single and very abstract ("transcendental") definition of the human will is replaced by *multiple and more concrete models of human self-reference.*

"Materialities of communication" represents the desire for a theory that integrates these three tendencies—toward less anthropocentric (less spiritual), less antitechnological, and less transcendental forms of human self-reference. The fact that we have to refer to each of these changes with a negative formula makes it clear that we still find ourselves in a stage of actively problematizing our heritage of theories rather than of working toward its substitution. And it could well be the case that there is no possibility of a continuous transition or transformation between the self-problematization and the self-substitution of the humanities.[4] If, *today*, we see "theory" as a place where figurations of human self-reference are being negotiated and where transformations of institutionalized knowledge may originate, our desire for theory may lead toward a situation without a form of self-reference that is exclusively "human," without a construction of "time" through which we can follow its transformations as a narrative—and hence toward *a future without theory*. Perhaps the fate of theory is connected to a period of transition within our larger cultural environment; perhaps we find ourselves in a moment of de-temporalization (if "time" is the operating space of the subject); of de-referentialization (if the existence of an outside world as a "world of reference" is dependent on its being opposed to the subject as a coherent figuration); and of de-totalization (if theory's connotation of abstractness is an effect of the subject's transcendental status).[5]

Exteriority

But before theory vanishes, we should enjoy it as a principle of productive instability and as a device capable of generating multiple and impossible questions* rather than as a source of answers. It is up to us to play with theory by formulating such unsolicited questions as a potential for variation in our assumptions about reality—and in our realities themselves.[6] The chronological simultaneity between the "students' revolution" in Europe and North America during the late 1960's and the emergence of the philosophical position we now call "deconstruction" provides the most striking illustration of this principle. The political dreams of those years were based on Marxism as a set of certainties, and their ideological

---

*In his contribution to this volume, Lyotard defines "philosophical questions" as questions without possible answers.

criticism functioned upon substantialistic truth-claims. If there was any question that remained open, it was the question concerning a strategy through which the political order could be changed in a way that corresponded to "truth." To problematize the philosophical traditions that had yielded such truth claims, as Jacques Derrida's did in his first three books,[7] was the least welcome and most unsolicited of all possible positions. Nevertheless, Derrida's questions not only outlived the students' revolution and its theoretical certainties, but have in the meantime begun to unfold so strong an impact on the extra-academic world that they ridicule the early criticism of deconstruction's "unpolitical" character.

Doubtlessly, Derrida's thought was originally motivated by his discontent with a group of assumptions that functioned as a common denominator for structuralism, phenomenology, and Marxism as the then dominant positions on the European intellectual scene, especially in France.[8] Arguing that these assumptions were the result of a continuous privileging of speech over writing as a totalizing model for human communication and interaction within the tradition of Western thought, Derrida presented one side of his own position as the critique of such "logocentrism." He only occasionally offered, as a complementary side in his early work and under the guiding concept of "écriture," speculations about a different kind of thought repressed under logocentrism. Both as an illustration of theory as "unsolicited questioning" and as a possibility of clarifying our concept of "materiality," I want to briefly recall the main elements of deconstruction's antilogocentric side. Derrida argued that only speech provides the impression of a self-presence of thought and meaning (we hear ourselves speaking while we speak) on which any Western philosophy of consciousness is based, whereas the completion of meaning is infinitely deferred by the sequential character of any written or printed text. The aspect of self-presence functions as a precondition for the idea of a subject controlling its own acts and its own speech; in addition, by exempting language from the destabilizing effects of time as deferral (or "différance"), self-presence fosters the illusion that it is possible to attribute stable, self-identical meanings to individual texts and words—an illusion that strengthens the position of the subject, emphasizes its instrumental relationship to language, and confirms, through the idea of language as a mediating instrument, its claim to controlling a "world of objects." Only under the assumption of such meaning identity can we speak of *the* content of individual texts and can structuralism try to analyze content as constituted in binary semantic oppositions. Finally, given the ephemeral status of the sounds that constitute speech, logocentrism tends to neglect the physical side, the *"exteriority" of language*. Although the logocentric exclusion of exteriority is extremely important in understanding the absence of the human body as a topic within the humanities, Derrida pays astonishingly little attention to it[9]—and exteriority almost disappeared as an element of antilogocentrism from subsequent forms of deconstructive practice. It was not until very recently that David Wellbery, in a brilliant article (1992b), systematically elaborated the connection between the exteriority of the signifier and a principle of randomness in language that, by problematizing the subject's "interiority," further contributes to its emasculation. This exteriority, together with the human body (or, more precisely: the human bod*ies*), is a central point of reference for the research program named "materialities of communication."

I disagree, however, with Wellbery's thesis that the concept of "discursive exteriority," to which Michel Foucault gives special emphasis in his famous inaugural lecture on *L'ordre du discours*, is identical to Derrida's notion of exteriority; I don't believe the two are even close.[10] What Foucault wants to underscore is the independence of the discourses from any subjective interiority. Discourses—this is Foucault's central methodological principle— should never be seen as expressions of such interiority. But Foucault does *not* thematize exteriorities in Derrida's sense; indeed their repeated dissolution into the loftiness of discursive structures has recently emerged as one of the rare shortcomings of the innovative practice of history he invented (see Gumbrecht 1992a). Regarding the articles presented in this volume, it is their focus on the concreteness of exteriority/materiality that sets them apart from the intellectual style of New Historicism—even if, in some cases, they share with the New Historicists certain narrative and descriptive techniques.* From such a perspective, one can formulate the following paradox: what made it so easy for New Historicism to

*Among the authors in this volume, at least Martin Stingelin, Bernhard Siegert, Friedrich Kittler, and Wulf Halbach would disagree with my discussion of Foucault. On the other hand, Wlad Godzich remarks that I do not draw a

speak about the body and the economy and the structures of power was its exclusion of the epistemological resistance that these phenomena offer to our concepts. And while it might be a serious point of philosophical discussion whether this exclusion is not ultimately inevitable, it can certainly not be justified by reference to the work of Derrida.

If, then, "materialities of communication" as a field of reflection is much closer, on the map of contemporary epistemology, to deconstruction than to New Historicism, such closeness becomes particularly obvious in relation to Derrida's early books—whereas more recent developments oblige us to mark three perspectives of divergence between "materialities of communication" and contemporary forms of deconstructive practice (without thereby questioning the latter's epistemological legitimacy). Deconstruction has been adopted, especially in many American departments of literature, as a modality of literary interpretation whose only difference in comparison to the New Critical tradition resides in its assumption of a basic heterogeneity characterizing the texts to be interpreted—as opposed to the New Critical premise of harmony.[11] Mainly under the influence of Paul de Man's work—and without contributing to such interpretive domestication—deconstruction has, secondly, developed a strong interest in the analysis of those textual structures and rhetorical forms that generate effects of meaning and illusions of reference. While this position converges with the "materialities" program in its radical skepticism concerning the hermeneutic premise of an "always already given" meaning, it seems to focus on discursive phenomena in Foucault's sense rather than on the level of "exteriority" that I have been trying to emphasize in Derrida's early work. Finally, coping with the impossibility of articulating nonlogocentric forms of thought in logocentric language and under the premise that only literary texts can offer certain nonlogocentric openings (if such can be offered at all), the discourses of deconstruction, especially Derrida's own writing, have become more and more "literary"—to the point where a collapse of the difference between philosophical and literary language has been claimed.[12] The articles presented in this volume, as

---

sufficiently clear line of distinction between New Historicism and "materialities of communication." See Godzich 1992: xv.

stylistically ambitious as some of them might appear, do not participate in this "literary turn." It seems to be their—perhaps problematic—claim that at least some concerns of the antilogocentrism inaugurated by Derrida can be maintained and actively pursued in a discourse that is still logocentric.

Macro-mapping: The Nonhermeneutic

Our effort to circumscribe "materialities of communication" as a field of research and reflection neither necessarily questions the epistemological legitimacy of other contemporary theory-positions nor implies any claim of covering the totality of the space that the humanities has traditionally occupied. But how do "materialities of communication" refer to concurrent positions on the epistemological map? And what basic changes is this map undergoing at present? As an answer to such questions, it is my main hypothesis that a convergence—or at least a contiguity—of some recently emerging theory-positions can be seen in their common problematizing of that concept in which the humanities appear as hermeneutics, that is, as a group of disciplines grounded on the act of interpretation as their core exercise. The institutionally most influential description of "interpretation" as a practice and its implications goes back to Wilhelm Dilthey. I quote the very passage that makes the tension between "hermeneutics" and "materialities of communication" most obvious:

However, there is a certain, increasingly strong tendency inherent to the group of academic disciplines with which we are dealing to see the physical side of what is going on as a mere condition, as mere instruments of understanding. This is caused by the emphasis of these disciplines on self-reflection, on the directness of understanding—which goes from an outside to an inside. It is a tendency that uses every exteriorization of life for the comprehension of the very interiority out of which it emerges. (Dilthey 1983 [1910]: 251)

These sentences presuppose that "meanings" are always given—in the interiority of the subject's psyche. The articulation/expression of such meanings, however, on the material surface of a spoken or a written text is expected to remain necessarily incomplete and fragmentary. Within the basic hermeneutic topology, it is precisely this insufficiency that accounts for the need of interpretation and for the devaluation of any material surface as secondary in relation to subjective interiority. The hermeneutic paradigm is echoed by the most notorious concept of the linguistic sign—traditionally related to the name of Ferdinand de Saussure—in which the (material) signifier and the (spiritual) signified are inseparably related, although the function of the signifier lies exclusively in its offering access to the signified.

Among a multiplicity of contemporary departures from a concept of the humanities as hermeneutics (i.e., as based on the reciprocity of expression and interpretation), the project "materialities of interpretation" marks but one individual impulse. What these different departures from hermeneutics share and how they relate to each other can be shown by using the four notions with which Leo Hjelmslev complexified Saussure's sign concept.[13] Hjelmslev not only distinguished between "content" (the signified) and "expression" (the signifier), but also projected a second distinction—between "substance" and "form"—onto this binarism. The four concepts and the four fields of linguistic phenomena that he thus established—substance of content and form of content, substance of expression and form of expression—can be related to the main concerns of contemporary theory-positions. "Substance of content" is a level of communication where impressions, thoughts, memories, and associations are not yet structured; it seems to come close to Derrida's concept of "écriture" (and it would certainly include the sphere of the imaginary that has recently received renewed theoretical attention). "Form of content" refers to those structures that give shape to the substance of content and that are therefore a necessary precondition for any articulation of meaning; this is the place for the rhetorical forms analyzed in Paul de Man's work and for Foucault's notion of discourse. "Substance of expression" points to the physical dimensions out of which signifiers emerge, whereas the notion "form of expression" covers any set of structured and—by virtue of their structure—identifiable signifiers.

It is almost trivial to mention that the most obvious phenomena of reference for "materialities of communication" belong to the two fields of "expression."* The more important insight, how-

*Although not without exception. Recent theories (and empirical investigations) on imagination as a human faculty argue for a specifically close link between imagination and bodily functions. See Bahr 1988.

ever, that our use of Hjelmslev's concepts provides, is that the mutual isolation in the four above-mentioned fields causes a shift in our main perspective of investigation. Since none of them can independently refer to articulated meaning, although each of them includes necessary preconditions for the existence of articulated meaning, this shift goes *from interpretation as identification of given meaning-structures to the reconstruction of those processes through which structures of articulated meaning can at all emerge.*[14] An initial, schematic distinction between three stages of such constitution of meaning becomes immediately evident: substance of content has to adopt a form to become a potential content/signified; substance of expression has to adopt a form to become a potential expression/ signifier; and both sides have to be coupled in order to become articulated meaning. Under the premise that none of the four fields in question can independently constitute meaning, they would *all* satisfy a definition that describes "materialities of communication" as the totality of phenomena contributing to the constitution of meaning without being meaning themselves.[15] Thus it becomes evident that what "materialities of communication" ultimately point to is not only the thematization of a hitherto nonthematized phenomena but also—and above all—a change in the perspective with which we observe communication.

The identification of this new perspective helps to explain why, at least in the German context, the work of the sociologist Niklas Luhmann has had a particularly strong impact on the departure from hermeneutics. A decisive move in the architecture of Luhmann's theory lies in his setting apart of social systems and psychic systems (whose definition corresponds roughly to the classical philosophical notion of "consciousness") as meaning-producing systems* from any other types of systems (e.g., machines, organisms). Only in meaning-producing systems do those operations that are the systems' basic elements ("thought" in psychic systems and "communication" in social systems) have the status of observa-

*For reasons of terminological economy within the architecture of his theory, Luhmann uses the word "Sinn" (and not "Bedeutung," which is closer to, although not synonymous with, the English "meaning"). In the context of this article, however, I think that it is legitimate to make a connection between Luhmann's concept of "Sinn" and what I have been referring to as "meaning." I mainly refer to chaps. 2, 4, and 6 in Luhmann 1984.

tions. Observations are operations that imply an "awareness" of other operations that *might* have taken place instead of those that actually occur—and it is this awareness of a selectivity that Luhmann calls "meaning." Therefore, the by-now-familiar question of *how it is possible at all that psychic systems and social systems constitute meaning* is also a crucial question for Luhmann's sociology. His contribution to this volume contains perhaps the most complex and certainly the most boldly counterintuitive answer he has offered so far.

Micro-mapping: Materialities of Communication

In the previous section, we have seen that there are two different points of convergence for the essays presented in this volume. First, they are a symptom for and a part of a reorientation in the humanities that replaces, as their central concern, "interpretation" with "meaning constitution." Second, they pay more attention to phenomena like the human body or the physical qualities of signifiers than has previously been the case in the history of our academic disciplines. Ultimately these two concerns are not unrelated. Different from interpretation as meaning identification, the project of analyzing the processes of meaning constitution literally obliges us to take into account those "nonspiritual" phenomena that used to be excluded from the thematic field of the humanities. On the following, final pages I will try to chart some of the more concrete and specific problems that result from their recent inclusion.

It seems to be a recurrent strategic device in the contemporary theory-scene "to start with a difference" (see Luhmann 1988). Instead of taking for granted the degrees of complexity under which certain systems present themselves to our everyday observations, theory can analytically separate their constitutive elements, underscore the initial improbability of the interplay between them, and thus start with the question of the specific conditions under which such an interplay—and the systems' complexity as their result—becomes at all possible. This very perspective explains the interest that systems theory has taken, during the past decade, in the systems' *autopoiesis* (their self-constitution and their independent functioning), and in the *coupling* between autopoietic systems.[16] Whatever appears as a condition facilitating such system couplings can be described and further analyzed as their potential of *resonance*.[17] The articles that we present in the section "Sounds, Colors, and Their Nonsemantic Functions" focus on the ways in which physical properties of signifiers make resonance and coupling possible, and on the emergence of meaning out of primary coupling-structures that do not yet include levels of meaning and observation. The concept of "coupling," therefore, marks an epistemological area where a number of hitherto underthematized "hardware" dimensions of communication become relevant. This *could* also be the case for aspects of sex and of gender (although they are not really addressed in this volume—perhaps because of the situation of gender studies in Germany). Another aspect of coupling and resonance is *speed*. The relationship between the levels of speed that certain operations adopt in different systems can turn out to be either an enhancement of or an obstacle to their integration. Whatever we call a "rhythm" is a level of speed that facilitates coupling.

Perhaps astonishingly, such reflections about coupling and its conditions allow us to rephrase the tendency in contemporary Western philosophy to *problematize concepts such as "agency" and "subjecthood"* as yet another outcome of the principle of "starting with a difference." They made the subject emerge out of specific couplings between psychic systems and social systems—and such emergence is always contingent upon specific frame-conditions under which the couplings are taking place.[18] Luhmann has gone so far to present a political—or perhaps rather, ethical—argument in favor of theories that purposefully avoid a transcendental status for the subject category. According to him, as long as theories are not based on a "transcendental subject," they are incapable of formulating those universal claims or obligations that have been frequently presented in its name—and that have often turned into legitimations of totalitarianism.[19] What the essays presented in our volume under the heading "Media of Communication and Historical Thresholds," then, bring into view are situations where couplings between human bodies, psychic systems, and new communications technologies (especially the printing press) produce specific subject-effects. With this perspective, they diverge from a historiographical tradition that describes technical innovations as motivated by collective needs and as "invented" by subjective genius.

Instead of confirming the deeply rooted belief in an instrumental relation between the subject and different technologies,* they encourage us to experiment with the inversion of this narrative pattern.

Seeing the subject from a perspective of contingency further enables us to discover—and to question—a relationship between the *three-dimensional concept of time* institutionalized in Western culture and the concept of agency. As long as we imagine time as a sequence of moments that link the past with the present, we presuppose that the observations, actions, and events attributed to subsequent moments on this continuum are connected by a principle of (however "soft") causality (see Luhmann 1990a). Understanding the "laws" of such causality appears, then, as a precondition for the subject's possibility of exerting control over the systems in its own environment. This, however, is precisely the central hope—or the central illusion—articulated in the concept of "agency." It is one of the more remarkable points of convergence between deconstruction and systems theory that both of them challenge such a construction of time, together with the concepts "subject" and "agency." Instead of being thematized as centers of agency, autopoietic systems are seen as maintaining their self-reproduction and a relationship of homeostasis with their environment—against "perturbations" originating in their environment. Time, then, is no longer perceived as the continuity of a transformation or of a development, but exclusively as breakdowns in self-reproduction and homeostasis. The contributions to this book collected in the section "Communication Systems and Their Discontents" discuss such a concept of time, and they seem to suggest further that moments of breakdown provide a specific opportunity for the observation and the analysis of those couplings that they discontinue.

The most flagrant shortcoming of the debates and experiments to which we refer by the title "Materialities of Communication" lies, so far, in their incapacity to overcome the conceptual dualism

---

*Walter Benjamin's famous article "Das Kunstwerk im Zeitalter seiner technischen Reproduzierbarkeit" fully—and very optimistically—relies on the possibility of such a relationship of instrumentality between subject and technology. This might be one of the reasons why most of its prophecies have been proved wrong—and why it enjoys such unbroken popularity in the humanities.

between spirit and matter, mind and body, materiality and meaning. Rethematizing a wide horizon of phenomena under the notions "matter," "body," and "exteriority/materiality of the signifier" is but a first step in overcoming this situation; and speaking about couplings that connect "materialities" to phenomena that we refer to as "spirit," "mind," and "meaning" not only does not guarantee that we can retrace, in each case, the specific operations of their interactions, but might even contribute to an ultimate preservation of the Cartesian dualism. The notion of "embodiment" in one of our volume's section titles points to a number of essays that outline different theory and discourse strategies in overcoming this heritage. Despite their efforts to develop and to expand phenomenological, Freudian, and Marxist theories for this purpose, it seems unlikely that any decisive progress can be made without an opening toward the state of the art in contemporary science.

But, as I briefly mentioned in my introductory remarks, we may fall prey to an illusion if we imagine the substitution of the conceptual repertoires and questions that have come upon us as "theory" without, at the same time, imagining the end of "theory" altogether. Perhaps we even jeopardize the most important option offered by the materialities approach if we dream of a new stability for renewed concepts in a future age of theory. This most important option might well be the possibility of seeing the world under a *radical perspective of contingency*—as a sphere of extremely short-lived phenomena and without any stable or general concepts for their description. Rather than overcoming the resistance that "materialities of communication" offer to our contemporary concepts and theories, we might profit from this resistance. It could help us to overcome the temptation to fall back into theories and discourses that are inhabited by such totalitarian specters as causality, philosophy of history, and the transcendental subject.[20]

REFERENCE MATTER

Notes

For complete author names, titles, and publication data for the works cited here in short form, see the Works Cited, pp. 413–39.

Assmann, Ancient Egypt

1. For the origin and early history of hieroglyphic writing, see especially Sethe 1939; Schott 1950; Kaplony 1966; Westendorf 1969; Helck 1985; and Schlott 1989: 95–118.

2. Compare an Egyptian tomb inscription of the later period that promises the visitors of the tomb certain blessings:

> When you meditate on this stela,
> enter into the inscriptions contained thereon,
> when you view the transfigurations of the ancestors in their
> place in unequaled abundance,
> when you hear those who quarrel, exchanging loud words with
> their companions,
> when you hear the singing of the musicians
> and the lamentations of those who mourn,
> when you find the name of every man above him in his offices
> given by name,
> the herds of cattle, the tree, and the herbs
> with their names above them . . .
> (Kuhlmann and Schenkel 1983, p. 72)

3. For a general overview of the complementary nature of image and writing, see (in addition to the previously cited works of Fischer 1977a and 1986, and Vernus 1985) Brunner 1979, Tefnin 1984, and J. Assmann 1987.

4. Compare A. Assmann 1980, 62: "The physically comprehensible manifestation gains a completely different meaning within the system of direct signification. The physical impulse, fixed as hieroglyph or emblem, represents a model of understanding to which a contemplative view as a determining orientation remains indebted. The hidden intellectual meaning must be uncovered in the physical manifestation. The principle of indirect signification uses the impulse of the senses merely as a kind of initial spark that stimulates and initiates the process of understanding. The paths of the intellect must diverge as far as possible from this initial point if the mind is to advance into the area of generality and universality. Not deciphering and interpretation but rather the abstraction of the manifest world leads to understanding. The real responsibility lies with the active, productive human intellect that is independent of the dictates of the senses and the impressions of the objective world."

5. Cf. the remarks of F. Junge concerning the late Egyptian "philosophy of writing" (Junge 1984: 270–72). For the transition from oral writing to sense writing, see Daumas 1978.

6. For Horapollon's original text, see Sbordone 1940; for a translation into English, see Boas 1950.

Pfeiffer, Dimensions of Literature

1. See Varagnac et al. 1959: 208; and Certeau 1975: 84–85, 103, 216–26, on the cultures of Mesopotamia, the Italian Renaissance, and the south of France from 1450. For ideal biographies, dialogues, instructions, etc., of the culture of ancient Egypt, see J. Assmann 1983: 71–86.

2. Cf. Weber 1963: 412, 559–60. See Needham 1977: 114–15, for the different cultural ramifications of printing; see Schluchter 1979: 202–3, 227–28, on the dualistic semantics of a political, economic, and religious nature in Europe.

3. Rösler 1983: 117–18; cf. generally Rösler 1980a; on Greek lyric between "symposion" and "reading," see 1980b: 40–41, 47–49, 54–55, 61, 91.

4. For modern analogies in the academic field, see Dreitzel 1972: 175–87, 215.

5. Cf. the term *poésie formelle* from R. Guiette; see also Friedrich 1964: 50–51; Warning 1982: 179–80.

Stingelin, Comments on a Ball

1. The 34 poems in "Joke, Cunning, and Revenge" for which typewritten draft versions are contained in folio Mp XVIII 3 are these: 3. "Un-

daunted"; 7. "Vademecum—Vadetecum"; 10. "Scorn"; 11. "The Proverb Speaks"; 12. "To a Light-Lover"; 13. "For Dancers"; 14. "The Good Man"; 15. "Rust"; 16. "Up"; 17. "The Maxim of the Brute"; 18. "Narrow Souls"; 19. "The Involuntary Seducer"; 20. "For Your Consideration"; 21. "Against Airs"; 22. "Man and Woman"; 23. "Interpretation"; 31. "The Disguised Saint"; 34. "Seneca et hoc genus omne"; 35. "Ice"; 36. "Juvenilia" (cf. *KGB* II. 5, 440); 38. "The Pious Retort"; 39. "In the Summer"; 42. "Principle of the Overly Refined"; 46. "Judgments of the Weary"; 48. "Against the Laws"; 49. "The Sage Speaks"; 50. "Lost His Head"; 51. "Pious Wishes"; 52. "Writing with One's Feet"; 53. "Human, All Too Human: *A Book*" (cf. *KGB* II. 5, 441); 54. "To My Reader"; 57. "Choosy Taste"; 58. "A Crooked Nose"; and 62. "Ecce homo." The 27 aphorisms in the second and third books of *The Gay Science* for which typewritten draft versions are contained in folio Mp XVIII 3 are these: 62. "Love"; 157. "Mentiri"; 159. "Every Virtue Has Its Age"; 185. "Poor"; 189. "The Thinker"; 190. "Against Those Who Praise"; 194. "The 'Openhearted' "; 195. "Laughable"; 196. "Limits of Our Hearing"; 197. "So Take Care!"; 198. "Chagrin of the Proud"; 199. "Liberality"; 200. "Laughter"; 205. "Need"; 216. "Danger in the Voice"; 217. "Cause and Effect"; 231. "The 'Thorough' "; 232. "Dreams"; 233. "Most Dangerous Point of View"; 243. "Origin of 'Good' and 'Bad' "; 247. "Habit"; 249. "The Sigh of the Search for Knowledge"; 252. "Better a Debtor"; 253. "Always at Home"; 258. "The Denial of Chance"; 259. "From Paradise"; and 264. "What We Do." Photographs of folio Mp XVIII 3 were kindly provided to me by Wolfram Groddeck, Basel. My thanks go as well to Hansmartin Siegrist, Basel, for his support, and to the Dubrovnik Discussion Group.

2. I was able to verify this for both typescript letters to Franz Overbeck that are now in the manuscript division of the Universitätsbibliothek in Basel: *KGB* III. 1, 174 (letter sent from Genoa, beginning of Mar. 1882), and *KGB* III. 1, 180 (letter sent from Genoa, Mar. 17, 1882). Both letters end thus: "I am always / yours and yours truly F.N."

3. "What happens when a proper name is written in quotes?" (Derrida 1984: 64). See Gumbrecht 1986b on the confrontation between Jacques Derrida and Hans-Georg Gadamer.

4. The most frequent mistakes in letter groups caused by the defect in the Malling Hansen are to be seen in Mp XVIII 3, 39.

5. The "original version" in Gerber is in italics: "*All words are sound pictures and are in reference to their meaning tropes in themselves and from the beginning*" (Gerber 1871: 333). My article "Nietzsche's Wordplay as a Reflection on Poet(olog)ical Procedure" (Stingelin 1988) contains a concordance put together with Anthonie Meijers, Utrecht, for the word-for-word appropriations and borrowings from Gustav Gerber's *Language as*

Art in Nietzsche's Rhetoric Lectures and in *Concerning Truth and Lying in the Extra-moral Sense.* The concordance is followed by a historical investigation by Meijers.

Elsner et al., Early German Television

1. *Der Telefunkensprecher,* no. 4 (May/June 1935): 96, cited in Reiss 1979: 35–36. Compare the different announcements of mass production by the Loewe AG company in *Funk,* Aug. 29, 1934, pp. 607–8.

2. On John Logie Baird, see Briggs 1985: 533, and Shiers 1975.

3. Max Dieckmann's patent DRP no. 420 567, from Jan. 28, 1931, cited in Goebel 1953, esp. pp. 279, 387.

4. See the "Extrablatt" in *Berliner Zeitung am Mittag,* Mar. 9, 1929.

5. See the speech given by Reichssendeleiter (Reich Program Director) Eugen Hadamovsky on Mar. 22, 1935, reprinted in *Mitteilungen der Reichs-Rundfunk-Gesellschaft,* no. 459 (Mar. 23, 1935): 1–3.

6. Reichssendeleiter Carl-Heinz Boese, *Funk: Die Zeitschrift des Funkwesens,* Apr. 15, 1935, p. 246.

7. Eugen Hadamovsky, "Der erste Fernsehprogrammbetrieb der Welt," *Mitteilungen der Reichs-Rundfunk-Gesellschaft,* no. 459 (Mar. 23, 1935): 4–5.

8. See the film *Das Auge der Welt* (1935), Bundesarchiv Koblenz, mag. no. 1111.

9. See, e.g., the cover of *Deutsche Allgemeine Zeitung,* Aug. 6, 1936.

10. See the description by the American author Thomas Wolfe of the atmosphere in Berlin during the Olympic Games, of the perfect organization, and of the National Socialist "art" of directing the masses, in *You Can't Go Home Again* (1940). National Socialist television was supposed to achieve the goal "of extending the circle of participants at important events" (Dr. Hoffmann, "Die fernsehtechnischen Aufgaben der Reichs-Rundfunk-Gesellschaft," *Mitteilungen der Reichs-Rundfunk-Gesellschaft,* no. 459 (Mar. 23, 1935): 3–4 (quotation on p. 4).

11. "Etappen des Fernsehens," *Die Sendung* 14, no. 20 (1937): 469.

12. Hadamovsky, speech of Mar. 22, 1935, in *Mitteilungen der Reichs-Rundfunk-Gesellschaft,* no. 459 (Mar. 23, 1935): 4–5.

13. See, e.g., Sheldon and Grisewood 1929: "Television cannot win its way foot by foot; it must come as a more or less finished product" (p. 189).

14. See Barnouw 1968, 2: 127–29, and Campbell 1976: 50–57.

15. Hadamovsky, speech of Mar. 22, 1935, in *Mitteilungen der Reichs-Rundfunk-Gesellschaft,* no. 459 (Mar. 23, 1935): 5.

16. This fascination marks one side of the "dichotomy of mind and body." See Gumbrecht 1986a: 36–37.

17. "Film und Fernsehen," *Der deutsche Film*, no. 5 (1936), cited in *Fernseh-Informationen*, no. 19 (1986): 587.

18. "Fernsehen vom Reichsparteitag," *Die Sendung* 13, no. 38 (1936): 1133.

19. Ludwig Kapeller, "Nürnberg ferngesehen," *Hier Berlin!* (1937), cited in *Fernseh-Informationen*, no. 18 (1987): 497.

20. See "Berlin sah und hörte Nürnberg!," *Berliner Tageblatt*, Sept. 8, 1937: "We heard and saw what happened in Nuremberg—we saw and heard it at the same moment that those things took place in Nuremberg. Not one minute, not one second, yes not even the thousandth part of a second was lost."

21. See the section on the medium of cinema, "The Immediacy Is an Illusion," in Virilio 1984b.

H. Pfeiffer, Girolamo Cardano

1. See Erasmus 1971: "If there is something characteristic for this genre, then I can, I think, define it no more concisely than by saying that the style of a letter should be similar to a conversation between friends" (p. 225).

2. H. Friedrich (1949: 451) describes the same phenomenon when he notes that Montaigne wanted "above all to be heard." R. W. Emerson (1850: 167) formulated the same thing even more plastically over 100 years earlier: "I know of no other book that appears to be less written. It is the language of conversation set into a book. Cut the words and they would bleed; they are as alive as the blood vessels of the body."

3. On the allied poetics of *vive représentation*, whose goal it was to conjure away the artifactual nature of art in light of the natural and alive, see Dubois 1984.

4. G. Defaux (1985: 47–48) recently formulated the semantic latitude of writing in Montaigne: "Instrument of philosophical examination, means of self-realization and self-control, portrait, mirror, body, friend, child—writing is the other and the whole for Montaigne." Friedrich 1949: 403, was more careful: "His grounding of writing makes up an indispensable part of the whole reflection of himself, because writing is itself an aid to this reflection. . . . As never before, the consciousness of being a writer is an essential part in the perception and self-awareness of individuality." Stierle 1984: 315, following Friedrich, formulates this succinctly: "Writing is not just a means for Montaigne's conversation with himself, it is a substantial element."

5. See the translator's introduction in Cardano 1914: xxxii; Buck 1956. On the historical context see Mandrou 1973, esp. pp. 116–17 (on Cardano).

6. Cardano 1914: 27–28. On the motif of fame in Cardano, see Buck 1956: 50. On the category of "modern fame" and its meaning for the Renaissance, the comments in Burckhardt 1966 are still helpful.

7. On the relationship between book printing and the order of knowledge, see (among others) Eisenstein 1979; Graff 1987; and Ong 1982.

8. The meaning of these systems for the Renaissance's organization of knowledge is comprehensively presented by Yates 1966.

9. See Wittkower 1965; and above all Klibansky, Panofsky, and Saxl 1964.

Gumbrecht, A Farewell to Interpretation

1. The famous final paragraph of Michel Foucault's *Les mots et les choses* (1966: 398) anticipated this crisis as a possibility: "On peut parier que l'homme s'effacerait, comme à la limite de la mer un visage de sable." Twenty-five years later, its multiple aspects motivated Jean-François Lyotard's book *The Inhuman: Reflections on Time* (1991, see esp. its introduction, "About the Human").

2. See David Wellbery's introduction to Kittler 1990: xiv, where a reference to the body as a central focus of concern is mentioned as a central premise of "post-hermeneutic criticism." The shocking thought, however, that European culture and philosophy might have lost touch with the human body as a dimension of experience goes back further in history. See Gumbrecht 1992.

3. Some of the problems that arise in addressing ecological concerns in institutionalized frameworks of discussion are analyzed in Luhmann 1989, esp. p. 115.

4. Toward the end of the first chapter in his *Of Grammatology* ("The End of the Book and the Beginning of Writing"), Derrida describes, in a similar way, the end of logocentrism and metaphysics as an end that may never come to an end. I have discussed the problem of such theory transitions with more detail in two articles: Gumbrecht 1993b and 1993c.

5. Under these three negative concepts, I have tried to describe the impact of the postmodern cultural situation on the humanities in Gumbrecht 1988b.

6. My discussion of the concept "theory" and of the social functions of theoretical practice tries to follow Luhmann 1990b.

7. They all appeared in 1967: *De la grammatologie, La voix et le phénomene, L'écriture et la différence*.

8. This thesis goes back to a Stanford seminar titled "Deconstruction

Contextualized" (fall 1991/92). For the larger intellectual context of the 1960's in France, see Descombes 1979.

9. See the very short remarks in Derrida 1973: 82, 87, 115.

10. See Wellbery's introduction to Kittler 1990: xii n. 2. My own distinction between Derrida's and Foucault's concepts of "exteriority" goes back to a seminar with Tim Lenoir titled "Technologies and Practices of Recording, 1830–1940" (Stanford, winter 1991/92).

11. See Hillis-Miller 1979: "The ultimate justification for this mode of criticism, as of any conceivable mode, is that it works. It reveals hitherto unidentified meanings and ways of having meaning in major texts. The hypothesis of possible heterogeneity in literary texts is more flexible, more open to a given work, than the assumption that a good work of literature is necessarily going to be 'organized' " (p. 252).

12. Derrida, Carte postale, and Bloom et al., Deconstruction & Criticism, can be important marks of transition, in this context. The most frequently quoted negative reaction to this "collapse" came from Habermas 1985: 219–47.

13. I follow the Hjelmslev interpretation (and its application to the contemporary theory scene) proposed by Frederik Stjernfelt (1992).

14. See, for a further point of convergence, Wellbery's introduction to Kittler 1990: ix.

15. See the programmatic formula on the cover of Gumbrecht and Pfeiffer 1988: "To thematize 'materialities of communication' means to ask for the non-meaning of constituted presuppositions, the place, the carriers, and the modalities of the emergence of meaning."

16. For the most accessible definition of these (and other) biological concepts that have become important for systems theory, see Maturana and Varela 1987.

17. See the definition in Luhmann 1989: "Resonance signifies that systems can react to environmental events only in accordance with their own structure" (p. 145).

18. The phrase "contingent upon" in this context refers to phenomena whose existence is not guaranteed by their sheer possibility. See the entry "Kontingenz" in Ritter and Gründer 1976, vol. 6. Also see Wellbery 1992a, who ends with the equally strong and interesting statement that the "realm of contingency is the space of our modernity."

19. See the interview with Franco Volpi in Luhmann 1987: 156–66, and Luhmann's preface to the forthcoming English translation of Luhmann 1984.

20. Godzich 1992: xv, speaks of "microphysics of history" as "revealing the folded-in dimensions of contingency, which include[d] those of

experience and of its description, very much in the noncausal and non-linear way in which the autopoiesis of systems takes place in the descriptions currently given of them."

I want to thank Helen Tartar, of Stanford University Press, for her intellectually invaluable—and constantly stimulating—help in conceiving this essay.

Works Cited

Adorno, T. W. 1970. *Ästhetische Theorie.* Frankfurt a.M. English translation, 1984. *Aesthetic Theory,* trans. C. Lenhardt. London.

Alonso, D. 1983 [1944]. *Hijos de la ira.* Ed. M. J. Flys. Madrid.

Alpers, S. 1983. *The Art of Describing.* London.

Ammianus Marcellinus. 1968. *Res gestae: Römische Geschichte.* Trans. W. Seyfarth. 3 parts. Darmstadt.

Anonymous. 1911a. "Schreibmaschine und Augenhygiene." *Schreibmaschinen-Zeitung* 157: 217.

———. 1911b. "Der tote Brief." *Schreibmaschinen-Zeitung* 157: 219.

———. 1935. "Das erste Fernsehsendespiel." *Fernseh-Informationen* 36, no. 10 (May): 298.

Aristides Quintilianus. 1963. *De musica.* Ed. R. P. Winnington-Ingram. Leipzig.

Aristotle. 1936. *De caelo.* Ed. D. J. Allan. Oxford.

———. 1956. *De anima.* Ed. W. D. Ross. Oxford.

Aristoxenus. 1955. *Elementa harmonica.* Ed. R. da Rios. Rome.

Assmann, A. 1980. *Die Legitimität der Fiktion: Ein Beitrag zur Geschichte der literarischen Kommunikation.* Theorie und Geschichte der Literatur und der schönen Künste 55. Munich.

———. 1988. "Die Sprache der Dinge: der lange Blick und die wilde Semiose." In Gumbrecht and Pfeiffer 1988, pp. 237–51.

Assmann, A., and J. Assmann. 1983. "Schrift und Gedächtnis." In A. Assmann, J. Assmann, and Ch. Hardmeier, eds., *Schrift und Gedächtnis: Beiträge zur Archäologie der literarischen Kommunikation* (1), pp. 265–84. Munich.

Assmann, J. 1983. "Schrift, Tod und Identität: Das Grab als Vorschule der Literatur im alten Ägypten." In A. Assmann, J. Assmann, and Ch. Hardmeier, eds., *Schift und Gedächtnis: Beiträge zur Archäologie der literarischen Kommunikation* (1), pp. 64–93. Munich.

————. 1987. "Heirotaxis: Textkonstitution und Bildkomposition in der altägyptischen Kunst und Literatur." In J. Osing and G. Dreyer, eds., *Form und Maß: Beiträge zur Literatur, Sprache und Kunst des alten Ägypten*, pp. 18–42. Festschrift Gerhard Fecht.

Auerbach, E. 1971 [1946]. *Mimesis*. Bern.

Augustine. 1911 [412–26]. *De civitate Dei. Über den Gottesstaat*. Trans. A. Schröder. Kempten.

————. 1947. *De musica*. Ed. and trans. G. Finaert and F. J. Thonnard. Bruges.

Bacon, F. 1982 [1620]. *Das neue Organon (Novum Organon)*. Ed. Manfred Buhr. 2nd ed. Berlin. English translation, 1960. *The New Organon*. Ed. F. H. Anderson. New York.

————. 1984 [1627]. *Neu-Atlantis*. Berlin. English translation, 1974. *The Advancement of Learning and New Atlantis*. Ed. A. Johnston. Oxford.

Bahr, A. 1988. "Imagination und Körperleben." In Gumbrecht and Pfeiffer 1988, pp. 680–702. Frankfurt a.M.

Bann, S. 1976. "Adriatics—à propos of Brice Marden." *20th Century Studies* 15/16: 116–29.

————. 1989. *The True Vine*. Cambridge, Eng.

Barnouw, E. 1968. *A History of Broadcasting in the United States*. New York.

Barthes, R. 1966. "The Activity of Structuralism." In *Form* 1: 1.

————. 1976. *S/Z*. Frankfurt a.M.

————. 1982. *L'obvie et l'obtuse*. Paris.

————. 1984. *Le bruissement de la langue: Essais critiques IV*. Paris.

————. 1985. "Analyse textuelle d'un conte d'Edgar Poe." In R. Barthes, *L'aventure sémiologique*, pp. 329–59. Paris.

Barzizius, G. 1972. *Orthographia*. Ed. Swierk.

Battaglia, S. 1967. *Mitografia del personaggio*. Naples.

Baudrillard, J. 1976. *L'échange symbolique et la mort*. Paris. German translation, 1982. *Der symbolische Tausch und der Tod*. Munich.

————. 1983. *Les stratégies fatales*. Paris.

————. 1985. "The Ecstasy of Communication." In H. Foster, ed., *Essays on Postmodern Culture*, pp. 126–33. Washington, D.C.

————. 1986. *Amérique*. Paris.

————. 1987a. *L'autre par lui-même*. Paris.

————. 1987b. *Forget Foucault/Forget Baudrillard: An Interview with S. Lothringer*. New York.

Baum, W. 1967. "Regierung Dönitz und deutsche Kapitulation." In Hillgruber 1967: 347–78.

Bazin, A. 1967. "The Ontology of the Photographic Image." In *What Is Cinema*, trans. H. Gray, pp. 9–16. Berkeley, Calif.

Beaujour, M. 1980. *Miroirs d'encre*. Paris.

Bec, C. 1967. *Les marchands écrivains: Affaires et humanisme à Florence (1375–1434)*. Paris.

Beckett, S. 1957. *Proust*. New York.

Bénédite, G. 1922. "Signa Verba: Les jeux d'écriture dans l'image." In *Rec. d'ét. égypt. Champollion*, pp. 23–24.

Benjamin, W. 1980 [1928]. "Einbahnstraße." In T. Rexroth, ed., *Walter Benjamin: Kleine Prosa. Baudelaire-Übertragungen*, pp. 83–148. Frankfurt a.M. English translation, 1979. In *"One-way Street" and Other Writings*, trans. E. Jephcott and K. Shorter. London.

Benn, G. 1984 [1944]. "Roman des Phänotyp." In B. Hillebrand, ed., *Gottfried Benn: Prosa und Autobiographie in der Fassung der Erstdrucke*, pp. 149–91. Frankfurt a.M.

Benveniste, E. 1966. "La notion de 'rythme' dans son expression linguistique." In *Problèmes de linguistique générale*, pp. 327–35. Paris.

Bischoff, F. W. 1984 [1926]. "Die Ästhetik des Rundfunks." In I. Schneider, ed., *Radio-Kultur in der Weimarer Republic*, pp. 72–74. Tübingen.

Blanch, L. 1987. *The Wilder Shores of Love*. London.

Bloch, E. 1976. *Das Materialismusproblem: Seine Geschichte und Substanz*. Frankfurt a.M.

———. 1980. "Utopische Funktion im Materialismus." In R. Traub and H. Wieser, eds., *Gespräche mit Ernst Bloch*. Frankfurt a.M.

Bloch, O. 1985. *Le matérialisme*. Paris.

Bloom, H., et al. 1979. *Deconstruction and Criticism*. New York.

Blum, W. 1969. "Curiosi und regendarii: Untersuchungen zur Geheimen Staatspolizei der Spätantike." Ph.D. diss., Munich.

Boas, G. 1950. *The Heiroglyphica of Horapollo*. Bollingen Ser. 23. Princeton, N.J.

Boelcke, W. A., ed. 1969. *Deutschlands Rüstung im Zweiten Weltkrieg: Hitlers Konferenzen mit Albert Speer 1942–1945*. Frankfurt a.M.

Boese, C.-H. 1940. "So fingen wir an." *Welt-Rundfunk* 4: 14–17.

Bolz, N. 1985. "Verwandlung des Lebens in Schrift: Walter Benjamins Variationen über ein jüdisches Motiv." In D. Boueke and N. Hopster, eds., *Schreiben—Schreiben lernen: Rolf Sanner zum 65. Geburtstag*. Tübingen.

Borch-Jacobsen, M. 1988. *The Freudian Subject*. Trans. C. Porter. Stanford, Calif.

Borges, J. L. 1964–66. *Obras completas*. Buenos Aires.

Bower, T. 1987. *The Paperclip Conspiracy: The Hunt for the Nazi Scientists*. Boston.

Brant, S. 1968 [1494]. *Das Narrenschiff*. Ed. M. Lemmer. Tübingen.

Brassicanus, J. A. 1525. In *Gallum nuper profligatum atque captum . . . epinikion: Eiusdem epigrammata ad . . . consiliarios Austriae. . . .* Vienna.

Braun, Chr. v. 1985. *NichtIch-IchNicht*. Frankfurt a.M.

Brendel, F. 1845. "Zur Einleitung." *Neue Zeitschrift für Musik* 22: 1–12.

Breton, A. 1925. *Les pas perdus*. Paris.

Briggs, A. 1965. *The History of Broadcasting in the United Kingdom*, vol. 1, *The Golden Age of Wireless*. London.

———. 1977. "The Pleasure Telephone: A Chapter in the Prehistory of the Media." In I. de Sola Pool, *The Social Impact of the Telephone*, pp. 40–65. Cambridge, Mass.

Brody, J. 1982. *Lectures de Montaigne*. Lexington, Ky.

Brown, P. 1986. *Die letzten Heiden: Eine kleine Geschichte der Spätantike*. Trans. H. Fliessbach. Berlin. English translation, 1978. *The Making of Late Antiquity*. Cambridge, Mass.

Bruch, W. 1967. *Kleine Geschichte des deutschen Fernsehens*. Berlin.

Brunner, H. 1979. "Illustrierte Bücher im alten Ägypten." In H. Brunner, R. Kannicht, and K. Schwager, eds., *Wort und Bild*, pp. 201–18. Munich.

Bruyne, E. de. 1946. *Etudes d'esthétique médiévale*. Vol. 2. Bruges.

Buck, A. 1956. "Das Lebensgefühl der Renaissance im Spiegel der Selbstdarstellungen Petrarcas und Cardanos." In *Formen der Selbstdarstellung: Festgabe für Fritz Neubert*, pp. 35–52. Berlin.

Buffier, C. 1724. *Traité des premieres véritéz et de la source de nos jugemens*. Paris.

Bunke, H. 1986. "Über die Bildung mathematischer Modelle und deren deduktive Überprüfung." *Deutsche Zeitschrift für Philosophie* 2: 135–42.

Burckhardt, J. 1966 [1859]. *Die Kultur der Renaissance in Italien: Ein Versuch*. Stuttgart.

Burkholder, J. P. 1985. *Charles Ives: The Ideas Behind the Music*. New Haven, Conn.

Burnet, M. 1959. *The Clonal Selection Theory of Acquired Immunity*. Nashville.

Bury, R. de. 1960 [1345]. *Philobiblon*. Trans. E. C. Thomas. Ed. M. Maclagan. Oxford.

Büscher, H. 1938. "Zukunftsphantasie: Das werden wir erleben." In *Radio-Web*, ed., *Jeder Rundfunkinteressent muß wissen was . . .*, pp. 9–10. Berlin.

Calvet, J. L. 1973. *Roland Barthes: Un regard politique sur le signe*. Paris.

Campbell, R. 1976. *The Golden Years of Broadcasting: A Celebration of the First 50 Years of Radio and Television on NBC*. New York.

Camus, R. 1981. *Auteur de journal d'un voyage en France*. Paris.

Cardano, G. 1914 [1663]. *Des Girolamo Cardano von Mailand, Bürgers von Bologna, eigene Lebensbeschreibung*. Ed. H. Hefele. Jena.

Carr, D. 1967. "Maurice Merleau-Ponty: Incarnate Consciousness." In G. A. Schrader, Jr., ed., *Existential Philosophers: Kierkegaard to Merleau-Ponty*, pp. 369–429. New York.

Cartier, R. 1985. *Der Zweite Weltkrieg*. Munich.

Cassiodorus, F. M. A. 1973 [537–38]. *Variarum libri XII*. Turnhout.

Catalogue de la fonte hiéroglyphique de l'imprimerie de l'IFAO. 1983. Cairo.

Cazeneuve, J. 1958. "La connaissance d'autrui dans les sociétés archaïques." *Cahiers internationaux de sociologie* 25: 75–99.

Certeau, M. de. 1975. *L'écriture de l'histoire*. Paris.

Ceserani, R., and L. de Federicis. 1979. *Il materiale e l'immaginario*. Vol. 3. Turin.

Châteaubriand, F. R. 1849. *Itinéraire de Paris à Jerusalem: Suivi du voyage en Amérique*. Vol. 1. Paris.

Chesterton, G. K. 1966. *Un nommé Jeudi*. Paris.

Chrisman, M. U. 1982. *Lay Culture, Learned Culture: Books and Social Change in Strasbourg, 1480–1599*. New Haven, Conn.

Christ, K., ed. 1986. *Der Untergang des römischen Reiches*. 2nd ed. Darmstadt.

Chuikov, V. 1966. *Das Ende des Dritten Reiches*. Munich. English translation, 1967. *The End of the Third Reich*, trans. R. Kisch. London.

Claessens, D. 1980. *Das Konkrete und das Abstrakte: Soziologische Skizzen zur Anthrolpologie*. Frankfurt a.M.

Classen, P. 1955. "Kaiserreskript und Königsurkunde: Diplomatische Studien zum römisch-germanischen Kontinuitätsproblem." Part 1. In *Archiv für Diplomatik, Schriftgeschichte, Siegel- und Wappenkunde 1*, pp. 1–87.

———. 1956. "Kaiserreskript und Königsurkunde: Diplomatische Studien zum römisch-germanischen Kontinuitätsproblem." Part 2. In *Archiv für Diplomatik, Schriftgeschichte, Siegel- und Wappenkunde 2*, pp. 1–115.

Codex Theodosiani libri XVI cum constitutionibus sirmondianis. 1971 [439]. Ed. T. Mommsen. Zurich.

Cohen, A. 1971. " 'La Supposition' and the Changing Concept of Dissonance in Baroque Theory." *Journal of the American Musicological Society* 24: 63–84.

Comolli, J.-L. 1980. "Machines of the Visible." In T. deLauretis and S. Heath, eds., *The Cinematic Apparatus*, pp. 121–42. New York.

Corneille, P. 1950 [1662]. "Sertorius." In P. Lièvre and R. Caillowis, eds., *Théâtre complet*, vol. 2. Paris.

Correa, G., ed. 1980. *Antología de la poesía española (1900–1980)*. 2 vols. Madrid.

Costa Lima, L. 1984. *O Controle do Imaginário: Razão e imaginação no*

Ocidente. São Paulo. English translation, 1988. *Control of the Imaginary: Reason and Imagination in Modern Times*. Minneapolis.

Coutinho, A., and F. Varela. 1990. "Immune Networks: The Latest on a Growing Field." *Immunology Today*.

Coutinho, A.; L. Forni; D. Holmberg; F. Ivars; and N. Vaz. 1984. "From an Antigen-Centered, Network Perspective of Autonomous Activity in a Self-Referential Immune System." *Immunology Review* 79: 151–68.

Cy Twombly: Paintings and Drawings 1954–1977. 1979. Whitney Museum of American Art.

Dahl, P. 1978. *Arbeitersender und Volksempfänger Proletarische Radiobewegung und bürgerlicher Rundfunk bis 1945*. Frankfurt a.M.

———. 1983. *Radio: Sozialgeschichte des Rundfunks für Sender und Empfänger*. Reinbek bei Hamburg.

Dahlhaus, C. 1962. "Domenico Belli und der chromatische Kontrapunkt um 1600." *Die Musikforschung* 15: 315–40.

———. 1967. *Untersuchungen über die Entstehung der harmonischen Tonalität*. Kassel.

Danto, A. 1979. "Moving Pictures." *Quarterly Review of Film Studies* 4: 1–21.

Daumas, F. 1978. "Du phonème au symbole dans l'écriture hiéroglyphique ptolémaïque." *Le courrier du CNRS* 29: 14–21.

Debord, G. 1983. *Society of the Spectacle*. Detroit.

Defaux, G. 1985. "Rhétorique et représentation dans les *Essais*: De la peinture de l'autre à la peinture du moi." In F. Lestringant, ed., *Rhétorique de Montaigne*. Paris.

De Man, P. 1986. *The Resistance to Theory*. Minneapolis.

Derrida, J. 1967. "Freud et la scène de l'écriture." In J. Derrida, *L'écriture et la différence*, pp. 293–340. Paris.

———. 1973. *Speech and Phenomena (and Other Essays) on Husserl's Theory of Signs*. Evanston, Ill.

———. 1974 [1967]. *Of Grammatology*. Trans. Gayatri Chakravorti Spivak. Baltimore, Md.

———. 1974/75 [1972]. "White Mythology: Metaphor in the Text of Philosophy." *New Literary History* 6: 15–74.

———. 1976. "Signatur Ereignis Kontext." In *Randgänge der Philosophie*, trans. D. W. Tuckwiller. Frankfurt a.M.

———. 1978. *Writing and Difference*. London.

———. 1979. *La carte postale: De Socrate à Freud et au-delà*. Paris.

———. 1980. "Nietzsches Otobiographie oder Politik des Eigennamens." In *Fugen*. Olten, Germany.

———. 1984. "Guter Wille zur Macht (II)." In P. Forget, ed., *Text und Interpretation*, pp. 62–77. Munich.

―――. 1990. *Lacan, the Absolute Master.* Trans. Douglas Brick. Stanford, Calif.

Descombes, V. 1980. *Modern French Philosophy.* Trans. L. S. Fox and J. M. Harding. Cambridge, Eng.

Dilthey, W. 1983 [1910]. "Der Aufbau der geschichtlichen Welt in den Geisteswissenschaften." In U. Lessing, ed., *Texte zur Kritik der historischen Vernunft.* Göttingen.

Dirscherl, K. 1986. "Fragmente bildnerischen Denkens: Der Maler Antoni Tàpies als Schrifsteller." *Iberoamericana* 10, no. 2/3: 71–86.

Dornberger, W. 1953. *V 2: Der Schuß ins Weltall.* Esslingen.

Dreitzel, H. P. 1972. *Die gesellschaftlichen Leiden und das Leiden an der Gesellschaft: Vorstudien zu einer Pathologie des Rollenverhaltens.* Stuttgart.

Dubois, C.-G. 1984. "Itinéraire et impasses de la 'vive représentation.'" In M. Soulié, ed., *La littérature de la Renaissance: Mélanges offerts à Henri Weber,* pp. 405–25. Geneva.

Ducrot, O., and T. Todorov. 1973. *Dictionnaire encyclopédique des sciences du langage.* Paris.

Dumas, A. 1980. *Le Comte de Monte Cristo.* Ed. J.-H. Bornecque. Paris.

Dumézil, G. 1968. *Mythe et épopée: L'idéologie des trois fonctions dans les épopées des peuples indo-européens.* Paris.

―――. 1977. *Les dieux souverains des Indo-européens.* Paris.

Düring, I. 1934. "Ptolemaios und Porphyrios über die Musik." *Göteborgs Högskolas Årsskrift* 40: 1–293.

Durth, W. 1987. *Deutsche Architekten: Biographische Verflechtungen 1900–1970.* 2nd ed. Braunschweig.

Eckert, G. 1953. *Die Kunst des Fernsehens.* Emsdetten.

Einrauch, V., and L. Kurzawa. 1983. "Baudrillard und die Medien." *Spuren* 2: 31–34.

Eisenstein, E. 1979. *The Printing Press as an Agent of Change: Communications and Cultural Transformations in Early-Modern Europe.* 2 vols. Cambridge, Eng.

Ekschmitt, W. 1964. *Das Gedächtnis der Völker: Hieroglyphen, Schrift und Schriftfunde auf Tontafeln, Papyri und Pergamenten.* Berlin.

Elias, N. 1978. *Was ist Soziologie?* 3rd ed. Munich.

Emerson, R. W. 1850. *Representative Men.* Boston.

Enzensberger, C. 1968. *Größerer Versuch über den Schmutz.* Munich.

Erasmus. 1971. *Opera omnia.* Vol. 1.2. Amsterdam.

Felperin, H. 1985. *Beyond Deconstruction: The Uses and Abuses of Literary Theory.* Oxford.

Festinger, L. 1978. *Theorie der kognitiven Dissonanz.* Bern.

Fischer, H. G. 1977a. *Egyptian Studies II: The Orientation of Hieroglyphs, I, Reversals.* New York.

———. 1977b. "Hieroglyphen." In *Lexikon der Ägyptologie*, 2: 1189–99.

———. 1986. *L'écriture et l'art de l'Egypte ancienne*. Paris.

Flaubert, G. 1986 [1849/50]. "Voyage en Egypte." In C. Meyer, ed., *Photographies de Maxime du Camp*. Paris.

Foerster, H. v. 1981. *Observing Systems*. Seaside, Eng.

Földes-Papp, K. 1984. *Vom Felsbild zum Alphabet: Die Geschichte der Schrift von ihren frühesten Vorstufen bis zur modernen lateinischen Schreibschrift*. Stuttgart.

Fónagy, I. 1983. *La vive voix*. Paris.

Foster, K. 1984. *Petrarch: Poet and Humanist*. Edinburgh.

Foucault, M. 1966. *Les mots et les choses*. Paris.

———. 1979. "Was ist ein Autor?" In *Schriften zur Literatur*, pp. 7–31. Frankfurt a.M.

———. 1986. *Archäologie des Wissens*. Trans. U. Köppen. 2nd ed. Frankfurt a.M.

Franco von Köln. 1974 [ca. 1280]. *Ars cantus mensurabilis*. Ed. G. Reaney and A. Gilles. Corpus scriptorum de musica, vol. 18. Rome.

Frank, M. 1980. *Das Sagbare und das Unsagbare*. Frankfurt a.M.

———. 1983. *Was ist Neo-Strukturalismus?* Frankfurt a.M.

Freud, S. 1952. *Totem und Tabu*. In *Gesammelte Werke*. London.

———. 1975. "Trauer und Melancholie." In S. Freud, *Psychologie des Unbewußten*, Studienausgabe, vol. 3, pp. 193–212. Frankfurt a.M.

Friedell, E. 1969 [1927–31]. *Kulturgeschichte der Neuzeit: Die Krisis der europäischen Seele von der schwarzen Pest bis zum Ersten Weltkrieg*. Munich.

Friedrich, H. 1949. *Montaigne*. Bern.

———. 1964. *Epochen der italienischen Lyrik*. Frankfurt a.M.

Fuchs, J. 1978. "Friedrich Nietzsches Augenleiden." *Münchner Medizinische Wochenschrift* 18: 631–34.

Fuchs, W. 1973. *Todesbilder in der modernen Gesellschaft*. Frankfurt a.M.

Galitz, R. 1986. *Literarische Basisöffentlichkeit als politische Kraft: Lesegesellschaften des 17. bis 19. Jahrhunderts unter besonderer Berücksichtigung des 18. Jahrhunderts*. Frankfurt a.M.

Gautier, T. 1870. *Voyage en Espagne*. Paris.

Gehlen, A. 1957. *Die Seele im technischen Zeitalter: Sozialpsychologische Probleme in der industriellen Gesellschaft*. Hamburg.

———. 1961. *Anthropologische Forschung: Zur Selbstbegegnung und Selbstentdeckung des Menschen*. Reinbek.

———. 1975. *Urmensch und Spätkultur: Philosophische Ergebnisse und Aussagen*. 3rd ed. Frankfurt a.M.

———. 1978 [1931]. *Wirklicher und unwirklicher Geist: Philosophische Schriften 1*. Frankfurt a.M.

Geisler, E. 1985. "Leere, Schrift, Vielheit der Sprachen: Überlegungen zum Werk von Antoni Tàpies." *Iberoamericana* 9, no. 1: 38–63.

Geldner, F. 1961. "Zum ältesten Missaldruck." In *Gutenberg-Jahrbuch*, pp. 101–6.

Gendolla, P. 1991. "Phantasien der Askese: Über die Entstehung innerer Bilder am Beispiel der 'Versuchung des heiligen Antonius.'" Heidelberg.

Gerber, G. 1871. *Die Sprache als Kunst*. Bromberg.

Gerke, W. 1988. "Destabilisieren Computerprogramme die Aktienkurse?" *Spektrum der Wissenschaft*, Jan., pp. 24–31.

Gerson, J. 1973 [1423]. "De laude scriptorum." In J. Gerson, *Oeuvres complètes*, 9: 423–34. Paris.

Gesner, C. 1966 [1545]. *Bibliotheca Universalis* and *Appendix*. Zurich.

Geyer, M. 1984. *Deutsche Rüstungspolitik 1860–1980*. Frankfurt a.M.

Gibbon, E. 1909–14 [1776–88]. *The History of the Decline and Fall of the Roman Empire*. London. German translation, 1987. *Verfall und Untergang des römischen Reiches*. Ed. D. A. Saunders. Trans. J. Sporschill. Nördlingen.

Giehlow, K. 1915. *Die Hieroglyphenkunde des Humanismus in der Allegorie der Renaissance*. Jahrbuch der kunsthist. Sammlg. 32, Heft 1. Vienna.

Gil de Biedma, J. 1985. *Las personas del verbo*. Barcelona.

Gilgenmann, K. 1986. "Sozialisation als Evolution psychischer Systeme." In H.-J. Unverferth, ed., *System und Selbstproduktion: Zur Erschließung eines neuen Paradigmas in den Sozialwissenschaften*, pp. 91–165. Frankfurt a.M.

Gimbel, J. *Science, Technology, and Reparations: Exploitation and Plunder in Postwar Germany*. Stanford, Calif.

Glanville, R. 1984. "Distinguished and Exact Lies." In R. Trappl, ed., *Cybernetics and Systems Research 2*, pp. 665–67. Amsterdam.

Glasersfeld, E. von. 1985. "Konstruktion der Wirklichkeit und des Begriffs der Objektivität." In H. Gumin and A. Mohler, eds., *Einführung in den Konstruktivismus*, pp. 1–26. Munich.

Godzich, W. 1992. "Figuring Out What Matters; or: The Microphysics of History." In H. U. Gumbrecht, *Making Sense in Life and Literature*, pp. vii–xvi. Minneapolis.

Goebel, G. 1953. "Das Fernsehen in Deutschland bis zum Jahre 1945." *Archiv für das Post- und Fernmeldewesen* 5, no. 5 (Aug.): 259–393.

———. 1978. "Der Fernsehstart in Deutschland." *Funkschau* 19: 62–65.

Goldberg, J. 1990. *Writing Matter: From the Hands of the English Renaissance*. Stanford, Calif.

Goldin, D. 1981. *Boncampagno da Signa: Testi*. Venice.

González, A. 1986. *Palabra sobre palabra*. Barcelona.

Goody, J. 1977. *The Domestication of the Savage Mind*. Cambridge, Eng.

Graff, H.-J. 1987. *The Legacies of Literacy: Continuities and Contradictions in Western Culture and Society*. Bloomington, Ind.

Grapow, H. 1924. *Die bildlichen Ausdrücke des Ägyptischen*. Leipzig.

Greene, T. 1982. *The Light in Troy: Imitation and Discovery in Renaissance Poetry*. New Haven, Conn.

————. 1986. *The Vulnerable Text: Essays on Renaissance Literature*. New York.

Greenfield, K. R. 1967. "Die amerikanische Luftkriegführung in Europa und Ostasien 1942–1945." In Hillgruber 1967, pp. 292–311.

Guglielminetti, M. 1977. *Memoria e scrittura: L'autobiografia di Dante a Cellini*. Turin.

Gumbrecht, H. U. 1983. "Schriftlichkeit in mündlicher Kultur." In A. Assmann, J. Assmann, and Ch. Hardmeier, eds., *Schrift und Gedächtnis: Beiträge zur Archäologie der literarischen Kommunikation* (1), pp. 158–74. Munich.

————. 1986a. " 'Dabeisein ist alles': Über die Geschichte von Medien, Sport und Publikum." *Arete: The Journal of Sport Literature* 4, no. 1: 25–43. See also Gumbrecht 1992.

————. 1986b. "Déconstruction Deconstructed." *Philosophische Rundschau* 1/2: 1–35.

————. 1988a. "Beginn von Literatur/Abschied vom Körper." In G. Smolka-Koerdt, P. M. Spangenberg, and D. Tillmann-Bartylla, eds., *Der Ursprung von Literatur: Medien, Rollen, Kommunikationssituationen zwischen 1450 und 1650*, pp. 15–50. Munich.

————. 1988b. "Flache Diskurse." In Gumbrecht and Pfeiffer 1988: 914–23.

————. 1992. "It's Just a Game: On the History of Media, Sport and the Public." In *Making Sense in Life and Literature*, pp. 272–87. Minneapolis.

1993a. "Beyond Foucault/Foucault's Style." *Representation* (University of Tokyo).

1993b. "Ende des Theorie—Jenseits?" In R. Maresch, ed., *Zukunft oder Ende: Standpunkte, Analysen, Entwürfe*, pp. 40–46. Munich.

1993c. "Schrift als epistemologischer Grenzverlauf." In Gumbrecht and Pfeiffer 1993.

Gumbrecht, H. U., and K. L. Pfeiffer, eds. 1986. *Stil: Geschichten und Funktionen eines kulturwissenschaftlichen Diskurselements*. Frankfurt a.M.

————. 1988. *Materialität der Kommunikation*. Frankfurt a.M.

————. 1993. *Schrift*. Munich.

Habermas, J. 1985. *Der philosophische Diskurs der Moderne: Zwölf Vorlesungen*. Frankfurt a.M.

Haensel, C. 1952. *Fernsehen—nahegesehen: Technische Fibel—Dramatur-gie—Organisatorischer Aufbau*. Frankfurt a.M. and Berlin.

Hagemeyer, F. W. 1979. "Die Entstehung von Informationskonzepten in der Technik in Industrie- und Kriegsforschung." Ph.D. diss., Berlin.

Hahn, A. 1968. *Einstellungen zum Tod und ihre soziale Bedingtheit*. Stuttgart.

———. 1987. "Sinn und Sinnlosigkeit." In H. Haferkamp and M. Schmid, eds., *Sinn, Kommunikation und soziale Differenzierung: Beiträge zu Luhmanns Theorie sozialer Systeme*, pp. 155–64. Frankfurt a.M.

Hahn, F. 1963. *Deutsche Geheimwaffen 1939–1945*. Heidenheim.

Hallowell, I. 1960. "Ojibwa Ontology: Behavior and World Views." In S. Diamond, ed., *Culture in History: Essays in Honor of Paul Radin*, pp. 19–57. New York.

Hamerton-Kelly, R. G. 1987. *Violent Origins: Walter Burkert, René Girard, and Jonathan Z. Smith on Ritual Killing and Cultural Formation*. Stanford, Calif.

Hardorn, W., and M. Cortesi. 1986. *Man and Media: History of Mass Communication*. Stuttgart.

Harris, M. 1979. *Cultural Materialism: The Struggle for a Science of Culture*. New York.

Hartmann, N. 1949 [1933]. *Das Problem des geistigen Seins: Untersuchungen zur Grundlegung der Geschichtsphilosophie und der Geisteswissenschaften*. Berlin.

Hattori, T. 1967. "Japans Weg aus dem Weltkrieg." In Hillgruber 1967, pp. 389–436.

Havelock, E. A. 1963. *Preface to Plato*. Cambridge, Mass.

———. 1978. "The Alphabetization of Homer." In E. A. Havelock and J. P. Hershbell, eds., *Communication Arts in the Ancient World*, pp. 3–21. New York.

———. 1982. *The Literate Revolution in Greece and Its Cultural Consequences*. Princeton, N.J.

Hegel, G. W. F. 1955. *Asthetik*. Ed. F. Bassenge. Berlin.

———. 1975. *Phänomenologie des Geistes*. Frankfurt a.M.

Heidegger, M. 1972. "Die Zeit des Weltbildes." In *Holzwege*, pp. 69–104. Frankfurt a.M.

———. 1977. "The Question Concerning Technology." Trans. W. Lovitt. In M. Heidegger, *Martin Heidegger: Basic Writings*. Ed. D. F. Krell. New York.

Heidenheimer, H. 1925. "Das Begleitgedicht zum Justiniani Institutiones-Drucke von 1468." In A. Ruppel, ed., *Gutenberg-Festschrift: Feier des 25 jährigen Bestehens des Gutenberg-Museums in Mainz*, pp. 108–17. Mainz.

Heider, F. 1959 [1926]. "Thing and Medium," *Psychological Issues* 1/3: 1–

34. Abridged translation of "Ding und Medium," *Symposium* 1: 108–57.

Heims, S. 1982. *John von Neumann and Norbert Wiener: From Mathematics to the Technologies of Life and Death*. Cambridge, Mass.

Helck, W. 1985. "Gedanken zum Ursprung der ägyptischen Schrift." *Bibl. d'Et.* 97: 395–408.

Herb. 1907. "Schreibmaschine und Presse." *Schreibmaschinen-Zeitung* 103: 12.

Herbst, L. 1982. *Der Totale Krieg und die Neuordnung der Wirtschaft: Die Kriegswissenschaft im Spannungsfeld von Politik, Ideologie und Propaganda 1939–1945*. Stuttgart.

Herzlich, C., and J. Pierret. 1984. *Malades d'hier, malades d'aujourd'hui: De la mort collective au devoir de guérison*. Paris.

———. 1987. "Le phénomène SIDA: Discours autours d'une maladie." In E. Hirsch, ed., *Le SIDA: Rumeur et faits*, pp. 17–34. Paris.

Hickethier, K. 1986. "Beschleunigte Wahrnehmung." In J. Boberg, T. Fichter, and E. Gillen, eds., *Die Metropole: Industriekultur in Berlin im zwanzigsten Jahrhundert*, pp. 144–55. Munich.

Hillgruber, A., ed. 1967. *Probleme des Zweiten Weltkriegs*. Cologne.

Hillis-Miller, J. 1979. "The Critic as Host." In Bloom et al. 1979.

Hirsch, R. 1967. *Printing, Selling and Reading 1450–1550*. Wiesbaden.

Hirschfeld, O. 1893. "Die agentes in rebus." In *Sitzungsberichte der Königlich Preussischen Akademie der Wissenschaften zu Berlin*, 2nd half vol., pp. 421–41.

Hodges, A. 1983. *Alan Turing: The Enigma*. New York.

Hoffmann, K. O. 1965. *Die Geschichte der Luftnachrichtentruppe*. 2 vols. Neckargmünd.

Holmberg, E. J. 1933. "Zur Geschichte des Cursus publicus." Ph.D. diss. Uppsala.

Homo, L. 1950 [1927]. *Les institutions politiques romaines de la cité à l'état*. Paris.

Homze, E. L. 1967. *Foreign Labour in Nazi Germany*. Princeton, N.J.

Horkheimer, M. 1931. *Die gegenwärtige Lage der Sozialphilosophie und die Aufgaben des Instituts für Sozialforschung*. Frankfurt a.M.

Horkheimer, M., and Th. W. Adorno. 1969 [1944]. *Dialektik der Aufklärung*. Frankfurt a.M.

Huetz, F.; F. Jacquemart; C. Peña-Rossi; F. Varela; and A. Coutinho. 1988. "Autoimmunity: The Moving Boundaries Between Physiology and Pathology." *Journal of Autoimmunity* 1: 507–18.

Humbert, G. 1962 [1887]. "Cursus publicus." In *Dictionnaire des antiquités Grecques et Romaines*, vol. 1.2, pp. 1645–72. Graz.

Husserl, E. 1966 [1905]. "Die Vorlesungen über das innere Zeitbewußtsein aus dem Jahre 1905." In E. Husserl, ed., *Zur Phänomenologie des inneren Zeitbewußtseins (1893–1917)*, pp. 3–98. The Hague.

Hymes, D. 1975. "Breakthrough into Performance." In D. Ben Amos and K. S. Goldstein, eds., *Folklore, Performance and Communication*. The Hague.

Ihde, D. 1979. *Experimental Phenomenology: An Introduction*. New York.

———. 1990. *Technology and the Lifeworld: From Garden to Earth*. Bloomington, Ind.

Illich, I., and B. Sanders. 1988. *The Alphabetization of the Popular Mind*. San Francisco.

Innis, H. A. 1972. *Empire and Communications*. Toronto.

Iser, W. 1977. "Literaturwissenschaft in Konstanz." In H. R. Jauß and H. Nesselhauf, eds., *Gebremste Reform: Ein Kapitel deutscher Hochschulgeschichte. Universität Konstanz 1966–1976*, pp. 181–200. Konstanz.

———. 1982. "Das Literaturverständnis zwischen Geschichte und Zukunft." *Der Deutschunterricht* 34: 8–25.

———. 1987. *Laurence Sterne's Tristram Shandy: Inszenierte Subjektivität*. Munich.

———. 1991. *Das Fiktive und das Imaginäre: Perspektiven literarischer Anthropologie*. Munich.

Ishagpour, Y. 1983. "Le resprésentable." *Traverses* 29: 20–33.

Iverson, E. 1961. *The Myth of Egypt and Its Hieroglyphs in the European Tradition*. Copenhagen.

Ives, C. 1972. *Memos*. Ed. J. Kirkpatrick. New York.

Jakobson, R. 1979 [1960]. "Linguistik und Poetik." In R. Jakobson, *Poetik: Ausgewählte Aufsätze 1921–1971*, pp. 83–121. Frankfurt a.M.

Jameson, F. 1984. "Postmodernism, or The Cultural Logic of Late Capitalism." *New Left Review* 146 (July–Aug.): 53–94.

Jan, C. v. 1895. *Musici Scriptores Graeci*. Leipzig.

Janssen, J. M. A. 1974. "Les listes des signes hiéroglyphiques." In *Textes et languages—Hommage Champollion*, 1: 57–66. Cairo.

Jaume, L. 1989. *Le discours jacobin et la démocratie*. Paris.

Javitch, D. 1978. *Poetry and Courtliness in Renaissance England*. Princeton, N.J.

Jay, M. 1984. *Marxism and Totality: The Adventures of a Concept from Lukács to Habermas*. Berkeley, Calif.

Jaynes, J. 1976. *The Origin of Consciousness in the Breakdown of the Bicameral Mind*. Boston.

Jeanneret, M. 1976. "Rabelais et Montaigne: L'écriture comme parole." *L'esprit créateur* 16: 78–94.

Jerne, N. 1974. "Towards a Network Theory of the Immune System." *Annuel Immunologique Institut Pasteur* 125C: 373–89.

———. 1984. "Idiotypic Networks and Other Preconceived Ideas." *Immunology Review* 79: 5–24.

Jodl, A. 1982 [1946]. "Der Einfluß Hitlers auf die Kriegführung." In Schramm, 4: 1714–21.

Jones, R. O. 1972. *A Literary History of Spain: The Twentieth Century.* London.

Joyce, J. 1986 [1922]. *Ulysses.* New York. German translation, 1982. *Ulysses.* Trans. H. Wollschläger. Frankfurt a.M.

Junge, F. 1984. "Zur 'Sprachwissenschaft' der Ägypter." In *Studien zu Sprache und Religion Ägyptens: Festschrift W. Westendorf,* pp. 257–72.

Jungk, R. 1956. *Heller als tausend Sonnen: Das Schicksal der Atomforscher.* Bern.

Kamper, D., and C. Wulf, eds. 1982. *Die Wiederkehr des Körpers.* Frankfurt a.M.

Kant, I. 1983a [1787]. *Kritik der reinen Vernunft.* In *Immanuel Kant, Werke,* vol. 4. Darmstadt.

———. 1983b [1788]. *Kritik der praktischen Vernunft.* In *Immanuel Kant, Werke,* vol. 6. Darmstadt.

Kaplony, P. 1966. "Prinzipien der Hieroglyphenschrift." *Chron. d'Eg.* 41/81: 60–99.

Keel, O. 1980. *Das Böcklein in der Milch seiner Mutter und Verwandtes.* Freiburg.

Kern, S. 1983. *The Culture of Time and Space: 1880–1918.* Cambridge, Mass.

Kittler, F. A. 1985a. "Nietzsche, der mechanisierte Philosoph." *kultuR-Revolution* 9:25–29.

———. 1985b. "Die Zeit der anderen Auslegung: Schreiben bei Rilke und in der Kunsterziehungsbewegung." In D. Boueke and N. Hopster, eds., *Schreiben—Schreiben lernen: Rolf Sanner zum 65. Geburtstag,* pp. 40–56. Tübingen.

———. 1986. *Grammophon Film Typewriter.* Berlin.

———. 1987. *Aufschreibesysteme 1800/1900.* 2nd ed. Munich. English translation, 1990. *Discourse Networks 1800/1900,* trans. M. Metteer with C. Cullens. Stanford, Calif.

Klibansky, R.; E. Panofsky; and F. Saxl. 1964. *Saturn and Melancholy.* London.

Koestler, A. 1967. *The Ghost in the Machine.* New York.

Koppe, F. 1977. *Sprache und Bedürfnis: Zur sprachphilosophische Grundlage der Geisteswissenschaften.* Stuttgart.

Kornhuber, H. H. 1984. "Von der Freiheit." In M. Lindauer and A. Schöpf, eds., *Wie erkennt der Mensch die Welt? Grundlagen des Erkennes, Fühlens und Handelns: Geistes- und Naturwissenschaftler im Dialog,* pp. 83–112. Stuttgart.

Korzybski, A. 1958. *Science and Sanity: An Introduction to Non-Aristotelian Systems and General Semantics*. 4th ed. Lakeville, Mass.

Kraft, J. 1977 [1934]. *Die Unmöglichkeit der Geisteswissenschaft*. Hamburg.

Krausse, J. 1987. "Limbo—die Vorhölle: Auf dem Weg zum elektronischen Raum." *Bauwelt* 12: 439–44.

Kritzman, L. 1980. *Destruction/Découverte: Le fonctionnement de la rhétorique dans les 'Essais' de Montaigne*. Lexington, Ky.

Kuhlmann, K. P., and W. Schenkel. 1983. *Das Grab des Ibi, (Theb. Grab. Nr. 36)*. AV 15. Mainz.

Lacoue-Labarthe, P. 1986. "Der Umweg." In W. Hamacher, ed., *Nietzsche aus Frankreich*, pp. 75–110. Frankfurt a.M.

Lactantius. 1754–59 [ca. 300]. *Divinae institutiones*. Rome.

Landon, B. 1987. "Cyberpunk: Future So Bright They Gotta Wear Shades." *Cinefantastique* 18, no. 1 (Dec.): 27–31.

Lanham, R. A. 1973. *Tristram Shandy: The Games of Pleasure*. Berkeley, Calif.

Larsen, E. 1929. "Fernsehen in Sicht!" *Film und Volk* 2, no. 4 (May): 9.

Le Goff, J. 1985. *Les intellectuels au moyen âge*. Paris. German translation, 1986. *Die Intellektuellen im Mittelalter*. Stuttgart.

Leishman, J. B. 1963. *Themes and Variations in Shakespeare's Sonnets*. 2nd ed. London.

Lerg, W. B. 1967. "Zur Entstehung des Fernsehens in Deutschland." *Rundfunk und Fernsehen* 15, no. 4: 349–75.

Leroi-Gourhan, A. 1980 [1964/65]. *Hand und Wort: Die Evolution von Technik, Sprache und Kunst*. Frankfurt a.M.

Libanius. 1967 [381]. "Oration II." In *Autobiographische Schriften*, trans. P. Wolf. Zurich.

Link, J. 1976. "Das lyrische Gedicht als Paradigma des überstrukturierten Textes." *Funkkolleg Literatur: Studienbegleitbrief* 4: 36–67.

Ludwig, K.-H. 1979. *Technik und Ingenieure im Dritten Reich*. Königstein/Taunus.

Luhmann, N. 1978. "Interpenetration bei Parsons." *Zeitschrift für Soziologie* 7: 299–302.

———. 1984. *Soziale Systeme: Grundriß einer allgemeinen Theorie*. Frankfurt a.M. English translation, forthcoming. Stanford, Calif.

———. 1985a. "Die Autopoiesis des Bewußtseins." *Soziale Welt* 36: 402–46.

———. 1985b. "Complexity and Meaning." In *The Science and Praxis of Complexity*, pp. 99–104. Tokyo.

———. 1985c. "Läßt unsere Gesellschaft Kommunikation mit Gott zu?" In Bogensberger and Kögeler, eds., *Grammatik des Glaubens*, pp. 41–48. Vienna.

————. 1986a. "Das Kunstwerk und die Selbstreproduktion der Kunst." In Gumbrecht and Pfeiffer 1986, pp. 620–72.

————. 1986b. "Das Medium der Kunst." *Delfin* 7: 6–15.

————. 1987. *Archimedes und wir: Interviews*. Berlin.

————. 1988. "Über Kreativität." In H. U. Gumbrecht, ed., *Kreativität— ein verbrauchter Begriff?*, pp. 13–20. Munich.

————. 1989. *Ecological Communication*. Chicago.

————. 1990a. "Gleichzeitigkeit und Synchronisation." In *Soziologische Aufklärung 5: Konstruktivistische Perspektiven*, pp. 95–130. Oppladen.

————. 1990b. *Die Wissenschaft der Gesellschaft*. Frankfurt a.M.

Lukács, G. 1963. *Die Eigenart des Ästhetischen*. 2 vols. Neuwied.

Lundqvist, I.; A. Coutinho; F. Varela; and D. Holmberg. 1989. "Evidence for the Functional Interactions Among Natural Antibodies." *Proceedings of the National Academy of Science (USA)*.

Lusar, R. 1971. *Die deutschen Waffen und Geheimwaffen des Zweiten Weltkrieges und ihre Weiterentwicklung*. 6th ed. Munich.

Lycosthenes, C. 1551. *Elenchus scriptorum omnium*. Basel.

Lyotard, J.-F. 1983. *Le différend*. Paris.

————. 1985. *J.-F. Lyotard mit anderen: Immaterialität und Postmoderne*. Berlin. See also Lyotard et al. 1985.

————. 1991. *The Inhuman: Reflections on Time*. Trans. G. Bennington and R. Bowlby. Stanford, Calif.

Lyotard, J.-F., et al. 1985. *Les immatériaux*. 3 vols. Paris.

Machiavelli, N. 1984. *Lettere*. Ed. F. Gaeta. Vol. 3 of N. Machiavelli, *Opere*. Turin.

Mandrou, R. 1973. *Des humanistes aux hommes de science (XVIe et XVIIe siècles)*. Paris.

Marlowe, C. 1968. *The Poems*. Ed. M. Maclure. London.

Marquard, O. 1986. "Über die Unvermeidlichkeit der Geisteswissenschaften." In *Apologie des Zufälligen*, pp. 98–116. Stuttgart.

Martin, E. 1949. *Die Schreibmaschine und ihre Entwicklungsgeschichte*. Pappenheim.

Martín-Santos, L. 1982 [1961]. *Tiempo de silencio*. Barcelona.

Martinet, A. 1960. *Eléments de linguistique générale*. Paris.

Marx, K. 1953 [1859]. *Grundrisse zur Kritik der politischen Ökonomie*. Berlin.

————. 1958 [1845]. *Die deutsche Ideologie*. Vol. 3 of *Marx-Engels Werke*. Berlin.

————. 1962 [1867]. *Das Kapital*. Vol. 23 of *Marx-Engels Werke*. Berlin.

————. 1977 [1844]. "Ökonomisch-philosophische Manuskripte." Part 1, vol. 3 of *Marx-Engels Werke*. Berlin.

Massenkeil, G. 1963. "Zur Frage der Dissonanzbehandlung in der Musik des 17. Jahrhunderts." In *Le 'baroque' musical*, pp. 151–67. Paris.

Mathiae, P. 1961. "Il motivo della vacca che allatta nell'iconografia del Vicino Oriente antico." *RSO* 36: 21–23.

Mattenklott, G. 1985. "Bergwerk, Tintenfluß, Palimpsest: Phantasien der Schrift." In D. Boueke and N. Hopster, eds., *Schreiben—Schreiben lernen: Rolf Sanner zum 65. Geburtstag*, pp. 14–39. Tübingen.

Maturana, H. R. 1982a. "Biologie der Sprache: Die Epistemologie der Realität." In Maturana 1982b, pp. 236–71.

———. 1982b. *Erkennen: Die Organisation und Verkörperung von Wirklichkeit.* Braunschweig.

———. 1986a. "The Biological Foundations of Self Consciousness and the Physical Domain of Existence." Manuscript.

———. 1986b. "Evolution: Phylogenetic Drift Through the Conservation of Adaptation." Manuscript.

Maturana, H. R., and Varela, F. 1987. *Der Baum der Erkenntnis: Die biologischen Wurzeln des menschlichen Erkennens.* Bern. English edition, 1992. *The Tree of Knowledge: The Biological Roots of Human Understanding.* Trans. R. Paolucci, Boston.

McCulloch, W. S. 1965. *Embodiments of the Mind.* Cambridge, Mass.

McLuhan, M. 1964. *Understanding Media: The Extensions of Man.* New York.

McNeill, W. H. 1982. *The Pursuit of Power: Technology, Armed Forces, and Society Since A.D. 1000.* Chicago.

Mead, G. H. 1969 [1929]. "Die Philosophie der Sozialität." In G. H. Mead, ed., *Philosophie der Sozialität: Aufsätze zur Erkenntnisanthropologie*, pp. 229–71. Frankfurt a.M.

Meibom, M. 1652. *Antiquae musicae auctores septem.* Amsterdam.

Meier, Ch. 1980. *Die Entstehung des Politischen bei den Griechen.* Frankfurt a.M.

Melchinger, S. 1979. *Aischylos. Sophokles.* Vol. 1 of *Die Welt als Tragödie.* Munich.

Meredith, G. 1962. *Selected Poems.* Ed. and with an Introduction by G. Hough. London.

Mérimée, P., O.J. N.d. *La Guzla, ou Choix de poésies illyriques recueilleies dans la Dalmatie, la Bosnie, la Croatie et l'Herzogowine.* Strasbourg.

Merleau-Ponty, M. 1964. "Eye and Mind." Trans. C. Dallery. In J. Edie, ed., *The Primacy of Perception*, pp. 159–90. Evanston, Ill.

———. 1968. *The Visible and the Invisible.* Trans. A. Lingus. Evanston, Ill.

Mertens, D. 1983. "Früher Buchdruck und Historiographie." In B. Moeller et al., eds., *Studien zum Städtischen Bildungswesen des späten Mittelalters und der frühen Neuzeit*, pp. 83–111. Göttingen.

Michaux, H. 1948. *Un barbare en Asie.* Paris.

Milward, A. S. 1967. "Hitlers Konzept des Blitzkrieges." In Hillgruber 1967, pp. 19–40.

Mitscherlich, A. 1976. *Sinnieren über Schmutz.* St. Gall, Switzerland.

Moltmann, G. 1967. "Die Genesis der Unconditional-Surrender-Forderung." In Hillgruber 1967, pp. 171–202.

Montaigne, M. 1978. *Essais.* Ed. P. Villey. Paris.

Morin, E. 1969. *Le vif du sujet.* Paris.

———. 1973. *Le paradigme perdu: La nature humaine.* Paris.

Mulas, L. 1982. "La scrittura del dialogo: Teoria del dialogo tra cinque e seicento." In G. Cerina et al., eds., *Oralità e scrittura nel sistema letterario,* pp. 245–63. Rome.

Müller, H. 1986. *"Ich bin ein Neger": Diskussion mit Heiner Müller.* Darmstadt.

Müller, K.-J. 1987. *Armee und Drittes Reich 1933–1939: Darstellung und Dokumentation.* Paderborn.

Musil, R. 1978. *Gesammelte Werke.* Ed. A. Frise. 9 vols. Reinbek.

Nassehi, N., and G. Weber. 1989. *Tod, Modernität und Gesellschaft: Entwurf einer Theorie der Todesverdrängung.* Opladen.

Needham, J. 1977. *Wissenschaftlicher Universalismus: Über Bedeutung und Besonderheit der chinesischen Wissenschaft.* Frankfurt a.M.

Negt, O. 1983. "Die Geschichte der lebendigen Arbeit: Diskussion mit O. Negt und A. Kluge." *Ästhetik und Kommunikation* 13, no. 48: 79–109.

Neumann, J. von, and O. Morgenstern. 1972. *Theory of Games and Economic Behavior.* Princeton, N.J.

Nietzsche, F. 1912 [1872/73]. "Rhetorik." In O. Crusius, ed., *Nietzsche's Werke: Unveröffentlichtes zur Litteraturgeschichte, Rhetorik und Rhythmik,* pp. 237–68. Leipzig.

———. 1969a [1873]. "Erkenntnistheoretische Einleitung über Wahrheit und Lüge im außermoralischen Sinne." In *Das Philosophenbuch,* pp. 170–214. Paris.

———. 1969b. *Umwertung aller Werte.* Ed. Friedrich Würzbach. Munich.

———. 1975–. *Briefwechsel.* Ed. G. Colli and M. Moninari. Berlin.

———. 1980. *Sämtliche Werke.* Ed. G. Colli and M. Moninari. Munich.

Noël, B. 1978. "La pensée visible." In F. Collin et al., eds., *Le récit et sa représentation,* pp. 71–76. Paris.

———. 1980. *URSS aller retour.* Paris.

Nonner, T. 1975. *Identität und Idee: Laurence Sternes "Tristram Shandy."* Heidelberg.

Norbrook, D. 1984. *Poetry and Politics in the English Renaissance.* London.

Oberkommando der Kriegsmarine, Amtgruppe Technisches Nachrichtenwesen, im Einvernehmen mit dem Reichsluftfahrtministerium,

Chef Nachrichtenverbindungswesen, eds. 1943. *Würzburg-Fibel*. 2 parts.

Odington, W. 1970. *Summa de speculatione musicae*. Ed. F. Hammond. Corpus scriptorum de musica, vol. 14. Rome.

Ogilvie, B. 1984. "Voyager, voyager toujours . . . ?" In *Oui, la philosophie*, 3: 4–10.

Ong, W. J. 1971. *Rhetoric, Romance and Technology: Studies in the Interaction of Expression and Culture*. Ithaca, N.Y.

————. 1977. *Interfaces of the Word: Studies in the Evolution of Consciousness and Culture*. Ithaca, N.Y.

————. 1982. *Orality and Literacy: The Technologizing of the Word*. London.

————. 1985. "Writing and the Evolution of Consciousness." *Mosaic* 18, no. 1: 1–10.

Ooteghem, J. van. 1959. "Le service postal à Rome." *Les études classiques: Revue trimestrielle d'enseignement et de pédagogie* 27: 187–97.

Ory, C. E. de. 1975. *Basuras (1945–1973)*. Madrid.

Pask, G. 1981. "Developments in Conversation Theory: Actual and Potential Applications." In G. E. Lasker, ed., *Applied Systems and Cybernetics*, vol. 3. New York.

Pavis, P. 1981. *Problèmes d'une sémiologie du texte théâtral*. Urbino.

Paz, O. 1982. *Der sprachgelehrte Affe*. Frankfurt a.M.

Perelson, A., ed. 1988. *Theoretical Immunology*. 2 vols. Redwood City, Calif.

Pfeiffer, E., ed. 1970. *Friedrich Nietzsche—Paul Rée—Lou von Salomé: Die Dokumente ihrer Begegnung*. Frankfurt a.M.

Pfeiffer, K. L. 1979. "Zur Theorie des Tragischen in der Tragödie der frühen Stuart-Zeit." *Germanisch-Romanische Monatsschrift* 29: 170–84.

Picht, G. 1981. *Hier und Jetzt: Philosophieren nach Auschwitz und Hiroshima*. 2 vols. Stuttgart.

Plato. 1990. *The Theaetetus of Plato*. Ed. M. Burnyeat. Indianapolis.

Pleynet, M. 1977. "La peinture par l'oreille." In *Art et littérature*, pp. 304–23. Paris.

Pöggeler, O., ed. 1972. *Hermeneutische Philosophie*. Munich.

Polanyi, M. 1964. *Personal Knowledge: Towards a Post-Critical Philosophy*. New York.

Polidori Vergilii Urbinatis. 1502. *De inventoribus rerum opus*. Paris.

Pollak, M. 1987. "Identité sociale et question d'un risque de santé: Les homosexuels face au SIDA." *Actes de recherches en sciences sociales* 68: 77–106.

————. 1988. *Les homosexuels et le SIDA: Sociologie d'une épidémie*. Paris.

Porphyry. 1932. "Kommentar zur Harmonielehre des Ptolemaios." In J. Düring, ed., *Göteborgs Högskolas Årsskrift* 38, no. 2: i–lxiii, 1–217.

Pothast, U. 1987. "Etwas über 'Bewußtsein.'" In K. Cramer et al., eds., *Theorie der Subjektivität.* Frankfurt a.M.

Ptolemy, C. 1930. "Die Harmonielehre." In J. Düring, ed., *Göteborgs Högskolas Årsskrift* 36: i–cvi, 1–147.

Pynchon, T. 1973. *Gravity's Rainbow.* New York.

Raabe, P. 1986. "Die Notwendigkeit der Buchkultur." *Universität* 41: 1219–34.

Ramsey, P. 1979. *The Fickle Glass: A Study of Shakespeare's Sonnets.* New York.

Rathert, W. 1989. *Charles Ives.* Darmstadt.

Reiser. 1930. "Bildfunk, Fernsehen und Tonfilm." In Reichs-Rundfunk-Gesellschaft, ed., *Rundfunk-Jahrbuch 1930*, pp. 299–306. Berlin.

Reiss, E. 1979. *"Wir senden Frohsinn": Fernsehen unterm Faschismus. Das unbekannteste Kapitel deutscher Mediengeschichte.* Berlin.

Rhein, E. 1930. "Es ist ein weiter Weg. . . ." *Fernsehen* 1, no. 9: 413–15.

Riedel, H. 1985. *Fernsehen: Von der Vision zum Programm.* Berlin.

Riedel, M. 1965. "Grundzüge einer Theorie des Lebendigen bei Hegel und Marx." *Zeitschrift für philologische Forschung* 19, no. 4: 577–600.

Riemann, H. 1901. "Zur Theorie der Konsonanz und Dissonanz." In *Präludien und Studien*, 3: 31–46. Leipzig.

Riepl, W. 1972 [1913]. *Das Nachrichtenwesen des Altertums: mit besonderer Rücksicht auf die Römer.* Leipzig; reprint, Darmstadt.

Ritter, J., and K. Gründer, eds. 1976. *Historisches Wörterbuch der Philosophie*, vol. 4. Basel and Stuttgart.

Roche, D. 1972. *Le mécrit.* Paris.

Rohwer, J., and J. Eberhard Jäckel, eds. 1979. *Die Funkaufklärung und ihre Rolle im Zweiten Weltkrieg: Eine internationale Tagung in Bonn-Bad Godesberg und Stuttgart vom 15.–18.9.1978.* Stuttgart.

Rosenberg, H. 1962. *The Tradition of the New.* London.

Rösler, W. 1980a. *Dichter und Gruppe: Eine Untersuchung zu den Bedingungen und zur historischen Funktion früher griechischer Lyrik am Beispiel Alkaios.* Munich.

———. 1980b. "Die Entdeckung der Fiktionalität in der Antike." *Poetica* 12: 283–319.

———. 1983. "Schriftkultur und Fiktionalität: Zum Funktionswandel der griechischen Literatur von Homer bis Aristoteles." In A. Assmann, J. Assmann, and Ch. Hardmeier, eds., *Schrift und Gedächtnis: Beiträge zur Archäologie der literarischen Kommunikation (1)*, pp. 109–22. Munich.

Roth, G. 1982. "Conditions of Evolution and Adaptation in Organisms as Autopoietic Systems." In D. Mossakowski and G. Roth, eds., *Environmental Adaptation and Evolution*, pp. 37–48. Stuttgart.

———. 1986. "Selbstorganisation—Selbsterhaltung—Selbstreferentialität: Prinzipien der Organisation der Lebewesen und ihre Folgen für die Beziehung zwischen Organismus und Umwelt." In A. Dress et al., eds., *Selbstorganisation: Die Entstehung von Ordnung in Natur und Gesellschaft*, pp. 149–80. Munich.

Rothacker, E. 1965 [1927]. *Logik und Systematik der Geisteswissenschaften*. Munich.

Rothschild, A. de. 1984 [1880]. *Histoire de la poste aux lettres et du timbre-poste depuis leurs origines jusqu'à nos jours*. Paris.

Ruben, P. 1978. *Dialektik und Arbeit der Philosophie*. Cologne.

Rubio, F. 1976. *Revistas poéticas españolas, 1939–1975*. Madrid.

Ruland, B. 1969. *Wernher von Braun: Mein Leben für die Raumfahrt*. Offenburg.

Rumelhart, D.; J. McClelland; and the PDP Research Group. 1986. *Parallel Distributed Processing: Explorations in the Microstructure of Cognition*. Vols. 1–3. Cambridge, Mass.

Ruskin, J. 1903. *Modern Painters*. London.

Sabato, E. 1982. *Le tunnel*. Paris.

Salvian. 1935 [ca. 450]. *De gubernatione Dei: Von der Weltregierung Gottes*. Trans. A. Mayer. Munich.

Sanz Villanueva, S. 1976. In V. Pozanco, ed., *Nueve poetas del resurgimiento*, pp. 261–77. Barcelona.

Sasso, C. R. 1982. *Soviet Night Operations in World War II*. Combat Studies Institute, U.S. Army Command and General Staff College, Fort Leavenworth.

Sauneron, S. 1982. *L'écriture figurative dans les textes d'Esna*. Esna 8. Cairo.

Sbordone, F. 1940. *Hori Apollinis Hieroglyphica*. Annotated. Naples.

Schäfer, A. 1989. "Drogen und Krieg." In F. A. Kittler and G. C. Tholen, eds., *Arsenale der Seele: Literatur- und Medienanalyse seit 1870*, pp. 151–69. Munich.

Schechner, R. 1982. *The End of Humanism: Writings in Performance*. New York.

Scheffer, B. 1985. "Schreiben hinter Gittern." In D. Boueke and N. Hopster, eds., *Schreiben—Schreiben lernen: Rolf Sanner zum 65. Geburtstag*, pp. 115–41. Tübingen.

Schelsky, H. 1963. *Einsamkeit und Freiheit: Idee und Gestalt der deutschen Universität und ihrer Reformen*. Reinbek bei Hamburg.

Schenda, R. 1970. *Volk ohne Buch: Studien zur Sozialgeschichte der populären Lesestoffe 1770–1910*. Frankfurt a.M.

Schenkel, W. 1971. "Zur Struktur der Hieroglyphenschrift." *Mitt. dt. Archäol. Inst. Kairo* 27: 85–98.

———. 1981. "Rebus-, Buchstabiersilben- und Konsonantenschrift." *Göttinger Miszellen* 52: 83–95.

————. 1984. "Schrift." In *Lexikon der Ägyptologie*, 5: 713–35.

Schlaffer, H. 1986. "Einleitung." In J. Goody, I. Watt, and K. Gough, eds., *Entstehung und Folgen der Schriftkultur*, trans. F. Herborth, pp. 7–23. Frankfurt a.M.

Schlott, A. 1989. *Schrift und Schreiber im Alten Ägypten*. Munich.

Schluchter, W. 1979. *Die Entwicklung des okzidentalen Rationalismus: Eine Analyse von Max Webers Gesellschaftsgeschichte*. Tübingen.

Schmandt-Besserat, D. 1982a. "The Emergence of Recording." *American Anthropologist* 84: 871–78.

————. 1982b. "How Writing Came About." *Zeitschrift für Papyrologie und Epigraphik* 47: 1–5.

Schmied-Kowarzik, W. 1981. *Die Dialektik der gesellschaftlichen Praxis: Zur Genesis und Struktur der Marx'schen Theorie*. Munich.

————. 1984. *Das dialektische Verhältnis des Menschen zur Natur: Philosophiegeschichtliche Studien zur Naturproblematik bei Marx*. Munich.

Scholz, H. 1923. *Die Schreibmaschine und das Maschinenschreiben*. Leipzig.

Schönberg [Schoenberg], A. 1921. *Harmonielehre*. Vienna.

————. 1975. *Style and Idea: Selected Writings of Arnold Schoenberg*. Ed. L. Stein. New York.

Schott, S. 1950. *Hieroglyphen: Untersuchungen zum Ursprung der Schrift*. Wiesbaden.

————. 1961. *Kanais: Der Tempel Sethos' im Wadi Mia*. NAWG. Göttingen.

Schottenloher, K. 1931. "Handschriftenforschung und Buchdruck im 15. und 16. Jahrhundert." *Gutenberg-Jahrbuch*, pp. 73–106.

Schrage, Wilhelm. 1930. *Fernsehen, ein praktischer Wegweiser: Wie es vor sich geht und wie der Radiohörer daran teilnehmen kann*. Munich.

Schramm, Percy E., ed. 1982. *Kriegstagebuch des Oberkommandos der Wehrmacht (Wehrmachtsführungsstab) 1940–1945*. Reprint, Hersching.

Schreber, D. P. 1973 [1903]. *Denkwürdigkeiten eines Nervenkranken*. Frankfurt a.M.

Schreiner, K. 1984. "Laienbildung als Herausforderung für Kirche und Gesellschaft." *Zeitschrift für historische Forschung* 11: 257–345.

Schucht, J. 1848. "Der überwundene Standpunkt der Tonkunst: Zweiter Artikel." *Allgemeine Musikalische Zeitung* 50: 755–59.

Schücking, J. L. 1935. "Gefahren des Fernsehens." *Das Deutsche Wort*, no. 19 (May 12): 13.

Schuller, W. 1975. "Grenzen des spätrömischen Staates: Staatspolizei und Korruption." *Zeitschrift für Papyrologie und Epigraphik* 16: 1–21.

Schütz, A. 1960. *Der sinnhafte Aufbau der sozialen Welt: Eine Einführung in die verstehende Soziologie*. Vienna.

Seeck, O. 1901. "Cursus publicus." In G. Wissowa, ed., *Paulys Real-*

Enzyklopädie der classischen Altertumswissenschaft, vol. 1.4, col. 1846–63. Stuttgart.

——. 1966. *Geschichte des Untergangs der antiken Welt*. 6 vols. Darmstadt.

Serres, M. 1973. "Laplace et le romantisme (Esquisse)." In *Romantisme*, pp. 319–57.

Sethe, K. 1939. *Vom Bilde zum Buchstaben: Die Enstehungsgeschichte der Schrift*. UAÄG 12. Leipzig.

Sheldon, H. H., and N. E. Grisewood. 1929. *Television: Present Methods of Picture Transmission*. New York.

Shiers, George. 1975. "Television 50 Years Ago." *Journal of Broadcasting* 19, no. 4: 387–400.

Sibyllinische Weissagungen. 1951 [5th–6th cent.]. Trans. A. Kurfess. Munich.

Sloterdijk, P. 1983. *Kritik der zynischen Vernunft*. 2 vols. Frankfurt a.M. English translation, 1987. *Critique of Cynical Reason*. Minneapolis.

Snell, B. 1960. *The Discovery of the Mind: The Greek Origins of European Thought*. New York.

Sobchack, V. 1987. *Screening Space: The American Science Fiction Film*. New York.

——. 1992. *The Address of the Eye: A Phenomenology of Film Experience*. Princeton, N.J.

Söllner, A. 1979. "Erfahrungs- und Geschichtsabhängigkeit der Wahrheit: Horkheimers Begründung der materialistischen Gesellschaftstheorie und Sozialforschung (1929–1933)." *Philologisches Jahrbuch* 86, no. 1: 113–46.

Sontag, S. 1980. *Krankheit als Metapher*. Munich.

——. 1989. *AIDS und seine Metaphern*. Munich.

Soupault. 1985. *Le nègre*. Paris.

Southall, B. 1982. *Abbey Road: The Story of the World's Most Famous Recording Studio*. Cambridge, Eng.

Spangenberg, P. 1988. "TV, Hören und Sehen." In Gumbrecht and Pfeiffer 1988, pp. 776–98.

Speer, A. 1989. *Erinnerungen*. Berlin. English translation, 1970. *Inside the Third Reich: Memoirs*. Trans. R. and C. Winston. New York.

Spencer Brown, G. 1971. *Laws of Form*. 2nd ed. London.

Spengler, O. 1972 [1923]. *Der Untergang des Abendlandes: Umrisse einer Morphologie der Weltgeschichte*. 2 vols. Munich.

Spiegelberg, H. 1965. *The Phenomenological Movement: A Historical Introduction*. 2nd ed. 2 vols. The Hague.

Spremberg, P. 1963. *Entwicklungsgeschichte des Staustrahltriebwerkes*. Mainz.

Stein, E. 1928. *Geschichte des spätrömischen Reiches von 284 bis 476 n. Chr.* Vienna.

Steiner, F. 1963. *Die Armee der Geächteten*. 2nd ed. Göttingen.

Steiner, G. 1962. *Der Tod der Tragödie*. Munich.

Stierle, K. 1984. "Gespräch und Diskurs—Ein Versuch im Blick auf Montaigne, Descartes und Pascal." In K. Stierle and R. Warning, eds., *Das Gespräch*, pp. 297–334. Munich.

Stingelin, M. 1988. "Nietzsches Wortspiel als Reflexion auf poet(olog)ische Verfahren." *Nietzsche-Studien* 17: 336–68.

Stjernfelt, F. 1992. "Hjelmslev and the Form of Writing." In *Culture and Society*.

Suetonius Tranquillus. 1985 [ca. 120]. "Kaiserbiographien." In Suetonius Tranquillus, *Werke*. Ed. W. Krenkel, ed. Berlin.

Sulzer, J. G. 1792. *Allgemeine Theorie der Schoenen Kuenste, Erster Theil: Neue vermehrte zweyte Auflage*. Leipzig.

Swierk, A. 1972. "Johannes Gutenberg als Erfinder in Zeugnissen seiner Zeit." In H. Widmann, ed., *Der gegenwärtige Stand der Gutenberg-Forschung 1*, pp. 79–90. Stuttgart.

Tacitus. 1969 [104–10]. *Historiae: Historien*. Ed. J. Borst. Munich.

Tàpies, A. 1976. *Die Praxis der Kunst*. St. Gall, Switzerland.

———. 1983. *Memoria personal: Fragmento para una autobiografía*. Barcelona.

Taubes, J. 1983. "Zur Konjunktur des Polytheismus." In K. H. Bohrer, ed., *Mythos und Moderne*, pp. 457–70. Frankfurt a.M.

Tavernier, J. B. 1981. *Les six voyages en Turquie et en Perse*. Vol. 2. Paris.

Tefnin, R. 1984. "Discours et iconicité dans l'art égyptien." *Göttinger Miszellen* 79: 55–72.

Tertullian. 1952 [198]. *Apologeticum: Verteidigung des Christentums*. Ed. and trans. C. Becker. Munich.

———. 1980 [191/200]. "De testimonio animae: Das Zeugnis der Seele." In Tertullian, *Werke*, ed. J. H. Waszink, vol. 1. Zurich.

te Velde, H. 1985/86. "Egyptian Hieroglyphs as Signs, Symbols and Gods." *Visible Religion* 4/5: 63–72.

———. 1988. "Egyptian Hieroglyphs as Linguistic Signs and Metalinguistic Informants." *Visible Religion* 6: 169–79.

Thompson, M. 1979. *Rubbish Theory: The Creation and Destruction of Value*. Oxford.

Thun, R. 1930. "Bemerkungen zum Fernsehprogramm." *Fernsehen* 3.

———. 1932. "Die Bedeutung des Programmes für einen Erfolg des Fernsehens." *Fernsehen und Tonfilm* 3: 134–39.

Tinctoris, J. 1975 [1477]. "Liber de arte contrapuncti." In J. Tinctoris, *Opera theoretica*, ed. A. Seay, 2: 11–157. Corpus scriptorum de musica, vol. 22. Rome.

Trevor-Roper, H. R. 1947. *The Last Days of Hitler*. London.

Trithemius, J. 1973 [1494]. *De laude scriptorum: Zum Lobe der Schreiber.* Ed. and trans. K. Arnold. Würzburg.

Tusa, M. C. 1985. "Die authentischen Quellen der 'Eroica.'" *Archiv für Musikwissenschaft* 42: 121–50.

Urbain, J. 1986. "Idiotypic Networks: A Noisy Background or a Breakthrough in Immunological Thinking?" *Annuel Immunologique Institut Pasteur* 137C: 57–64.

Vaillé, E. 1947. *Histoire des postes français,* vol. 1, *Des origines à la fin du moyen âge.* Paris.

Valente, J. A. 1972. *Palabras de la tribu.* Barcelona.

———. 1980. *Punto cero: Poesía 1953–1979.* Barcelona.

———. 1985. *Entrada en materia.* Ed. J. Ancet. Madrid.

Varagnac, A., et al. 1959. *L'homme avant l'écriture.* Paris.

Varela, F. 1979. *Principles of Biological Autonomy.* New York.

Varela, F., and A. Coutinho. 1991. "Second Generation Immune Networks." *Immunology Today* 12: 159–67.

Varela, F.; A. Coutinho; B. Dupire; and N. Vaz. 1988. "Cognitive Networks: Immune, Neural and Otherwise." In Perelson 1988.

Varela, F.; V. Sánchez; and A. Coutinho. 1988. "Viable Strategies Gleaned from Immune Systems Dynamics." In P. Sauders and B. Goodwin, eds., *Epigenetic and Evolutionary Order in Complex Systems: A Waddington Memorial Symposium.* Edinburgh.

Vaz, N., and F. Varela. 1978. "Self and Nonsense: An Organism-Centered Approach to Immunology." *Medical Hypothesis.*

Vernus, P. 1977. "L'écriture de l'Egypte ancienne." *L'espace et la lettre: Cahiers Jussier* 3: 60–77.

———. 1985. "Des relations entre textes et représentationes dans l'Egypte pharaonique." In M. A. Christin, ed., *Ecritures II,* pp. 45–69. Paris.

Veyne, P. 1981. *Der Eisberg der Geschichte: Foucault revolutioniert die Historie.* Trans. K. Tholen-Struthoff. Frankfurt a.M.

———. 1988. "Ein Inventar der Differenzen: Antrittsvorlesung am Collège de France." In F. Weinert, trans., *Die Originalität des Unbekannten: Für eine andere Geschichtsschreibung.* Frankfurt a.M.

Virilio, P. 1984a. *L'espace critique.* Paris.

———. 1984b. *Guerre et cinéma I: La logistique de la perception.* Paris.

———. 1984c. *L'horizon négatif.* Paris.

———. 1986. "Geschwindigkeit—Unfall—Krieg: Gespräch mit Virilio." *TAZ,* May 3, 1986, pp. 12–13.

Voigt, W. 1985. *Dissonanz und Klangfarbe: Instrumentationsgeschichtliche und experimentelle Untersuchungen.* Bonn.

Volkmann, L. 1923. *Bilderschriften der Renaissance.* Leipzig.

Volten, A. 1945. *Zwei altägyptische politische Schriften.* Copenhagen.

Wagenführ, K. 1938. "Im verdunkelten Zimmer: Der Programmaufbau des Fernsehsenders." *Deutsche Allgemeine Zeitung*, Feb. 15.

———. 1983. *Anmerkungen zum Fernsehen 1938 bis 1980.* Ed. A. Kutsch. Mainz and Stuttgart.

———. 1985. "Fünfzig Jahre Deutsches Fernsehprogramm 1935 bis 1985: Das erste Fernsehspiel der Welt war nur ein Bunter Nachmittag." *Fernseh-Informationen* 36, no. 10: 293–97.

Walther, J. G. 1953 [1732]. *Musikalisches Lexikon oder musikalische Bibliothek.* Kassel.

Warning, R. 1982. "Imitatio und Intertextualität: Zur Geschichte lyrischer Dekonstruktion der Amortheologie—Dante, Petrarca, Baudelaire." In W. Oelmüller, ed., *Kolloquium Kunst und Philosophie 2. Ästhetischer Schein*, pp. 168–207. Paderborn.

Warschauer, F. 1930. "Die Zukunft der Technisierung." In L. Kestenberg, ed., *Kunst und Technik*, pp. 409–46. Berlin.

Watt, I. 1957. *The Rise of the Novel: Studies in Defoe, Richardson and Fielding.* Harmondsworth, Eng.

Weber, M. 1963. *Gesammelte Aufsätze zur Religions-soziologie.* Vol. 1. 5th ed. Tübingen.

Webern, A. v. 1912. "Schönbergs Musik." In A. Berg et al., eds., *Arnold Schönberg*, pp. 22–48. Munich.

Weck-Erlen, L. van der. 1978 [1907]. *Das goldene Buch der Liebe: Ein Eros-Kodex für beide Geschlechter.* Reprint, Reinbek.

Weimar, K. 1975. *Historische Einleitung zur literarwissenschaftlichen Hermeneutik.* Tübingen.

Weitz, H. P. 1930. "Fernsehprogramm?" *Fernsehen* 11/12.

Welchman, G. 1982. *The Hut 6 Story: Breaking the Enigma Codes.* New York.

Wellbery, D. 1992a. "Contingency." In A. Fehn, I. Hoestery, and M. Tatar, eds., *Neverending Stories: Toward a Critical Narratology*, pp. 337–57. Princeton, N.J.

———. 1992b. "The Exteriority of Writing." *Stanford Literature Review* 9, no. 1: 11–24.

Westendorf, W. 1969. "Die Anfänge der altägyptischen Hieroglyphen." In *Frühe Schriftzeugnisse der Menschheit*, pp. 56–87. Göttingen.

Widmann, H. 1970. "Kontinuität und Wandel in der Herstellung des Buches." *Archiv für die Geschichte des Buchwesens* 10: xxxv–xlviii.

———. 1972. "Gutenberg im Urteil der Nachwelt." In H. Widmann, ed., *Der gegenwärtige Stand der Gutenberg-Forschung 1*, pp. 251–72. Stuttgart.

Wiener, N. 1961. *Cybernetics or Control and Communication in the Animal and the Machine.* Cambridge, Mass.

Wildhagen, K.-H., ed. 1970. *Erich Fallgiebel: Meister operativer Nachrichtenverbindungen. Ein Beitrag zur Geschichte der Nachrichtentruppe.* Wennigsen/Hannover.

Winckel, F.; A. Wellek; and C. Dahlhaus. 1958. "Konsonanz—Dissonanz." In F. Blume, ed., *Die Musik Geschichte und Gegenwart,* 7: 1482–516. Kassel.

Winnicott, D. W. 1973. *Vom Spiel zur Kreativität.* Stuttgart.

Wittkower, R. 1965. *Künstler: Außenseiter der Gesellschaft.* Stuttgart.

Wood, A. E. 1985. *Knowledge Before Printing and After: The Indian Tradition in Changing Kerala.* Delhi.

Yates, F. 1966. *The Art of Memory.* London.

Zarlino, G. 1966 [1558]. *Istituzioni harmoniche.* New York.

Zelle, C. 1987. *"Angenehmes Grauen": Literaturhistorische Beiträge zur Ästhetik des Schrecklichen im achtzehnten Jahrhundert.* Hamburg.

Zumthor, P. 1983. *Introduction à la poésie orale.* Paris.

———. 1985. "Le geste et la voix." *Hors-cadre* 3: 4–17.

———. 1987a. "Chansons médiatisées." *Etudes françaises* (Montréal) 22: 13–20.

———. 1987b. *La lettre et la voix.* Paris.

Index

In this index an "f" after a number indicates a separate reference on the next page, and an "ff" indicates separate references on the next two pages. A continuous discussion over two or more pages is indicated by a span of page numbers, e.g., "57–59." *Passim* is used for a cluster of references in close but not consecutive sequence. Entries are alphabetized letter by letter, ignoring word breaks, hyphens, and accents.

Library of Congress Cataloging-in-Publication Data

Materialities of communication / edited by Hans Ulrich Gumbrecht
and K. Ludwig Pfeiffer.
    p. cm.—(Writing science)
    "With the exception of . . . three chapters and the closing
chapter . . . the other chapters in this book were translated from the
German versions originally published in either . . . Materialität der
Kommunikation . . . or Paradoxien, Dissonanzen,
Zusammenbrüche"—T.p. verso.
    Includes bibliographical references and index.
    ISBN 0-8047-2263-3 — ISBN 0-8047-2264-1 (pbk.)
    1. Communication—Philosophy. 1. Gumbrecht, Hans Ulrich.
11. Pfeiffer, Karl Ludwig. 111. Materialität der Kommunikation.
Selections. English. 1994. IV. Paradoxien, Dissonanzen,
Zusammenbrüche. Selections. English. 1994. v. Series.
P91.25.M364 1994
302.2—dc20   93-4911
                                                  CIP
                                                REV

∞This book is printed on acid-free paper.